Trusting and its Tribulations

TRUSTING AND ITS TRIBULATIONS

Interdisciplinary Engagements with Intimacy, Sociality and Trust

Edited by
Vigdis Broch-Due and Margit Ystanes

berghahn
NEW YORK • OXFORD
www.berghahnbooks.com

First published by
Berghahn Books
www.berghahnbooks.com

© 2016, 2020 Vigdis Broch-Due and Margit Ystanes
First paperback edition published in 2020

All rights reserved. Except for the quotation of short passages for the purposes of criticism and review, no part of this book may be reproduced in any form or by any means, electronic or mechanical, including photocopying, recording, or any information storage and retrieval system now known or to be invented, without written permission of the publisher.

Library of Congress Cataloging-in-Publication Data

Names: Broch-Due, Vigdis, editor. | Ystanes, Margit, editor.
Title: Trusting and its tribulations: interdisciplinary engagements with intimacy, sociality and trust / edited by Vigdis Broch-Due and Margit Ystanes.
Description: New York: Berghahn Books, [2016] | Includes bibliographical references and index.
Identifiers: LCCN 2015045558 | ISBN 9781785330995 (hardback: alk. paper) | ISBN 9781785331008 (ebook)
Subjects: LCSH: Trust--Social aspects--Case studies. | Social interaction.--Case studies. | Intimacy (Psychology)--Case studies.
Classification: LCC BJ1500.T78 T79 2016 | DDC 302/.14--dc23 LC record available at http://lccn.loc.gov/2015045558

British Library Cataloguing in Publication Data
A catalogue record for this book is available from the British Library

ISBN 978-1-78533-099-5 (hardback)
ISBN 978-1-78920-840-5 (paperback)
ISBN 978-1-78533-100-8 (ebook)

Contents

List of Illustrations   vii
Preface   viii

Introduction: Introducing Ethnographies of Trusting   1
Vigdis Broch-Due and Margit Ystanes

1. Unfixed Trust: Intimacy, Blood Symbolism and Porous Boundaries in Guatemala   37
   Margit Ystanes

2. Witchcraft: The Dangers of Intimacy and the Struggle over Trust   60
   Peter Geschiere

3. Trusting the Untrustworthy: A Mongolian Challenge to Western Notions of Trust   84
   Paula Haas

4. The Puzzle of the Animal Witch: Intimacy, Trust and Sociality among Pastoral Turkana   105
   Vigdis Broch-Due

5. 'Sharing Secrets': Gendered Landscapes of Trust and Intimacy in Kenya's Digital Financial Marketplace   131
   Misha Mintz-Roth and Amrik Heyer

6. Eddies of Distrust: 'False' Birth Certificates and the Destabilization of Relationships   148
   Jennifer M. Speirs

7. Intimate Documents: Trust and Secret Police Files in Post-socialist Mongolia   170
   Chris Kaplonski

8. Trustworthy Bodies: Cashinahua Cumulative Persons as Intimate Others   191
   Cecilia McCallum

9 Habitus of Trust: Servitude in Colonial India   213
   Radhika Chopra

10 'You Can Tell the Company We Done Quit': The Destruction
   and Reconfiguration of Trust in the Appalachian Coalfields
   in the Early Twentieth Century   235
   Gloria Goodwin Raheja

Index   259

 **Illustrations**

9.1	British Bungalow with Servants, 1870s	218
9.2	'Our Bedroom', Capt. G.F. Aitkinson	219
9.3	Bombay Servants	221
9.4	'A Gentleman With His Hookah-Burdar, or Pipe-Bearer'	224

 # Preface

This volume was born out of a long-standing interest in the intricacies of trusting and its tribulations shared by the two editors. Coming to the problem with fieldwork experience on trust formation from different continents and communities – Ystanes from Central America and Broch-Due from Africa – but having both grown up in Norway, a country that ranks on the top of all trust barometers, it was abundantly clear from our compiled experiences that trust could not be taken for granted, even in close-knit relationships. Examples range from the deep suspicion fracturing Ladino Guatemalans projecting a family façade of pure trust and solidarity (Ystanes 2011) to the trusting modalities of pastoralists in Northern Kenya, which fail to neatly discriminate between distant and close relationships in terms of blood, but rather extend trust and belonging to those who are linked by cattle transfers, including the beasts themselves (Broch-Due 2005).

Moving closer to home we experience yet another scenario of trusting. A highly visible instance of Norway's levels of taken-for-granted trust is the fact that Norwegian parents often leave sleeping babies alone in their strollers outside homes and cafés during all weathers and seasons. This can be a rather shocking sight for those coming from places where the dangers of kidnapping and abuse are always highlighted in the media, with the result that social mistrust soars in the public imagination. Many foreigners are likewise puzzled by the apparent willingness of Scandinavians to pay high taxes, trusting their government to deploy the public purse wisely and justly, redistributing services, benefits and resources evenly throughout society (Skirbekk 2012). In short, *tillit* [trust] has become a defining feature of everything Nordic, deeply embedded in an egalitarian ethos that is still visible and pervasive, both arising from and creating high levels of social trust.

Whatever the case, the relatively homogeneous composition of the Scandinavian citizenship, combined with a remarkable consensus across the political spectrum about core values, has probably served as a shield against the most rampant waves of social anxiety that have engulfed larger, more complex and less cohesively constituted

Western societies in a 'self-endangering civilization', the term coined by sociologist Ulrich Beck in his seminal *Risk Society* (1992 [1986]). The postmodern notion that risk is no longer chosen and controllable, but ubiquitous and unavoidable seems particularly penetrating in Anglo-Saxon cultures. Mary Douglas and Aaron Wildavsky capture this corrosive mistrust well in *Risk and Culture* (1982: 10):

> What are Americans afraid of? Nothing much, really, except the food they eat, the water they drink, the air they breathe, the land they live on, and the energy they use. In the amazingly short space of fifteen to twenty years, confidence about the physical world has turned into doubt. Once the sources of safety, science and technology have become sources of risk.

Just from this handful of examples it became clear to us that the social conditions for trust formation are not only highly variable, but remain elusive and are certainly not exhausted by the rather obvious explanations we can draw from the social sciences. The very opaqueness of trust as a human condition becomes even more palpable if we venture into the intimate sphere where, despite commonplace notions that trust coagulates naturally from shared blood and genes, human experiences also bear evidence that the underbelly of intimacy bleeds mistrust too. Misgivings and betrayal of close kin has been the mainstay of literature as far back as the Greek tragedies. Ancient myths, works of fiction and feminist critiques have long reminded us that the most intimate relations can also be deeply troubling and difficult, even violent. Paradoxically, myth and fiction constitute the only spaces in which the strong association of intimacy as embedded in trust, harmony, altruism and nurture are interrogated and challenged. The Scandinavian literary tradition has been particularly notable for its focus on the friction of family life, with playwrights such as Henrik Ibsen and August Strindberg famously depicting it as fraught with suffocating and unrealistic expectations, dark secrets, deception and handed-down personal flaws. These topics appear to have had a lasting appeal throughout time, and today feature in both ideological struggles over the role of the family and in psychoanalytical approaches to it. The fundamental conflicts of the biological nuclear family scrutinized by the ancient Greek myth of Oedipus and later adopted by Freud, as well as the limiting and infantilizing role assigned to women in married life which Ibsen criticized in *A Doll's House*, continue to be the subject of literary and feminist critique in a large number of contexts.

Perhaps it is an understanding of such tensions as particular to 'Euro-American' or 'Western' notions of family life and the particular, historically situated struggle for women's emancipation in the 'West' that has led anthropologists to largely disregard this problematic when they venture into more exotic terrain. Ethnographic studies of witchcraft, kinship, gender, morality and the self indicate in fact that domestic bliss can be hard to come by in most societies. Yet these findings have not lead to a critical debate on the notion of intimacy in anthropology, nor have they inspired a critical discussion of the theorizations of trust that rest upon an idyllic, all-embracing image of domestic life. As an unchallenged supposition in mainstream anthropology, the notion of intimacy continues to be associated with reciprocity and trust – indeed, with the safe haven of the kinship group, family or community. Whether this notion of intimacy accurately reflects what goes on in close relationships in any context is rarely explored, but is, nevertheless, a frequently unquestioned premise across the entire interdisciplinary field of trust scholarship – in philosophy, economics and sociobiology.

Instead, in much trust research it is taken for granted that trust can be explored through universalizing conceptions, that trust is mainly an aspect of symmetrical relationships, and that the domestic sphere is the quintessential example of a domain marked by trust. Because of this tendency, our knowledge about trust in hierarchical relationships – including within families – is missing. So is our insight into how different conceptions of intimacy necessarily lead to different ways of producing and understanding trust and mistrust. Our knowledge about intimacy and trust formation is therefore limited and leaves much to be explored.

We invited a collection of anthropologists to address the topic, and it is our hope that the present volume will enhance the discussions in this field. Our starting point is that in order to expand our knowledge about trust we must explore how it is produced in specific contexts, always in articulation with culturally elaborated notions of intimacy and sociality. It is crucial to take to task the tendency to approach trust with 'thinly' conceived concepts. As the introduction to this volume demonstrates, many of the concepts and premises upon which contemporary trust research rests tell us perhaps more about the ideas prevalent at the historical moment of their conception than about the phenomenon of trust. The chapters here thus answer the need for deeper understanding of how trust, sociality and intimacy are produced and understood in actual, 'thickly' conceived life-worlds, by presenting comparative ethnographic explorations of selfhood, intimacy, kinship, sociality and trust.

In particular, we focus on the intimate sphere, as the family is the most important location where notions of intimacy and sociality are elaborated, reproduced and also challenged in virtually all societies. The chapters call into question the conventional understanding of intimacy and the domestic sphere as marked by idyllic harmony, and instead draw out the complexities and tensions of these relations and the ways in which these mark the formation of trust in different societies. However, because of our emphasis on 'thick description', these chapters also address a wider spectrum of trust relations than those found in the intimate sphere. Necessarily, embodied experiences, the cultural milieu and forms of sociality in which intimate relations are forged must be drawn upon in order to account for the way trust and mistrust is formed and experienced in different life-worlds. What we find is that trust relations in the so-called 'private' and 'public' spheres are closely interconnected and profoundly impact upon one another. Together, the chapters will advance the anthropological theorizing of trusting as a formative, affective and intersubjective phenomenon with its own specificity that cannot only be subsumed under the generic category of 'sociality'.

In sum, our topic is the nebulous quality of trust and trusting, its relations to both the intimate and personal, but also to the public and social. This is an interdisciplinary field, in which economics, philosophy and political science dominate theorizing about the 'public' face of trusting, whilst neuroscience, psychoanalysis and sociobiology dominate theorizing about its 'personal' face. Curiously anthropology has remained silent in this influential debate. Crucially, the important debates about trust are being waged not only in seminar rooms but probably more significantly in the popular media and public arenas. The terms of that debate, unfortunately, tend to be highly ethnocentric, taking Western notions of trust uncritically as universally given and valid. The significance of ethnography in this context is exactly its power to open up the conversation by introducing complexity, but without erasing the shared quality of trusting across human diversity. Again, our aim is precisely to contribute to larger inquiries beyond anthropology, not simply to produce more ethnography organized around the idea of 'trust'.

We seek to move beyond current debates within anthropology to engage much wider scholarly and public debates around this absolutely fundamental but rather amorphous issue of trusting. We hope that this volume demonstrates the huge relevance and significance of anthropology when willing to engage with other disciplines in debates about the human condition.

Vigdis Broch-Due
Margit Ystanes

Acknowledgements

We would like to acknowledge the generous contribution of the Research Council of Norway's Mental Health programme, which funded the research activities that underpin this scholarly enquiry.

References

Beck, U. 1992 [1986]. *Risk Society: Towards the New Modernity*. London: Sage.
Broch-Due, V. 2005. *Violence and Belonging: The Quest for Identity in Post Colonial Africa*. London: Routledge.
Douglas, M. and A. Wildavsky. 1982. *Risk and Culture: Essays in the Selection of Technological and Environmental Dangers*. Berkeley: University of California Press.
Skirbekk, H. 2012. *Tillit i Norge*. Res Publica.
Ystanes, M. 2011. 'Precarious Trust: Problems of Managing Self and Sociality in Guatemala', PhD Dissertation. Bergen: University of Bergen.

 Introduction

INTRODUCING ETHNOGRAPHIES OF TRUSTING
Vigdis Broch-Due and Margit Ystanes

It has become a truism that trust is the 'glue' binding together the many social networks of modern democracy. From the intimate relationships of family, the web of trust stretches outside the home into the public realm: helping neighbours cooperate about school runs; making customers feel safe to consume the food displayed in supermarkets; persuading citizens vote in elections and pay their taxes; and making those who can afford it invest their savings in the global stock market. These expansive networks of trusting are immensely complex and take considerable time and effort to evolve. And yet, as has become abundantly clear during the last decade of financial trouble in Western economies, trust can dissolve rapidly, burning deep holes in the social fabric. The already massive interest in trust prior to the full-blown financial crisis of 2007 (Cook et al. 2005: 1) has grown, perhaps because of these experiences, into a situation in which 'everybody talks about trust' (Corsín Jiménez 2011: 177). Nevertheless, trusting remains an opaque phenomenon.

Trusting is a disposition, a powerful affect, a stance towards the world expressed in a confident reaching out to others. It is a social orientation towards the future nurtured by the gradual accumulation of positive experience and sometimes revealed in a leap of faith. Trust is an often-unquestioned background whisper of well-being occasionally surfacing in more conscious deliberations when events bring it into question. Trust weaves together intersubjective worlds. It is sometimes unspoken, can be suspended and, of course, trust networks can collapse altogether. The spaces trust builds are of different scale, complexity and duration depending on the specific geographical, cultural and historical location. Trusting is built over time and always vulnerable to the countervailing forces of mistrust, which can overwhelm some social spaces and biographies.

We are thus confronted with an elusive social phenomenon that is nonetheless essential for the workings of any relationship and institution. Despite its immense significance and ubiquity in our everyday existence, the complex workings of trust are poorly understood and theorized. Trust is simply *taken for granted* not only by most human subjects, but also by scholars (Ystanes 2011). Perhaps this unquestioned quality is a side effect of the nature of trusting itself. Serving as a supporting mesh onto which other affects and emotions are wired, trust seldom surfaces in the mind of subjects as a distinct feeling distinguishable from its twinned emotions of love, hope and well-being. Rather, it tends to surface into consciousness as *an absence* precisely in those moments when trust is in doubt, a lingering suspicion that triggers thought and deliberation, both rational and irrational. It is precisely this conscious calculation that has caught the interest of philosophers, economists and political scientists, whilst the more inchoate, embodied and sensual substrata have been relegated to neuroscience and psychoanalysis. The dominant schools of trust research in the social sciences have largely ignored these primary aspects of trusting. In the tradition of Western scholarship, trust has simply been fragmented and fallen through the fault lines that divide body and mind, nature and nurture, biology and sociology.

The Emerging Field of Trust Research

While trust has a long genealogy as an academic concern, especially within the 'Western' philosophical tradition, the more recent surge in interest has led to a proliferation of publications exploring this phenomenon. Indeed, trust research has emerged as a field in its own right. Spanning academic disciplines such as philosophy, political sciences, sociology, economy and evolutionary biology, trust research is a truly interdisciplinary field, in which contributors struggle to communicate across disciplinary and methodological boundaries. There is little agreement among researchers as to what exactly trust is and how we can study it (see, e.g., Grimen 2009), or even what kind of concept it is (Corsín Jiménez 2011). It is therefore very unclear what we actually know about trust.

Indeed, reading across different arenas of the humanities and social sciences, we found 'trust' entering into equations with other concepts like 'risk', 'contract', or the game playing of rational actors. In this sort of abstract theorizing, trust was typically removed from any contamination by the complexities of intimate and public life. Trust from the perspective of the library was essentially seen as either a taken-for-granted property of the 'intimate' domain or a free floating, pure element of the 'social', a virtual domain with little location in history, culture or the other messy realities in which ordinary people face specific problems of relationship. By browsing through reports on the topic of trust from the laboratory of natural sciences, a different kind of abstraction and omission leapt out of the page. Since genes and neurons by necessity are embodied, the biological approaches are indeed steeped in a sort of 'intimacy' but of a seriously reduced sort, involving either an individual entity only or a rudimentary collective cut from relations of consanguinity. Here the serious puzzle concerning 'trust' is not its intimate source, but rather its undeniable 'social' character. For if one believes that natural selection in the Darwinian sense can only work on single organisms or at the level of genes, and if those genes or organisms are also perceived as intrinsically 'selfish', how can one then account for the perpetuation of the altruistic properties of collectives that precisely bind trust into expansive forms of sociality. The debate waged in the laboratories about whether the evolution of trust is best understood as a matter of individual or group 'selection' is as fierce as the debate waged among scholars of a more humanistic bent, who argue from the comfort of their armchairs the finer points of contracts and risks as the foundation of trust.

Despite the large variety of approaches to trust in these disciplines, a couple of features can be observed in many of them. Firstly, there is a tendency to assume that trust is essentially produced in the same way everywhere. What surprised both editors of this volume during our encounter with contemporary thinking about 'trust', and its links to such diverse notions as 'risk', 'reciprocity', 'contract', 'obligation', 'gene' and 'neuron', was how 'thinly' it was conceived. Despite its different guises across the domains of scholarship, 'trust' seemed to be spun out of the minds of philosophers, economists and political scientists as a 'thing in itself', a universal essence, which could be easily defined, quantified, calibrated and compared. The 'trust' of the biological sciences did not seem to fare much better, being reduced to the rapid firing of neurons or the slow evolving of genes. The multifaceted, ever-evolving life-worlds in which trusting and its negation take place are therefore often ignored or superficially treated.

Secondly, and related to the tendency to treat social orders superficially, it is often assumed that we can study trust with reference to a singularly conceived subject, often referred to as 'the Truster'. This makes it difficult to conceptualize that even 'Western' selves usually do not conform to the types of self envisioned in much of this research – especially in the neoliberal version of self-governable, rational selves (Hardin 2002, 2006; see, e.g., Cook et al. 2005). As the rich ethnographic material presented in the chapters of this volume illustrates, such thinly conceived conceptualizations are ill suited to unpack the complex, manifold ways in which trust is conceptualized, formed and lived around the world. Indeed, if we are to understand trust, we must dissolve the singularly conceived subject and focus our attention on trust not as a 'thing' that can be easily defined and accounted for, but as a composite social phenomenon arising in the interplay between bodies, minds and intersubjectivity. Trusting subjects inhabit complex social landscapes, and observe and engage with their surroundings from a variety of social positions. We must therefore explore the very conditions for trust and mistrust in each social order and take into consideration how self, sociality and subject positions are constituted in specific life-worlds. These are of course not new points in social theory per se. There has long been a concern with 'thick descriptions' (Geertz 1973) and the integration of different subject positions into the analysis – for example in postmodern experimental writing. For some reason, however, trust research appears to be excessively marked by an epistemological individualism, which takes various forms and is reflected in conceptions, methodologies and approaches to social and writing styles within the field (see, e.g., Hardin 2002, 2004, 2006; Ostrom and Walker 2003; Cook et al. 2005). The source to such a deep trust in the individual stems from the premise of economics and philosophy.

Capitalizing on Trust: Selfish or Social?

In the *Wealth of a Nation* (1776), Adam Smith asserted that it was an essential 'self-love' in search of profit that drove the individual to 'truck, barter and exchange' (Smith 2008 [1776]: 12). The claim that human beings by nature were motivated by self-interest, not only in commerce but also in all other social activities, was a well-established idea of the time. The alluring purity of Smith's deductive argument, however, that this personal desire was not only the primary cause of market activity but also the driving force behind the division of labour and thus the very foundation of society itself, has had a lasting effect on subsequent sociological and economic theory.

Karl Marx was famously concerned with the classical labour theory of economic value rather than the market. However, on those pages of *Capital* where he did discuss market behaviour he notably failed to take his colleague Smith to court for his reductionist proposition of the inherent egotism of economic behaviour. Marx seemingly accepted that people bought and sold goods out of rational self-interest, but he rejected vehemently the idea that self-interest was the best driver of increased production. Rather, he argued that the bourgeoisie developed markets in a destructive fashion by warping the system of monetary exchange in ways that confused the proper use value of commodities with their fetishized exchange value. That the working class seemingly trusted these ruinous arrangements Marx simply put down to 'false consciousness', thereby inadvertently being the first scholar to question the notion that trust is invariably beneficial (Marx 1990 [1867]). We will return the various ramifications of trust later.

Ever since Smith, however, ideologically and morally laden debates about whether markets are 'good' or 'bad' for subjects and sociality have raged in scholarly discourse. On the one hand, neo-classical economists like Milton Friedman argue that social and political freedom is fostered by the individual's ability to buy, sell and accumulate freely. James Manyard Keynes, on the other hand, is representative of the opposing school of thought of the 1930s, being of the opinion that markets need to be regulated by the state to prevent the unbridled speculation that can cause financial chaos and widespread economic crisis. Echoing this sober position are seminal voices like Ferdinand Tönnies (2001 [1887]) and Max Weber (1978 [1904]) who blamed the market for breaking up the medieval *gemeinshaft*, conceived of as circles of social trust and communion, and replacing these havens with *gesellshaft* – a pared down and disenchanted form of sociality that fostered individualism and the structural conditions for capital accumulation and modernity.

Most significantly, whether they condemned or promoted the effects of markets, none of these scholars seriously questioned the premise of the rational 'self-interest' at the heart of the matter. The only difference was that while formal economists located selfishness in nature, the sociologists had a more nostalgic interpretation, insisting that the selfish individual was the product of capitalism and had replaced a more communitarian antecedent. From the privileged position of the present day, with more theoretical sophistication at hand, it is easy to see how flawed this thin modelling of pure self-interest really was. We know that the buying and giving of goods participates in complex circuits of motivation and meaning, but such empirically informed insights were not available to earlier scholars. Clearly, they were all speaking of their historical moment and reflecting the dominant evolutionary views of their society and class. Seated most often in private libraries, they also shared a mode of desk study that was conducted from the rather speculative purview of the armchair.

Equipped with better methods and inspired by theorizing in contemporary anthropology, including *Money and the Morality of Exchange*, the influential volume edited by Jonathan Parry and Maurice Bloch (1989), historians have recently embarked on a revisionary project of market behaviour in early modern England. This new look on the past has revealed a starkly different picture than the older 'thin' European accounts, but one which is more in line with contemporary East Africa in its nuanced depiction of the social fabric of entrustments (Shipton 2007; Broch-Due, this volume). By painstakingly sifting through archives, letters, memoirs, bulletins, court files and ledgers of tax and commerce, Craig Muldrew helps us to understand why it is that 'trust' in its dictionary usage slides so easily between personal character, credit and a cooperation of sorts.

His magisterial book, *The Economy of Obligation: The Culture of Credit and Social Relations in Early Modern England* (1998), is turning conventional wisdoms on their head. Muldrew's stage is the revolution in the English economy of the sixteenth century brought about by the explosion of credit relations, in turn spurred by a chronic shortage of coins in circulation. Credit became a barometer of trust in society. Outstanding claims consisted of a 'system of judgements about trustworthiness' which involved the entire household of individual debtors. Communities might be split by politics or religion, kith and kin might backbite one another in order to advance their personal position and remunerations, but the inescapable necessity of employing credit forced everyone to trust that those with whom they traded would honour their word and repay their outstanding debts. 'People were constantly involved in tangled webs of economic and social dependency', Muldrew writes, 'which linked their households to others within communities and beyond, through the numerous reciprocal bonds of trust in all of the millions of bargains they transacted' (1998: 97). Since attracting credit meant butter on their toast for the better off and the means of sheer survival for those on the margins, keeping a good reputation was thus of paramount concern. In the absence of regulatory instruments, personal forms of impression management, rather than the pure desire for profit, motivated both merchant and shopkeeper. The threat in these networks of loans and debts was the potential domino effect of defaults, which put a strain on relationships, though moralizing pressure was exerted on those likely to fail their repayments. Many, mostly among the poorer segments of society, were simply ejected from networks of trust and credit altogether, ending up in the debtors' prisons familiar to us from Dickens novels. Neighbours often tried to mediate disputes before they ended in such tragic incarceration but if that failed the courts stepped in to enforce the justice of keeping promises. Of course for most debtors, their defaults were not a matter of morality but simply of empty pockets.

Muldrew found little evidence from Tudor voices that they would stress private desire for profit over mutual interdependence in their own reflections on the meaning and motives of what they were doing. On the contrary, he argues that as the market expanded so too did religious and cultural stress on the ethics of credit, resulting in a new flexible law of contract with emphasis on trusting. Thus, contrary to Weber's idea that the 'spirit of capitalism' was to be found in the Calvinist diligence, thrift and frugality expected of market-oriented individuals, Muldrew demonstrates that moral guidance was more concerned with social standing, and thus oriented 'outward into the community, not inwards, concerning belief' (ibid.: 1–2). This moral bolstering of market relations continued well into the eighteenth century. However, throughout this period we discern a gradual and subtle shift away from social trust towards more individualistic values, with the development of more anonymous form of paper credit. Moreover, a sharpening of class and gender divides takes place with the development of a firmer distinction between the public and private domains and with the advent of the middle class.

In 'The Moral Economy of the English Crowd' (1971), E.P. Thompson succinctly captured the turning point occurring in the second half of the eighteenth century, showing that 'self-interest' did not filter into classical theory from 'nature' but from culture. He demonstrated that during years of dearth, popular consensus about the entitlement of the poor to locally produced grain came into conflict with a new, more absolute, utilitarian ideology of free trade. This was promoted by a new type of middleman who used the shrinking supply of wheat to speculate in higher prices. Mobilizing on the basis of entrenched communitarian values of obligation and trust, the poor took to the streets during the famous 'bread riots', seizing the grain destined for export and selling it locally at a lower and fairer price. They thus regulated the market through social action rather than the mysterious 'invisible hand' of Adam Smith's theory.

Whatever the case, the historical ethnographies of Muldrew and Thompson demonstrate that what operated in the economies of the time was *not* the calculating, autonomous, inward-looking individual envisaged by the philosophers of risk and contract, but rather 'the public perception of the self in relation to a communicated set of both personal and household virtues' (Muldrew 1998: 156). And yet the narrow focus on the individual agent continues unabated in the economic models of Western philosophy.

Trust Research and the Enquiring 'I'

The appearance of the singularly conceived subject, the Truster, is related to the origin of the academic interest with trust in philosophy.

Contemporary accounts often trace this interest back to Thomas Hobbes's book *Leviathan* (1996 [1651]). Here Hobbes argues that human beings are first and foremost driven by a concern with their own needs, desires and fears. In order to avoid a conflict of all against all, or what Hobbes refers to as the state of nature, it is necessary to establish a social contract. For Hobbes, this involves giving up our natural freedom to an absolute sovereign power, which can enforce peace, justice and distribution. Hobbes thus assumes that human beings are fundamentally untrustworthy, and that only an absolute sovereign power can secure the conditions for social trust.

The philosopher Trudy Govier (1997) points to an interesting aspect of Hobbes's argument. That is, Hobbes read humankind in himself. As he tried to estimate what motivated other people, he looked inside himself, and asked what he would do in similar circumstances, and why. This mode of knowing points to the way Western philosophers have tended *not* to conceive of themselves as Western, but rather as representative members of humankind, making arguments valid for all of its members. This epistemological starting point is reflected in much contemporary research on trust, where subjects are conceived of as identifiable with the enquiring 'I' and referred to as 'I' or 'we'. These enquiries are thus premised on the unspoken assumption that 'I' or 'we' can include all human beings. This sweeping universalism is, of course, a problematic feature for anthropologists attempting to use existing conceptions of trust to analyse their ethnographic material. The chapters in this volume illustrate that not only is there considerable variety in the behaviours and attitudes that help produce trust in each context, but the people inhabiting these contexts have radically different ways of understanding what trust is. That is, the words we normally translate into 'trust' may refer to concepts and attitudes that are quite radically different from the connotations of the English word.

Paula Haas's chapter is a case in point. The Barga Mongols she has worked with consider trust to be a virtue in and of itself: a sign that one is a good person trying to produce positive effects in the world. In contrast to the concepts of trust arising out of 'Western' philosophical traditions, the Barga Mongol understanding is entirely unrelated to the trustworthiness of others, and purely a reflection of the inner attitude of those extending trust. Indeed, to trust is associated with 'not having bad thoughts about anybody', and *being* honest and trustworthy. Extending trust towards others, even clearly untrustworthy persons, is thus conceived of as morally good and making an effort to create favourable outcomes. This latter point is related to how Barga Mongols not only understand trusting as morally good in and of itself, but also as a way of asserting control of the people they extend their trust towards, and *making* them trustworthy.

This is significantly different from the concepts of trust formulated by academics working in Western contexts. According to these theorizations, the attitude favoured by the Barga Mongols would be considered gullible and perhaps even immoral, considering the possibility that such trust relationships are based on deception (e.g., Baier 1986).

Haas teases out the Barga Mongol notion of trust by exploring a case in which a family's land tenant has stopped paying rent and has bribed local government officials to have his name put in the cadastral register instead of theirs. Despite struggling for years to turn the situation around and regain their land, the family continued to trust the corrupt officials who clearly had no intentions of resolving their problem. They even emphasized the importance of doing so. Indeed, to not trust in this situation would be unthinkable. Because of the Barga Mongol emphasis on trusting as a moral act infused with the power to influence others towards trustworthiness and to divert misfortune, not to trust would signify resignation and make one vulnerable to misfortune. This case illustrates the analytical problems that arise when we take conceptions produced with one particular social order in mind as a starting point for exploring what trust is and the social work it does around the world. By taking this undying trusting, apparently against all reason, as her lead, Hass opens up pathways and boundaries of the landscape of trust that are much more complex and open-ended than 'Western' theorising has imagined. This not only forces us to widen our empirical scope in explorations of trust, but also to question whether the myriad words that dictionaries translate into 'trust' can be meaningfully understood to be about the same social phenomenon.

Two different approaches may arise from this question. We can rigorously define the concept we wish to explore, in any given society, regardless of how it relates to the semantic and phenomenological intricacy of words usually translated into 'trust'. This is the approach often taken in contemporary trust research, where the search for 'conceptual clarity' (Cook et al. 2005: 19) guides the investigations and produces reductionist analyses of this multifaceted phenomenon. Alternatively, we might take a more open and exploratory approach, and allow for empirical findings to guide the search for definitions. This, we argue, is the most productive and sensible approach – despite the Pandora's Box of complexity that inevitably follows. Being faithful to the values of 'thick' description does not, as some might argue, mean an end to large-scale comparison or the possibility of general theory. It simply means a different way to tackle them. Indeed, as Haas's study of the Barga

Mongol notion of trust demonstrates, it is necessary to problematize epistemological individualism and sweeping universalism if we are to deepen our understanding of the multitude of ways in which trust is formed and works on social fabrics around the world.

Trust, Hierarchy and Intimacy

Anthropologists are not alone in challenging the universalism commonplace in trust research. Some philosophers have problematized it by engaging feminist critiques, and pointing to how power differences are indeed part of the intimate sphere so often idealized as a locus of trust and mutual support, both in trust research and in the folk theories of many societies. Trudy Govier (1992) and Annette Baier (1986), for example, point out that hierarchized gender relationships are usually left out of philosophical enquiries into trust. Baier (1986) attributes this blind spot in 'Western' philosophical traditions to the fact that it is mainly contractual philosophy that has concerned itself with trust. Here, it has largely been taken for granted that contracts represent agreements between equal men. Dependent women, children, slaves and proletarians have therefore not been included in the analyses. The legacy of this origin in contemporary trust research can be observed in how trust in hierarchical relationships is often ignored or simply assumed to not exist. This is of course particularly so in game-theory experiments where trust is explored without any context whatsoever.

The political scientist Russell Hardin, who has published extensively on trust in the last couple of decades (Hardin 2004, 2006; see also, e.g., Cook et al. 2005; Hardin 2003), is very explicit about this. He argues that substantial power differences wreck the possibility and meaningfulness of trust. This view is a logical consequence of his understanding of trust as encapsulation of interests. That is, I can only trust those who have encapsulated my interests into their own, simply because they are *my* interests.

This means that for Hardin, trust depends mainly on affection, and exists almost exclusively in the private sphere of intimate relationships. He takes trust to be a type of knowledge: the conscious assessment that the persons we trust have linked our interests to their own. Trust can therefore not exist among the anonymous strangers that together constitute a complex society, or in hierarchical relationships marked by diverging interests. This is also the main premise for the argument developed in *Cooperation without Trust?*, which Hardin co-authored with Karen S. Cook and Margaret Levi (Cook et al. 2005). The central claim of this book is that trust plays a limited role in the production of social orders in the modern era because it is so difficult to achieve outside of intimate relationships. Institutions – not trust – therefore function as guarantors for cooperation (Cook et al. 2005: 19).

There are a number of problems with such an analysis of trust. One of the most important is perhaps that it is based on a reductionist understanding of personal, professional and public relationships. By taking the smooth workings of trust in the intimate sphere for granted, as an underlying, unexplored premise, the analysis falls apart in the encounter with the kind of complex and at times troublesome intimacy presented in the chapters of this volume. Cook et al. (2005) take the idea that intimate relationships are essentially harmonious refuges from a calculating and self-serving world to its logical conclusion, and thus represent a radical position on the role of trust in complex societies. Nevertheless, the premise of their argument is not that far removed from the epistemological individualism underlying most trust research, and thus it illustrates clearly the importance of unpacking notions and experiences of intimacy and sociality as they appear in different contexts. As our chapters show, there is great variation in the ways in which people conceptualize intimacy, engage in trust relationships or find their trust in intimate others shattered.

Radhika Chopra's chapter speaks to the feminist critique of trust research by exploring trust relations in a highly hierarchical context: the relationships between colonial masters and their local servants in India. The case of domestic servants is interesting, as relations between them and the employers are usually not intended to be intimate; yet as Chopra shows, considerable, even 'unspeakable' intimacies, complicity and trust may develop through the servants' tending to the masters' physical, emotional and practical needs, as well as continuous physical proximity. Drawing upon the British colonial masters' conceptualizations of their role, their local subjects and the moral universe they inhabited, Chopra teases out the complex web of relationships between masters and servants, bonds that wavered between moralities of contract and family ties and generated different forms of trust. She shows how intimacies and trust created their own hierarchies of value within the household. Chopra brings attention to the peculiarity of the colonial household, in which intimate proximity did not automatically translate as blood kinship or family but included servitude of various kinds in a tightly controlled network of trust.

Whilst such inclusive colonial households resembled the big halls of medieval Europe, as a *habitus* of home it was rather moulded on the aristocratic mansions of later centuries in which shared space was built and subdivided in corridors and separate quarters. Through performing their daily chores in such organized space, servants would incorporate into the rhythms of their body movement social distinctions sedimented in the structural layout of colonial homes; in addition they would also learn how to handle invisibility. These 'body technologies', in a Maussian sense, were particularly elaborated in colonial India where one not only had to behave 'properly' in spatial terms according to class and gender, but also according to race and caste. Within the interiors of the colonial bungalow, distance and invisibility were orchestrated to convey and consolidate the racial and class divides between 'white' masters and 'black' servants. Architectural innovations of domestic spaces consigned the servant to a phantom existence, a silent figure whose presence, despite being privy to all the secrets of the home, was without acknowledgement. Nevertheless, while there was an enormous cultural and spatial divide within the household, it was also clear that the 'white' members of the household were a minority within their own walls and thus had to trust their servants' discretion in private matters. Masters and mistresses were thus compelled, despite their elevated positions, to entrust their daily lives and those of their children to their native servants, including intimate acts such as being dressed, washed and fed. Despite the absolute nature of colonial power that fixed the servants into positions of virtual enslavement, the fact that servants' work and lives were intertwined into everyday domestic worlds often created the illusion of a fictive kinship and familial bonds. Feelings of intimacy bled into distinctions of class, race and caste, often becoming relations of strong affection and even love between nannies and the children in their care. Thus, sovereignty met intimacy in the kitchens and nurseries of empire, blurring the distinctions between dependence, dominance, distance and trust. The persistent familiarity induced by intimacies of care translated into a strange tension between trust and mistrust. This form of intimacy and proximity, the author concludes, still persists in contemporary India, where the huge divides in wealth make the presence of servants common in most middle-class homes.

Chopra's analysis not only challenges the widespread idea that trust cannot exist in hierarchical relations (see, e.g., O'Neill 2002; Cook et al. 2005; Hardin 2006), but also illuminate how trust and intimate relations are shaped and moulded by the social, economic, moral and spatial landscapes in which they are played out. Indeed, by paying close attention to the complexity and variety of human life-worlds, we learn that the connection between intimacy and trust is unstable, difficult to pin down, and may arise even in the relationships that people consider to be the most inappropriate for the openness and affection that may follow. It is also clear from this case that the presumption that trust cannot exist in hierarchical relationships, that is so commonly observed in trust research (O'Neill 2002; Cook et al. 2005; Hardin 2006), is too simplistic and based on unexplored, taken-for-granted premises rather than being subjected to serious empirical scrutiny.

This exploration should not only take place in the public sphere, where it is most commonly recognized that hierarchical relations exist, but also within the intimate sphere of domestic relations, as Baier (1986) and Govier (1992) point out. For indeed, families and kinship networks are widely considered a realm of trust in many, if not most societies, despite the hierarchization of intimate relationships that inevitably follow from the power asymmetry between children and adults, and often also from the stratification of gender and unequal access to resources, networks of influence and so on. Interestingly, this association between intimate relationships and trust appears to be most explicitly pronounced in societies where family and kinship relations are most hierarchical, such as China or Latin America (Fukuyama 1996). Nevertheless, as several of the chapters here show, intimate relationships, even in contexts where they are highly idealized in the local culture, are not without complication, disappointment and estrangement.

Margit Ystanes's chapter, for example, critiques the stereotypical notion that Latin American families constitute such a tightly knit and enclosed web of trust relations that it hinders the formation of societal trust. Indeed, the *ladino* Guatemalans she has worked with do usually consider family and kin to constitute a realm of trust and intimacy, and the public sphere is marked by mistrust and confrontation. Nevertheless, in reality this boundary is highly permeable, and rests precariously on family members' continuous adherence to moral norms idealizing symbolic closures. Spatially, this distinction is epitomized in the opposition between *la casa* [the house] and *la calle* [the street], the doorway serving as the material mediator. Just as the house cannot function without a passage to the world, so the separation between these spheres is highly porous, with elements from each bleeding into the other. Ladino conceptualizations of trust and mistrust draw, among other things, upon a symbolism of blood. Those who are considered most trustworthy are related by blood; this bodily substance provides the connection that bind people together as kin, and, in the most intimate sense, to a house. Blood is a powerful, yet ambiguous symbol, evoking both good and evil within the body: life and procreation, violence and death. Blood is thus not just a vehicle for intimacy, kinship and trust, but also for embodied notions of superiority and inferiority, social distance and mistrust.

The ways in which the blood metaphor seeps into all domains of living in the Guatemalan social imaginary is coloured by their own internal colonial history and concerns to create a racial purity in the dominant population similar to that of the European Empires. There was simultaneously a concern with the 'mixed' as 'matter out of place', and ambitions to 'whiten' the population through European immigration, strict control of elite 'white' women and their sexual and reproductive lives and 'race improvement', that is, making indigenous women pregnant by 'white' men. Needless to say, these practices produced numerous kinds of violent intimacies; from the assumption that ladino boys would practice sex with young domestic workers to plantation owners' traditional rights to the 'first night' of their female indigenous employees (Hale 2006: 160), as well as the sexual control of elite women. In such ways, private desire and public status merged in concerns over kinship and heredity, often conceptualized as 'blood relations'.

As the ladino Guatemalan conception of trust rests upon this highly equivocal foundation, this creates ambiguity in intimate relationships. It also reinforces mistrust towards those considered to be of a different kind of blood: the indigenous people. The formation of trust and mistrust in this context takes place against a backdrop of the management of sexuality, respectability and social pre-eminence, and cannot be reduced to the presence of tight-knit intimate relations. Rather, the ambiguity marking these entities means that trust formation within the family rests on an unstable foundation that reaches into the public sphere, affecting trust formation there also. Ystanes argues that rather than being an outcome of solid trust relations in the intimate domain, the arid ground for the formation of societal trust in Guatemala is related to the precariousness of trust relations amongst family and kin. Her analysis thus challenges existing notions about trust, family and intimacy in Latin societies (see, e.g., Fukuyama 1996), and thereby, the idea that trust in its essence is a taken-for-granted aspect of the intimate sphere. Such presumptions should not form an unquestioned premise upon which analysis is based, but rather, be approached as an empirical question to be explored in its own right.

Similarly, Peter Geschiere's contribution goes right to the core of intimacy, trust and the social, and forcefully illustrates how problematic it is to assume that trust usually flows naturally and unhindered in relationships between people who are connected by blood, affection and domestic proximity. Drawing on more than forty years of ethnographic engagement with Maka of Southeast Cameroon, he explores intimacy and trust in the context of 'witchcraft of the house' – that is, witchcraft that strikes from within one's most intimate relationships. Maka, like so many others, consider kinship to be a source of trust and solidarity. However, this intimacy has a flipside: the possibility of jealousy and betrayal represented by the witch who strikes from within the kinship group. His study of Maka witchcraft also pays attention to notions of the body and worlds of both sensuous pleasure and suffering. Witchcraft is understood to be an evil creature residing in someone's belly, giving him or her special powers to transform into an animal or spirit. These abilities allow witches to participate in cannibalistic, transgressive banquets in which they each offer a relative to be devoured by the other witches. In daily life, such treason from within will manifest itself in illness or even death unless healers are able to discover the source of the illness and force the witch into the open. Maka witchcraft discourse, then, is fundamentally about the betrayal of kin to outsiders.

As Geschiere argues, witchcraft discourse can be read as the realization that intimacy is ambiguous – an essential anchor for social relations, yet burdened with suspicion and menace. From this perspective, the preoccupation of many peoples in present-day Africa with the proliferation of witchcraft no longer appears that exceptional; the fear of intimacy as potentially dangerous is ubiquitous. A case in point is the way that feminist philosophers remind us that power differences, and sometimes also violence, are part of intimate relationships, and that 'Western' philosophers' inability to engage with this fact in their explorations of trust reflects first and foremost their own distancing from the kinds of domestic complications that mark most people's lives (Govier 1992; Baier 1986). This close link between 'witchcraft' and 'intimacy' inevitably raises the question of how to maintain 'trust' in close relations if they can be so poisonous. It also emphasizes how problematic it is to take folk theories about the family and kinship network, as entirely harmonious spheres of mutual support, as an unquestioned premise for explorations of trust, regardless of whether these theories are 'Western', Latin American or African in their origin. Indeed, as the ethnographies provided by Chopra, Ystanes and Geschiere illustrates, intimacy has a darker flipside of power differences, subjugation, ambiguity, violence or betrayal, which must also be taken into consideration.

Biological Trusting

One of the fascinating linkages the phenomenon of trusting can make is to the realm of the biological and some of the new discoveries of neuroscience. Here we are dealing with debates about the ways in which trusting may be hard-wired into our cognitive and physiological make-up, opening up the spaces of human intersubjectivity. As the expert on early baby talk and dialoguing styles between infant and mother, the psychobiologist Colwyn Trevarthen, sums up: 'the idea of infant intersubjectivity is no less than a theory of how human minds, in human bodies, can recognize one another's impulses intuitively with or without cognitive or symbolic elaboration' (1998: 17).

In *The Interpersonal World of the Infant* (1985), which bridges the divide between psychoanalysis and cognitive psychology, Daniel Stern emphasizes the significance for a child's development of the preverbal relations of early life, which envelop the infant in an intersubjective embrace with its caretaker. During childhood and adolescence, affects and behaviour linked to a neurobiological unfolding combine with epigenetic processes related to each subject's personal experiences, leading to specific emotional habits and traits. And yet all subjects grow up within specific cultural contexts and child-rearing regimes (Broch-Due, this volume). The variation in trusting we see across the essays in this volume speaks precisely to the entanglement of trust and mistrust with different cultural styles and different ways of shaping subjects and sociality. As Siri Hustvedt so succinctly puts it: 'we become ourselves through others, and the self is a porous thing, not a sealed container. If it begins as a genetic map, it is one that is expressed over time and only in relation to the world' (2012: 70).

Having established that human infants are naturally born with social skills that are shaped within biographical and cultural frames, the next breakthrough of great relevance for anthropology is the *plasticity* of the brain itself, creating new connections in its wiring along with the maturing of the experiencing subject. The human brain is a vast, elaborated edifice and scientists are only now beginning to develop adequate tools to explore it.

At the heart of this new thinking about the faculties hard-wired into our being is a discussion which bears very directly on the phenomenon of trusting: altruism. As against the old idea that humans are born as 'blank slates' on which culture then writes its various codes for sharing, trust and cooperation, more recent research suggests that humans are indeed born with these propensities. It seems that trust, cooperation and the moral emotions play a huge role in infant psychology and are not cultural scripts that have to learnt. However, psychology and neuroscience share with philosophy an unfortunate ethnocentric tendency to generalize their findings globally. All the brains and behaviours studied in this kind of research seem to belong to subjects brought up within Western cultures. Anthropology, in contrast, has access to a vast cross-cultural array of intersubjectivities with their different cooperative and trusting behaviours. Given the elasticity of the brain, there are thus good reasons to assume that such vast differences in habitus and experiences would affect its wiring too. This is a possible avenue for cooperation between ethnography and cognitive science.

Perhaps less attractive to the topic of this volume and puzzling to many social anthropologists is the disagreement in evolutionary biology about whether altruism, and thus trust, is possible at all. This question could only seriously be asked after Charles Darwin's *On the Origins of the Species* (1859). Before this watershed in scholarship it would have been utterly nonsensical. If anything, most would have contended that there was not enough altruism in the world. The Scottish philosopher David Hume, for example, emphasized the human propensity 'to sympathize with others' in his *A Treatise of Human Nature* (1739). On this score, Darwin himself was more aligned with Hume than with many 'Darwinists', proclaiming in *The Decent of Man*: 'Any animal whatever, endowed with well-marked social instincts, the parental and filial affections being here included, would inevitably acquire a moral sense or conscience as soon as its intellectual powers had become as well developed, or nearly as well developed, as in man' (2004 [1871]: 71–72).

For Darwin, the evolution of human beings from primates depended precisely on the *continuation* of certain traits across species, emotions and empathy included. His strong belief that animals like his own dog, whose affective behaviour he scrutinized, had feelings and intentions like humans, though less sophisticated, was mocked by later generations of animal scientists. Darwin has recently been exonerated on this point of the continuity between animal and human affect. There is now widespread agreement that the evident fact that human empathy can stretch far beyond blood relatives to include even other species, is simply an incidence of 'natural' behaviour. The entrenched view of Western thinking that morality is only a thin veneer laid down by the advent of civilization to cover up an ingrained human savagery and bestiality has simply gone out of date in animal research.

One of the world's leading primatologists, Frans de Waal, takes contemporary moral philosophers to task for their holding on to the so-called 'Veneer Theory' in their conceptualization of morality and trust. Western philosophy flowing from Descartes shares with religious authorities an a priori faith in human uniqueness and separation from animals, thus rejecting evidence that points to the animal origins of human empathy, trust and rudimentary sociality. For example, monkeys and children show a marked aversion to inequity. Whilst many scholars would reject interpretive analogies drawn between human and animals as anthropomorphism, de Waal claims that the larger danger is what he terms 'anthropodenial' – the a priori rejection of shared characteristics between humans and animals – 'which leads to a wilful blindness to the human-like characteristics of animals, or the animal-like characteristics of ourselves' (de Waal 2009: 44–49).

As anthropologists who are inclined to believe in the affective interface between animal and human but do not easily trade in universals, we would rather reserve the term 'morality' for its specific elaborations of meanings and matters in a human cultural context. Turkana for their part, as Broch-Due's essay details, would enthusiastically support the idea of an 'animal morality', the very trait that makes cattle into such powerful gifts since they are moulded to embody the 'moral spirit' of their human caretakers. Similar notions of the porous boundaries between human and animal are widespread among Amazonian Indians. In her chapter for this volume, entitled 'Trustworthy Bodies: Cashinahua Cumulative Persons as Intimate Others', Cecilia McCallum gives us a window onto a culture that entrusts sociality to a physio-logic, expressing itself in a corporeal idiom. The corporality the Cashinahua have in mind is one of extraordinary capacities, for the body not only incorporates other bodies (human, animal, plants, spirit), but is also cumulative in biographical time. Their brand of phenomenology is almost an inversion of Darwin's evolutionary theory. Rather than a shared nature from which springs a diversity of species and cultures, Amerindians rather think that the world consists of a single shared culture and a diversity of natures. Being human is the overarching subject position and style of perception. Those species that are conceptualized as such self-identifying humans are ascribed a 'soul'. These souls are not seen as immaterial, as in Western thought, but substantial and active in the world. Sometimes alone and sometimes accompanied, the soul is present in a body whose flesh can easily be shed, allowing the soul to take flight and settle into another form of corporality.

Here appearance deceives; it is only by assessing behaviour that an Amerindian knows for sure one kind of body from another. Thus, a person who eats raw meat is, perhaps, a jaguar; a child who grinds her teeth whilst sleeping is changing into a peccary. By 'becoming animal' almost in a perfect Deluzeian sense (Deleuze and Guattari 1987), Cashinahua take on another perspective congruent with a different style of behaviour and sensory awareness. In emphasizing not the immutability of matter but rather its instability, this indigenous epistemology agrees with evolutionary thinking particularly on the generative force of time. By believing in the transformability of bodies into bodies or things, matter into those forms of non-matter that may be felt or known through the senses (wind or sounds or sights or smells), McCallum argues, we see the defining contours of a phenomenology rooted in temporal flow – past, present and future.

Cashinahua treat trustworthiness as embodied too: that is, as materially integrated into organs and physiologies as thought, emotion and memory. Mental faculties are believed to be liquid and to circulate in the body in the form of blood. Thoughts generate particular kinds of actions, which impinge on others, thereby moulding them. At the same time, however, thoughts originate from interactions with others and become a sort of 'experience made flesh'. Thus if someone has good thoughts, which transform into acts of generosity and kindness, prolonged contact with this kind of person will create positive memories of love and affection. These 'memories' will be integrated into the body, and subsequently generate sweet and positive thoughts and actions. However, since transformative interactions include those with other species and spirits, bodies may contain conflicting thoughts, both social and anti-social, good and bad, which emerge in behaviour at different points in time. Most interestingly, this Amazonian thinking seems to be in agreement with the power of trusting as an act, a performance, and thus with Barga of Mongolia and Turkana of Northern Kenya.

Whatever the case, for some contemporary sociobiologists any feeling or act directed at others, in human or animal, runs counter to the hard-programmed belief about the selfish gene: that natural selection works through sexual reproduction only and in ways that leads to the survival of the fittest (Wilson 1980). Typically, this notion of the 'fittest' seems to be taken quite literally, conjuring up on the page a feisty, muscular, testosterone-driven individual pushing evolution ahead by outcompeting everybody else who does not carry his own genes. Violence seems to be the order of the day, filtering even into descriptions of human pregnancy, which Richard Dawkins recently imagined as a 'womb in warfare', where the selfish organisms of mother and foetus were apparently engaged in lethal strife. There is not much space left for intersubjectivity, sociality or any kind of emotional complexity in such a vocabulary about the brute nature of being.

To solve this self-created enigma of altruism, some evolutionary biologists have come up with the notion of 'group selection' in which individuals sacrifice personal fitness on behalf of other members of the kin group (Hamilton 1996). An example would be a warrior sacrificing his life to protect his clan on the grounds that his nephews, sharing parts of his gene pool, will ensure the survival of his own selfish genes through his kinsmen's own procreation. In this version of altruistic group behaviour we are not allowed to imagine that some advanced types of hominids developed language as a tool of communication since that gave them a competitive advantage over those without. On the contrary, it would boil down to a single individual, having a greater linguistic capacity than others, who would, as a consequence, leave more offspring. But since 'the best talkers don't necessarily make the best listeners', as a reviewer succinctly pointed out, we would need two sorts of selection simultaneously, which only compounds the problem in evolutionary circles (Lewontin 1998).

There are more sophisticated versions of sociobiology, like the one proffered by Sarah Blaffer Hrdy, who focuses on evolution from the 'perspective of oestrogen' as it were, but is convinced that parturition does not inevitably lead to female nurturing. Since she straddles the whole spectrum of trusting from intimate to social from an evolutionary perspective, it is worthwhile for our discussion to take a closer look at her argument.

In her magnum opus *Mother Nature: A History of Mothers, Infants, and Natural Selection* (2000), Hrdy draws on literature, history, anthropology and evolutionary biology to buttress her tough-minded thesis that motherhood is not the tender state so often envisioned but rather a minefield. Her journey across species, and deep into human evolution, is littered with aborted foetuses, infanticide and abandoned infants. What drives her argument is the gendered quality / quantity of genes dilemma so favoured by sociobiology. In this narrative, the female of the species is primed to consider quality when choosing how many offspring to nurture. A human baby, for instance, requires a high calorie intake to grow up: thus a mother is inclined to choose fewer offspring or none at all, contingent upon personal and familial gains. The male of the species, in contrast, not burdened with long-term caring responsibilities, is primed to go for quantity: spreading his sperm widely around to sire as many offspring as possible in order to pass on his genes.

Hrdy's revisionist take on mothering, which she claims is not instinctive, contra her male colleagues in evolutionary biology, is curiously inspired by William Hamilton's theory of 'group selection' too. Hrdy needs to close this explanatory gap: aside from the tiny corpses left in the wake of women's tough reproductive choices during evolution, mothers are also known to love their babies fervently even if not unconditionally. On the other side of the equation, baby love is absolutely unconditional, desperately vying for all the attention it can muster from its mother. Babies are built in flesh and behaviour to appeal to adult hearts. These calculations of love on the parts of mothers and babies,

Hrdy claims, reflect the genetic logic of kin helping kin when the benefit outweighs the cost. However, the overlap in interest of mother and child is not complete. The mother needs to spread her devotion over her whole family, to those already born, but also save some energy for having another baby in the future.

From the perspective of social science, however, which takes as point of departure that individuals are born into a *habitus* organized by specific physical, social and linguistic structures, the design of which varies across the spectrum of livelihoods and throughout human history, this circular debate of whether altruism exists beyond the gene leaves a rather curious reverberation. There is an interesting echo of the universalistic and egoistic tenets of popular versions of evolutionary biology in economic thinking. Here the 'invisible hand' of the market plays a similar role as the selfish gene in natural selection, whether it concerns the survival of the 'fittest', the 'greediest', the 'nastiest' or the 'nicest'.

Trust and Anthropology

So far we have used ethnography from the chapters of this volume to problematize approaches to trust formulated within other disciplines. We might ask why anthropologists should concern themselves with this field, which appears to be going in directions far removed from anthropological methods and theorising. Our contention is that anthropology has much to contribute to trust research, mainly by giving a more serious treatment to the diversity and intricacy of notions of self and social order. Furthermore, we also argue that by approaching classic anthropological topics such as notions of self, intimacy, sociality, embodiment, kinship, morality and political processes through the lens of trust, new insights will arise.

Regarding the first point, by introducing us to a notion of trust so radically different from the often risk-oriented conceptions we find in Euro-American trust research, and using it to critique the unquestioned assumptions contained in them, Paula Haas makes a very convincing case for the contributions of ethnography in this field. Russell Hardin has pointed out that much of the literature on trust is in reality about trustworthiness, not trust (1996). As such, Haas's focus on the Barga Mongol act of trusting as something entirely unrelated to trustworthiness represents a new and unexplored angle in the study of trust. By focusing on this, Haas also opens up a social landscape where power and the act of trusting interact in ways that one might think impossible based on conventional trust research, in which hierarchies are either disregarded, or their possible coexistence with trust relations dismissed. Similarly, Chopra, Ystanes and Geschiere deconstruct common unquestioned premises in trust research by showing respectively how trust and intimacy is formed in hierarchical relationships where the people involved strive to maintain distance, how trust in ladino Guatemalan families rests on a precarious foundation, and how intimacy among Cameroonian Maka is both idealized and feared. By attending to such messy complexities of daily life, our understanding of both trust and intimacy will become more comprehensive.

As it stands, existing approaches are analytically ill-equipped to help us advance our insights into exactly how personal and social trust is produced, and what intimacy consists of in particular contexts. By simplifying the complex nature of the biological, the intimate and the social, as well as the intricate links between them, they contribute little to our understanding of intimacy and trust, or the multiple entanglements of the personal and the social. Classic anthropological concerns such as notions of self, intimacy, sociality, embodiment, kinship, morality and political processes, on the other hand, are at the core of the matter. By exploring how trust and mistrust are produced in actual landscapes of multiple subjectivities, rather than in highly abstracted, notions of 'society', we can further our understanding of trust and its social role. Indeed, as Corsín Jiménez points out, a theory that reaffirms our trust in anthropological comparison will make a useful antithesis to the way 'social and politic theory has called upon trust as a placeholder for robust public knowledge and prudential political choice' (Corsín Jiménez 2011: 179). This kind of comparative contribution to the field of trust research is precisely the aim of this volume.

In this ethnographic comparison, it is nevertheless necessary to depart from traditional anthropological approaches to trust and intimacy. The scant theorizing on trust formation per se found amongst our older school seems as refractory and thinly conceived as in other disciplines. Most vintage anthropologists of 'trust' typically dig themselves deep into the realm of the intimate, where 'trust' is supposed to originate and remain pure. It is in the safe haven of family, kin group or community that anthropological models assume trust is most intense. Here 'trust' is a property of reciprocity, as exemplified by Marshal Sahlins's seminal model (1974 [1965]) – it is assumed to be highest at home and to diminish gradually the further out in the social network you get (see also Ingold [1986] for a more recent application). Such general modelling, bent towards the 'idyllic small-scale' of localized kinship relations, seems particularly ill-suited to explain the workings of trusting across complex modern societies in a globalized age, but also, as the examples above illustrate, even within such small entities as households and kinship networks. There are of course noteworthy exceptions to this general disinterest in theorizing and exploring trust in its own right, and the few examples that exist come out of fine-grained ethnography. A superb contribution, and an inspiration for this volume, is Parker Shipton's monograph *The Nature of Entrustment: Intimacy, Exchange and the Sacred in Africa* (Shipton 2007). Based on the complex exchange practices amongst the Luo of Western Kenya, Shipton develops the idea of *entrustment* as a multiparous phenomenon. Taking hold of indigenous practises of entrusting children, animals, objects, money and spiritual dimensions with others throughout the whole social network of kith and kin, Shipton shows how Luo collapse the firm 'Western' distinctions between the domains of economy and religion, insurance and sacrifice, the material and immaterial, the intimate and the social. For them, credit depends on a close relationship between lender and borrower buttressed by the production of trust over time by means of frequent acts of entrustment of persons and things. In the face of modern bankers and developers who insist that the economic sphere should be ruled by rationality, profit, robust property rights and self-interest, Luo customers continue to prioritise claims emanating from the social obligations of entrustment before they will settle their bank accounts or pay their a tax bill. This study exemplifies how kin relations can indeed form the basis for mutually supportive relationships of trust, but also that such relations require conscious work to be maintained as such through ever-evolving acts of entrustment.

In so far as the ethnographic focus on trust and trusting has taken our authors along similar pathways to those envisioned in this complex notion of entrustment, it has led them to depart from the main avenue of contemporary trust research in other disciplines that seeks to pinpoint trust in a firm, unequivocal definition. Indeed, because trust continues to be an elusive concept, there is a tendency to define it as anything from social capital, expectations about the future, encapsulated interests or the willingness to trade, cooperate or take risk (see, e.g., Luhmann 1979; Roniger 1985, 1990; Fukuyama 1996; Putnam 2000; Hardin 2003; Levi 2003; Ostrom 2003; Ostrom and Walker 2003). Most approaches to trust are tied to the notion of risk and actors' calculations of other people's trustworthiness. In the ethnographic cases presented here, however, different ways of understanding, experiencing and creating trust emerge – all of them deeply embedded in local understandings and practices concerning morality, sociality and intimacy.

Towards an Anthropology of Trusting

The language used in any analysis is a good indicator of the kind of theorizing it is built upon. Classical philosophy typically employs trust in the noun mode, as an idea or essence sometimes qualified by an adjective. In contrast, we suggest that the case studies in this volume make it clear we should focus more on trust as a verb, and on *acts of trusting*. This is because trust, as a noun, tends to emphasize an individual subject's deliberation to enter a contract or take risk, while trust as a verb conjures up an intersubjective space of social anticipation binding subjects together. Adjectives conjure up how subjects inhabit a world; verbs reveal the way subjects interact with the world through endeavour and emotion. Trusting is a social phenomenon saturated with sentiment, motivation and meaning which goes far beyond any pure, cool calculation by individuals. In other words, to capture analytically this experiential complex we need to move away from a representational stance, focusing on the correspondence between phenomena like 'trust' and 'risk', and develop more performative approaches to trusting, which focus on various forms of agency.

In addition to matters of grammar, the vocabulary of trusting is also indicative of motivation, meaning and social orientation. For example, the English word 'trust' stems from medieval Scandinavia where the Old Norse *traust* connoted a person who was steadfast and sturdy as a 'pillar'. Etymologically 'trust' also sprang from *traustr* and thus 'faith'. Whilst these days the proper translation of 'trust' would be *'tillit'*, the Nordic roots of the English word 'trust' are a reminder of the shared ethos of Scandinavian peoples, who collectively score the highest on all available trust barometers worldwide. In Scandinavia, *tillit* is still intimately bound up with the 'personal' and the 'social', evoking moral qualities and acts across diverse arenas of life. This, then, marks a divergence from the English 'trust', which in its contemporary definitions focuses extensively on the contractual. According to the Merriam-Webster web dictionary, 'trust' has historically drawn a number of seemingly disparate meanings around itself. Archaic meanings evoke a person with characteristics such as ability, strength, truth and hope. But 'trust' then became associated with an array of legal and financial relationships. A trustee, for instance, is someone awarded the custody of a child or the care of an office, while a 'trust' in the pecuniary sense can be everything from a loan given in anticipation of future repayment, a property interest held by one person for the benefit of another, or an assembly of firms formed by legal agreement for the purpose of reducing competition.

Outside of Europe, we find that in Guatemala, for instance, the Spanish word *confianza*, which is usually translated as 'trust', also connotes familiarity, informality, confidence and faith. In contrast to the English term, the Spanish one is geared towards matters of sociality, kinship and closeness rather than towards contracts and finance. To say that one has trust in someone [*tener confianza con alguien*] is to say that one has a close relationship of some kind with that person. The languages of the Luo and Turkana provide yet more meanings in the vocabulary of trust. Here, there are no words that fall neatly into Western categories of the personal or contractual and it would be hard to come up with a simple translation of the word 'trust'. Local terms for 'trusting' consist of a broader range of meanings and acts. And yet it is precisely by paying attention to these cultural nuances and couplings between emotions, acts and domains of experience that we can hope to come closer to the diverse experience of trusting. This, in turn, would be the empirical basis for building sounder cross-cultural models of trust.

The Problem of the Moral

We argue that sound models of trust cannot be built on taken-for-granted and 'thinly' conceived premises, but rather, on comprehensive empirical studies of how people come to trust in different contexts. While this effort may appear to some as hopelessly anti-theoretical, we maintain that this is not the case and that there is a common thread running through all of our chapters which presents an interesting theoretical lead for an ethnography of trusting, namely the problem of the moral. For example, Vigdis Broch-Due recounts the trouble that ensued when normally inalienable cattle, whose existence is profoundly intertwined with that of human beings, were channelled into the market as commodities. This violation of Turkana moral economy has produced a relatively new phenomenon in the Kenyan hinterland: the presence of animal witches amongst their livestock. The metaphorical interweaving of person, animal and the wider world among Turkana is not simply a semantic or conceptual artifice but a lived reality: a vital flow charged with bodily and sensory power, in which self, group, other species and world are brought together. Here trusting is a cross-species affair. When Turkana treat their cattle as social beings, this reflects not merely a metaphoric or symbolic relation but a deeper, participatory, metonymic and material involvement in each others' lives. Cattle are a crucial part of Turkana social landscapes; they provide sustenance for human bodies and 'pathways' to the formation of new relationships through sharing, giving and trading milk, meat and animals. Broch-Due argues that the emergence of cattle witches testifies to the challenge to this social and moral universe brought about by the increasing commodification of cattle – a process that not only affect economic life, but also brings about a reconfiguration of intimacy, trust and sociality. This relates to how the Turkana social universe is marked by the intimate interconnection of bodies and substances; without animals no trust formation is possible, according to the pastoralist ethos and cultural logic. Removing animals from their traditional sphere and inserting them into the market economy thus causes significant trouble in the realm of trust formation. By drawing on Bourdieu's concept of *habitus*, psychoanalysis and Julia Kristeva's notion of the abject, Broch-Due illustrates how reactions to changes at a societal level are deeply grounded in the formation of trust in the intimate sphere. It is in the context of the household and family that the harmful consequences of cattle commodification manifest themselves and unleash destructive forces. Consequently, this chapter emphasizes the significance of understanding local forms of morality, sociality and physical intimacy if we are to comprehend larger societal processes. Broch-Due's contribution also reminds us of how interconnected economic processes are with the moral, and the potential they have to create rifts in the social fabric.

Gloria Goodwin Raheja's chapter is another case in point. She presents us with a painful account of the introduction of mining in Appalachia and its destructive effects on trust relations, both in intimate relationships, among kin and community, and the wider social order. In the past, Appalachian identity was rooted in the landscape itself: each self-sufficient community occupied a distinct valley separated from its neighbours by a rim of hills. This mountain scenery shaped forms of sociality by knitting kith and kin into an intimate mesh of mutual dependency and trust. The arrival of the mining companies literally exploded this physical and social landscape, polluting rivers and flattening forests and hills. Along with these natural signposts, layers of social inscription also disappeared, such as place names, community structures and stories that anchored social memory in the landscape. Conflicts in West Virginia's Logan County in the 1920s, between miners and coal operators, over the right to unionize, were the most violent labour struggles in American history.

The oppressive nature of coal-mining labour enhanced trust formation among families as they closed ranks against capitalist incursion. In the process, however, the bonds of intimate trust became fractured, as men and women adopted sometimes conflicting and contradictory perspectives on economic and social transformation; on the ways that family intimacy should be maintained; on masculinity; and on the nature of the trust that could be placed in local and state-level government, in representatives of organized religion and in union organizers. There were also new forces pushing people together in unexpected ways. For the labour demands of mining brought African-American migrants to the mountains, and with them came new styles of music and storytelling that mingled with the Appalachian modes into a new medley of sounds and tales, black and white. In her evocative and eloquent prose, Raheja teases out of these fusions of music and stories not only the social history of mining, but also the ways in which new networks of trust and solidarity were forged by an emergent class-consciousness that stretched across racial lines. Thus, Raheja illustrates the importance of not ignoring social and moral universes while studying trust in the context of economic relations. The rich material outlined here speaks about losses and gains – of intimacy, trust and social coherence – which can never be captured by game-oriented models of trust.

Similarly, the chapter by Misha Mintz-Roth and Amrik Heyer emphasizes the profound intertwining of economic processes with the realm of emotions. The authors explain the expansion of state-sponsored corporate capitalism in Kenya into locally embedded relations of exchange, focusing on the mobile money transfer service, M-Pesa, developed by the leading national telecom operator, Safaricom. Unlike many European nations, Kenyans have problems in imagining a truly national community. Already before the Second World War, the inaugural narrative of modern Kenyan nationalism, Jomo Kenyatta's *Facing Mount Kenya* (1938), had repeatedly underlined the wholeness and completeness of traditional Kikuyu life. When Kenyatta was inaugurated in 1963 as the first president of an independent country, the 'imagined community' (Anderson 1983) of his Kikuyu tribe became the model for the nation as a whole, thereby erasing its huge ethnic diversity. This image of a nation based on the narrative of the dominant group alone has recently exploded with a vengeance to violently fragment both the idea of a homogenous nation and the privileged position of the Kikuyu within it.

Nonetheless, based on an ambitious business model whose goal was national dominance in e-finance, Safaricom set out to create an 'imagined community', if not of citizens, then at least of subscribers. Through the use of radio, billboards and print advertisement featuring landmarks, songs and snapshots of the country's huge ethnic diversity, Safaricom rallied people around the slogan 'send money home'. The company supplied a narrative with a vision of Kenya as a nation of migrants and remitters – the slogan itself echoing the rhetoric of the legendary Jomo Kenyatta. Safaricom pictured itself as a responsible provider that would support both local migrants and households, and the nation, in one great sweep of financial service.

The authors point to the irony that Safaricom apparently succeeded in using the experience, images and sentiments of nationhood, otherwise fractured by political corruption and ethnic violence, to appeal to Kenyan consumers. At the launch of the company on the stock exchange, this 'imagined community' of mobile communicators and remitters had achieved widespread salience, judging from the long queues of people nationwide eager to purchase shares. This initial exuberance was soon dampened as the stock price quickly fell, and the bitter loss left many disenchanted, feeling that Safaricom was just as deceitful as any other government agency. The trust so rapidly built up in an enthusiastic fervour of speculation evaporated, echoing the many past narratives of such financial bubbles, from the South Sea Company to the spectacular collapse on a world scale of Lehman Brothers.

Despite the initial disappointment of speculators, mobile financial services have nevertheless gone on to become a resounding success by contrast to the preceeding telecom arena, which was a sprawling morass of inefficiency, corruption, poor coverage and bad service. Companies like Safaricom have brought millions of Africans into the formal financial market, brought down crime by substituting pin-secured virtual accounts for cash, and created tens of thousands of jobs among local agents. They have also built more solid imagined communities of trust around the M-Pesa money-transfer service, not cut along the lines of the 'nation' or the 'tribe', but rather along gendered lines. Sending money home, as the initial propaganda proposed, was largely directed towards male migrants working in the city, who needed to transfer savings back to the countryside where their wives were in charge of children, farms and petty trade. While in the past, more cumbersome ways of sending money back went through the hands of men, the advent of transfer via the mobile phone circumvented this and put things directly in the hands of women. Through the mere 'touch of a button', there has been a significant transformation in the gendered flows of money and service, mainly from men to women. The power of digital technology to effect 'time-space compression' (Harvey 1991) by money transfers electronically means that men more seldom travel to rural homes. Male absence weakens the marital bond and lessens dependency on land controlled by the clan, but empowers female decision making and economic freedom. Through products such as M-Pesa, women can claim financial support from children working far away and can more easily free themselves from the control of husbands and fathers by demanding direct access to electronic savings.

Trust networks multiplied by means of such mobile finance, Mintz-Roth and Heyer discovered, but their formation was similarly gendered, with male transfers more in line with the contractual mode of obligations that otherwise characterized patrifocal transactions. Women, in contrast, expressed their bonds with each other in a more emotional vocabulary of care and responsibility; their trust networks were matrifocal in orientation. These different sentiments were evident in their relationship to the phone itself. Whereas women personalized the device by selecting ring-tones, men saw it as a symbol of alienation and insecurity. Interestingly, men from those ethnic groups in Kenya with a strong patriarchal bent feared that women's intimate bonding with their phones and the new finance opportunities they offered would fracture male authority. Such possibilities have paved the way for new ties of intimacy and trust between women, and have undermined male dominance in family and economic matters. The authors thus argue that the M-Pesa mobile technology has opened up new social geographies of trust and intimate relations – landscapes that could not be captured by reductionist theorizing about trust we so often find in the study of transactions and economic processes.

The significance of the phones as personalized objects and technologies that contribute to reconfiguring the social landscape of trust and intimacy illustrates how the problem of the moral not only resides in interpersonal spaces, but also in objects and bodily substances. Our approach to the relationship between trusting, intimacy and the material world is inspired by Marcel Mauss' *The Gift* and his ideas about how the giving of gifts contribute to the weaving together of persons in relationships marked by reciprocity and obligation. Mauss argued (2002 [1925]) that the gift carried the 'spirit' of the giver out into the social world, making people feel 'the obligation to give, the obligation to receive, and the obligation to reciprocate'. In other words, donors give something of their personal being with their gifts, a potential danger to the well-being of any recipient who fails to make a return. Thus, 'the spirit of the gift' joins persons and objects in an intimate fashion. Contained within this intimacy, however, is an ambivalent tension surrounding the *obligation* to reciprocate. This disguised hint of an expected return flavours the relationship between the subjects joined by the exchange of the objects. Just as with trust, the gift has its own downsides and dangers. Broch-Due's chapter is a good example of the ways in which gifting in certain instances is a prerequisite for trusting, but also of the ways that the spirit of the gift, in this case a cow, can turn sour, destroying not only trust but the health of the persons affected. Witchcraft accusations are intimately connected to gifting-gone-wrong across contemporary Africa and in medieval Europe too (see Geschiere, this volume), and are fused with concerns about morality and sociality.

Chris Kaplonski's contribution to this volume explores the social role of a particular kind of official papers: secret police files in post-socialist Mongolia. The uncanny paradox of this case is that in the reconciliation process, which occurred decades after the terrible events of the former repressive Soviet regime, the dignity and lifework of the long-deceased could only be pieced together from fragments and narratives left in the archives of the perpetrators. In other words, the mourning relatives had to trust in otherwise treacherous sources. It was simply the only means available to open up a path to the past and recover the wronged dead for social memory. Interestingly, Kaplonski shows that not only are the papers produced by the deeply mistrusted regime now trusted, they also become embodiments of relationships and important links to the past for the families he writes about. In a profound way, these fragments of paper served as small 'gifts', each providing a piece of the memory puzzle of reconstituting the 'spirit' of the dead and restoring them as social persons, who could then live on in public imagination as proper moral selves. Again, we find that between trusting and gifting there can be tension and unpredictability.

By exploring these processes, Kaplonski not only adds layers to the ethnographic exploration of trust and the material world, he also illustrates the usefulness of thinking about anthropological puzzles through the lens of 'trust' – by taking this approach, new insights may develop. In this case, it allows us to examine the multiple aspects of rehabilitation processes in Mongolia, rather than seeing them as single-layered and paradoxical. Furthermore, by focusing on 'trust' rather than 'respect', as previous studies have done, overlooked aspects of sociality and society in Mongolia are teased out.

Broch-Due's story about the trouble that ensued when normally inalienable cattle were channelled into the market as commodities parallels the problems of such 'new' gift phenomena as organ donations. Because the body is universally the seat of personhood, an organ is as inalienable as an object can be. In today's practice, when organs are either transacted commercially or given to total strangers, this gift of oneself can easily be turned into a commodity and dramatically confuse the boundaries between 'self' and 'other'.

A telling case of such gift-trouble surrounding the question of sperm donation by anonymous donors is discussed in Jennifer Speirs' chapter. Physicians in the UK have carried out artificial insemination with donated human semen since the late 1930s, as a means of bypassing male infertility and helping childless women achieve pregnancy. Medical practitioners insisted on donor anonymity in order to ensure the legitimacy of children and avoid the possible consequences for the recipients if the husband was not treated as the 'real' father. The birth certificates of these children recorded the mother's husband as the father of the child, not the donor. In effect, as pointed out by Speirs, this entailed an illegal act by the person registering the birth. While the Human Fertilisation and Embryology Act of 1990 enshrined the anonymity of donors in law, it was circumvented soon after by the regulations of 2005 that stated that donor-conceived children for the future should enjoy access to information about their donors. The whole legislation process spurred fierce debate.

Riding on the new wave of biological reductionism in the public imagination, donor-conceived activists reasoned that it was a human right to know one's genetic heritage, and lobbied for gamete donors' real names to be recorded on birth certificates. Adopted people, they argued, had already won the right to access their original birth certificate. Infertility clinicians opposed such revelations, claiming donors needed protection from potential emotional and financial claims from their donor offspring. It would further be a breach of contract since they had gifted their sperm on the condition of anonymity. Many parents of donor-conceived children joined commentators who also disagreed that what constitutes a parent, particularly a father, could be reduced to a matter of semen and genes only. Rather, they focused on social fatherhood, the shaping influence of the daily upbringing and the love of children in your care. This sensitive issue of donors' anonymity sparked a climate of mutual distrust between infertility specialists, parents and donor-conceived people.

Whether they were pressing for the reinstatement of anonymity, support for education programmes or annotated birth certificates, they all aimed at swaying the opinion of policy makers to their own advantage. Most significantly, Speirs goes on to argue, the state itself was acquiring the status of a person with responsibility. As in other instances of gifts-gone-wrong in the public domain, it became a question of state: whether the legal documents issued by the state on behalf of its citizenry could really be trusted. In her analysis, Speirs draws upon British notions of kinship, masculinity, fatherhood and respectability, thus locating the issue of trust also in this context firmly within a framework of morality and sociality. The fact that gamete donation can bring out such controversies involving a whole range of social institutions illustrates that bodily substances can serve as a useful lens for exploring the social. We see this significance of flesh echoed in many cultural theories of trust in this volume, ranging from Scotland, Northern Kenya and the Amazon. Similarly, the exchange of bodily substances as an expression of the core idea of sociality is commonly understood through the idiom of gifting. Without such gifting of thoughts and actions, neither trust nor mistrust is possible, as it constitutes the very foundation of personhood, sociality and moral reasoning.

Concluding Thoughts

Our ethnographic cases highlight the nebulous quality of trust and trusting – its relations to the intimate, corporeal and personal, but also to the public and social. The problem of trust constitutes an interdisciplinary field, in which economics, philosophy and political science dominate theorizing about the 'public' face of trusting, while neuroscience, psychoanalysis and sociobiology dominate theorising about its 'personal' face. Not only has there been little cross-fertilization among these different disciplines, but contemporary anthropology has also been curiously absent from this influential debate. Crucially, the important debates about trust are being waged not only in seminar rooms but probably more significantly in the popular media and public arenas. The terms of that debate, unfortunately, tend to be highly ethnocentric, taking 'Western' notions of trust uncritically as universally given and valid.

The quintessential theoretical contribution of this volume to the evolving scholarship in this field is that trust formations in the 'public' and 'private' spheres are intrinsically interlinked. Because trust works across this broad canvas of human existence, extending through the whole lifecycle and across different domains, it becomes entangled with other emotions and experiences; the shape of this entanglement will by necessity vary across personal and social biographies, along with the diversity of cultural forms of sociality. In short, trust is an experiential multitude, being both a general and particular phenomena. By extension, this implies that any deep analysis of trusting needs to pay particular attention to the specificities of context, history and the wider connectivity of each case to translocal and global networks.

What can be drawn from the chapters of this volume is not primarily robust knowledge about what trust is. If anything, the variety of ways in which this phenomenon is conceptualised and experienced across different life-worlds illustrates the difficulty in establishing a universally valid theory about what trust is without further investigation of its local manifestations. Any existing theorization of trust may capture and crystallize something specific, but it may not correspond to what people in other contexts think about, accept or translate as trust. The reasoning about situations and behaviours that are likely to enhance and produce trust underlying most contemporary trust research is too narrowly focused on 'Western' contexts – and often an abstraction of an imagined, generic version of such societies and relationships.

Rather, by providing a contrast to such theorizations of trust, this volume illustrates the multitude of ways in which people come to trust or mistrust intimate others, allowing ethnographic diversity rather than conceptual unity to guide the analyses. We consider this a contribution to an ethnography of trusting, emphasizing the moral aspects of such acts and the kinds of situations that enable or thwart them in complex, 'thickly' described life-worlds. Being faithful to the values of 'thick' description does not, as some might argue, mean an end to large-scale comparison or the possibility of general theory. It simply means a different way to tackle them. By placing the ethnographic cases in this volume on a broader theoretical and interdisciplinary canvas, we have tried to tease out a few variables that could generate such a variation-centred model of the triangulation of intimacy, trust and the social.

The most significant fact about trusting is that it realizes itself in the intersubjective space *between* persons. As trust scholars we need to fill this intersubjective space with matters of nature and materiality, not only the matter of discourse. We are arguing for a shift from a representational stance on 'trust' and the questions of correspondence between, for example, 'trust' and 'risk' or 'neurons', to a *performativity* of 'trusting', of practices, doings and actions. If performativity is linked not only to the formation of the subject but also to the production of the matter of bodies, as the physicist Karen Barad (2003) has so succinctly theorized on the basis of quantum physics, we can explore how 'flesh' and 'word' together forge subjects into their shape in ways that are historically, culturally and socially specific. The horizon of trusting is a promising field for exploring 'the entanglement of matter and meaning' through this brand of performative studies (2003: 3).

We have indeed arrived at the core idea behind this volume, which is precisely that anthropology offers a vital and hitherto neglected discourse that can bind together the disparate studies and ideas of trust being carried out in different disciplines, ranging from neuroscience and biology to philosophy.

References

Anderson, B. 1983. *Imagined Communities*. London: Verso.
Baier, A. 1986. 'Trust', *Ethics* 96(2): 231–260.
Barad, K. 2003. 'Posthumanist Performativity: Toward an Understanding of How Matter Comes to Matter', *Signs* 28(3): 801– 831.
Cook, K.S., R. Hardin and M. Levi. 2005. *Cooperation without Trust?* New York: Russell Sage Foundation.
Corsín Jiménez, A. 2011. 'Trust in Anthropology', *Anthropological Theory* 11(2): 177–196.
Darwin, C. 1859. *On the Origin of the Species*. London: John Murray.
—— 2004 [1871]. *The Descent of Man*. London: Penguin.
de Waal, F. 2009. *Primates and Philosophers: How Morality Evolved*. Princeton: Princeton University Press.
Deleuze, G. and F. Guattari. 1987. *A Thousand Plateaus: Capitalism and Schizophrenia*. Minneapolis: University of Minnesota Press.
Fukuyama, F. 1996. *Trust: The Social Virtues and the Creation of Prosperity*. New York: Free Press.
Geertz, C. 1973. 'Thick Description: Toward an Interpretive Theory of Culture'. In *The Interpretation of Cultures*, 3–30. New York: Basic Books.
Govier, T. 1992. 'Trust, Distrust, and Feminist Theory', *Hypatia* 7(1): 16–33.
—— 1997. *Social Trust and Human Communities*. Montreal: McGill-Queen's University Press.
Grimen, H. 2009. *Hva er tillit*. Oslo: Universitetsforlaget.
Hale, C.R. 2006. *Más Que un Indio [More Than an Indian]: Racial Ambivalence and Neoliberal Multiculturalism in Guatemala*. School of American Research Resident Scholar Book. Santa Fe, New Mexico: School of American Research Press.
Hamilton, W.D. 1996. *Narrow Roads of Gene Land vol. 1: Evolution of Social Behaviour*. Oxford: Oxford University Press.
Hardin, R. 1996. 'Trustworthiness', *Ethics* 107(1): 26–42.
—— 2002. *Trust and Trustworthiness*. New York: Russell Sage Foundation.
—— 2003. 'Gaming Trust'. In E. Ostrom and J. Walker (eds), *Trust and Reciprocity: Interdisciplinary Lessons from Experimental Research*, 80–101. New York: Russell Sage Foundation.
—— (ed.). 2004. *Distrust*. New York: Russel Sage Foundation.
—— 2006. *Trust*. Cambridge: Polity Press.
Harvey, D. 1991. *The Condition of Postmodernity: An Enquiry into the Origins of Cultural Change*. Malden: Wiley-Blackwell.
Hobbes, T. 1996 [1651]. *Leviathan*. Oxford: Oxford University Press.
Hrdy, S. 2000. *Mother Nature: Maternal Instincts and How They Shape the Human Species*. New York: Ballantine Books.
Hume, D. 2000 [1739]. *A Treatise of Human Nature*. Oxford: Oxford University Press.
Hustvedt, S. 2012. *Living, Thinking, Looking: Essays*. New York: Picador.

Ingold, T. 1986. *The Appropriation of Nature: Essays on Human Ecology and Social Relations*. Manchester: Manchester University Press.
Levi, M. 2003. 'The Transformation of a Skeptic: What Nonexperimentalists Can Learn from Experimentalists'. In E. Ostrom and J. Walker (eds), *Trust and Reciprocity: Interdisciplinary Lessons from Experimental Research*, 373–380. New York: Russell Sage Foundation.
Lewontin, R.C. 1998. 'Survival of the Nicest?', *New York Review of Books*, October 22.
Luhmann, N. 1979. *Trust and Power*. Chichester: John Wiley.
Marx, K. 1990 [1867]. *Capital, Volume I* (trans. Ben Fowkes). London: Penguin Books.
Mauss, M. 2002 [1925]. *The Gift: The Form and Reason for Exchange in Archaic Societies*. London: Routledge.
Muldrew, C. 1998. *The Economy of Obligation: The Culture of Credit and Social Relations in Early Modern England*. London: Palgrave Macmillan.
O'Neill, O. 2002. *A Question of Trust: The BBC Reith Lectures 2002*. Cambridge: Cambridge University Press.
Ostrom, E. 2003. 'Toward a Behavioral Theory Linking Trust, Reciprocity, and Reputation'. In E. Ostrom and J. Walker (eds), *Trust and Reciprocity. Interdisciplinary Lessons from Experimental Research*, 19–79. New York: Russell Sage Foundation.
Ostrom, E. and J. Walker (eds). 2003. *Trust and Reciprocity: Interdisciplinary Lessons from Experimental Research*. New York: Russell Sage Foundation.
Parry, J., and M. Bloch. 1989. *Money and the Morality of Exchange*. Cambridge: Cambridge University Press.
Putnam, R.D. 2000. *Bowling Alone: The Collapse and Revival of American Community*. New York: Simon & Schuster.
Roniger, L. 1985. 'Institutionalized Inequalities, the Structure of Trust, and Clientelism in Modern Latin America'. In E. Cohen, M. Lissak and U. Almagor (eds), *Comparative Social Dynamics: Essays in Honor of S.N. Eisenstadt*, 148–163. Boulder: Westview Press.
—— 1990. *Hierarchy and Trust in Modern Mexico and Brazil*. New York: Praeger.
Sahlins, M. 1974 [1965]. 'On the Sociology of Primitive Exchange'. In E.M. Banton (ed.), *The Relevance of Models for Social Anthropology*. London: Tavistock.
Shipton, P. 2007. *The Nature of Entrustment: Intimacy, Exchange, and the Sacred in Africa*. New Haven: Yale University Press.
Smith, A. 2008 [1776]. *An Inquiry into the Nature and Causes of the Wealth of Nations: A Selected Edition* (ed. K. Sutherland). Oxford Paperbacks.
Stern, D. 1985. *The Interpersonal World of the Infant*. New York: Basic Books.
Thompson, E.P. 1971. 'The Moral Economy of the English Crowd in the 18th Century', *Past and Present* 50: 76–136.
Tönnies, F. 2001 [1887]. *Community and Civil Society* (ed. J. Harris). Cambridge: Cambridge University Press.
Trevarthen, C. 1998. 'The Concept and Foundations of Infant Intersubjectivity'. In S. Braten (ed.), *Intersubjective Communication and Emotion in Early Ontogeny*, 15–46. Cambridge: Cambridge University Press.

Weber, M. 1978 [1904]. *Economy and Society* (ed. G. Roth and C. Wittich). Berkeley: University of California Press.
Wilson, E.O. 1980. *Sociobiology: The Abridged Edition*. Cambridge, MA: Belknap Press.
Ystanes, M. 2011. 'Precarious Trust: Problems of Managing Self and Sociality in Guatemala'. PhD dissertation. Bergen: University of Bergen.

Vigdis Broch-Due is Professor of Social Anthropology and International Poverty Studies, University of Bergen. She is currently employed as Scientific Director at Centre for Advanced Study (CAS), Oslo. Her academic career has taken her from teaching positions in anthropology at the Universities of Oslo and Washington (Seattle), to the Directorship of a Poverty and Prosperity Research programme at the Nordic Africa Institute, Uppsala, to senior research positions at the Universities of Cambridge, SOAS and Rutgers. Her books include the co-edited volumes, *Carved Flesh/Cast Selves: Gendered Symbols and Social Practices* (Oxford: Berg, 1993); *The Poor Are Not Us: Poverty and Pastoralism in Eastern Africa* (Oxford: James Currey, 1999); *Producing Nature and Poverty in Africa* (Uppsala: the Nordic Africa Institute Press, 2000); and *Violence and Belonging: The Quest for Identity in Postcolonial Africa* (Abingdon: Routledge, 2005). She has published articles on gender and embodiment, trauma, pastoral development, cultural models of the relations between animals and people and changing property relations.

Margit Ystanes is Associate Professor at the Faculty of Social Science and History at Volda University College. She obtained her PhD from the University of Bergen in 2011. Her dissertation is titled *Precarious Trust: Problems of Managing Self and Sociality in Guatemala*. Her work explores how local forms of sociality and intimacy give rise to culturally specific ways of forming and experiencing trust and mistrust – both in the intimate sphere of family life and in the public sphere. Ystanes' current project, *Trust as a Precondition for Socio-economic Development: What Can We Learn from the Case of Brazil?*, continues to investigate how trust and mistrust are formed in both private and public lives. Her research interests include trust, poverty, development, gender and conceptions of nature.

 1

Unfixed Trust
Intimacy, Blood Symbolism and Porous Boundaries in Guatemala

Margit Ystanes

'*En la calle solo encuentra uno enemigos*' [In the street one only finds enemies], don Santiago told me in his usual soft-spoken manner, as we shared coffee and sweet bread in his kitchen. A man now in his sixties, he emphasized the importance of making sure the members of his family fulfil each other's social needs so that they do not have to search elsewhere for friends. Thus, sitting in the most intimate and most protected space of his house, the place for nourishment, nurture and most family gatherings, he emphasized the dangers of the outside world. He told me it is necessary to shield his grandchildren from outside influence, '*para que crezcan rectos*' [so that they will grow up to be righteous], and underlined his statement by raising his underarm so that it resembled the stem of a plant growing straight up from the ground.

Don Santiago is not the only Guatemalan to perceive the world outside the home as dangerous. Rather, his statements resonate with widespread concerns about the moral risks associated with the world beyond family and kin, as well as the possibilities of falling victims to violent crime. Luisa, a woman in her thirties, explained that she never goes anywhere by herself unless absolutely necessary, and that the fear of doing so has been engrained in her throughout her upbringing:

> I was never allowed to do anything, no matter how much I begged. So I got used to living shut away [*encerrada*], and whenever I had to do errands outside the house it made me scared.

These examples illustrate how in Guatemala, as in other Latin-American societies, the realm of family and kin is considered one of trust, respectability and intimacy. The public realm of outsiders, on the other hand, is considered the location of mistrust, confrontation, conflict and moral risk. This conceptual boundary is often referred to as a distinction between *casa* [house] and *calle* [street], and it rests upon the assumption that close, mutually supportive relationships are more easily developed among kin. In contrast, it is considered that close relationships cultivated in the public domain may turn out to be deceptive.

However, as feminist philosophers have already argued (Baier 1986; Govier 1992), domestic intimacy and trust relationships are far from uncomplicated. Guatemalans also recognize this, for as Oscar, a man in his thirties, put it, 'family is also a kind of prison'. On the other hand, close friendships can be cultivated outside of the family, despite the folk theory claiming the opposite. Thus, in this context, the separation between the private and public spheres is highly porous, with elements from each bleeding into the other.

In this chapter I explore the unfixed nature of trust and mistrust in intimate relationships among *ladino* Guatemalans – people of mixed origin who foreground the European part of their heritage and identify with national culture, while shoving the indigenous part into the background (Hale 1999, 2006; Nelson 1999; Ystanes 2011). I will critique the commonly reiterated idea that public trust is low in Latin-American societies because people locate trust mainly in the intimate sphere or in clientelistic relationships (e.g., Roniger 1985; Fukuyama 1996). Instead, I will argue that public trust is low among *ladino* Guatemalans because trust amongst family and kin *also* finds a very precarious foundation in this context; for as people enter public life they bring with them their intimate experiences of trust and mistrust, and the lessons about their social world thus produced. Hence, the formation of trust in the intimate sphere makes the basis for the formation of public trust, rather than constituting its opposite (see also Ystanes 2011).

Ladino conceptualizations of trust and mistrust that associate the former with kin and the latter with strangers draw, among other things, upon a symbolism of blood. Those who are considered most trustworthy are related by blood – this bodily substance provides the connection that bind people together as a family, and in the most intimate sense, to a house. This is not a uniquely Guatemalan conception, but is widespread in Latin America. Indeed, the Chilean expression *casa de sangre* [house of blood], which refers to one's place of primary intimate relations (Han 2012: 16), articulates the connection between home and kinship very literally.

Blood is a powerful yet ambiguous symbol, evoking both good and evil within the body; life and procreation, violence and death. In Guatemala, the way blood has traditionally been associated with both kinship and 'race' through the notion of *pureza de sangre* [blood purity] connects the intimate sphere of the body and kin with public entities such as honour, status and respectability. Ever since colonization, the Euro-Guatemalan elite has thus used marital endogamy to reproduce their privilege and power – both awarded them by a social order in which 'blood purity', understood as 'whiteness', has been a prerequisite for inclusion into the upper echelons (Casaús Arzú 2007). Blood is thus not just a vehicle for intimacy, kinship and trust but also for embodied notions of superiority and inferiority, social distance and mistrust. During Guatemala's long civil war, which ended after more than thirty years with the signing of a peace agreement in 1996, these notions took on devastating meanings as the army massacred numerous indigenous villages they considered to be allied with the insurgent guerrillas (e.g., Hale 2006; Nelson 2009). However, the disappearances of political activists and others the army considered a threat to the status quo also left deep wounds in intimate relationships. For the relatives left behind, talking and sharing information about the events was too dangerous, thus isolating each person with their grief and terror (e.g., Hale 2006). While the effects of war is not the focus of this chapter, it is important to acknowledge that the traumas produced during this period, both to individuals and the social body, are likely to have contributed to the precariousness of trust relations described here (Ystanes 2011).

However, just as the symbolism of blood is ambiguous, the formation of trust and mistrust does not follow the culturally defined schema according to which it should fall neatly into two separate spheres. Rather, people are well aware that intimacy is unruly and does not always appear in appropriate spaces or contain the idealized warmth and safety assumed. Indeed, very close friendships can be cultivated in the domain of the street, while family relationships may bring both deception and disappointment. Experiences of trust and mistrust thus weave their way into different places and relationships, connecting intimate and public domains in ways that the conceptual distinction between *casa* and *calle* does not account for. Trust and mistrust, intimacy and distance, are thus unfixed entities, which succeed and replace each other, and are never finally settled within persons, spaces or the social body.

Approaching Trust Ethnographically

While trust research is emerging as a field in its own right, this field is marked by lack of agreement as to what exactly trust is and how we can study it (e.g., Grimen 2009), or what kind of concept it is (Corsín Jiménez 2011). Indeed, the illusive character of trust can readily be observed in the tendency to define it as anything from social capital to expectations about the future, encapsulated interests or the willingness to trade, cooperate or take risk, or simply the common-sense understanding of trust may be applied.[1] No theory has established itself as dominant or paradigmatic, and the different conceptions we have do not necessarily travel well across methodological and disciplinary boundaries. This great variety of ways in which trust is conceptualized, illustrates that the phenomena we refer to when we evoke 'trust' analytically are manifold. The same goes for the people we work with, whose experiences and understanding of trust are shaped and moulded by the life-worlds they inhabit. The great variety of ways in which the topic of trust is approached both analytically and empirically in the chapters of this volume illustrates the difficulty of pinning down this phenomenon once and for all.

Differences between languages constitute another challenge. For example, when discussing the way he includes Spanish words and expressions in his English writings, the Dominican-American author Junot Díaz explains: 'For a Spanish speaker *confianza* signifies a deep feeling of trust and a close, pseudo-familial bond. I don't know how anyone would be capable of expressing in English that they trust someone to the extent that *confianza* implies' (Gustavsson 2013: 36, my translation from Norwegian). For anthropologists as well as fiction writers, then, translating between different contexts and modes of being is a complicated task. Often we conflate the multitude of meanings words such as *confianza* may have for the people who use them with the significance that *trust* has for us. Indeed, Haas (this volume) illustrates that investigations of the local concepts we translate into trust may constitute a powerful critique of theories that do not take cultural difference into account.

Traditionally, however, the latter approach has marked trust research to a large extent. Its origins are usually traced back to Thomas Hobbes' book *Leviathan* (1996), first published in 1651. Here the main argument is that human beings are fundamentally untrustworthy, and that it is only by entering a social contract with an absolute sovereign power that the conditions for social trust can be secured. This origin of trust research in contract philosophy brings with it a problematic way of phrasing the issues at hand; trusting subjects are very often, if not usually, conceived of as identifiable with an enquiring 'I', and referred to as either 'I' or 'we'. This is very much in line with Hobbes' own approach, which was to read mankind in himself; as he tried to estimate what motivated other people, he looked inside himself, and asked what he would do in similar circumstances, and why (Govier 1997: 48–49). This introspective mode of knowing exemplifies the way Western philosophers have tended *not* to conceive of themselves as specifically Western, but rather as representative members of mankind, making universal claims for all human beings.

Many contemporary enquiries into trust are therefore premised on the unspoken assumption that 'I' or 'we' can include all human beings. To the extent that there is comparison in trust research, it is very often centres on how much or little trust there is in different societies. Typically, it is argued that Latin America and southern Europe have very low degrees of societal trust – with trust first and foremost located within the family or in clientelistic relationships (Roniger 1985; Fukuyama 1996). In contrast, northern Europe is considered to have high degrees of both personal and societal trust (Sellerberg 1982; Miller and Listhaug 1990; Fukuyama 1996).

However, implicit in such comparisons is of course not only the idea that trust is thought about in the same way everywhere, but also that it is formed in identical ways across cultural boundaries.[2] This is problematic, as the types of behaviour that allow people to feel at ease in different contexts are not the same. For example, in Guatemala people consider it very important to be able to show proper respect, treat others with ritualized politeness, and conceal inappropriate behaviour – even in close relationships such as within a family. For young people, mastering this mode of behaviour is crucial for establishing *confianza* with their parents. And if their parents feel *confianza* towards them, they will be able to enjoy greater freedom of movement and less chaperoning. The idea here is not to deceive the parents, but for the youth to show that they can manage themselves in a way that makes them trustworthy – they will not harm the family reputation (Ystanes 2011).

This is in contrast to philosophers such as Baier, who argue that trust relationships built on concealment are morally rotten (1986: 255). So if we try to use dominant Western conceptions of trust to analyse non-Western societies, we very quickly end up moralizing rather than understanding the forms of sociality that produce trust in those contexts.

This brings us to another but related problem: existing theories about trust commonly reject the idea that trust can exist in hierarchical relationships. For example, O'Neill argues that trust can only exist when all have equal rights and duties (2002). Hardin, Cook and Levi (Hardin 2002, 2006; Cook et al. 2005) argue that trust can only exist in relationships between people who have encapsulated each other's interests. That is, I have encapsulated your interests into mine simply because they are your interests. This means that trust hinges mostly on affection, and that trust outside of the intimate sphere of domestic life plays a minimal role in the formation of complex societies (Cook et al. 2005). These scholars make it very explicit that they reject the idea that trust can exist in hierarchical relationships, yet many others do so indirectly. For example the prisoner's dilemma game is frequently applied in the study of trust (e.g., Ostrom and Walker 2003), and here all players have equal status and knowledge. As Baier argues, the prevalence of the Prisoner's Dilemma game points to an 'obsession with moral relations between minimally trusting, minimally trustworthy adults who are equally powerful' (1986: 252).

Baier's argument is that the Western academic tradition has ignored the possibility of trust in hierarchical relationships because of its origin in contractual philosophy. Here it has been taken for granted that contracts were agreements made between equal men, and people of inferior positions have not been included in the analyses (1986: 247–248). However, as she points out (ibid.: 252):

> [S]laves [have been] trusted to cook for slave owners; women, with or without marriage vows, [have been] trusted with the property of their men, trusted not to deceive them about the paternity of their children, and trusted to bring up their sons as patriarchs, their daughters as suitable wives or mistresses for patriarchs.

As is clear from the above, domestic relationships, which are usually considered to be marked by trust, both in Western societies and elsewhere, are also hierarchical (see also Baier 1992; Govier 1992). Indeed, intimacy is hierarchical, as gender and age usually ascribe different roles, rights and duties to members of a household. However, the assumptions about intimacy and sociality that are implicit in most conceptions of trust – for example, that the private sphere does not contain these complications – do not allow us to unpack the complexities that domestic trust relationships involve.

Finally, most conceptions of trust are marked by cognitivism to some degree or other (Grimen 2009). That is, they take trust to be something we make more or less conscious decisions about. This is of course particularly so in game-theoretical approaches where trust is to a large extent collapsed with the willingness to accept risk or cooperate (e.g., Ostrom and Walker 2003), and more context-oriented approaches inspired by game theory (e.g., Hardin 2002; Gambetta and Hamill 2005). Other approaches are cognitivist to lesser degrees – for example those emphasizing the kinds of characteristics that make a person trustworthy, such as competence, good will, etc. (Govier 1997; Grimen 2009). However, such approaches tend to ignore the way that experiences of trust are not simply and straightforwardly produced by the conscious evaluation of available information, but also reach deeply into human experience and life-worlds – as many of the chapters in this volume illustrate.

Daniel and Knudsen (1995a) take such insights seriously, as they consider trust to be not something we experience after careful evaluation of risk but rather what we experience when we do not think about whether or not we trust. That is, trust is defined as an ingrained, taken-for-granted, largely unconscious experience of comfortable being; something akin to what Pierre Bourdieu has called 'habitus'. This means that trust prevails in relationships, situations and contexts in which we feel comfortable, and which do not make us consciously evaluate if we are putting ourselves in harm's way. Daniel and Knudsen's concern is situations in which the conditions for trust break down (see Daniel and Knudsen 1995b), yet by emphasizing the role of culture and society, their approach also opens the way for a genuinely ethnographic examination of how trust is produced in actual life-worlds.

My concern here is not to demonstrate that any particular theory of trust is in operation among *ladino* Guatemalans, but rather to critique claims about public and private trust in Latin America that do not take the complications of the intimate sphere into account. In doing this, I will use the folk theories about what kinds of relationships *confianza* normally prevails in, and outline the kinds of situations and experiences that people consider to make *confianza* difficult or impossible. I take inspiration from Daniel and Knudsen's (1995a) emphasis on life-worlds in the formation of trust, and from the contributions of feminist philosophers who have problematized the domestic sphere as a locus of trust (Baier 1986; Govier 1992). I will start by outlining how the *ladino* notion of sociality – which constitutes the conditions for trust in both the intimate and public spheres – is highly ambiguous. Thereafter, I will discuss the meanings associated with blood symbolism in the Guatemalan context, and the way they connect private and public concerns. Finally, I will briefly comment upon the potential contribution of anthropology to trust research.

Sociality, Intimacy and Spatio-moral Domains in *Ladino* Life-Worlds

The understanding of trust as produced in articulation with specific life-worlds encourages a focus on sociality and how the world is perceived and constituted. How are such experiences created? In order to answer this question, we must outline the building blocks of the social in each context. The most central feature for the constitution of sociality among *ladinos* is a gendered symbolism of openness and closure. This symbolism is by no means unique for the Guatemalan context, but can be observed among *mestizos* as well as people of African and European heritage all over Latin America. The analysis below is therefore inspired by studies of gender, sexuality, morality, the domestic and public spheres, social space, national identity and 'racial' concerns, from various Latin American contexts and moments in history.[3]

The emphasis placed on the maintenance of boundaries – between *ladinos* themselves and the indigenous populations, the private and public domains, inside and outside, kin and non-kin and between the self and the world – reflect both the high value placed on 'closedness' and the depreciation of openness. This symbolism is expressed in virtually any context, and has profoundly contributed to moulding aspects of sociality such as gender identities and conceptualizations of intimacy, as well as public life and social space. The emphasis on closure and privacy is for example mirrored in architecture, which is usually constructed so as to shield domestic life from the intruding gazes of neighbours and passers-by. Similarly, practices of visiting involve separating between different categories of visitors with regard to how far they can be led into the house. Only kin or other intimately connected persons are invited all the way into the most intimate location of the house – the kitchen.

For *ladino* Guatemalans, as many other Latin Americans, being a competent social actor involves concealing certain feelings and aspects of the self and outwardly displaying respectful and decent behaviour. Thus, hiding feelings, thoughts, intentions or acts that are inappropriate in a given situation allows people to form relationships with others by making them feel good about the interaction. This is of course an aspect of sociality anywhere, but the emphasis placed on it in many Latin American contexts, and in Guatemala in particular, stands out. Indeed, Guatemalans have a reputation among Central Americans for being 'closed off or turned inward like a snail in its shell' (Nelson 2009: 21). Nelson's research participants underline that an effect of the civil war has been to increase this tendency. As a young ladina woman explains (ibid.):

> People, families, they shut down. They don't talk about things. There's a generation gap because young people don't know what happened in their families, if people were involved.

People I have worked with in Guatemala would tend to agree with the assessment that they close themselves off from the world, although they have not personally experienced violence or violations during the war. The following situation is illustrative: Jennifer, a student in her early twenties, had told her family that she was going to visit me during an afternoon, thus providing an alibi for something they did not allow her to do. I was not aware of this, so when her aunt phoned my house and asked to speak to her, I simply told her the truth; that I had not seen Jennifer and had no idea where she was. Later, when I told Jaime, a student in his early twenties, about the phone call, he could not hide his frustration with my inability to manage such situations with what he referred to as *mentiras blancas* [white lies]:

> I don't know why you [foreigners] are unable to lie like us Latinos;[4] we can manage a situation like that very well by lying, no problem. But you guys always have to tell the truth, without even thinking about it. For us Latinos lying comes very naturally, we hardly think about it at all. We can manage any situation through lies, any time.

Managing situations in this way may provide relationships with valuable social glue because the ability to do so demonstrates a person's respect for social norms and understanding of what it is appropriate to say in different situations. We could say that it establishes a person as socially intelligent and a reliable friend. The way I had managed the situation, in contrast, had demonstrated to Jaime that our friendship might put his reputation at risk. He therefore instructed me, and explained how to close oneself off from the intruding inquires of others, even very close persons like family members or intimate friends:

> There are lies that we can never reveal, that we take to the grave with us. When you tell the first lie, you break down this barrier, and as you go along with it, the lie becomes an integral part of you, it stops being a lie and is transformed into truth. For example, if I were to get caught telling a lie, I would never admit to it. I'd rather avoid the problem by continuing to lie, and claim that what this other person has said about me is a lie, I have not lied; if you don't believe me, that's your problem, I know I'm telling the truth.

Managing situations through concealment and closing oneself off not only facilitates social relationships by demonstrating respect, decency and social intelligence, it can also produce a profound sense of loneliness in the individual. It may be important, Jaime explains, to avoid discussing a problem with your parents, if seeking their help or comfort involves exposing inappropriate behaviour on your part. He admits that this may make you feel awful on the inside, but produces good relationships and encourages people to trust you. It is of course contradictory to all of this that Jaime shares these highly private thoughts with me, part of a group of friends he has never introduced into his family sphere nor indicated an inclination to do so. For him, I am a relation of *la calle*, someone he should ideally not speak so openly with – yet he did so with all of us in this group. This illustrates both the idealization of the self-contained person, and the impossibility of producing such bounded selves. Just like intimacy cannot be contained to the domain of *la casa*, selves cannot be completely closed off from others.

The mode of behaviour Jaime favours can nevertheless be observed in all sorts of contexts, ranging from the intimate and private to the public. Closure is thus highly valued, and openness is depreciated. Value is also placed upon the creative ability to symbolically break open the closures produced by others, for example by challenging their right to respectful deference, or by deceiving them into opening up. The fact that conquest is a frequently used metaphor for seduction indicates that there is a component of confrontation and struggle for dominance in this social universe, also in very intimate relationships. For example, when a woman is being courted by a man, she is well aware that his displays of emotion may be absurdly exaggerated, to the point of bearing no resemblance to reality. This awareness is reflected in the frequently evoked expression *'los hombres te bajan la luna, las estrellas y el sol'* [men will fetch you the moon, the stars and the sun]; behind their beautiful words, deception, a broken heart and a tainted reputation may very well await.

The gendered aspects of this symbolism turn on the ways in which openness and closure are associated with men and women in distinctive ways – hierarchical gender relations are moulded by the association of women with the depreciated openness, and the association of men with the highly valued closure as well as the ability to creatively and symbolically break others open. Analytically, this dichotomy is often traced back to the Mexican philosopher Octavio Paz's *The Labyrinth of Solitude* (1990), first published in 1961. Here, Paz takes *la conquista*, the conquest of the New World, as a starting point, and places the origins of what he calls 'the Mexican personality' firmly within the historical events of the colonial encounter. He claims that the Mexican, or more specifically, the *mestizo*, is the result of treason and rape, an ambiguous origin that the *mestizo* has never managed to reconcile himself with and feels ashamed of. The rape Paz refers to is both the symbolic rape of the continent by the *conquistadores* and their actual rape of the women who lived on it. The treason is personified in the myth of the indigenous woman Malinche, who was given as a gift to the *conquistador* Hernán Cortés and eventually became his mistress, translator, advisor and intermediary.[5] Thus, Paz argues, Malinche came to be emblematic of the open, the deceitful, the passive and the feminine: a counterpart to the closed, the stoic, the active and the masculine, which the culture idealizes.

While Paz's work has been criticized for being biased with regards to both class and gender (e.g., Limón 1989; Lomnitz-Adler 1992), it is also praised for its use of imagery, symbolism, metaphor and paradox (Chavarría 1971). Indeed, the way Paz describes the symbolism of openness/depreciation and closure/appraisal and its association with the feminine and the masculine respectively corresponds to the way several anthropologists have analysed gender relations and sexual symbolism in various Latin American contexts. For example, it is often pointed out that traditionally, Latin American conceptualizations of homosexuality centred on the act of penetration. Mainly it was men who allowed other men to penetrate them who were categorised as homosexuals and stigmatized because of their 'passive' role in the sexual encounter – symbolically, they were associated with the depreciated openness.[6] In contrast, men who engaged in same-sex relation by penetrating other men were not necessarily considered to be homosexuals, and were not stigmatized; symbolically they were associated with the idealized 'closedness' (Lancaster 1988; Prieur 1994, 1996; Kulick 1998). Indeed, as Lancaster (1988) points out, men who penetrate other men may boast about their sexual contact with men to emphasize their virility and masculinity. Kulick makes a similar point, and argues that this is so fundamental for the constitution of identities that the gender binary among the Brazilian *travestis* he works with is most meaningfully understood not as men and women, but as men and non-men. That is, their most important conceptual distinction with regards to gender identity is between people who desire to penetrate others and people who desire or allow themselves to be penetrated. The way gender classification can thus shift according to behaviour illustrates well the ambiguity of the open/closed symbolism that social relations, and hence trust, is built on.

In heterosexual relationships the symbolic association of women with openness makes it necessary to both protect and control them from being symbolically 'opened up' by men, through romance, intercourse, inappropriate welcoming of catcalls or friendships, or through sexual violence. Avoiding excessive openness is crucial for maintaining a good reputation. Consequently, decent women are strongly associated with the closure of the house, with protected family life and sexual purity. This symbolic association remains strong even though many respectable *ladinas* these days spend large parts of their time outside the home, as workers, students, politicians, activists or in other public roles. Writing about Brazil, McCallum points out that 'although control of female sexuality is discursively located in the past, a striking aspect of contemporary social relations in the Baixa is the pressure on women and girls to control themselves, sexually, psychologically and spatially' (1999: 287). This is an observation that is highly relevant also for Guatemalan *ladinas*, who continue to be associated with *la casa* even as they now increasingly occupy *la calle*.

As Jaime's comments illustrate, Guatemalan men must also find ways of controlling themselves psychologically, yet sexually and spatially they enjoy far greater freedom than their female counterparts. Their excesses should be contained to the street, however – the unprotected sphere of public, anonymous life and confrontation. This is the space in which they can demonstrate their ability to manipulate and symbolically break open the closures produced by others, through the use of skill and creativity. Indeed, if *la casa* is considered a female domain, *la calle* constitutes its male complementary domain.

Gender relations are not only hierarchized through the association of men and women with valued and depreciated entities respectively, but also through men's ability to symbolically break others open. While such behaviour is considered highly inappropriate in *la casa*, in *la calle* men may actively challenge the closures produced by others through confrontation, catcalls and sexual conquest, attempting to break them open in the search for masculinity, dominance and virility. Such challenges are directed at both women and other men, as the common catcall ¡*Hola cuñado!* [Hi, brother-in-law!] shows. This is often shouted after young men walking with a young woman on the street, be she a girlfriend, sister, cousin, colleague or friend. The implication is that the catcaller has a sexual relationship with the woman in question, and he thus simultaneously challenges the man's ability to protect the sexual purity of the woman associated with him *and* the woman's respectability. While the catcall is at the same time a compliment to her, it is important that the woman responds with a display of polite disinterest – she has been accused of being excessively open, but by demonstrating that she is in fact closed, she may refute this challenge to her reputation. In this way, both men and women engage with the symbolism of openness and closure in everyday street encounters, yet their roles are different, and it is mainly men who may assert themselves though the creative and skilful opening up of the closures produced by others.

However, as I have already pointed out, this symbolism represents an ideal that is extremely difficult to reproduce as lives and situations unfold. Women, selves and houses (which have been evoked as symbolic of the self in Latin-American literature; see, for example, Allende [1994]) represent entities that should ideally be closed, protected from the intrusions of the world outside. However, intrusive elements constantly find their way in, and the closures people produce around their selves are imperfect at best. Awareness of this, and the uncertainty it produces, can be observed in a jealous guarding of family and close friends – which is considered a sign of affection – and in the chaperoning of women to protect their reputations and respectability. Elements belonging to the street may also be introduced into the house: for example, someone may get drunk on a celebration taking place in the kitchen, or a young daughter may sneak her boyfriend into her room without asking for her parents' permission.

It is noteworthy that despite the idealization of family life, many *ladino* Guatemalans consider domestic violence and sexual abuse by family members to be commonplace. Whether this reflects reality or not, such negative images of intimacy are part and parcel of their social imaginary, and contribute to making *la casa* unreliable as a location for trust. The widespread assumption that stepfathers are more likely to sexually abuse children than other relatives further emphasizes this point while pointing out the ambiguities: blood relations are perceived as vehicles for trust in the domestic sphere, and non-kin are perceived as threats to such idealized trust relations. Ideally, non-kin should not be present in *la casa*, yet, for the ideal family to be established and reproduced, it must include in-laws. The efforts to produce symbolic closures, then, may never be fully successful, but they remain a constant concern.

This symbolism constitutes the foundation for the life-world of Guatemalan *ladinos*, yet it produces ambiguities and double messages rather than a coherent experience of the world. It presents *ladinos* with a contradiction and a dilemma, for the valuation of 'closedness' is attributed to both individuals and groups such as families. By closing oneself off from the world as a person, it is difficult to form a group that can do the same. This contradiction is reflected in how the idealization of the intimacy of family life is accompanied by a widespread assumption that family life may also bring disappointment, deceit, suffering and abuse – especially for women and children (see also Melhuus 1997). Furthermore, the social boundaries that are considered so crucial for the maintenance of the *ladino* life-world are continuously emphasized and yet at the same time contradicted, manipulated and contested by the value placed upon breaking others open while remaining closed. The ensuing ambiguities give rise to double messages and contradictions as people engage the foundation of their social world in their daily interaction. This makes the conditions for trust very precarious, as the experience of comfortable being is frequently interrupted by displacements: that is, the introduction of elements into places they do not belong (DaMatta 1991).

Approaching trust in this way allows us to look past the conventional view of why public trust is considered to be so low in Latin America: that people in this region mainly reserve their trust for family, kin, close friends and clientelistic relationships (e.g., Roniger 1985; Fukuyama 1996). Rather, we here see that the symbolic foundations of the *ladino* life-world produce conditions for trust that are precarious not only in the public sphere but also in intimate relationships. Furthermore, just as notions of intimacy are marked by ambiguity, so are conceptions of societal relations, as we shall explore shortly. Trust – its conditions and formation – can therefore be used as a lens though which we can explore important aspects of a social order. In the following I will continue to do this by outlining how blood symbolism, which connects the intimate and public domains, contains a similar ambiguity as that described above, as it makes statuses and positions uncertain.

Blood Symbolism: Ambiguity, Kinship and Social Status

Blood symbolism is crucial to consider in the exploration of trust among *ladino* Guatemalans. It constitutes an important aspect of the conception of kinship, and trust is assumed to arise more easily amongst those sharing the same blood. Blood symbolism also produces links between the intimate and public spheres, as personal desire and public status merge in concerns over kinship and heredity. Such concerns can create considerable mistrust among kin and contribute to reinforcing the emphasis on 'closure' discussed above.

Ever since the Americas became colonized by European states, ideas about human 'races' have served as vehicles for hierarchization (Martinez-Alier 1989; Stepan 1991; Twinam 1999; see also, e.g., Wade 1997; Nelson 1999; Hale 2006; Casaús Arzú 2007; Milton 2007). In Spanish America, the notion of *pureza de sangre* [blood purity] was perhaps the most central concept guiding colonial hierarchization. This concept derives from a Catholic doctrine dating back to the thirteenth century (Stolcke 1993). Until then, Christians, Muslims and Jews were presented as living harmoniously together on the Iberian Peninsula and intermarriage was common. From the thirteenth century onwards, however, the doctrine of *pureza de sangre* was introduced to segregate Christians from non-Christians. It was originally based on medieval physiological theories: it was believed that the mother's blood fed the child while in the womb and continued to do so after birth by being transformed into milk. A child's substance was thus provided by the mother's blood, and purity of blood meant descent from Christian women. During the expulsion of Jews and Moriscos (converted Muslims) from the Spanish Empire during the sixteenth century, however, the doctrine of blood purity started to take on new meanings. While previously referring to a religious/cultural discrimination that could be overcome through conversion to Christianity, it was now transformed into a racist doctrine of original sin; descent from Jews or Muslims was regarded as a permanent and indelible stain (Stolcke 1993: 31–32). When later applied in the colonial setting, the doctrine of blood purity 'found expression in a heightened concern among Europeans and their descendants over endogamous marriage and legitimate birth as a means to ensure and attest racial-cum-social purity as prerequisites for social pre-eminence' (Stolcke 1993: 32).

A number of studies (Martinez-Alier 1989; Stepan 1991; Stolcke 1993; Nelson 1999; Casaús Arzú 2007) show that the reproduction of a 'pure European' elite, or in reality the idea of such purity, depended on different sexual practices for men and women. Sexual purity, premarital virginity and motherhood were important ideals for 'white' women, and their sexuality was fiercely guarded. For 'white' men it was considered important not only to produce legitimate, 'white' offspring with their wives, but also to spread their 'white genes' among the indigenous population – often by rape – in order to 'improve the race' through *blanqueamiento* [whitening]. This practise stretches into Guatemala's very recent history, as expressed by one Guatemalan plantation owner in the late 1970s: 'For many years I had a German administrator on my plantation, and for every *india* he got pregnant I paid him 50 dollars extra' (Casaús Arzú 2007: 251). His motivation for doing so is his conviction that 'the only solution for Guatemala is to improve the race, to bring Aryan studs to improve it' (ibid.).

This idea still holds relevance. Several contemporary *ladinos* pointed out to me that they consider Guatemala's problems of crime, violence and corruption (see, e.g., O'Neill and Thomas 2011) to be caused by a lack of '*pureza*'. Mirroring some of Casaús Arzú's interviewees perfectly, they claimed it would have been better if Guatemala had been colonized by the Germans or the English, because they were even 'purer' than the Spaniards – and hence better people. The social importance of the notion of *pureza de sangre*, and the gender hierarchization upon which it depends, is therefore not limited to the colonial era. Indeed, it is clear that even as *ladinos* now mostly reject overt biological racism, human difference continues to be conceptualized in ways that include and intertwine ideas from the natural and cultural domains (Hale 2006). These conceptions and the practices they have helped legitimize continue to produce mistrust between people considered to be of different blood – as well as between those sharing blood.

For example, many *ladinos* are of the opinion that *somos todos mezclados* [we are all mixed], and that genetically there is no difference between Mayans and *ladinos*. At the same time, however, *ladinos* widely consider Mayans to have a number of inherent traits by which their culture is negatively influenced: laziness, vindictiveness, irrationality, ignorance and an incapacity for independent thinking. The latter assumption helps *ladinos* justify the chronic poverty and marginality in which the majority of indigenous people in their country still live, while the former makes their own position in the social hierarchy highly uncertain. *Ladinos* therefore tend to carefully guard the boundary between themselves and indigenous Guatemalans, as the almost complete absence of intermixing in the networks of those who have become my friends and research contributors throughout the years illustrates.

The porousness of this boundary can nevertheless be observed in the way in which certain characteristics, for example darker skin tones, poverty and submissiveness, will make a *ladino* person more closely associated with the indigenous population. Lighter skin tones, wealth and access to masculine domains of prestige and influence, on the other hand, will make the claim to *ladino* identity more solid. *Ladinos* are thus constantly involved in negotiations over status and position and they evaluate, include and exclude each other based on such associations. It is not surprising, perhaps, that it is often those who find themselves in a more uncertain position who strive hardest to maintain a clear boundary between themselves and indigenous people, the quintessential others.

For example, Antonio, an elementary schoolteacher in his late twenties, characterizes some of his acquaintances as 'ninety-nine per cent indígena' because of their dark skin colour and short stature. The people in question, however, strongly identify as *ladinos*, and regularly make depreciatory comments about Mayans. Most likely, they would not be pleased to hear Antonio's perception of them. Antonio, on the other hand, is by many considered to be taller and more light-skinned than is common in Guatemala, and he has kinship ties to an elite family. Ironically, perhaps, it was one of the persons he considers to be 'ninety-nine per cent indígena' who pointed out to me that he belongs to a 'very important family in the capital'. Because of these characteristics, Antonio never faces the challenge to his *ladino* identity that he himself presents to others, and marking the boundary between himself and the indigenous population is less urgent for him than for many others. Indeed, he appears to experience 'comfortable being' in many more social encounters than do his 'ninety-nine per cent' *indigena* acquaintances.

Blood thus symbolizes both highly valued entities such as kinship, procreation and family, and strongly depreciated entities such as 'racial' otherness and impurity, strangers and even enemies. Because of this, there is considerable concern with the correct management of blood relations, as distancing oneself from the stigma of indigenous blood that all *ladinos* carry in their bodies depends on it. Lighter-skinned persons are therefore considered to be particularly attractive marriage partners as they carry with them the potential for lighter-skinned children, and by extension a distancing from stigma. Darker-skinned *ladinos*, however, risk being met by the family of a new girlfriend or boyfriend with considerable suspicion and mistrust, especially if they do not have other qualities to 'compensate', such as a good job or a university degree.

Ladinos commonly consider marriage to an indigenous person as particularly problematic, and kin may fiercely guard their claim to superiority by controlling each other's romantic choices. For example, Juliana, a student in her early thirties, told me that she had a cousin who had married an indigenous man. Her cousin's decisions to do so had been met with strong sanctions from the extended family, which had completely broken off contact with her. Juliana related how this cousin had attempted to greet her during the Easter celebrations, but she refused to acknowledge her. The cousin had reacted with anger and disappointment, something which Juliana interpreted as her cousin having become 'just as *abusiva* [outrageous, abusive] as them, *pura india*'.[7] When I queried Juliana about why she and the rest of her family had taken such a drastic measure as cutting ties and even refusing all civility towards this woman, she tried to make me understand by emphatically declaring: 'Her mother-in-law sells *atol* at the market, can you imagine?'

Atol is a traditional Guatemalan drink usually made with maize and often sold by Mayan women at street markets. Juliana considered affinal ties to such an obviously lower-class indigenous person a serious problem. This must be seen in light of her project of social mobility, achieved through years of sacrifices to obtain a university degree. Juliana feared that the prospect of an easier future for herself and her family, without the burdens of economic worries and social inferiority, would be made very uncertain should they welcome such ties. Social mobility has multiple vehicles in the Guatemalan context: success in education and work is one, removing one's family from the stigma of indigenous blood through marriage is another. In such ways, private desire and public status merge in concerns over kinship and heredity, conceptualized as 'blood relations'. The idealization of the self-contained person, which reflects the high value placed on 'closedness' is mirrored in the need of families to make their social status more stable by closing themselves off from those who might associate them more closely with the stigma of indigenous blood. The ambivalences here consists of the simultaneous interest in making the nation 'whiter' to enhance national prestige and at the same time maintaining strict boundaries between Mayans and *ladinos*; the instability and multifaceted nature of *ladino* identities; and the ways in which concerns over this can sever trust relationships between kin. In the case of Juliana's cousin, had she not established sufficient trust with an indigenous man to marry him, she would not have been excluded from her kin's circle of trust. Her story therefore illustrates both the fragility of trust relations based on blood, and the possibilities for building trust with 'racial others'.

The most fundamental symbols of their life-world thus equip *ladinos* with highly ambiguous and contradictory ways of thinking about intimacy, hierarchization and their own identity. Although conceptualized as discrete domains, *la casa* and *la calle* are intrinsically tied to one another by the notion of blood as a mediator of kinship and 'race', stigma and prestige. Hence, double messages are produced, underlining the potential for stigma and making positions uncertain. The conditions for trust, both private and public, among *ladinos* are therefore precarious.

Unfixed Trust: Trust, Intimacy and Spatio-moral Domains

Family and kinship are considered the most fundamental basis for trust among *ladinos*, and the world outside the home and kin is conceptualized as a domain of mistrust. Yet working to maintain this boundary represents a never-ending and impossible task, as experiences of trust and mistrust weave their way into places and relationships where they do not belong. Close friendships may be cultivated in *la calle*, and deception and disappointment inevitably appear also in family life. And has we have seen, the hierarchization of difference through a notion of inherently distinct kinds of blood also contributes to placing those who are differently positioned in this respect well outside the domain of trust and intimacy – even when they are family. In this way, the intimate and the public domains are connected and intertwined in ways that the conceptual distinction between *casa* and *calle* does not account for. Crucially, the idealization of the self-contained person as well as the self-contained family makes the notion of intimacy complex and ambiguous, for as people are well aware, it is difficult to realize both simultaneously. Consequently, experiences of trust and mistrust cannot be pinned down to specific spaces like the domestic sphere.

Indeed, the ethnography presented here demonstrates that trust and intimacy are not unproblematically connected. Indeed, if trust is the experience of comfortable being, as Daniel and Knudsen (1995a) take it to be, in this context it is frequently interrupted by experiences of mistrust, deceit and preoccupation – also in intimate relations. Furthermore, *ladino* Guatemalans present us with a conceptualization of sociality that is radically different from how it appears in most trust research. O'Neill (2002), for example, argues that trust can only be produced by mutual obligations among all members of society. She bases her argument on the Kantian notion that all human beings are moral equals, and therefore have equal rights and duties. We know, however, that in many, perhaps even most, societies, people do not have equal rights and duties. The *ladino* life-world is a case in point, where complementarity and hierarchy constitute guiding principles for sociality.

In the book *Trust* (2006), Hardin introduces his topic by an account of life in a French village in the tenth century, over a thousand years ago. Here we meet Bodo, whose life in a village of about eighty people is taken as a contrast to later developments and larger, more complex societies. By treating the history of humankind as a unified process of evolution, and trust as hinging on the encapsulation of interests, Hardin presents his conception of trust as universally valid. Scale and time appears to be the only relevant variables among societies in his account of how trust is formed. Mistrust is more widespread in complex, modern societies than in Bodo's village, he explains, because there are more strangers and hence more people whose interests are unknown to us.

However, as anthropologists we are uneasy with this lack of concern with the different ways life-worlds are constituted. Our practise has taught us that specificity is necessary if we are to produce valid accounts of anything pertaining to the social. If we are to understand how trust is formed anywhere, we cannot start from the point of view of a singularly conceived 'I' or a universal 'we', and we need to ground our analysis in specific contexts. Thus, I will argue that in order to enhance our knowledge about trust we must focus our attention on how it is produced in each context. In the *ladino* life-world the relationships, situations and contexts in which people feel comfortable, and which do not make them consciously evaluate if their reputations, feelings or bodies are somehow at risk, do not arise so easily. This does not mean that the *ladino* social world is without trust, for certainly trust must 'coexist with mistrust' (Daniel and Knudsen 1995a: 1). The conditions for trust among *ladino* Guatemalans rest upon a precarious foundation that is often unsettled, even in the spatio-moral domain of *la casa*, where it should be most solid. By accounting for the ways in which people transport lessons learned about sociality and trust in the intimate domain into public life, however, we can begin to untangle the complex relationship between sociality, intimacy, trust, life-worlds and social orders – as well as the stereotypical images of impermeable Latin American family ties as a hindrance for a wider societal trust.

Notes

1 See, for example Luhmann (1979), Roniger (1985, 1990), Miller and Listhaug (1990), Fukuyama (1996), Putnam (2000), Hardin (2003) and Ostrom and Walker (2003).
2 It must be pointed out that Fukuyama's (1996) approach is more complex than this, and does take cultural difference into account. However, his analysis is macro oriented, and he does not critically scrutinize the intimate sphere of the societies he discusses. Thus, he ends up reproducing the notion that a cultural emphasis on trust within the family produces low trust in the public sphere.
3 See, for example, Paz (1990 [1961]), Lancaster (1988), Martinez-Alier (1989), Robben (1989), DaMatta (1991), Stepan (1991), Prieur (1994), Melhuus and Stølen (1996), Melhuus (1997), Kulick (1998), Franco (1999a), McCallum (1999), Nelson (1999), Twinam (1999) and Milton (2007).
4 Jaime here uses the category Latino, not *ladino*. The two have very different meanings: whereas *ladino* is a specifically Guatemalan identity notion based on local conceptualizations of 'race' and culture, by using the world Latino Jaime means to evoke Latin Americans more generally.
5 See also Franco (1999b) for a feminist reading of this historical character and representations of her.
6 However, conceptualizations of homosexuality more similar to those prevalent in Euro-America are now increasingly widespread in contemporary Latin American contexts. In Brazil, for example, the traditional definition of homosexuality, which centred on the act of penetration, has been partially displaced by a new identity, *gai*, defined as 'sexual orientation' and linked to global gay culture (Parker, cited in Edmonds 2010: 247).
7 *Indio/india* is a derogatory term for indigenous people.

References

Allende, I. 1994. *The House of the Sprits*. London: Transworld Publishers.
Baier, A.C. 1986. 'Trust and Antitrust', *Ethics* 96(2): 231–260.
—— 1992. 'Trusting People', *Philosophical Perspectives* 6, Ethics: 137–153.
Casaús Arzú, M.E. 2007. *Guatemala: Linaje y Racismo*. Ciudad de Guatemala: F & G Editores.
Chavarría, J. 1971. 'A Brief Inquiry into Octavio Paz's Laberinto of Mexicanidad', *The Americas* 27(4): 381–388.
Cook, K.S., R. Hardin and M. Levi. 2005. *Cooperation without Trust?* New York: Russell Sage Foundation.
Corsín Jiménez, A. 2011. 'Trust in Anthropology', *Anthropological Theory* 11(2): 177–196.
DaMatta, R. 1991. *Carnivals, Rogues, and Heroes. An Interpretation of the Brazilian Dilemma*. Notre Dame: University of Notre Dame Press.
Daniel, E.V. and J.C. Knudsen. 1995a. 'Introduction'. In E.V. Daniel and J.C. Knudsen (eds), *Mistrusting Refugees*. Berkeley: University of California Press, 1–12.
—— (eds). 1995b. *Mistrusting Refugees*. Berkeley: University of California Press.
Edmonds, A. 2010. *Pretty Modern: Beauty, Sex and Plastic Surgery in Brazil*. Durham: Duke University Press.
Franco, J. 1999a. 'Killing Priests, Nuns, Women, Children'. In M.L. Pratt and K. Newman (eds), *Critical Passions. Selected Essays by Jean Franco*. Durham: Duke University Press, 9–17.
—— 1999b. 'La Malinche: From Gift to Sexual Contract'. In M.L. Pratt and K. Newman (eds), *Critical Passions. Selected Essays by Jean Franco*. Durham: Duke University Press Pratt, 66–83.
Fukuyama, F. 1996. *Trust: The Social Virtues and the Creation of Prosperity*. New York: Free Press Paperbacks.
Gambetta, D. and H. Hamill. 2005. *Streetwise: How Taxi Drivers Establish Their Customer's Trustworthiness*. New York: Russell Sage Foundation.
Govier, T. 1992. 'Trust, Distrust, and Feminist Theory', *Hypatia* 7(1): 16–33.
—— 1997. *Social Trust and Human Communities*. Montreal: McGill-Queen's University Press.
Grimen, H. 2009. *Hva er tillit*. Oslo: Universitetsforlaget.
Gustavsson, H. 2013. 'Et Kart over Mannligheten', *Morgenbladet*: 36–37.
Hale, C.R. 1999. 'Travel Warning: Elite Appropriations of Hybridity, Mestizaje, Antiracism, Equality, and Other Progressive-Sounding Discourses in Highland Guatemala', *The Journal of American Folklore* 112(445): 297–315.
—— 2006. *Más Que un Indio (More Than an Indian): Racial Ambivalence and Neoliberal Multiculturalism in Guatemala* (School of American Research Resident Scholar Book). Santa Fe, New Mexico: School of American Research Press.
Han, C. 2012. *Life in Debt: Times of Care and Violence in Neoliberal Chile*. Berkeley: University of California Press.

Hardin, R. 2002. *Trust and Trustworthiness*. New York: Russell Sage Foundation.
—— 2003. 'Gaming Trust'. In E. Ostrom and J. Walker (eds), *Trust & Reciprocity: Interdisciplinary Lessons from Experimental Research*. New York: Russell Sage Foundation, 80–101.
—— 2006. *Trust*. Cambridge: Polity Press.
Hobbes, T. 1996 [1651]. *Leviathan*. Oxford: Oxford University Press.
Kulick, D. 1998. *Travesti: Sex, Gender and Culture among Brazilian Transgendered Prostitutes*. Chicago: The University of Chicago Press.
Lancaster, R.N. 1988. 'Subject Honour and Object Shame: The Construction of Male Homosexuality and Stigma in Nicaragua', *Ethnology* 27(2): 111–125.
Limón, J.E. 1989. '"Carne, carnales", and the Carnivalesque: Bakhtinian "batos", Disorder and Narrative Discourses', *American Ethnologist* 16(3): 471–486.
Lomnitz-Adler, C. 1992. *Exits from the Labyrinth: Culture and Ideology in the Mexican National Space*. Berkely: University of California Press.
Luhmann, N. 1979. *Trust and Power*. Chichester: John Wiley.
Martinez-Alier, V. 1989. *Marriage, Class and Colour in Nineteenth-Century Cuba: A Study of Racial Attitudes and Sexual Values in a Slave Society*. Ann Arbor: The University of Michigan Press.
McCallum, C. 1999. 'Restraining Women: Gender, Sexuality, and Modernity in Salvador da Bahia', *Bulletin of Latin American Research* 18(3): 275–293.
Melhuus, M. 1997. 'The Troubles of Virtue: Values of Violence and Suffering in a Mexican Context'. In S. Howell (ed.), *The Ethnography of Moralities*. London: Routledge, 178–202.
Melhuus, M. and K.A. Stølen (eds). 1996. *Machos, Mistresses, Madonnas: Contesting the Power of Latin American Gender Imagery*. London: Verso.
Miller, A. H. and O. Listhaug. 1990. 'Political Parties and Confidence in Government: A Comparison of Norway, Sweden and the United States', *British Journal of Political Science* 20(3): 357–386.
Milton, C.E. 2007. *The Many Meanings of Poverty: Colonialism, Social Compacts, and Assistance in Eighteenth-Century Ecuador*. Stanford: Standford Universty Press.
Nelson, D.M. 1999. *A Finger in the Wound: Body Politics in Quincentennial Guatemala*. Berkeley: University of California Press.
—— 2009. *Reckoning. The Ends of War in Guatemala*. Durham: Duke University Press.
O'Neill, K.L. and K. Thomas (eds). 2011. *Securing the City: Neoliberalism, Space and Insecurity in Postwar Guatemala*. Durham: Duke University Press.
O'Neill, O. 2002. *A Question of Trust: The BBC Reith Lectures 2002*. Cambridge: Cambridge University Press.
Ostrom, E. and J. Walker (eds). 2003. *Trust & Reciprocity: Interdisciplinary Lessons from Experimental Research*. New York: Russell Sage Foundation.
Paz, O. 1990 [1961]. *The Labyrinth of Solitude*. London: Penguin Books.
Prieur, A. 1994. *Iscenesettelser av kjønn. Transvestitter og Macho-menn i Mexico By*. Oslo: Pax Forlag A/S.
—— 1996. 'Domination and Desire: Male Homosexuality and the Construction of Masculinity in Mexico'. In M. Melhuus and K.A. Stølen (eds), *Machos,*

Mistresses and Madonnas: Contesting the Power of Latin American Gender Imagery. London: Verso, 83–107.
Putnam, R.D. 2000. *Bowling Alone: The Collapse and Revival of American Community*. New York: Simon & Schuster Paperbacks.
Robben, A.C.G.M. 1989. 'Habits of the Home: Spatial Hegemony and the Structuration of House and Society in Brazil', *American Anthropologist* 91(2): 570–588.
Roniger, L. 1985. 'Institutionalized Inequalities, the Structure of Trust, and Clientelism in Modern Latin America'. In E. Cohen, M. Lissak and U. Almagor (eds), *Comparative Social Dynamics: Essays in Honor of S.N. Eisenstadt*. Boulder: Westview Press, 148–163.
―――― 1990. *Hierarchy and Trust in Modern Mexico and Brazil*. New York: Praeger.
Sellerberg, A.-M. 1982. 'On Modern Confidence', *Acta Sociologica* 25: 39–48.
Stepan, N.L. 1991. *"The Hour of Eugenics": Race, Gender, and Nation in Latin America*. Ithaca: Cornell University Press.
Stolcke, V. 1993. 'Is Sex to Gender as Race is to Ethnicity?'. In T. del Valle (ed.), *Gendered Anthropology*. London: Routledge, 17–37.
Twinam, A. 1999. *Public Lives, Private Secrets: Gender, Honor, Sexuality, and Illegitimacy in Colonial Spanish America*. Stanford: Stanford University Press.
Wade, P. 1997. *Race and Ethnicity in Latin America*. London: Pluto Press.
Ystanes, M. 2011. 'Precarious Trust: Problems of Managing Self and Sociality in Guatemala'. PhD dissertation. Bergen: University of Bergen.

Margit Ystanes is Associate Professor at the Faculty of Social Science and History at Volda University College. She obtained her PhD from the University of Bergen in 2011. Her dissertation is titled *Precarious Trust: Problems of Managing Self and Sociality in Guatemala*. Her work explores how local forms of sociality and intimacy give rise to culturally specific ways of forming and experiencing trust and mistrust – both in the intimate sphere of family life and in the public sphere. Ystanes' current project, *Trust as a Precondition for Socio-economic Development: What Can We Learn from the Case of Brazil?*, continues to investigate how trust and mistrust are formed in both private and public lives. Her research interests include trust, poverty, development, gender and conceptions of nature.

 2

Witchcraft
The Dangers of Intimacy and the Struggle over Trust

Peter Geschiere

The focus of the present collection (and the conference on which it is based), on the entanglement of intimacy and trust as crucial for understanding the social, relates very well to a theme in my research among the Maka of Southeast Cameroon that has puzzled me since I started my fieldwork there, more than forty years ago. One of the first things my new Maka friends taught me was that the 'witchcraft of the house' [*djambe le ndjaw*] was the most dangerous one; this clearly had a troubling impact on people's everyday relations. For the Maka the family is the self-evident core of trust and solidarity; yet precisely this inner circle is haunted by the image of the witch who strikes from close by (see also Broch-Due, this volume). Margit Ystanes' emphasis (in this volume) that 'trust and mistrust ... are ... unfixed entities, which succeed and replace each other' speaks directly to this uneasy balance. Moreover, I soon came to realize that this conceptual knot is certainly not just a local issue, an obsession of a closed village society. In my recent book[1] I try to show how these intimate dangers can assume global dimensions with the growing mobility of people – transcontinental migrants still feeling pursued by the dangers of the house (see also McCallum, this volume). Indeed, in African contexts, the stretching of kinship and 'the house' – now including people in different parts of the globe, yet still retaining its coherence – seems to attain impressive dimensions. What does such an increase of scale of the intimate imply for the struggle over trust?

Witchcraft and Intimacy

Let me start by giving a more substantial image of this link between witchcraft and intimacy, notably within the family, that confused but also fascinated me so much during my fieldwork among the Maka in the forest region of Southeast Cameroon. A brief sketch of the context must suffice here. In precolonial times people in this area lived in small patrilineal hamlets under the authority of an elder, and practiced slash-and-burn agriculture; no fixed position of authority developed above the hamlet level. In 1905 they were subjected by the Germans, who were beaten by the French in 1914/15; independence followed in 1960. Since the 1940s food agriculture was complemented by cash-cropping (cocoa and coffee); however these products suffered heavily from collapsing prices on the world market at the end of the 1980s. Nowadays most young men and women try to find jobs in the cities.

The intrusion of *djambe* [witchcraft] into my research in this area came as a sort of surprise. My plan as a political anthropologist was to study local effects of state formation. However, whenever I wanted to discuss issues of authority and politics, my informants referred sooner or later to this *djambe*. Clearly to them, the politics in daylight were only understandable in relation to the nightly shadow-world of this occult force to which almost everybody seemed to have access in one way or another. People linked this *djambe* to kinship (the *djambe le ndjaw*, witchcraft of the house, mentioned before) as some sort of self-evident truth. Rumours of witchcraft attacks – that in this region were only rarely translated into public accusations – always pointed to people of the same compound, or from within the same family. Urban elites complained that, despite all their commitment to the village of origin, they were really afraid to go back since 'those people will eat us' – and 'eating' in this context is associated with the cannibalistic tendencies of the *djambe*. *Nganga* [healers] would emphasize that they could only heal someone if the family wanted to cooperate and, indeed, they always discovered that the main source of danger lay 'inside'. My anthropological training had made me see kinship and witchcraft as opposites – witchcraft as an attack on the order imposed by kinship – but to my interlocutors they seemed to be completely intertwined: witchcraft as the flipside of kinship rather than its opposite. I learned also quite quickly that neither witchcraft nor kinship presented themselves as closed systems. The poly-interpretability of kinship relations – in practice each and every relation appeared to allow for contestation and different interpretations – matched the surprising dynamics of conceptions concerning the *djambe*. Precisely the relation between these two poles – each equally volatile and constantly changing, and even more uncertain in their mutual articulation – seems to give shape to the representations and practices of occult aggression, not as a fixed essence but rather as an ongoing 'event.'

The link with kinship is central to an image that is at the core of Maka notions of witchcraft: the nightly meeting of the witches.

Elsewhere I have extensively described the Maka imaginary around *djambe* (Geschiere 1997), so a short sketch has to suffice here. People describe the *djambe* as an evil creature living in someone's belly which gives its owner (*djindjamb* – the one who has the *djambe*) special powers. The main power is the capacity to transform oneself into an animal or a spirit. Especially at night when the owl calls, the *djambe* will leave the body and fly off into the night – 'along the cobwebs of the *djambe*' – to the *sjoumbou*, the nightly meetings of the witches. There, terrible cannibalistic banquets are being staged. The stories about the debaucheries of these nightly meetings – marked by shocking transgressions, violent encounters and devious victories – are many.[2] But one element recurs all the time: each witch has to offer a relative in his or her turn to be devoured by the other witches; in daily life the victim of this nightly treason will fall ill and die unless the *nganga* [healer] is called in, who can 'see' the guilty witches and force them. Basic to Maka witchcraft discourse is that it is about the betrayal of one's kin to outsiders. In many respects witchcraft is at the interface of the private and the public: between intimate world of kinship or the house, on the one hand, and the outer world and its fascinating opportunities for self-enhancement, on the other. Witches are supposed to have a special hold over their relatives but they used it to hand over their victims to outsiders.

The inherent link with kinship is cogently conveyed by a recurrent motif in witchcraft stories, as a kind of further elaboration of this basic scheme: it concerns the notion of the witch as a martyr who sacrifices him/herself rather than betraying another relative. The sad case of Eba's death was the first time I stumbled upon this kind of interpretation – a trope I was to encounter many more times. During one of the first months of my fieldwork in the village of Logboud (1971), Eba, a man in the strength of his life, suddenly succumbed to a heavy attack of malaria. His family was in shock: one day Eba seemed to be still in good health and the next he was dying! So they made furious but as yet unspecific hints at witchcraft: they clearly were looking for someone to blame. However, other people said the very suddenness of his death showed that he must have been himself a witch. After all, everyone knows that when an 'innocent' – that is, someone who does not 'go out' in the *djambe* – is attacked, (s)he will die slowly. Only between witches does an attack lead to a sudden death: they can 'see' who is attacking them, and then it becomes a battle of life and death. Therefore, some people whispered that Eba must have been a witch himself who in his turn had the worst of the eternal fights among the witches; or, to put it differently: he got what he deserved.

But friends of Eba opted for another interpretation. Maybe he was a witch – after all, he had been very successful in the outlay of cocoa and coffee plantations, which suggested he knew how to defend himself against jealousy – but then it was clear that he had sacrificed himself since he did not want to offer yet another relative to his witch-companions. This image of the witch – recurrent in many parts of Africa – as a person of special courage returns in proverbs about the terrible loneliness of the witch who has neither 'brother nor sister, father nor mother'. If he refuses to give yet another relative, he has to face the wild crowd of witches all alone; people shudder before such an image. Eba might have been a witch but he was also a martyr who, despite earlier betrayals, had made a final stance by refusing to give up yet another kinsman. His tragic courage offered again a powerful expression of the close link people make between witches and kin – witchcraft as the betrayal of kinship – which seemed to be self-evident to my spokesmen, but came to me as a shock.

Especially in present-day contexts, this continuing link with the local realities of kin and village is all the more striking since this imaginary shows an impressive ability to link up with modern developments that far exceed the limits of the village. As one of my Maka spokesmen told me back in 1973: 'We have our own planes, much quicker than yours – our witches fly to Paris and back within a single night'. The zombie spirits, who in the 1960s and 70s were supposed to be put to work on 'invisible plantations' on Mount Kupe in West Cameroon by the nouveaux riches through a novel kind of witchcraft, are now said to be sold off to the mafia, Mount Kupe becoming only a relay station in global circuits of labour exploitation (see de Rosny 1981; Geschiere 1997). But, in the end, even such vertiginous speculations about dark global conspiracies are linked to the familiar, albeit shifting, theme of the betrayal of kin to outsiders.

This new zombie witchcraft highlights the paradoxical combining of the global and the local in a particularly pregnant way. People tend to emphasize the novelty of this form of witchcraft, opposing it to older forms of witchcraft in which the witches would cannibalize their victims. Instead they are now supposed to turn them into zombies to exploit their labour, or even (as people say) 'sell' them. De Rosny traces the obvious link with traumatic memories of the slave trade, but he relates all the excitement over this new form of witchcraft also to people's bewilderment by the capriciousness of the new inequalities and the vagaries of the world market: why do a few people become so rich while all the others invariably fail in their plans? Rumours about zombies provide at least a possible explanation for the shocking wealth of the new elites. Yet even this 'modern' form of witchcraft is linked to similar ideas as the Maka obsession with the *djambe le ndjaw* [witchcraft of the house]. In his fascinating study of how the *nganga* [healers] try to deal with this new threat, Eric de Rosny shows that they always insist that the whole family has to be reunited. This is quite remarkable since it often concerns urbanites who have lived in the city for generations and sometimes really have to search for their kin in the faraway countryside. Despite all novelty and increase of scale, the most dangerous attack is still supposed to come from inside, and the family is still the obvious locus of this inside. This ongoing articulation of witchcraft and intimacy stands out all the more starkly because of this increase of scale of social relations.

The link with intimacy – in this context especially with family – is certainly not an invariable or straightforward premise. For instance, at first sight the role of the *nganga* among the Maka and other groups in the forest of southern Cameroon seems to contradict this, since they are supposed to work outside kinship. The *nganga* should use the forces of the *djambe against* all the witches, thus surpassing kinship. Sometimes people will even say that *nganga* should not live with their family since their powers are so frightening that they would be too much of a danger for their own kin. In many respects they are beyond the framework of kinship. However, at a deeper level kinship is nonetheless there as an essential condition for enhancing their occult powers. People will whisper that in order to be initiated into this dangerous knowledge, a *nganga* had to sacrifice a close relative, who has to be 'given' to his/her 'professor' as reward for all the lessons (see also de Rosny 1981).

Even more important is the recent but quite general trend throughout the African continent to complain that witchcraft is breaking though the boundaries of kinship: supposedly in present times it has lost its old moorings in the family; hence people's worry about witchcraft 'running wild'. Indeed, the link between witchcraft and kinship may seem to become ever more stretched with modern changes and a constant increase of scale of social relations. New forms of witchcraft are seen as particularly shocking since they seem to be effective against anybody, kin or non-kin. For instance, in his recent study of *feymen* (Cameroon's equivalent of the Nigerian 419s, who are involved in global computer fraud, false money schemes and other illicit practices), Basile Ndjio (2006, 2012) emphasizes that the current association of the mysterious success of these swindlers – and some of them do become amazingly rich – with particular forms of witchcraft is no longer tied to kinship. Their *mokoagne moni* [magical money] rather helps them to find their victims – businessmen or politicians eager to invest in dubious schemes – on a transcontinental scale: their *fronts* are in Europe, South Asia and the Gulf states, far outside the reach of kinship. Their occult powers seem to become truly global.

Still, when one follows Ndjio's rich case studies in detail it is striking that references to witchcraft always seem to point back ultimately to the close environment of kin and locality: the helpers of a *feyman* are suddenly bewitched when they accompany him to the village, which in most effective ways takes revenge for the unwillingness of their ungrateful son to share his new wealth; a local community in Douala raises a magical barrier to another *feyman*'s activities by closing its ranks. This is symptomatic. Witchcraft may be supposed to work now in new circuits on a much wider, even global scale – this is one of the reasons for people's worries about it getting ever more out of bounds. Yet in most of these global witchcraft stories there is ultimately a pointer back to the local realities of neighbourhood and family. 'The village' and its emotional intimacy may, at least in some respects, become an almost 'virtual' reality to many Cameroonians – modern urbanites with a global outlook – but it is still is deeply engraved in witchcraft visions.

The Congolese anthropologist Joseph Tonda (now in Libreville) insists even more strongly that since the colonial encounter *la sorcellerie* largely surpasses the old lineage order (it is from then on 'beyond what is thinkable and possible in the lineage order' [Tonda 2002: 237]). Yet in his books the link with the family is everywhere. Even *Mammywata* – the beautiful lady, often white, with blond hair, who captures young men with evil promises of unheard riches – asks her followers to sacrifice a close parent, often a child (Tonda 2002: 85, 2005: 177). *Mammywata* may be the very symbol of modernity and its promises of unlimited consumerism, but she is apparently not completely outside kinship. The general relevance of Tonda's insistence on a complete *déparentélisation* of society as a logical outcome of the colonial moment is problematic.[3] In many parts of Africa the remarkable elasticity of kinship claims grafting themselves upon completely novel relations remains quite striking (not to say worrying). Even African migrants in Europe and America fear the telephone calls from home with their endless demands that can be underlined with hidden threats. Precisely the ongoing association of family with witchcraft as a serious threat among migrants far away from home shows the impressive elasticity of the family/witchcraft complex. Tonda is certainly right that in such novel contexts witchcraft takes on new guises, but its precarious yet inherent link with kinship and the family is in many contexts constantly reaffirmed despite staggering distances. Apparently the map of intimacy can constantly be redrawn, stretching the witchcraft/family complex to a breaking point, yet without destroying its grasp.[4]

This basic link with intimacy – and in many African contexts this means the family from which one is born, and the soil in which one has to be buried – brings out the full horror of witchcraft. In most parts of Africa the family is still celebrated as the basic circle of sociability and trust – even though in practice things may be very different. Yet witchcraft introduces lethal aggression into the very heart of the community, where only solidarity and serenity should reign. It expresses the shocking realization that there is not only harmony inside, but also jealousy and therefore aggression. Moreover, this aggression is all the more dangerous since there is hardly any protection against it. As said, this fear of aggression from close by is certainly not special to Africa or to other regions marked by poverty and crisis. On the contrary. I am always surprised that to Westerners this theme in many African stories of witchcraft – for instance on the betrayal of your own father or mother – is so shocking. After all, Freud warned us already that the family is not just a happy enclave in society, but also a primal hotbed of aggression. With their deep worries about witchcraft, Africans and others raise a universal issue: how to deal with aggression from close by – with intimacy that is not just a haven of peace but at the same time a lethal source of threat and betrayal?

The Struggle over Trust

Linking witchcraft to intimacy automatically raises the issue of trust. As said, intimacy is in many respects the very core of the social. Yet how can one establish trust in people who are close, how can one live and work with them, if they can be so dangerous? Clearly, intimacy – in whatever sense – family, neighbourliness, regular collaboration – does not necessarily breed trust, in contrast to what so many anthropologists and other social scientists seem to assume. This means that trust is always contingent; even inside the smallest circle of social relations it is never an ontological given. A witchcraft reading of intimacy and trust can have challenging implications, of broader relevance. Both intimacy and trust have recently become buzzwords in anthropology and social science in general. Yet more recent reflections on these notions often give intimacy a surprisingly positive charge, linking it in quite simplistic ways to trust, as some sort of given. Elsewhere I tried to show that such a positive interpretation can have its limitations for the notion of intimacy. Here I want to focus especially on trust, and the dangers of simplistically associating it with closeness as more or less a given in the inner circle of social relations.

It is hardly surprising that the notion of trust has experienced a new boost of life since the 1990s. This was the time of an unprecedented flowering of 'management studies', as a new shoot of organization sociology, which used 'trust' as some sort of magical wand. Moreover, the growing insecurities of capitalism as a supposedly rational system – the increasing dominance of finance capitalism, that according to some rapidly deteriorated into a kind of 'casino capitalism' (J. and J. Comaroff 2000) – seemed to require an ever wider stretching of current forms of trust. Of course, in hindsight (certainly after the dramatic collapse of 2008 and 2009) one can speak of clearly an over-stretching. Urgent reasons, also for economists, to take the concept of trust seriously.

The challenge of the concept in present-day contexts will be clear: it marks the limits of the rational choice approach so dear to economy and related disciplines. As a long line of thinkers, from Georg Simmel through Niklas Luhmann, Herbert Frankel and Anthony Giddens has highlighted, trust is based on a complex mixture of knowledge and uncertainty (Simmel's *Wissen und Nicht-wissen*), but it always contains also an element of affect that gives it – even in situations of very weak knowledge – particular force, possibly stronger than purely rational choice. It is impossible, therefore, to exclude culture, affect, emotion or morality – whatever term one prefers – from the analysis (see Ystanes, present volume). For many of the leading authors in trust studies this seems to result in uncomfortable compromises. Yet, as Guido Möllering notes in his seminal article (2001), the impact of rational choice remains strong: there is a constant tendency in trust studies to return to a mapping of 'good reasons' as the main strategy to understand why in a given situation people do, or do not, trust.

Möllering rightly opposes this to the strong emphasis by Georg Simmel – in both his study of money and his essay on the secret and secret societies – on the key role in trust relations of a 'further element' beyond knowledge and calculation. Striking are Simmel's terms for this mysterious element: he called it *Glauben*, equating it to religious faith (Simmel 1990: 216). For Simmel, trust had to be understood first of all as combining sound reasons with faith. Following up on this, Möllering – also inspired by Luhmann – translates this by *Aufhebung* [suspension] of doubt: the willingness to suspend doubt and leap over ignorance. For Möllering, the great merit of Simmel is to condense this in his emphasis on a 'further element'. Hence Möllering's depiction of this 'suspension' as a leap over the gorge that separates 'the land of interpretation' from 'the land of expectation':

[D]espite precarious knowledge and uncertain interpretation this suspension lifts a person by a 'mental leap' into the land of firm expectation (whether positive or negative). (Möllering 2001: 412–414)

However, Simmel's approach to trust in terms of a leap of faith is not only a good cure for rational choice addicts when they have to understand, for instance, the vagaries of casino capitalism. It may be as salutary for anthropologists, at least for those who still have a tendency to entrench themselves in a bastion of gift-giving and reciprocity when addressing trust. This can become a problem when one wants to address the paradox of how intimacy can breed trust despite the hazards of inherent jealousy and witchcraft. A classical example is the way Marshall Sahlins evacuated the darker sides from Mauss' vision of gift-giving – the gift that can kill, possibly linked to witchcraft – in the famous concentric circles model of 'primitive exchange' (Sahlins 1974 [1965]). The crux of the model is the movement from 'generalized reciprocity' in the inner circle to ever more 'negative reciprocity' in the wider circles. The more general implication is clear: reciprocity and therefore trust reigns inside. Of course, there have been numerous criticisms on this somewhat one-dimensional model. Tim Ingold (1986: 232), for instance, insists that even in 'hunter-gatherer societies' negative reciprocity exists at the very core of the system in the form of 'demand sharing'. Thus, Ingold proposes a concentric circles model that looks the same as Sahlins' one, but has a crucial twist: in the inner circle ('relatives') there are now two signs: +sharing, but also – demands. With 'demands' we are close to jealousy, and thus to witchcraft.[5] In a more general sense feminist anthropologists have furnished powerful contributions for destabilizing the assumption of the domestic circle as a safe core.

Yet the power of Sahlins' model – building on a kind of commonsense assumption that kinship is synonymous with trust – should not be underestimated. This assumption returns, for instance, even with a sophisticated author with a keen historical sense like Charles Tilly. In his book on *Trust and Rule* (2005), kinship figures as some sort of primal example of trust networks. This may be understandable in the context of Tilly's large-scale historical project that aims at understanding the global processes through which more restricted networks of trust – 'kinlike solidarity' – were integrated into broader 'public politics' (Tilly 2005: 7, 9). Yet the aplomb with which he declares that 'participants in kinship and other trust networks usually take them for granted' is striking (Tilly 2005: 6). This runs straight against the obsession in many parts of Africa (and elsewhere) with witchcraft as festering within the family. And even within Tilly's own society there are long traditions of violent strife and deep hatred precisely *within* the family (compare the programmatic title of François Mauriac's famous 1932 novel *Le noeud des vipères*).

It may be important, moreover, to emphasize that these are not merely academic quibbles. Consider, for instance, the central role this image of the family as a safe haven of solidarity and trust continues to play in development sociology, notably for Africa. In the 1980s Goran Hyden's notion of an 'economy of affection' that still allowed Africa's 'uncaptured peasantry' to take an 'exit option' – a singularly inapt term to designate the precariously balance of relations inside the village – was hailed by many as the key to understand Africa's crisis (Hyden 1980). It is striking also that the neoliberal turn in development thinking brought a comeback of such ideas. In Africa (and elsewhere) neoliberal development experts have a surprising tendency to combine a solid belief in the blessings of the market with an equally categorical appeal to the old idea of 'the' community as a starting point for new style development projects.[6] The role family and village economy continue to play in many development schemes for the continent indicates also that these neoliberal experts still tend to see the sector as some sort of safe refuge – indeed, an economy where only affection reigns. A 'witchcraft reading' of intimacy as always ambiguous can help to recognize the severe limitations of such one-sided views.

There may be good reasons, therefore, to question the self-evidence with which many anthropologists use the term 'reciprocity'. It would be interesting to follow the genealogy of the notion in our discipline – how it came to take such a central place in the anthropologist's tool-kit. Yet that would lead us too far here.[7] The great advantage of Simmel's emphasis on 'the further element' as crucial to any form of trust is that it can serve to relativize implicit assumptions that so easily creep into the anthropological predilection for reciprocity. The contingency of this 'further element' means that trust is never a given, not even in the most intimate surroundings. Precisely there the appeal to 'generalized reciprocity' always has a counterpoint in the potential danger of intimacy. Thus Simmel's approach suggests concrete questions rather than fixed answers – questions that have to be addressed ethnographically and historically in order to tackle the complicated knot of witchcraft, intimacy and trust. When are people willing to suspend their doubts in the face of omnipresent danger? What encourages such 'a leap of faith', and when it is bound to fail? Some ethnographic examples may give an idea of how these questions can be tackled in a constantly changing context.

Trust and Doubt: The Recourse to the *Nganga* [Healer]

An obvious option for my Maka friends – as for most Cameroonians – in case of growing distrust within 'the house' is to go and visit the *nganga*. This is logical since such healers are supposed to be experts at 'seeing' what the witches are plotting. They all have acquired 'a second pair of eyes' [*miesj meba*] as the first step in their painful initiation. This allows them to 'surprise' these evil-doers, and force them to lift their spell. All this is supposed to make the *nganga* experts at reconciling tensions within the family. Let me give an example.

A few weeks after I had started my fieldwork in 1971 in 'my' Maka village I heard that Mbili was ill. I had taken quite a liking to him because of the way he played his guitar, and sang little songs he heard on the radio. Clearly he wanted to be 'modern' in some sort of artistic way. *Mbili* [arrow] was his nickname because of his impressive rushes at the football field, and he clearly loved to be called this. The next day people said he was still ill, so I decided to go and see how he was doing. But on the way to his family's house we met Mendouga, who had been pointed out to me already several times as the greatest *nganga* of the whole district. She was accompanied, as always, by her dog – a whitish animal, quite friendly – and a little boy. She seemed quite happy to see us – earlier on she had already tried to contact the 'new *ntangue* [white man]' of the village. So we walked down together, Mendouga explaining to me with her somewhat mocking smile that Mbili's people had called her in to 'resolve things'. When we got to the compound – a rambling complex of buildings of poles and mud walls, some of them in a state of approaching collapse – Mendouga was offered a big cockerel. She told the little boy who accompanied her to hold the bird. Then we entered Mbili's room. Clearly Mendouga had no problems with me going in with her.

Mbili was in bed, looking a bit weak and upset. She sat at his bed, held his hand and stroked his head. Then she started to talk in a low voice. The main message seemed to be that everything was going to be all right. But there was also a note of warning: she had 'seen' that some people were plotting evil things, but they should know now that she had spotted them, so they had better turn back. Clearly the warning was addressed to 'someone' inside the house, but no further details were given. After delivering this warning, Mendouga chuckled – I had come to dread her giggling by now – stood up and left. On the way out she explained to me that this was the way to put an end to evil: now the witches would think twice because they knew that she would be after them if they did not refrain from further mischief. After one more giggle – clearly very satisfied that I had seen her demonstration of good intentions – she left with her dog, the boy running after her dragging the protesting cockerel by the neck.

This little sketch gives an image of how a healer should behave. *Nganga* can be men or women. They are supposed to have learned their secrets through a long initiation with their 'professor' who taught them 'to see', to 'tie up the witches', and rob their *djambe* [witchcraft] of its powers.[8] Thus *nganga* can nip dangerous threats in the bud and re-establish trust in a family that risks to be torn by hatred and jealousy. But this, of course, depends on people trusting the *nganga*. I soon was to understand that precisely this is a big issue.

Ambiguities of the *Nganga*

Mendouga's small performance in my presence – it was clear that she welcomed the opportunity for showing me that all sorts of nasty rumours about her were unfounded – indicated why people should trust a *nganga*. She had the capacity to 'see', and the reputation of her 'professor' (to whom she kept referring without ever going into details about his identity) should further guarantee that she had 'the power'. All this clearly impressed the villagers. Yet a problem is that to the Maka it is self-evident that the *nganga* themselves must be deeply involved in the very *djambe* they are supposed to combat. How else could they be able to heal? In the beginning I was a bit disconcerted that my friends would insist so blandly that 'of course' a *nganga* like Mendouga was a *djindjamb* (someone who has the *djambe* – that is, a witch). A big *nganga* of her calibre would even have a *djambe* that 'beats all records'. And, indeed, the other *nganga* I was to talk to later, also all confirmed that their 'professor' had helped them to develop the *djambe* in their belly in order to give them exceptional powers. But they would always add that, of course, the professor had bound them with heavy oaths – *itsi* [interdictions] that kill someone as soon as (s)he transgresses them – to use their powers only to heal and never to kill. Yet the Maka are never sure of that. After all, a *djambe* is a *djambe*, and there is always the danger that its basic instinct – to betray and kill the people who are in its power – will get the upper hand. Moreover, there are persistent rumours (as noted above) that *nganga* have to offer a close relative to their professor in order to fulfil their initiation. On top of that there are all sorts of sayings that an ambitious pupil will end up killing his *nganga*-professor. This is why a pupil always has to go away once his initiation has been completed (see also de Rosny 1981). Or, to put it more succinctly, one has to kill in order to be able to heal. *Nganga* are deeply respected – certainly as long as they seem to have 'the' power – but they are at the same time seen as highly dangerous persons who can always direct their formidable knowledge against you. This vicious circle – the main protection against the *djambe* is to be sought in the very field of this *djambe* itself – makes any form of trust highly uncertain and situational. The *nganga* can only heal and restore trust if people are willing to trust him/her. But complete trust is very difficult since the *nganga* themselves are such ambiguous and potentially dangerous figures.

It is on this point – central to the conundrum of witchcraft, intimacy and trust – that my earlier book on witchcraft (Geschiere 1997) has been severely criticized.[9] For instance, John Hund (now at the University of the North, South Africa) attacked me even more forcefully by quoting me as an outstanding example of the fact that academic writers are 'unfortunately some of the worst perpetrators of confusion'. He was clearly shocked that I repeated my informants' view of the *nganga* being a kind of 'super-witch' who can only heal by using the same powers as witches do. For Hund this is an 'overwhelming misunderstanding' (Hund 2000: 369–370). He insists instead that healers (for him especially the *sangoma* of South Africa) should be radically kept apart from the witches.

Of course, the whole witchcraft conundrum would be a lot easier to solve if such a separation could be applied so simply. The problem is, again, the subversive character of witchcraft discourse that so easily erodes all such nice conceptual distinctions – in Africa, just as elsewhere in the world.[10] It is clear that there are wide differences as to how African societies view central actors in the occult domain – like the healers or the chiefs – and to what extent they try to separate these leaders from the hidden powers. It is also true that in the forest societies in Cameroon where I did my main fieldwork, the central notions (*djambe* among the Maka and *evu* among the Beti) are extremely broad and fluid, covering a wide array of different expressions of the occult, from highly negative to fairly positive ones – *djambe*/*evu* being potentially lethal but also essential for healing, exercising authority or accumulating wealth. Elsewhere in Cameroon – for instance, in the more hierarchical societies of the country's western highlands (Bamileke, Bamenda) – there is a determined effort to 'compartmentalize' the sphere of the occult through clear terminological distinctions between more negative and more positive forms. In these societies, the chief may be associated with occult powers, but he is normally rigidly separated from the darker manifestations of these powers. However, it is important to emphasize that such distinctions are always precarious and never self-evident. It seems to require a constant struggle to maintain them against the inherent fluidity of any discourse on the occult. For instance, in the 1990s, when many chiefs from the Cameroonian highlands got into trouble with their subjects for continuing to support the hated regime of President Biya, people were quick to accuse them of being real witches, setting fire to their palaces and damaging their Pajeros – all things that were supposed to be impossible only a few years before, but that were now seen as legitimate since clearly the chiefs had strayed off the right path and started to make alliances with the witches.

There are also good reasons not to take the distinctions that are often emphasized in, for instance, the literature on South Africa between 'witch' and *sangoma* – or between the *sangoma* as a 'priest-diviner' and the *inyanga* as his disreputable colleague – too easily for granted. Even Hund (ibid.: 373) emphasizes that they all use 'the same occult forces', but he insists that there is an 'ontological' difference. One can sympathize with his effort to separate the *sangoma* as a reliable ally in these dark struggles. But who makes this 'ontological difference' between actors that are so closely involved with the same forces? And how can such a distinction be maintained in practice? It is clear that widely different views of the *sangoma* pertain in daily life. In the famous Ralushai report (Ralushai Commission 1996) on the bloody witch hunts unleashed by young men who called themselves 'ANC comrades' during the last years of the Apartheid regime in Transvaal, people say quite nasty things about *sangoma* (e.g., 'with a lust for blood and easy money' [ibid.: 268]). Indeed, it is quite clear that the young comrades gave the healers an impossible dilemma. They were the first ones to be suspected of being involved with the horrible *muti* murders (the practice of maiming especially children – preferably while still alive – in order to use their vital organs for 'medicine'). Often the healers could only escape being lynched if they were willing to use their powers in order to 'smell out' other witches. Thus the notorious diviner Ramaredi Shaba in Sekhukuneland would give drugs to the comrades and then put up her 'African Television', a big screen on which the dazed comrades would recognize the faces of 'witches' who had to be necklaced (Delius 1996: 195).

Rather than taking such terminological distinctions – between witch and *sangoma*, or between 'bona fide' and 'mala fide' healers – as givens, it might be more urgent to study how exactly such compartmentalization is maintained, through which struggles and by what means.

Apparently maintaining such distinctions will always entail a highly precarious struggle against the blurring tenor of discourses on the occult. And, as said, it might be this subversive charge, undermining any clear-cut distinction between good and evil, that can help to understand the impressive resilience of these discourses in the face of modern changes.

A New Solution: God's Work as the Basis for Ultimate Trust

The 1980s brought in many parts of Africa a new approach to witchcraft and the conundrum of intimacy and (dis)trust: Pentecostalism. Indeed, one of the great attractions of Pentecostalism in Africa is that it promises a radical break with both witchcraft and family. Of course, Pentecostal missionaries, especially American ones, were active in Africa already long before this. But the 1980s brought a quite sudden proliferation of Pentecostal churches, sects and movements all over Africa. The switch in Pentecostal preaching, around that time, from 'asceticism to accumulation', as Robert Akoko calls it in his book on Pentecostalism and the economic crisis in Cameroon (2007), was very important for the rapidly increasingly popularity of the Pentecostal message throughout Africa. The new 'gospel of prosperity', to which most churches shifted, preached that true believers did not have to wait until the hereafter, they would get rich here and now. Apparently this was a major boost for many believers.

Even before the switch to the 'prosperity gospel', Pentecostalism brought a completely new approach for the struggle against witchcraft (see Meyer 1999). While the established churches – to which most Pentecostal converts belonged earlier in their life – tended to deny the reality of witches, the Pentecostals have always taken witchcraft most seriously. Particularly important was that throughout Africa they equate it with the Devil. Thus the struggle with witchcraft, as a major manifestation of Satan himself, became the basic theme in their version of Christianity. No wonder that in Africa the public confessions that form one of the climaxes of Pentecostal services mostly centre on former escapades in witchcraft from which the speaker was saved by a dramatic conversion. While the older churches, established by missionaries in colonial times, have great difficulty promising a cure against witchcraft (since they tend to deny its very existence), the Pentecostals offer definitive certainty that they are able not only to protect against witchcraft, but also to protect anybody who does not stray from the right path (or overtly repents) from this evil. Their cure is simple: the moment of conversion – the archetype of which is, as said, Paul's shattering experience on the way to Damascus when God spoke to him and turned him from an unbeliever into the new Church's most zealous apostle – will save the true believer from witchcraft in any form.

Of special interest to our topic is that the Pentecostal solution for witchcraft differs basically not only from that of the missionary churches but also from the approach of the *nganga*. The latter mostly see it as their task to repair relations, notably inside the family. In contrast, the Pentecostals advocate 'a complete break with the past' (Meyer 1998). In practice this means a break with the family, since this is seen as the very seat of the Devil. Indeed, many authors emphasize that central to Pentecostalism in Africa is its determination to liberate the believer from the pressures of kinship.[11] Thus the new message seems to bring a decisive turn exploding the coherence of the whole triangle of witchcraft, intimacy and (dis)trust. The solution seems to be as simple as it is drastic: the believer has to leave the family behind and will thus be liberated from its witchcraft-infested intimacy. Instead (s)he will enter a new intimacy, that of the global Pentecostal community, in which trust is guaranteed since it is based on Faith.

The question is of course whether this radically new approach succeeds in puncturing the whole witchcraft issue in practice, establishing a definitive victory of trust. The answer is far from clear yet. A complicating factor is the constantly contested position of the pastor, who is, of course, vital for the establishment of new forms of trust that would surpass the old predicaments. One thing that Pentecostals throughout Africa – and probably not only there – seem to have in common is that preachers are constantly scrutinized to see whether they live up to their own preaching. Of course this raises endless rumours that they have been found wanting. Already in 1999 I could buy at Ekok, the Cameroonian border-station with Nigeria, far out in the bush, one of those eloquent Nigerian posters, picturing a short strip of a successful Pentecostal preacher arriving in his own plane, where his Mercedes is already waiting for him. His driver takes the road, but he is stopped by at a police control. The policemen open the boot and it is full of skulls! Clearly the reverend himself is a witch!

But the main problem, emphasized by almost all the authors quoted above, is that in everyday life Pentecostalism seems to strengthen witchcraft rather than achieving a definitive victory over it. The constant confessions and admonitions to inspect oneself for guilty secrets only reaffirms the fear of witchcraft as an omnipresent danger. Pentecostalism may call for a final eradication of witchcraft, but in practice it seems to need this counterpoint for its own reproduction.

The Radical Approach versus the Everyday

There are many more openings for people to try and establish trust in the slippery world of witchcraft (see Geschiere 2013). But the opposition between the approach of the *nganga* and that of the Pentecostalist preacher might already allow certain tentative conclusions. Of interest is especially the opposition between the radicalism of the Pentecostal approach – witchcraft is the devil and therefore it has to be eradicated – to the much more resigned attitude of the *nganga*. De Rosny, the Cameroonian Jesuit-cum-*nganga* mentioned before, quotes a proverb from the Douala (a coastal group in Cameroon): 'you have to learn how to live with your *sorcier*' (de Rosny 1992: 114); this is much closer to the *nganga* approach. In this view, witchcraft as such can hardly be eradicated, but it can be neutralized in special settings and thus contained. We saw already that the Pentecostal solution, a most vivid example of a radical approach, only seems to reinforce people's obsession with the proliferating of this horrible threat in new forms. In contrast the approach in terms of 'learning how to live with' witchcraft seems to have in everyday practice a more quieting effect – remember Ms Mendouga's way of solving Mbili's plight (for further discussion see Geschiere 2013: ch. 3 and 6).

However, such contrasts have again to be historicized. It is clear that the adage of 'learning to live with your witch' and the role of the *nganga* have been subject to drastic changes, even during the relative short span of time of the forty years that I can follow developments in Makaland. The everyday approach has clear implications for how one can 'live with one's witch'. The main one is 'just redistribution'. As elsewhere, witchcraft discourse contains a powerful appeal to share; it is only by sharing that the rich and the powerful can avoid the deadly dangerous jealousy of their kin. However with the new opportunities for enrichment – or rather the new gap between the few who get rich and the others whose poverty becomes ever more glaring in contrast – the very idea of 'just redistribution' becomes ever more virtual. As elsewhere in Africa (and beyond), consuming is deeply serious to the new elites among the Maka. It expresses a constant struggle for affirming one's status. And precisely because the lines of stratification are so unclear – the inexplicable enrichment of some, their equally sudden fall – it seems all the more important to underline success with ostentatious spending. But how to combine this with people's deep worry about jealousy from close by?

Still regularly visiting the Maka villages for over forty years now, I remain surprised by the apparent complacency with which people live with such potential dangers from close by. Even when tensions become more manifest in hints, insistent rumours or even horrible accusations, things can often quieten down surprisingly quickly, and life in the family or among neighbours may go on as before. Yet such stressful moments are never completely forgotten. Accusations can suddenly re-emerge, enriched with details that hark back over longer periods of time. This uneasy balance has important implications for social relations. Even relations inside the house require constant maintenance. Good understanding is never a given; even with the closest of kin the relation has to be kept up with great prudence. But precisely because of this pressure, distrust and anger can suddenly flare up in noisy and sometimes even violent confrontations that afterwards have to be massaged with great care and repaired by all sorts of exchanges. Typically the big village palaver – the 'village tribunal' as people sometimes called it – where such suspicions had to be brought into the open and discussed, was not so much a court that tried to decide on guilt and punishment, but rather an arena for repairing social relations, striving to make the opposed parties again partners in ongoing exchanges. In such a context, the question is not so much whether you trust or distrust someone (cf. Haas, this volume). At stake is how you can maintain a relation, and this requires constant 'work'. It is clear also that the new inequalities and increasing openings for ostentatious consumption have made this 'work' ever more difficult.

One blatant sign of such changes was the further mercantilization of the *nganga* profession. In the 1980s I was surprised by the emergence of a new type of 'modern' *nganga*. While the *nganga* I knew in the 1970's – like Madame Mendouga mentioned before – kept a low profile in everyday life, often living in simple houses, at the margins of the village, these new *nganga* made themselves much more conspicuous. They lived in bigger houses, often in the middle of the village, with big signs. They were keen to show their familiarity with modern life, sporting sunglasses and urban style of dressing, adorning their *bureau* with books on religion and magic, and claiming scientific knowledge. In the same years, more successful *nganga* could claim official prestige: they would be called up as witnesses in the new processes before the state courts against 'witches' (see Fisiy and Geschiere 1990) and they could become involved in official health projects. This new recognition of the *nganga* profession triggered fierce competition and seemed to inspire a much more aggressive approach to potential clients. Ambitious younger *nganga* would come up to people warning them of terrible dangers and proclaiming quite startling and aggressive accusations. The therapies they prescribed often lacked the calming aspect described for Ms Mendouga above. They seemed to upset social relations rather than restoring them.

Such changes, of direct consequence for the way trust could be established, went together with an increase in the scale of witchcraft rumours. In the 1970s the distance between village and city was supposed to bring substantial protection against the jealousy of the villagers and their witchcraft. One of the new elites of the village where I lived, who had made his career in the city, decided to return and live again with his 'brothers' in the village. However he immediately fell ill and was only cured by a powerful *nganga*, who admonished him to return immediately to the city and thereafter keep his distance from village life. Other people commented that, of course, he had been most imprudent venturing again into the intimacy of his family 'at home'. Yet in the 1990s a cousin of this elite person also became involved in a witchcraft affair. But this time people supposed that he had brought an urban form of witchcraft into the village. By then, village and city had become so intertwined that the geographical distance between the two was certainly no longer seen as an effective protection against witchcraft attacks. In the 1980s, people in another part of Cameroon – the Southwest, colonized by the British and therefore Anglophone – would often tell me that 'witchcraft does not cross the water' (see also Goheen 1996). Yet in this respect also witchcraft discourse proved to be surprisingly flexible. Since the 1990s people in this area have become obsessed with the idea of 'bush-falling' – a new and quite surprising notion since 'bush' stands for Europe (or in general the richer parts of the world) while people relate 'falling' to the image of a hunter who has luck and returns with large amounts of booty. However, the metaphor of the hunter has its ambiguities since everybody also knows the stories of hunters who stumbled upon an attractive spot in the forest and chose to create a new village there. So the families who are often very actively involved in enabling younger members to leave for 'bush' set great store on making sure 'they will not forget' (Alpes 2011), and they have their own means for this. Talliani's seminal article on the heavy pressure on Nigerian prostitutes in Italy not to 'forget' the family at home shows how heavy the burden can become (Talliani 2012). In a study on Ghanaians in Tel Aviv, Galli Sabar (2010) shows most graphically how transcontinental migrants can come to fear angry phone calls from home reminding them of their obligations to share. Apparently witchcraft threats are now supposed – and most emphatically so – to cross the ocean. Clearly, the scope attributed to witchcraft threats can change over time in important ways, marking people's changing perceptions of what counts as intimacy.

Such a dramatic increase of scale puts the old adage of 'learning to live with your witch' to a heavy test. Yet all this does not seem to affect the coherence of the family, now stretching over ever-growing geographical and social distances. The Pentecostal approach equating witchcraft with a cosmic battle against the Devil may appear to be better equipped to deal with such increasing scale of relations. However, at least in African contexts, it locates this evil in the heart of the family, thus strengthening the very counterpoint it sets out to eradicate.

It is against the background of such incisive changes that trust has to be understood as an ongoing struggle. A witchcraft reading of the link between intimacy and trust can help to get beyond implicit assumptions linking closeness to reciprocity. The challenge is rather to study trust as a suspension of doubt that is always precarious.

Notes

1 *Witchcraft, Intimacy and Trust: Africa in Comparison* (Geschiere 2013); the present text contains element from various chapters of this book.
2 Another recurrent theme, briefly mentioned above, in the Maka stories about the *sjoumbou* is same-sex intercourse: these nightly encounters are marked not only by cannibalism but also by sexual debauchery. Yet in the night world everything is turned upside down. So sex is same-sex intercourse, according to most Maka unheard of in everyday life (which remains to be seen): in the *sjoumbou* men do 'it' with men and 'even' women with women. This equation of homosexuality with witchcraft has taken on new vigour with quite dramatic effects now that recently (especially since 2005) not only the state and the Catholic Church but also the population at large have embarked – as elsewhere in Africa – on ferocious witch-hunts against homosexuals.
3 Regional differences may play an important role in this context. Striking is, for instance, that – as Tonda shows in rich detail (2005: 223) – in Brazzaville and Kinshasa (and probably in other cities in Congo) there is hardly any question of bringing back deceased urbanites to their home village to be buried there – this in striking contrast to other parts of the continent where the funeral at home (that is, in the village) is still a high point in the reaffirmation of belonging and the coherence of the family; it is also a moment deeply feared by many urbanites since their obligatory attendance at funerals in the village offers the villagers a moment of choice to get even with their 'brothers in town' who neglected their duty to redistribute (see further Geschiere 2009: ch. 6). In the two Congos the general practice of burying in the city itself (where funerals are increasingly monopolized by unruly youths) might be a sign of a much further weakening of urban–rural ties: indeed a true *déparentélisation* (see also de Boeck 2006 and his 2010 film on funerals in Kinshasa).

4   See Beneduce (2012) and Taliani (2012) on Nigerians and Cameroonians in Turin; and Sabar (2010) on Ghanaians in Tel Aviv.
5   See also Gregory (1993: 925). Cf. the contrast with, for instance, the romantic tenor of Sahlins' image of reciprocity within small circles among 'Congo Pygmies' (and 'hunters and gatherers' in general) – an image that is strikingly unhelpful for understanding violent tendencies within these communities nowadays (see Appendix A to Sahlins 1972: 231 and 233).
6   Striking examples are to be found in Juan Obarrio's recent book (2014) on the emergence of what he calls the 'Structural Adjustment state' in Mozambique. In his thesis (2007) on which the book is based, Obarrio describes how, for instance, during a meeting a senior American UNDP official angrily replied to the doubts of a few social scientists about the ease with which he took 'the' local community as the starting point for projects: 'These communities know who they are and know also their boundaries perfectly well'. Similarly a British USAID consultant insisted that communities 'will be like corporations, unified single legal subjects under the new land law' (Obarrio 2007: 105).
7   An important moment in this genealogy might be the 1990 translation of Mauss' *Essai sur le don* that translates Mauss' '*rendre le don*' as 'to reciprocate the gift'. Of course, a more correct translation would be 'to return the gift' (this would also do more justice to Mauss' emphasis on the gift also having dangerous aspects, turning into poison and leading to witchcraft). Also since terms like *réciproque* or *réciproquer* hardly figure in Mauss' original text, one can wonder where the consequent use of 'to reciprocate' in the 1990 translation come from. Could it be from Sahlins' *Stone Age Economics* (1974)? It is striking that in the fourth chapter on Mauss, Sahlins does pay attention to the more negative sides of the gift in the Maussian view; while in the following chapter on 'primitive exchange' Sahlins' consequent use of the term reciprocity serves to evacuate these darker sides (cf. also Sahlins' recent book *What Kinship Is and Is Not* [2012] where 'reciprocity' is replaced by a similarly positive notion, 'mutuality of being', which again helps to evacuate the dangerous potentialities of kinship relations).
8   This is why witches who refuse to confess are seen as the really dangerous ones. Apparently, they want to hold on to their dangerous powers. Only if a witch confesses can the *nganga* neutralize their dangerous powers. In practice this means that an accused witch is under enormous pressure: a refusal to confess can trigger harsh sanctions.
9   See also Toulabor 1999. Yet I am certainly not the first to point to this circularity. Even an anthropologist like S.F. Nadel (1935: 436), whom one can hardly suspect of being sensationalist, stated categorically: 'In order to … fight witchcraft one must possess witchcraft oneself'. See also Bernault (2005) and Beneduce (2010: 119); the latter provides a haunting description of such ambivalences by a Baka (Pygmy) healer from South Cameroon who spoke about his sensations when walking in the forest and how the constant possibility of him or someone else becoming invisible makes it is no longer clear 'who is prey and who is predator'.

10　See for spectacular examples of such ambiguity Taussig (1987) on Columbia, and Favret-Saada (1977, 2009) on present-day Europe (for the latter see also Geschiere 2013: ch. 4). See also Ashforth (2000) on Soweto (South Africa).
11　See Meyer (1999) and van Dijk (2002) on Ghana; Marshall (2009) on Nigeria; Tonda (2002, 2005) on Congo-Brazzaville; Akoko (2007) on Cameroon and *passim* (for detailed bibliographies of the by now vast literature on Pentecostalism in Africa, see Marshall 2009 and de Witte 2008).

References

Akoko, R.M. 2007. *"Ask and You Shall Be Given": Pentecostalism and the Economic Crisis in Cameroon*. Leiden: African Studies Center.

Alpes, M.J. 2011. 'Bushfalling: How Young Cameroonians Dare to Migrate'. Ph.D. dissertation. Amsterdam: University of Amsterdam.

Ashforth, A. 2000. *Madumo, a Man Bewitched*. Chicago: University of Chicago Press.

Beneduce, R. 2010. 'Soigner l'incertitude au Cameroun – Le théra épique du nganga face à l'économie du miracle'. In L. Ladovic (ed.), *Le pluralisme médical en Afrique*. Paris / Yaounde : Karthala / UCAC (Université catholique de l'Afrique centrale.

—— 2012. Un imaginaire qui tue: Réflexions sur sorcellerie, violence et pouvoir (Cameroun et Mali). In J.Bouju and B. Martinelli (eds), *Sorcellerie et violence en Afrique*. Paris: Karthala, 309–328.

Bernault, F. 2005. 'Body, Power and Sacrifice in Equatorial Africa', *Journal of African History* 47: 207–239

Comaroff, J. and J. Comaroff. 2000. 'Millennial Capitalism: First Thoughts on a Second Coming', *Public Culture* 12: 291–344. Special issue, *Millennial Capitalism and the Culture of Neoliberalism*, edited by Comaroff and Comaroff.

De Boeck, F. 2006. 'Youth, Death and the Urban Imagination l: A Case from Kinshasa', *Bulletin des séances de l'Académie royale des sciences d'outre-mer* 52(2): 113–125.

—— 2010. *Cemetery State*. Brussels: Filmnatie.

Delius, P. 1996. *A Lion amongst the Cattle: Reconstruction and Resistance in the Northern Transvaal*. Johannesburg: Raven Press.

De Rosny, E. 1981. *Les yeux de ma chèvre - Sur les pas des maîtres de la nuit en pays douala*. Paris: Plon.

—— 1992. *L'Afrique des guérisons*. Paris: Karthala.

De Witte, M. 2008. 'Spirit Media: Charismatics, Traditionalists, and Mediation Practices in Ghana'. Ph.D dissertation. Amsterdam: University of Amsterdam.

Favret-Saada, J. 1977. *Les mots, la mort, les sors: La sorcellerie dans le Bocage*. Paris: Gallimard.

—— 2009. *Désorceler*. Paris: Seuil (Editions de l'Olivier).

Fisiy, C. and P. Geschiere. 1990. 'Judges and Witches, Or How is the State to Deal with Witchcraft? Examples from Southeastern Cameroon', *Cahiers d'Études africaines* 118: 135–156.

Freud, S. 2003 [1919]. 'The Uncanny'. In D. Mcclintock and H. Haughton (eds), *The Uncanny*. London: Penguin Classics.

Geschiere, P. 1997. *The Modernity of Witchcraft: Politics and the Occult in Postcolonial Africa*. Charlotsville: University of Virginia Press.

―― 2009. *The Perils of Belonging: Autochthony, Citizenship and Exclusion in Africa and Europe*. Chicago: University of Chicago Press.

―― 2013. *Witchcraft, Intimacy and Trust: Africa in Comparison*. Chicago: University of Chicago Press.

Goheen, M. 1996. *Men Own the Fields, Women Own the Crops: Gender and Power in the Cameroon Highlands*. Madison: Wisconsin University Press.

Gregory, C. 1994. 'Exchange and Reciprocity'. In T. Ingold (ed.), *Companion Encyclopedia of Anthropology*. London: Routledge.

Hund, J. 2000.Witchcraft and Accusations of Witchcraft in South Africa: Ontological Denial and the Suppression of African Justice. *Comparative and International Law Journal of Sothern Africa* 33: 369–389.

Hyden, G. 1980. *Beyond Ujamaa in Tanzania: Underdevelopment and an Uncaptured Peasantry*. London: Heinemann.

Ingold, T. 1986. *The Appropriation of Nature: Essays on Human Ecology and Social Relations*. Manchester: Manchester University Press.

Marshall, R. 2009. *Political Spiritualities: The Pentecostal Revolution in Nigeria*. Chicago: University of Chicago Press.

Mauriac, F. 1932. *Le noeud de vipères*. Paris: Grasset.

Mauss, M. 1950 [1923–4]. 'Essai sur le don. Forme et raison de l'échange dans les sociétés archaiques'. In *Sociologie et anthropologie*, 145–285. Paris: PUF.

Meyer, B. 1998. '"Make a Complete Break with the Past": Memory and Postcolonial Modernity in Ghanain Pentecostalist Discourse', *Journal of Religion in Africa* 28(3): 316–349.

―― 1999. *Translating the Devil: Religion and Modernity among the Ewe in Ghana*. Edinburgh: Edinburgh University Press.

Möllering, G. 2001. 'The Nature of Trust: From Georg Simmel to a Theory of Expectation, Interpretation and Suspension', *Sociology* 35(2): 403–420.

Nadel, S.F. 1935. 'Witchcraft and Anti-Witchcraft in Nupe Society', *Africa* 8(4): 423–437.

Ndjio, B. 2006. '*Feymania*: New Wealth, Magic Money and Power in Contemporary Cameroon'. Ph.D. dissertation. Amsterdam: University of Amsterdam.

―― 2012. *Magie et enrichissement illicite – La feymania au Cameroun*. Paris: Karthala.

Obarrio, J. 2007. 'The Spirit of the Law in Mozambique'. PhD dissertation. New York: Columbia University.

―― 2014. *The Spirit of the Law in Mozambique*. Chicago: University of Chicago Press.

Ralushai Commission. 1996. 'Report on the Commission of Inquiry into Witchcraft Violence and Ritual Murders in the Northern Province of the Republic of South Africa'. Pokwane: Ministry of Safety and Security, Northern Province, RSA.

Sabar, G. 2010. 'Witchcraft and Concepts of Evil amongst African Migrants Workers in Israel', *Canadian Journal of African Studies* 44(1): 110–141.
Sahlins, M. 1974 [1965]. 'On the Sociology of Primitive Exchange'. In *Stone Age Economics*, 185–277. London: Tavistock.
—— 1974. The Spirit of the Gift. In *Stone Age Economics*, 149–185. London: Tavistock.
—— 2012. *What Kinship Is and Is Not*. Chicago: University of Chicago Press.
Simmel, G. 1950 [1908]. *The Sociology of Georg Simmel* (translated, edited and introduced by K.H. Wolff). New York: Free Press.
—— 1990 [1900]. *The Philosophy of Money* (second edition). London: Routledge.
Taliani, S. 2012. 'Coercion, Fetishes and Suffering in the Daily Lives of Young Nigerian Women in Italy', *Africa* 82(4): 579–608.
Taussig, M. 1987. *Shamanism, Colonialism and the Wild Man: A Study of Terror and Healing*. Chicago: University of Chicago Press.
Tilley, C. 2005. *Trust and Rule*. Cambridge: Cambridge University Press.
Tonda, J. 2002. *La guérison divine en Afrique centrale (Congo, Gabon)*. Paris: Karthala
—— 2005. *Le souverain moderne, Le corps du pouvoir en Afrique centrale (Congo, Gabon)*. Paris: Karthala.
Toulabor, C. 1999. 'Sacrifices humains et politique: quelques exemples contemporains en Afrique'. In P. Konings, W. van Binsbergen and G.Hessling (eds), *Trajectoires de libération en Afrique contemporaine*, 207–223. Paris: Karthala.
Van Dijk, R. 2002. 'The Soul is the Stranger: Ghanaian Pentecostalism and the Diasporioc Contestation of "Flow" and "Individuality"', *Culture and Religion* 3(1): 49–67.

Peter Geschiere is Professor of African Anthropology at the University of Amsterdam. Since 1971 he has undertaken historical-anthropological fieldwork in various parts of Cameroon and elsewhere in West Africa. His publications include *The Modernity of Witchcraft: Politics and the Occult in Post-colonial Africa* (Virginia University Press, 1997) and *Perils of Belonging: Autochthony, Citizenship and Exclusion in Africa and Europe* (Chicago University Press, 2009). His latest book is *Witchcraft, Intimacy and Trust: Africa in Comparison* (Chicago University Press, 2013).

 3

Trusting the Untrustworthy
A Mongolian Challenge to Western Notions of Trust

Paula Haas

'We Barga Mongols don't have bad thoughts about anybody. We trust people, we are honest and trustworthy, that's what distinguishes us from others.' Such self-descriptive assertions about trust and trustworthiness as core elements of Barga Mongolian ethnic identity are of almost daily occurrence in the New Barga Right Banner in the far north-east of Inner Mongolia in China. Equally ubiquitous are normative statements which elevate trust and trustworthiness to a place of particular prominence among Barga Mongols' most important moral values. Yet social life is permeated by a strong sense of anxiety and mistrust, abuses of trust occur with saddening frequency and many people portray the present depreciatively as a time of social and moral disintegration.

Narratives of moral decay attribute the current state of affairs to the economic reforms which were inaugurated by Deng Xiaoping in 1978 and began to be implemented in the New Barga Right Banner in the early 1980s. As a result of the new policies, state farms in this primarily pastoral region were decollectivized and livestock and other assets distributed among herders. Trade across the nearby Russian and Mongolian borders was encouraged, thereby opening up new economic opportunities. Since then public transportation, telecommunications, health care, electricity and water supply systems have improved, and the average level of wealth has risen significantly, making the New Barga Right Banner one of the more affluent rural areas in China. From a material point of view life has thus become much better over the last decades.

Like most changes, however, the reforms have not only put an end to old discontents and problems but also created a series of new ones. In the mid nineties, long iron fences were erected to divide the pastureland into parcels [*nutag*] allotted to individual households for thirty to fifty years, and the population was sedentarized, which meant the end of what Barga people call their 'traditional nomadic lifestyle'. Many people feel that since then social problems, such as fights over land, corruption, unemployment, crime and alcohol abuse have been steadily increasing. Concerns about the rise of dishonesty, egotism and greed are equally widespread and cut across age, gender and professional groups. Yet people continue to place their trust in others, including those whose trustworthiness they doubt. Moreover, and more surprisingly perhaps, trust is also given rather frequently to individuals who have previously betrayed it and are likely to continue doing so. In other words, negative past experiences and otherwise gathered knowledge about a person's untrustworthiness do not necessarily deter people from trusting.

In this chapter, I wish to propose an answer to the anthropological puzzle constituted by 'trusting the untrustworthy', which I will illustrate with an ethnographic example in the following section. By comparing Western academic and popular conceptualizations of 'trust' with Barga Mongolian ones, I will show that the puzzle ceases to exist once one departs from universalist and strongly cognitivistic understandings of what trust is, how it is produced and what makes it desirable. Using an approach indebted to linguistic anthropology, which focuses on concepts shared by a speech community, I will suggest that the cognitive, emotional and behavioural processes subsumed under the Western notion of 'trust' may be mapped out differently in diverse sociocultural and historical contexts. Finally, I will raise a few thoughts about how such a finding can potentially contribute to anthropological understandings of the 'tensed relations between trust, intimacy and the social'.

'Of Course We Trust!'

Shortly after the division of pastureland, a family I was acquainted with had rented their *nutag* to a tenant. This was and still is a very common practice, which, according to local people, evolved as a result of demographic changes and because of the advantages it bears for both landlords and tenants. At the time of the division of pastureland, only households officially registered as 'herders' and residents in the New Barga Right Banner were entitled to a *nutag*, whereas non-residents, government officials and other professional groups were excluded. In the late 1990s and early 2000s the population increased due to in-migration from other regions in China, and while some households allegedly obtained pastureland that had not yet been allocated, many remained landless. Finally, as time passed, the children of the first generation of leaseholders set up their own families, but only few were able to lease a *nutag* on their own or to succeed their parents. The land rental system thus allows these various groups of landless people to make a living. It furthermore offers particularly enterprising herding families the possibility to rent land in addition to their own, in order to expand their herds with the help of shepherds or to engage in the highly profitable economic activity of haymaking. For the landlords, instead, renting out their land means increasing their access to cash while decreasing their workload, since many live in settlements on the rent and a possible additional income deriving from livestock which the tenant keeps for them. Despite its advantages, however, this arrangement hardly ever functions without serious disagreements between the parties involved. The allocation of pastureland furthermore constitutes one of the main arenas of corruption, and my acquaintances' story is an excellent example for how severe ensuing problems may be.

After a few years the tenant stopped paying rent, and when the family sued him it turned out that he had paid off some local government officials to have his name put in the cadastral register instead of theirs. The original maps were said to be untraceable, and since without documentary proof they could not show that the land had been theirs the judge dismissed the lawsuit. Not having any other income than the small pension of one member of the rather large household, the family did not give up the fight for their land. In 2009, at the time of my fieldwork, the Inner Mongolia Television (NMTV) was broadcasting a program aimed at making corruption cases public. Widespread corruption in Inner Mongolia had become a concern for both the provincial and the central government and numerous measures had been put in place to fight it. NMTV participated in the government's efforts to check corruption by interviewing people who had suffered at the hand of corrupt officials and airing their stories. The family thus called the TV station, which immediately sent a film crew to the New Barga Right Banner. Upon their arrival the reporters stayed in a hotel in the district centre, but left after a few days without having met the family in the countryside. Somewhat ironically, many people assumed that somebody had bribed them in order to prevent the interview from happening. The family, however, refused to surrender and called again. The second attempt was successful and their story was broadcasted. The public denunciation had its desired effect and the district government could no longer ignore the family's demand that their case be taken seriously. Soon after the broadcast in winter 2009, they had a meeting with the village authorities, some of whom were allegedly involved in the case and had accepted bribes from the tenant. The family was promised that the problem would very soon be taken care of and the tenant be evicted. However, because of the upcoming celebrations for the Chinese New Year they were asked to have a little bit of patience. A few weeks later, they returned to ask when action would be taken. 'In a few days', they were told, but nothing happened. The next time they inquired, the government official in charge was allegedly absent but expected to come back the following week. Like this, six months passed without anything happening except regular promises that the problem would soon be solved. After each meeting, the family was happy, almost exultant, and they seemed absolutely confident of getting their land back in the near future. Since none of the family members was able to engage in herding themselves, they started to search for a new tenant and chose an acquainted family whose lease for another pasture was due to expire a few months later. When they were ready to move with their herds to the new land, however, the old tenant had still not been evicted. Nor was he two months later, nor anytime during the following year. At some point, I asked the family why they were not going to talk to somebody higher up in the government hierarchy, such as the district governor. To me, it seemed that they were just being told lies and that they would never get their pasture back unless they tried to exert pressure from above. 'It's not necessary', they said, 'the village authorities promised that they will solve our problem'. 'How can you still trust them? Do you *really* trust them?', I asked, at that point myself very upset about the whole affair. 'Of course we do', was their reply, 'if we trust them they will do it [*itgel ögvöl hiine*]. If we trust everything will be all right [*itgevel büh yum bütne*]'. And their trust was very clearly real, even though in angry and exasperated conversations at home the local politicians were invariably referred to as 'untrustworthy' and 'immoral' [*yosgüi*].

Torsello (2008) observed a similar disjuncture between assessments of trustworthiness and trusting behaviour in a village in post-socialist Slovakia, where people tended to judge those who had previously collaborated with the socialist regime as untrustworthy, but nevertheless relied on them for all kinds of needs and favours. In order to make sense of this situation, he proposes distinguishing between a cognitive level of trust, which includes the social and cultural representations used to construct and assess trustworthiness, and trust as action. According to Torsello these two levels can be in contradiction with each other without social actors noticing the incoherence. He explains this inconsistency with the rapid social change Slovakia was undergoing at the time of fieldwork, which on the one hand heightened the need to trust while on the other hand it destabilized the expectations on which cognitive maps of trustworthiness were based. He concludes that in situations in which cognitive maps are constantly adapting to changing circumstances, the act of trusting might be 'situational', i.e., driven by immediate need and interest rather than based on an assessment of trustworthiness. Otherwise 'it would be insane to trust an untrustworthy party' (2008: 115). However, while in the cases Torsello describes situationally given trust does not seem to have been blatantly abused, in the above case the act of trusting was not only divorced from cognitive assessments of the government officials' trustworthiness, but it was also misplaced in the light of personally experienced previous abuses of trust. It indeed seemed 'insane', to borrow Torsello's terminology, that the family I described should continue to trust people who were responsible for the loss of their pastureland in the first place and who were very clearly giving them the run around.

When I first tried to understand their behaviour, the only explanation that came to my mind was based on the concept of cognitive dissonance (e.g., Gambetta 1988b; Cooper 2007). I thought that if people were stuck with each other in a small close-knit community from which they did not see any possibility of escape, they might not have another choice but to trust, thereby finding an emotional arrangement with an exasperating situation. I furthermore assumed that they were refusing to turn to the district governor for help because they deemed it inappropriate to approach such a high-ranking person and because of the high value placed on the moral injunction not to talk badly about people. However, they had already violated that moral norm by telling their story on NMTV. Even taking into account that human behaviour is often incoherent and contradictory, the situation remained a puzzle to me – until I considered the possibility that the meaning of the Barga word for 'trust' [*itgel*] might differ significantly from Western academic and popular conceptualisations of the term.

Trust in the Theoretical Literature

The notion of trust has had a long history in European thought, one which can be traced back to the Enlightenment. According to Seligman (1997), the development of its current meaning is intimately linked to Enlightenment reasoning about probability, risk and uncertainty, first in the realm of mathematics and later as an intrinsic aspect of human life. Trust became treated as the solution to the specific problem of risk, and in the mid seventeenth century it entered the lexicon of political and legal philosophy and their theories of rationality and reason. With the development of role-segmentation, social relations became fraught with new forms of risk which required new solutions in the form of new kinds of trust that were explicitly linked to expectations of role behaviour. Trust came to be seen as a necessary component of modern forms of solidarity, which were thought about in terms of the interaction between free and morally autonomous individuals. Trust started to matter for the smooth functioning of economic exchanges and political processes, and it became the foundation for the harmonious organization of the public as well as the private life (Seligman 1997).

Most authors agree that in the contemporary Western world trust in its various forms is ubiquitous and an essential aspect of many relationships, between people as well as between people and abstract organizations and processes. Especially in recent times, trust and mistrust have become important tropes in the discussion of social, economic and political problems, for the framing of possible solutions and for justifying certain actions and decisions. Due to its omnipresence, trust is an extremely complex social phenomenon and it has multiple meanings in everyday as well as scholarly discourse. As many scholars have pointed out, the elusiveness of the term complicates its use as an analytical concept and its definition as an object of theoretical enquiry (Cook 2001; Solomon and Flores 2001; Marková, Linell and Gillespie 2008). The above-described historical development of the notion of trust in the English-speaking Western context adds a further dimension to the problem, as it shows that the specific assumptions that underpin our understanding of what trust is and what it does are not necessarily transferable to other cultural contexts or historical periods. Yet this critical awareness is unfortunately lacking from much of the theoretical literature, which tends to treat trust as a universal phenomenon and a crucial aspect of life everywhere, allowing for cultural differences only with regards to definitions of trustworthiness and the social distribution of trust (e.g., Rabinowitz 1992; Menning 1997; Overing 2003; Li 2004, 2008; Choi and Han 2008; Sorge 2009), but not with regards to the concept of trust. This approach is also reflected in anthropological studies of trust, many of which are concerned with mapping social relations of trust and mistrust, describing practices that require, generate or break trust and analysing locally specific assessments of trustworthiness, without taking into account possible variations in the conceptualizations of trust itself.

Anthropology has overall contributed surprisingly little to the vast body of literature on trust, which is for the most part a conglomerate of studies carried out by psychologists, social psychologists, sociologists, behavioural scientists, economists, philosophers and internet scientists.

Approaches are diverse, not only due to different disciplinary interests and research questions, but also with regards to the scale of analysis and the assumed locus of trust, which for some is within the individual while others view trust as a property of social relationships. Nevertheless, there are a number of common themes that cut across the dividing lines, some of which are relevant for a discussion of Mongolian understandings of trust and therefore deserve closer attention.

The first unifying thread is the association of trust with risk and its calculability (e.g., Luhman 1979; Dasgupta 1988; Williams 1988; Seligman 1997; Coleman 1990; Sztompka 1999), which gives a calculative and cognitivistic quality to the way trust is theorized. Such a calculative element is inherent in the understanding of trust as a threshold point determined by a cognitive assessment of trustworthiness and the interest or need to trust (Gambetta 1988a), which is commonly accepted and used by trust theorists despite increasing anthropological criticism of overly cognitivistic approaches (e.g., Torsello 2008; Ystanes, this volume). The outcome of this process of evaluation of the risk involved in trusting in relation to its possible benefits is usually understood to be reflected in the feeling of trust or mistrust, which guides subsequent behavioural choices. From this perspective, trust is the outcome and an ideally truthful reflection of an individually specific judgement of relevant factors, and in its quality of *reaction* to such factors it often appears to be beyond wilful decisions and control. Since trustworthiness is often treated as an 'objective circumstance' (Gambetta 1988a), mismatches between individual behaviour and these allegedly objective factors are attributed to pathological traits such as gullibility or extreme suspiciousness, thus constituting exceptional cases that fall outside the definition of 'normal' or 'healthy' trust and mistrust (Isaacs, Alexander and Haggard 1963; Yamagishi, Kikuchi and Kosugi 1999). If trust and mistrust are mere indicators, as it were, they can only be changed by changing what they indicate, i.e., trustworthiness and/or the need or interest to trust. Even though it is acknowledged that trust can act in society and generate more trust and trustworthiness (Lahno 2001), when social trust declines what is targeted is thus usually trustworthiness, and as Hardin (1996) has cogently argued, most accounts of trust are in reality about trustworthiness. This conceptualization of trust also has repercussions on notions of morality. At the societal level, trust is considered to be an important social good, but as an individual act trust is 'good' only if it matches the perceived trustworthiness of the trustee, whereas mismatches are treated as 'silly' trust or 'pathological' mistrust (Baier 1994: 130–151). The primary locus of morality therefore lies in trustworthiness, without which trust is not very likely to develop.

The second major theme which unites different studies of trust is the association of trust with a lack of control. As has been mentioned above, trust and mistrust evade wilful control because they are considered to be a more or less accurate reflection of external circumstances. Second, trust is commonly defined as a deliberate relinquishment of control over certain aspects of the truster's life. As philosopher Annette Baier puts it, trust is 'an accepted vulnerability to another's possible but not expected ill will (or lack of good will) toward one' (1994: 99). Her widely accepted argument is that the act of trusting involves the truster giving the trustee 'discretionary powers' over something that the truster cherishes but cannot care for or do alone. As a result, the trustee has control over what has been entrusted, which can be anything ranging from an object or a task to the life and well-being of a person. Finally, it is commonly agreed that a lack of control in the sense of a lack of certainty is constitutive of the very phenomenon of trust, because it becomes necessary only in conditions of uncertainty. Trust is thus understood to function as a proxy for knowledge by enabling people to act in situations in which their knowledge is partial and insufficient (Gambetta 1988a). This makes trust particularly relevant with regards to the problem of future contingency, which for some scholars is so important that they consider it the defining trait of trust (e.g., Barber 1983, who refers to trust as an 'expectation').

The notion of a relinquishment of control is a common theme also in the literature on cooperation, which defines the cooperating act as one in which none of the involved parties has complete control over every single aspect of the common undertaking. Even though it is not at all clear whether trust really is a necessary component of cooperative relationships (Yamagishi 1996), cooperation has constituted the main context for the study of trust. It is likely that the origins of this intimate link between cooperation and trust lie in the historically specific development of the notion of trust outlined in the beginning of this section. As has been shown, trust became seen as the key ingredient for social solidarity in modern societies characterized by a complex division of labour, whose very existence is premised on cooperation. This might also explain why trust has mostly been approached from the perspective of its social functions. Luhman (1979) thus famously argues that trust reduces the complexity of social life, which would paralyse social actors if they were not able to trust the world to continue as they know it and other people to carry out their tasks within the complex division of labour in modern societies. Barber, instead, suggests that trust has the function of creating social solidarity and stability by 'providing cognitive and moral expectational maps for actors and systems', by acting as a mechanism of social control and by expressing shared social values (1983: 19–25). In both these definitions, trust is not only functional, but functional in a task-related sense. Put differently, trust is necessary when social actors need to rely on others for the accomplishment of certain tasks which they are not able to carry out themselves.

The focus on the functionality of trust within a complex division of labour might be at the origin of the commonly accepted theoretical notion that trust is never generalized, but given only with regards to certain tasks and not to others. While in everyday usages of the term trust might appear as a two-part relation between a truster and a trustee, scholars generally agree that a relation of trust always involves three variables which can be expressed as 'A trusts B to do X, but maybe not Y' (Hardin 2001). A simple example is that one might trust a heart specialist to cure heart disease but not necessarily to detect other illnesses not related to his or her field of expertise. In this case, trust is given on the basis of an assessment of competency, but it is also possible to imagine scenarios where a person is equally competent to carry out two or more tasks but not equally trustworthy with regards to all of them. Another example given by Annette Baier is that of a babysitter who has certain discretionary powers with regards to the well-being of the child entrusted to him or her, but would clearly act in untrustworthy ways if s/he decided to paint the nursery purple (1994: 101). Here, the scope of trust is defined not by the competency of the trustee, but by the limits of what has been entrusted. However, the threefold form of the trust relation appears to be related not only to its functionality but also to its taken-for-granted nature. As many scholars have pointed out, trust is never really thought about until it either becomes replaced by doubt or it is made explicit by the need to trust in order to achieve a desired goal (e.g., Baier 1994). As a result, the way trust is imagined is necessarily shaped by the goal or by the trigger of doubt in question.

Given the countless number of objects that can be entrusted and the expectations tied to them, attempts to use these as a basis for the distinction between different forms of trust have not been able to gain widespread acceptance (e.g., Sztompka [1999], who proposes a distinction between instrumental, axiological and fiduciary trust). Nevertheless, the desire to bring order into the fuzzy universe of trust by categorizing, defining and distinguishing between different kinds of trust is another common theme in the literature. The most commonly used distinction is based on the nature of the trustee and thus made between personal trust in people and impersonal forms of trust in processes, institutions, technologies and the like. Other categorizations include the distinction between trust in intentions and trust in actions (Dasgupta 1988), between micro- and macro-level social trust (Marková, Linell and Gillespie 2008) and between conceptual (i.e., conscious) and pre-conceptual (i.e., unconscious) trust (Marková, Linell and Gillespie 2008), to mention just a few.

Furthermore, there have been attempts to define distinctions between trust, reliance, familiarity, confidence, hope, belief, faith and other related concepts (e.g., Isaacs, Alexander and Haggard 1963; Hart 1988; Baier 1994; Heimer 2001). However, as the following discussion of Mongolian concepts of trust will show, these categories are heavily based on the English language and cannot be transferred to other cultural and linguistic contexts – not even within the Western world, differences within which are often neglected by trust theorists. German language, for example, does not distinguish between belief and faith, and it has two different words for trust, i.e., *trauen*, which indicates trust in somebody's honesty, and *vertrauen*, which can in addition also mean trust in a person's abilities. As will be shown in the following section, a similar linguistic distinction between two different kinds of trust is also known in Mongolian.

Despite the theoretical efforts to reach an agreement on what trust is, it remains an elusive concept. In the face of this problem, Jiménez suggests that the question today is not what trust is, but rather 'what kind of work the notion does' (2005: 65). Nonetheless, if the invocation of trust accomplishes something, it does so also because of the multiple associations and assumptions that are attached to our understanding of it and implicitly invoked at the same time (Jiménez 2011). In order to comprehend what trust does among Barga people in the New Barga Right Banner, it is therefore important to depart from universalizing definitions of trust and to allow for the possibility of the notion of trust being embedded within and shaped by a different associational field. An absolute and scientific definition of trust becomes then impossible not only because of the elusiveness of the term, but also because of locally specific interpretations of the universal phenomenon of trust. Yet acknowledging the contingency of the concept of trust does not make definition as such obsolete. While it is important not to formulate new universalizing ones, the following section will show that a critical examination and comparison of existing ones can be highly revealing.

Mongolian Concepts of Trust

Barga Mongols frequently refer to trust and trustworthiness as having 'good intentions/thoughts' [*sain sanaatai* or *sain sanah*] and to being suspicious and untrustworthy as having 'bad intentions/thoughts' [*muu sanaatai* or *muu sanah*]. The terms *sain sanah* or *sain sanaatai* encompass a large range of properties and thoughts of a person which are considered morally appropriate and whose core elements can be described as generosity, the absence of ill will toward others, trustworthiness and the absence of suspicions. Barga language possesses, however, also a more specific terminology. The most important words used to indicate notions related to trust are *naidah* (verb)/ *naidvar* (noun)/ *naidvartai* (adj., noun or verb); and *itgeh* (verb)/ *itgel* (noun)/ *itgeltei* (adj., noun or verb), which were employed in the previous ethnographic example.

The verb *itgeh* is usually translated as 'to trust' or 'to believe', the noun *itgel* as 'trust', 'belief', 'faith', 'hope' and 'trustworthiness', and *itgeltei* [lit. 'with *itgel*'] as 'trustworthy', 'confident', 'hopeful' as well as 'trusting' (Hamayon 2006). While in Halha Mongolian, spoken by the majority of the population in the independent state of Mongolia, the verb *naidah* occurs with the meaning 'to hope', in Barga and many other Inner Mongolian dialects it means exclusively 'to entrust someone with something' or 'to ask someone to do something'. *Naidah* furthermore entails a hierarchical relationship between the truster and the trustee, whereby the latter is superior in rank to the former (in the opposite case, Barga Mongols use the term *daalgah*, the meaning of which is more similar to 'ordering someone to do something'). The noun *naidvar* is usually translated as 'trust', 'trustworthiness' or 'hope', and it is often used in compound with the word *itgel*. *Naidvartai*, instead, can be translated as 'trustworthy', 'reliable', 'confident' or 'hopeful'.

The terms *itgel* and *naidvar* thus signify both trust and trustworthiness. The following analysis will nevertheless proceed from 'trust', because trust rather than trustworthiness appears to be the main locus of difference. When the words *itgeltei* and *naidvartai* are used in the sense of trustworthiness, they designate people who are deemed to be morally upright or otherwise capable and bound to perform specific tasks. Who is trustworthy and who is not are thus determined by local understandings of morality and obligation, but the concept of trustworthiness itself is not dissimilar from Western conceptualizations. With regards to the way trust is understood, however, differences are significant, and even though they partly stem from the conceptual conflation of trust and trustworthiness they can be elucidated only through a focus on trust rather than on trustworthiness.

The first discrepancy between Mongolian and Western theoretical concepts of trust lies in a peculiar distinction between different kinds of trust, which is obliterated in the English translations. The concept of *naidvar* refers to a specific trait, competency or act of a person. In other words, a person might be considered a liar and a cheater, but still thought to be trustworthy in the sense of *naidvartai* with regards to a specific task he or she is expected to perform. From the perspective of trust, instead, it means that the truster trusts the trustee to perform the task that has been entrusted, without thereby necessarily assuming that the trustee would also reliably perform others. It is thus very similar to the conceptualization of trust as a threefold relationship found in the Western literature. *Itgel*, instead, has strong moral connotations and indicates trust/trustworthiness in relation to the totality of a person's actions and character as known to the speaker. A person who is trustworthy in this sense is considered to be 'good' and morally upright. Also somebody who is trusting in the sense of *itgeltei* is considered to 'have a good heart', i.e., to be free from bad thoughts and suspicions. It is less about a task the trustee is expected to perform than about the quality and morality of the relationship within which the trusting expectation is formed, and it is often used to express an overall moral judgement of a person. Barga language thus distinguishes between different kinds of trust not on the basis of the nature of the trustee, as is common practice in Western theory, but on the basis of the moral import of trust. This is rather different from how trust is described in the literature, where, as has been shown above, trust is treated as an important social good, but morality resides in trustworthiness rather than in the act of trusting.

A further significant difference, which has already been touched upon several times but not yet been elaborated on sufficiently, is the lack of a conceptual distinction between trust and trustworthiness. *Itgeltei* and *naidvartai* mean both 'with trust' as well as 'with trustworthiness'. A person who trusts is thus at the same time trustworthy and a person who is trustworthy is also trusting. This identity of trust and trustworthiness suggests that the relationship in which the two stand to each other is crucially different from how it is treated in the Western literature. However, in order to fully grasp the implications of this conceptual conflation, it is necessary to first look at another important, maybe even the most important difference between Mongolian and Western theoretical ideas of trust.

As has been shown in the previous section, it is usually asserted that the act of trusting involves a deliberate relinquishment of control and that it hence increases the vulnerability of the truster. Yet, when in a discussion with Oyun, a Barga Mongolian philosopher, I began one of my questions with this assertion, it was met with incomprehension. At first I thought that I had expressed myself badly and tried to rephrase the question, but soon it turned out that the problem was not a linguistic but a conceptual one. 'Why do you think that someone who trusts relinquishes control?', I was asked; 'To trust means to assert control!'. 'But what happens if someone betrays my trust? Doesn't the very possibility of someone abusing my trust thereby harming me make me vulnerable?', I retorted. 'No, it doesn't', she answered. 'Those who give *itgel*, will find *itgel* [*Itgelee ögvöl itgel olno*]'. In other words, those who trust will be trusted because they are also trustworthy and at the same time their trust will be responded to with trustworthiness. Trusting someone thus means to *make* someone trust in return and at the same time to *make* someone trustworthy.

The inhabitants in the New Barga Right Banner have generally rather limited control over their lives. People are born into an intricate web of hierarchical relationships based on age, gender and seniority, each coming with a specific set of obligations (Sneath 1993), which can be a heavy burden and may severely restrict the possibility of control over the disposing of one's time. Social obligations and expectations are rendered particularly powerful by the impossibility of hiding from the public eye in this small and very close-knit community, where anonymity is unknown and the grapevine is constantly buzzing. The stark social hierarchy shapes interaction within the family as well as outside it and the degree of control and freedom one has to act autonomously decreases the lower one is positioned in relation to others. A superior social position confers, for example, the continuously used right to place demands, which the subordinate partner has the duty to carry out. The subordinate partner, instead, may politely ask the superior to perform a certain task, but does not have the right to make explicit requests nor the possibility to enforce action. Upward requests are thus usually phrased in terms of *guih* [to beg], or of the above-mentioned *naidah* [to entrust], and often result in situations of hopeful or anxious waiting which at first sight might appear as being at someone's mercy without the possibility to do anything but to trust, to hope and to wait. The Barga conceptualization of trust outlined above, however, also allows for an alternative interpretation. If trust *generates* trustworthiness, the act of 'entrusting' does not necessarily indicate helplessness and submissiveness, but it can conversely be understood as a way of acting assertively in a space where there is little margin for action. For people who have only very limited power, especially in interactions with superiors, trusting in the form of *itgeh* or *naidah* is thus one of the few things they can do and it becomes the vehicle for their attempts to exert a certain degree of control.

Annette Baier (1994) argues that depending on the context and nonverbal clues, the explicit assertion 'I trust you (will do X)' may not have a referential meaning, but a coercive, manipulative and morally questionable function by implicitly warning the interlocutor not to disappoint the speaker's expectation. Among Barga Mongols this function is inherent in the very way trust is conceptualized, but it is by no means morally questionable. On the contrary, trust is not only created and maintained through the affirmation of a person's morality, which seems to be a common theme across different cultural and social contexts (as shown by other chapters in this volume), but it is considered to be a moral act in itself, regardless of the trustworthiness of the trustee. Someone who trusts is seen to be as morally upright as someone who is trustworthy, if that distinction can be made at all considering the conceptual identity between the two. Trusting someone untrustworthy is not gullible, a pathological deviation from healthy trust and mistrust, but a good deed, which has the capacity to create trustworthiness. Trust thus becomes decoupled from trustworthiness as its necessary or at least strongly desirable condition. Trustworthiness produces trust as much as trust can produce trustworthiness. And even when trust fails to achieve its goal, as in the example given in the beginning of this chapter, precisely because it is a moral act it will have positive repercussions on one's own future. Many people in the New Barga Right Banner believe that immoral behaviour will bring about misfortune. This link between morality and well-being is, however, usually framed in positive rather than in negative terms: nothing bad will happen to those who act in morally good ways, and giving trust is one way of being a good person. By trusting and being trustworthy, people thus actively avert harmful events and bad fortune, thereby asserting control over their future. Even if the trustee betrays the trust bestowed on him or her, 'things will be fine' [*büh yum sain bolno*], people say.

In the light of the above, it is not surprising that assessments of trustworthiness and the act of trusting can be and often are in contradiction with each other. As has been said in the first part of this paper, one way of making sense of this inconsistency is by adopting Torsello's distinction between and cognitive level of trust and the act of trusting. However, even though he argues that trust and assessments of trustworthiness are more than goal-oriented social acts by helping to structure people's fields of expectation and action, his approach does not depart fundamentally from Gambetta's (1988a) definition of trust as 'threshold point' determined by subjective variables, assessments of trustworthiness and the need/interest to engage in an interaction that requires trust. It thus remains anchored in the assumption that an assessment of trustworthiness is an inseparable aspect of the phenomenon called 'trust', as clearly shown by his statement cited earlier that if trusting behaviour was not situationally driven by interest 'it would be insane to trust an untrustworthy party' (Torsello 2008: 115).

In the New Barga Right Banner, trust is often given to people who are assessed as *itgelgüi* and/or *naidvargüi* [lit. 'without *itgel/naidvar*'], who have abused trust previously, who are known to be liars and cheaters or who are known to be corrupt. Yet the above distinction between cognitive and performative trust does not seem to be particularly useful to explain these dynamics of trust. In order to be able to talk about a 'contradiction', as Torsello does, one has to assume, first, that an assessment of trustworthiness is an intrinsic part of 'trust', and second, that it logically precedes the act of trusting. However, since in Barga conceptualizations trustworthiness is not a necessary condition for trust because trust can generate trustworthiness, there is no contradiction that social actors would need to be aware of, no anthropological puzzle to be solved, no 'insanity'. Of course Barga Mongols assess people's trustworthiness and they prefer to give their trust to those whom they judge will not betray it. However, this moment of judgement and the related cognitive map are situated outside of what Barga Mongols mean by the terms of *itgel* and *naidvar*, which are understood as the *act* of giving trust and being trustworthy rather than as a cognitive, mental phenomenon.

In order to understand better this conceptualization of trust as action, it is useful to look at a similar idea concerning the notion of respect [*hündetgel*], which is considered to be at the basis of an orderly and harmonious world. Hierarchical relations are governed by a large number of rules of respect, which regulate the behaviour the subordinate has to display in front of the superior. The young are, for example, expected to show their respect for the elderly among other ways by performing a kowtow during the celebrations for the New Year. At the workplace, subordinates are expected to display a respectful behaviour by not contradicting their superiors and executing orders without hesitation, even if it means to work extra hours in the evenings, on weekends or during public holidays. Women have to show respect for men through a wide array of acts, including by not placing their clothes on top of men's garments, by serving men and by never asking men to carry out the ashes, which are considered to be the lowest of all forms of waste. Thinking of respect as having a threefold nature, i.e., (firstly) the feeling of respect, which reflects (secondly) the cognitive assessment of whether someone deserves to be respected and which can be expressed (thirdly) in the performance of respectful acts, I once asked a woman who was suffering continuous physical and verbal abuse at the hands of her husband whether she *really* respected him. She was clearly puzzled by my question. 'Of course', she said, 'don't you see how I cook for him, clean his clothes, ask him how he is and whether he needs anything?'. 'Yes, I see this', I replied, 'but do you feel it in your heart?'. 'Of course', she answered, 'how can it not be in my heart if I do it?' 'Do you think he deserves to be treated with respect?', I asked. 'No', she said, 'he doesn't deserve it, but I still respect him'. While she acknowledged that her husband did not deserve to be respected, for her this assessment was distinct from showing *hündetgel*. Respect is thus *not expressed* through respectful actions, but these acts *are* respect. Similarly, trust is not an *expression* of a positive cognitive assessment of trustworthiness, but trust is the *act* of trusting and simultaneously of being trustworthy itself. Such acts are performed whenever something is entrusted to someone and inquisitive or doubting behaviour suspended, independently from how the trustee's trustworthiness is judged. They may moreover also be shaped by explicit moral rules aimed at the public display of trust, such as the injunction not to lock the house or not to count money given by debtors, clients or as change. What the act of trusting is held to be an expression of or indicator for is the morality of a person, which is crucial not only for building and maintaining a good public reputation, but also for averting the occurrence of dangerous and harmful events in one's life.

To briefly recapitulate, in this section it has been argued that Barga conceptualizations of *itgel* and *naidvar*, two terms which can be translated with trust as well as with hope, differ significantly from what the Western literature on trust proposes as universal features of the phenomenon. The most important differences consist in: (1) the identity of trust and trustworthiness, as well as the identity of trust and hope; (2) the moral quality of the act of trusting independently from the trustworthiness of the trustee; (3) the imputed power of the act of trusting to make the recipient of trust trustworthy; (4) the assertion of control through the act of trusting; and (5) the dissociation of the act of trusting/being trustworthy from the cognitive assessment of a person's trustworthiness. In the light of these conceptual differences, the family's trust in the village authorities' promises does not constitute a riddle any more. If the act of trusting is not a reflection of an assessment of trustworthiness, but believed to be imbued with agentive power, it does not have to be explained by resorting to 'need' or 'cognitive dissonance'. Rather than behaving as powerless victims with no other choice but to trust, by continuing to trust the corrupt government officials despite everything they had done to them, the family was asserting control over them and trying to make them trustworthy. Furthermore, even if the village authorities failed to show themselves deserving of their trust, the family was still confident that as long as they remained *itgeltei*, thereby acting in a morally appropriate way, things would eventually be all right, no matter what happened.

Conclusion

To conclude, I first wish to elaborate further on what exactly is meant by 'different conceptualizations of trust' and then relate the above discussion to the anthropology of intimacy, trust and cooperation. In order to avoid misunderstandings, it is important to emphasize that I am *not* arguing that 'trust' as such is not universal or that people in the New Barga Right Banner do not feel in ways similar to those that are at the basis of Western understandings of trust. Rather, I wish to suggest that there are important differences in the way the complex processes that coalesce in the phenomenon of trust are thought about and linguistically expressed. As has been discussed earlier, the Western concept of 'trust' contains three (or possibly more) rather different processes: first, the cognitive assessment of trustworthiness; second, the reflection of this assessment in an emotional state; third, action that follows from these cognitive and emotional states. The semantic fields associated with the Barga Mongolian terms for trust and the way people use them in specific social situations, however, indicates that these three components of trust are mapped out differently, i.e., that they are included separately into various conceptual categories and/or conceptually merged with processes that in the Western context do not belong to the category of trust at all.

In the previous section, it has been argued that among Barga Mongols the act of trusting is not conditional on a positive assessment of a person's trustworthiness. This does not mean, however, that people in the New Barga Right Banner do not care about someone's trustworthiness or that an assessment thereof is completely irrelevant for social action, including that of trusting. On the contrary, people's ability to trust and to be trustworthy is of primary concern to Barga Mongols. It functions after all as an ethnic marker and core moral value. However, conceptually this assessment is thought of in terms of 'having good or bad intentions/thoughts' [*sain* or *muu sanaatai*], rather than of *itgel* or *naidvar*. Judging someone as untrustworthy and untrusting is understood as thinking badly about that person and conceptually merged with other thoughts that aim at harming others or at severing social ties. Judging someone as trustworthy and trusting, instead, is thought of as indicating the presence of good thoughts and intentions. This is conceptually differentiated from the act of trusting/being trustworthy, whose opposite is expressed by adding the negative suffix –*güi*, lit. 'without', to the terms *itgel* and *naidvar*. To be 'without trust' and by extension 'without trustworthiness' is not the same as being suspicious and mistrusting. Rather, they refer to not acting in a trusting or trustworthy manner. Emotional states are mapped across the cognitive and the performative realms, as both thoughts and acts are believed to originate from the mind/heart [*setgel*], which is also the seat of emotions. Negative assessments of somebody's trustworthiness are therefore accompanied by feelings of suspicion, while the act of trusting always coexists with a feeling of trust, which for the duration of the act of entrusting supersedes any other emotional state of the mind/heart and thus temporarily hinders the rise of suspicions as well as of other 'bad' thoughts and feelings about the trustee. The act of trusting and cognitive suspicion can therefore alternate, even at brief intervals, but not coexist in the very same moment.

Similarly to the case of 'anger' discussed by Lutz (1988), the issue is thus not whether the phenomena indicated by the term 'trust' are universal, but whether the Western way of thinking about it is. The example discussed in this paper shows that it is not, thereby raising the question of how the terms 'trust' and 'mistrust' should be used as an analytical category in the anthropological language if they can refer to culturally and socially specific assemblages of cognitive, emotional and behavioural processes. Furthermore, the very possibility of 'trust' being a culturally and historically contingent concept suggests that the Western notion might carry even more unquestioned assumptions that need to be carefully unpacked. The Barga examples of 'trust' and 'respect' as acts show, for instance, that people might despise and mistrust others, including their spouses, while still interpreting their own acts as 'trust', thereby problematizing the common association of trust with intimate relations (e.g., Overing 2003; Choi and Han 2008). It moreover illustrates that people's assertion that they 'trust' somebody does not necessarily indicate that the trustee does not abuse their trust, and that abuse does not always put an end to a relationship locally defined as 'trusting'. This complicates the already problematic relationship between trust and cooperation. If 'trust', or some of its components, are decoupled from an assessment of the probability of default and from practical experiences of abuse, does it still matter for cooperation? If it does not, what does? If it does, which components of 'trust' matter in what ways and are these relationships necessarily imbued with the positive feelings frequently associated with 'trust'?

The Barga example furthermore problematizes the way in which the breakdown of trust is theorized. When does abuse break trust and when does it not? Does it lead to the breakdown of all components of trust or only of some and if so of which? What is needed to rebuild what kind of trust once it is broken? Finally, what analytical tools and language have to be developed to capture the different emotional, cognitive, behavioural and social processes that constitute trust in radically diverse contexts?

Since trust in its various forms is an intrinsic aspect of social relations, it is implicitly present in many anthropological studies. However, due to the elusiveness of the concept, it has often been unwittingly conflated with more tangible social phenomena such as cooperation, closeness or social belonging (e.g., Gellner 1988; Roeber 1994; Harriss 2003; Overing 2003; Daryn 2007; Choi and Han 2008; Dasgupta 2009). While such studies have produced valuable insights, they also seem to have been informed by a number of theoretical entanglements, which the contributions to this volume attempt to unravel. An anthropology of trust, which analytically distinguishes 'trust' from the social realms, relations and practices that it is assumed to be part of and which critically engages with the great variety of culturally and historically specific ideas and practices of trust, has just started to develop. The above questions are by no means exhaustive nor can they be easily answered. However, they show how an anthropology of trust can shed new light on important areas of anthropological inquiry and contribute to our understanding not only of trust, but also of intimacy and cooperative relations.

References

Baier, A. 1994. *Moral Prejudices*. Cambridge: Harvard University Press.
Barber, B. 1983. *The Logic and Limit of Trust*. New Brunswick: Rutgers University Press.
Choi, S. and G. Han. 2008. 'Immanent Trust in a Close Relationship: A Cultural Psychology of Trust in South Korea'. In I. Marková and A. Gillespie (eds), *Trust & Distrust: Sociocultural Perspectives*, 79–104. Charlotte, NC: Information Age Publishing, Inc.
Coleman, J.S. 1990. *Foundations of Social Theory*. Cambridge: The Belknap Press of Harvard University Press.
Cook, K.S. 2001. 'Trust in Society'. In K.S. Cook (ed.). *Trust in Society*, xi–xxviii. New York: Russell Sage Foundation.
Cooper, J. 2007. *Cognitive Dissonance: Fifty Years of a Classic Theory*. London: Sage.

Daryn, G. 2007. 'Inversion Revisited: *Dai Halne* – a Himalayan Inversion of Hierachy and Trust', *Journal of the Royal Anthropological Institute* (N.S.) 13: 845–861.
Dasgupta, P. 1988. 'Trust as a Commodity'. In D. Gambetta (ed.), *Trust: Making and Breaking of Cooperative Relations*, 49–72. Oxford: Blackwell.
―――― 2009. 'Trust and Cooperation Among Economic Agents', *Philosophical Transactions of the Royal Society Biological Sciences* 364: 3301–3309.
Gambetta, D. 1988a. 'Can We Trust Trust?' In D. Gambetta (ed.), *Trust: Making and Breaking of Cooperative Relations*, 213–237. Oxford: Blackwell.
Gambetta, D. (ed.) 1988. *Trust: Making and Breaking of Cooperative Relations*. Oxford: Blackwell.
Gellner, E. 1988. 'Trust, Cohesion, and the Social Order'. In D. Gambetta (ed.), *Trust: Making and Breaking of Cooperative Relations*, 142–157. Oxford: Blackwell.
Hamayon, R. 2006. 'L'Anthropologie et la Dualité Paradoxale du 'Croire' Occidental', *Revue du MAUSS* 2(28): 427–448.
Hardin, R. 1996. 'Trustworthiness', *Ethics* 107(1): 26–42.
―――― 2001. 'Conceptions and Explanations of Trust'. In K.S. Cook (ed.), *Trust in Society*, 3–39. New York: Russell Sage Foundation.
Harriss, J. 2003. '"Widening the Radius of Trust": Ethnographic Explorations of Trust and Indian Business', *Journal of the Royal Anthropological Institute* (N.S.) 9(4): 755–773.
Hart, K. 1988. 'Kinship, Contract, and Trust'. In D. Gambetta (ed.), *Trust: Making and Breaking of Cooperative Relations*, 176–193. Oxford: Blackwell.
Heimer, C.A. 2001. 'Solving the Problem of Trust'. In K.S. Cook (ed.), *Trust in Society*, 40–88. New York: Russell Sage Foundation.
Isaacs, K.S., J.M. Alexander and E.A. Haggard. 1963. 'Faith, Trust, and Gullibility', *International Journal of Psychoanalysis* 44: 461–469.
Jiménez, A.C. 2005. 'After Trust', *Cambridge Anthropology*, Special Edition on 'Creativity or Temporality?' (ed. E. Hirsch and S. Macdonald), 25(2): 64–78.
―――― 2011. 'Trust in Anthropology', *Anthropological Theory* 11: 177–196.
Lahno, B. 2001. 'On the Emotional Character of Trust', *Ethical Theory and Moral Practice* 4(2): 171–189.
Li, L. 2004. 'Political Trust in Rural China', *Modern China* 30(2): 228–258.
―――― 2008. 'Filial Piety, Guanxi, Loyalty, and Money: Trust in China'. In I. Marková and A. Gillespie (eds), *Trust & Distrust: Sociocultural Perspectives*, 51–78. Charlotte, NC: Information Age Publishing, Inc.
Luhman, N. 1979. *Trust and Power*. Chichester: John Wiley & Sons.
Lutz, C.A. 1988. *Unnatural Emotions: Everyday Sentiments on a Micronesian Atoll and their Challenges to Western Theory*. Chicago: University of Chicago Press.
Marková, I., P. Linell and A. Gillespie. 2008. 'Trust and Distrust in Society'. In I. Markova and A. Gillespie (eds), *Trust & Distrust: Sociocultural Perspectives*, 3–28. Charlotte, NC: Information Age Publishing, Inc.
Menning, G. 1997. 'Trust, Entrepreneurship and Development in Surat City, India', *Ethnos* 62(1–2): 59–90.
Overing, J. 2003. 'In Praise of the Everyday: Trust and the Art of the Social Living in an Amazonian Community', *Ethnos* 83(3): 293–316.

Rabinowitz, D. 1992. 'Trust and the Attribution of Rationality: Inverted Roles amongst Palestinian Arabs and Jews in Israel', *Man* 27(3): 517–537.
Roeber, C.A. 1994. 'Moneylending, Trust, and the Culture of Commerce in Kabwe Zambia', *Research in Economic Anthropology* 15: 39–61.
Seligman, A.B. 1997. *The Problem of Trust*. Princeton: Princeton University Press.
Sneath, D. 1993. 'Social Relations, Networks and Social Organisation in Post-Socialist Rural Mongolia', *Nomadic Peoples* 33: 193–207.
Solomon, R.C. and F. Flores, 2001. *Building Trust in Business, Politics, Relationships, and Life*. New York: Oxford University Press.
Sorge, A. 2009. 'Hospitality, Friendship, and the Outsider in Highland Sardinia', *Journal of the Anthropology of Europe* 9(1): 4–12.
Sztompka, P. 1999. *Trust: A Sociological Theory*. Cambridge: Cambridge University Press.
Torsello, D. 2008. 'Action speaks Louder than Words? Trust, Trustworthiness and Social Change in Slovakia', *Anthropological Journal of European Cultures* 17: 96–118.
Williams, B. 1988. 'Formal Structures and Social Reality'. In D. Gambetta (ed.), *Trust: Making and Breaking of Cooperative Relations*, 3–13. Oxford: Blackwell.
Yamagishi, T. 1996. 'Trust and Cooperation'. In A. Kuper and J. Kuper (eds), *The Social Science Encyclopedia* (2nd edition), 367–386. London: Routledge.
Yamagishi, T., M. Kikuchi and M. Kosugi. 1999. 'Trust, Gullibility, and Social Intelligence', *Asian Journal of Social Psychology* 2: 145–161.

Paula Haas has a PhD in Social Anthropology from the Mongolia and Inner Asia Studies Unit, University of Cambridge. She now works as a consultant. Haas received her undergraduate degree in Chinese and Mongolian Studies from Ca'Foscari University of Venice, Italy. Following her graduation, she worked in Mongolia for several years, before returning to academia. Using an approach indebted to linguistic anthropology, her work explores the conceptual and discursive dimensions of trust and mistrust, as well as their impact on social dynamics among the Barga Mongols in Inner Mongolia (PR China). Her theoretical interests include language and social theory, trust and mistrust, post-socialism, China and Central Asia.

# 4

THE PUZZLE OF THE ANIMAL WITCH
Intimacy, Trust and Sociality among Pastoral Turkana

Vigdis Broch-Due

It is a dusty morning on the dry savannah that stretches towards the Daaba Mountains on the eastern frontier of Isiolo District, northern Kenya. I am sitting next to the old Turkana healer Ebei, who is eagerly inspecting the stomach of a slaughtered goat, which has been lifted out, gently placed on a cover of green leaves and folded out in its circular shape. We are gazing down at the Turkana diagnostic map of the state of their world graphically represented in the grains and swirls of the intestines, with tinges of red, black, and green visible against the whitish lining of the guts. Having served as an apprentice to this particular community of healers for years now, I know that the goat-belly map contains the entire natural and social world; each feature has its designated place – mountains, rivers, savannah, camp and community. In this soft, interior flesh is inscribed a total cosmography whose shifting configurations and colorations register what goes on in the outer world and in the interchanges among people, animals, divinity and nature; all stitched together on the surface of the belly map (Broch-Due 1990, 2004).

A young woman, embracing her sick toddler, has brought the white goat we are scrutinizing for divination and diagnosis. 'There, you see!', the healer exclaims, pointing to a long red line leading directly into the innermost coil of the colon, which signifies a wife's house [*ekol*], literally the 'embryo' of the Turkana social body. 'This is the enemy pathway [*erot emoit*] along which the animal witch now inside the camp has travelled from afar'. He turns to the patient and explains that the culprit is the black cow her husband recently bought on the market in Archers and placed in her corral. It has apparently bewitched the home, causing jealousy among co-wives and sickening her child. Clearly, the domestic trouble diagnosed from the belly map resonated with the young wife's recent experiences. For she went on adding layers of personal detail to the picture of strife between co-wives over unequal fortunes, and a husband who seemingly favoured one house over the other, or so it was perceived by the older, envious wife who had thus, in liaison with a black cow, turned the evil eye against the younger wife's son. The older wife, herself barren, had accused her husband of having carelessly given a camel, previously involved in a divorce case, as part of the bridewealth he gave for her. She was convinced that his neglect was the cause of her own misfortune. Clearly the trouble of this home had accumulated over some time, and Ebei had been consulted before without being able to heal the festering wounds.

Akai, the healer's own wife, fetched the special tortoise shell used for treatment, filled it with a mixture of water and white clay and washed the forehead and chest of the ailing child. The relieved mother was given instructions to continue the cure back in the homestead. In order to repair the ruptured trust, the black cow had to be killed not by spearing, but rather by putting a smooth sheepskin over its nose and slowly smothering it until its last breath was drawn. The meat had to be carved out, cooked and shared out in the manner prescribed for a sacrifice; everybody in camp eating together in the middle of the camp, the required portions of meat given to the elders who were to sit in the half circle under the community tree. As the crux of the ceremonial cure, everybody had to be purified by being smeared with the greenish chyme from the intestines of the sacrificial cow.

This healing case has a close bearing on the ambiguous relations that exist between intimacy, trust and sociality at the heart of this volume, but reconfigured in ways specific to the Turkana *habitus*. In Bourdieu's sense of the term (1977), this taken-for-granted social schemata is the result of values, dispositions, sensibilities and expectations being gradually incorporated over time through everyday experiences and practices. The Turkana habitus is moulded by the intimate presence of livestock in their lives and living quarters; it is a sensuous relationship of nurture, affection, play and mutual dependency. The goat-belly map, being the very epicentre of diagnosis and subsequent prescription for repairing the breached trust between spouses and co-wives, conjures forcefully the interface forged between animals and people. It also incarnates the cross-species relationship that is at the core of the creation of a form of sociality embedded in natural relations. I will return to the effects on trust of this intertwining of person and beast in a moment.

However, the ingredients involved in this particular act of divination are both typical and atypical, pointing to signs of a transformation of the Turkana habitus of trust, particularly on its margins where markets and money are now at work unstitching the social fabric of established ways. The surprising story element in the scenario presented here is that the animal, not the human, was cast as the primary witch. From being a sporadic phenomenon, witchcraft accusations have been steadily rising during the last decade in this area. More perplexingly, they are increasingly directed at animals rather than humans. In order to solve this puzzle, let us tease out firstly the habitus of trust and its inbuilt tensions and, secondly, trace the emergent fault lines in the existing social order and analyse what processes are possibly involved in its transformation. In one way or another the question of the animal as an active agent in Turkana world-making is at the heart of the matter but perhaps in unpredictable and changing ways.

Entangled Physiologies

What is striking about both the diagnoses and cure described above is the sheer visceral and sensuous materiality at play. It is a matter of flesh, blood, meat and digested grass, of white and red fluids comingled with black and green substances, of smoky, sweet and putrid smells, of interfaces between interiority and exteriority, of the animal incorporating the human world, and the human repairing breaches of that world by incorporating the animal in turn. This is not a union cast as mere metaphor: it is a physical digestive process of eating and being eaten, which results in an entangled embodiment of person and beast, brought together in an intimate, interspecies embrace.

In Turkana thought there is thus a sort of grand universal physiology of flows and processes which achieve a dual movement through which, on the one hand, bodies incorporate the exterior world, taking it in to establish a sort of interior bodyscape, and on the other, they externalize the multiple contents of the person and beast, projecting them out onto other bodies and things but also into the landscape itself – creating a series of 'affective assemblages' in the sense of Deleuze and Guattri (1987). Eating and excretion are one manifestation of this grand physiology, but it goes far beyond this. The incorporating movement creates an inventory of corporeal relationships of shared subsistence and substances that extends across different species and matters. The externalizing movement turns their dry savannah into a 'living landscape' in the pure sense of the term – shaped by Turkana, moulded by the affects, actions, memories and images of their bodies and those of their livestock (Broch-Due 1990).

This is how, concretely, it works. Imagine a cow nibbling on some tufts of grass, moving slowly but methodically through the savannah landscape. The cattle are gently directed along by a young herder singing to his favourite ox. The morning session ends at the riverbanks where the cow eagerly laps the water served in the wide, wooden vessel that Turkana girls bring to it from wells dug in the dry riverbed. The cow lays down with the herd to rest in the shade of a three. Its light skin has, etched upon it by human hands, dark concentric circles and patterns imitating plants and wild animals of the arid savannah. As the cow ruminates, the veins running from its throat down its belly to its udders swell, and stand out in stark relief under its tattooed skin. To every Turkana this is an immediate, visceral and outward sign of the essential interior transformation of grass and water into blood, milk, flesh and dung in the wake of digestion. The blood veins standing out on the cow's skin are seen as similar to the filigree of pathways its feet has imprinted on the surface of the hard baked earth, also seen as a 'skin' [ngajul]. Veins are like paths, and paths are like rivers, and rivers are perceived to be the 'blood veins' of the earth. These vital essences of life are connected by flows and sedimentations, simultaneously surface and depth, weaving together in a tight symbiosis nature and animal, animal and human, in an alimentary process that is as truly ecological as it is cosmological (Broch-Due 1993).

Humans are sustained, just as cattle are sustained and related to each other by grass and water from the land, by the constant sharing of milk, meat and blood. These 'food paths', as Turkana call them, grow bodies and relationships. Children and calves are thus in a very real sense kindred – a connection powerfully expressed in the idiom of conception, where the parental blood and semen are termed 'grass' and 'water', and the blend of these two is a mixed substance which 'grows' the child by being 'cooked' in the maternal womb. Indeed, cow and wife are honourably linked in having the same length of pregnancy, of being caring mothers, and forming genealogically complementary house-lines [ekol] of great significance in the bilateral kinship system. As will become clearer, these matching moral qualities of cows and women are at the centre of our witchcraft investigation.

The dominant physiological idea that the world is composed of a series of microcosmic and macrocosmic bodies, and that these bodies interpenetrate each other in some substantive way, is made real for Turkana in divination. Divination finds the perfect image of these multiple worlds curled up upon themselves in the guts of a goat, which we have seen the Turkana read to gain information about events in their world. Goats *incorporate* a complete configuration of everything Turkana. Since cattle are seldom killed, it is the assigned role of the voracious goat, whose tiny body brims with life in profusion, reproducing twice a year and consuming almost whatever one throws at it, to be the ultimate revealer of truth as it sacrifices its life. The term for goat [*akine*] is the same as for 'the gift' and the significance of goats clearly evokes that original Maussian meaning (Broch-Due 2004).

In contrast to Western mapping, the Turkana goat belly cartography is not just seen only as a representation of the world. It really registers the world's fluctuating states in the transient texture of blood bubbles, grains and the quality and texture of the digested grass in the animal's stomach and guts. These are visual signs of events and transformations in the external world. The data registered here helps in the evaluation of pasture and the planning of herd movements. It is also employed as a basis on which to formulate actions in the human world: the timing of weddings, birth and burial rituals; and the state of affairs in relationships. After the goat-belly map has been inspected and made known to everybody; it is cooked and eaten to ensure that the knowledge gained is stored in everybody. Turkana comprehend the world by literally 'taking it in'.

They are also passionately concerned with projecting out again into the exterior world what is being processed internally. Working on the surfaces of skin exhibits the interior, and a stranger cannot fail to be struck by the spectacular display of Turkana body decoration. Men, women and children alike while away the hot midday hours in the shade of trees, adorning themselves and each other. While keeping a watching eye on the livestock that graze in the vicinity, they create elaborate coiffures, they oil, paint and scarify their bodies, carve ornaments and utensils, thread beads and discuss their looks. Whenever the chance presents itself, individuals gaze at their reflections in a calm water surface (and in the wing mirrors of my car). In a profound way, their cattle adornment works alongside their own adornment to enhance the effects people strive to make on one another. Both are doctored and decorated with matching designs. An animal's body will be marked not only with fixed clan marks but also tattoos speaking of the deeds and exploits of its caretaker. Everybody has their favourite animals that are the focus of poems, songs and dances. As a personal touch, the possessor dips his or her finger into wet clay, chyme and dung and draws designs of their own skin and those of their cows and castrated oxen, copying intricate patterns drawn from the rich flora and fauna that surrounds them. This pair, person and beast, stand out in the world as a single, forceful image.

Towards a Habitus of Trust

So what has all this visceral and visual animal stuff to do with the Turkana habitus of trust? Simply put: without animals there is no trust formation possible, according to the pastoralist ethos and cultural logic. Not only is the quality of relationships monitored by inspecting the goat-belly map, but those relationships are created and maintained by the lavish giving and circulating of livestock and shared meals of meat and milk. Those who are placed outside 'the circle of trust' are simultaneously excluded from the circle of gift giving and meat consumption. The Turkana livestock ledger is so rich and subtle that it expresses not only the kind and amount involved in transactions but also what is precisely expected of the ensuing relation; whether it is purchase, barter, loan or gift. Memorialization is another function of the scripts etched into animal flanks, each cow carrying on its tattooed skin overlapping personal and social biographies. A herd of well-tended and beautifully decorated cattle dramatically enlarges the social space of the persons it represents. Livestock simply *embody* the relationship between overlapping pairs of donors and recipients. Exchanges are therefore about an intricate interweaving of person, animal and attributes. These all become partial signs for one another, as they are also partial signs for the social relationships they produce and reproduce. When cattle change hands, however, they act as an external carrier of not only those claims pushing people together, but also the counterclaims that pull them apart. This adds a precarious element to animal matters: although predicated on trust, doubt always lingers under the surface about the future intention of donor and recipient, powerfully summed up in the Turkana proverb 'Livestock speak louder than sweet words'.

Food sharing speaks volumes too; indeed, 'to speak from the belly' is an expression for speaking truth, of being particularly trustworthy. The eating pattern is as elaborate as is the exchange system: the cuisine for any occasion of collective meat consumption specifies methods for cooking and carving, the place for the shared meal, and which social category should get what portion of the slaughter. Since Turkana are intensely concerned with properly managing the entire digestive process from grass, blood, milk and meat to dung, bone and ash, the remains of the meals must be handled in prescribed ways and deposited in its right spatial position within the homestead (Broch-Due 1990).

Turkana have intricate notions of morality, trust and the emotions, and these are all expressed in the keenly observed colours of the fluids and solids produced in the animal body through feeding and digestion. After being chewed by the cow, grass enters the first stomach, the rumen, where it coagulates into chyme, a greenish and thick pre-digested substance, which is ruminated for hours. To Turkana, chyme therefore carries all the life-giving properties of the fresh grass. But animal digestion results in other products as well. The alimentary process is seen to consist of two intertwined colour loops. One circuit starts from green and yellow (grass), which are turned into white (milk and fat), and yellow (butter and oil); the second round is red (blood and meat). Both end in the colour black (animal dung). Chyme contains all these possibilities of transformation within it and is therefore an icon representing the vitality of the entire grand physiology which Turkana symbolism see so deeply embedded in nature. The smearing of putrid chyme on the human body is the most powerful method of purification, and it was exactly this blessed state that the healer's last prescription for a cure was designed to achieve in our opening case.

Animal physiology, with its range of pigmentations – green, white, red, black and yellow – serves as a template for transformation in all matters, including psychological and social. Perhaps Turkana deploys this bodily colour spectrum, which occurs both as surface on the skin and as depth beneath the skin, precisely because of the inherent potentiality for revealing what is hidden but also of concealing what has been revealed. In the struggle for scarce resources, there is a tension between common goods and personal goods, between collective liability and individual unpredictability, between what should be proper behaviour in contrast to how people actually behave. As pointed out by Haaland (1979), this tension between precariousness and coherence in social life is often the source for sign elaboration, and in his example from the Sudanese Fur, the moral qualities involved are represented by the colours white, red and black. This bears striking similarities with Turkana signification, although grounded in an agrarian idiom rather than a pastoral idiom, and with fewer colours in play.

The Turkana habitus of trust and its negation divides the cultural universe into corresponding categories of persons and acts, legitimized by the intimate analogies drawn between the social and the natural worlds. Just as right is superior to left, so is east superior to west, life to death, sweet to bitter, cool to hot, mothers' milk to blood, and so forth; so is 'insider' placed above 'outsider', senior above junior, the married above the unmarried, friends above enemies; and likewise herders above hunters, fishers and farmers, solidarity above competition, sociability above unsociability, and so forth. Such disparate qualities are placed on a colour continuum in which white and red represent the opposite poles (Broch-Due 1990).

The Colour of Your Heart

The colour white signifies actively auspicious qualities such as sociability, sharing, support, prosperity, and is thus located on the east and right sides of the cardinal axis. The space of the white is the patrilineal homestead [*awi*], properly constituted through marriage and encompassing both the livestock and people. Inside the homestead, there is one social relation where solidarity is taken for granted, and that is the mother–child bond. This is further bolstered by the principle of matrifiliation. Each wife is the founder of a houseline, through which her children inherit, and she builds a separate quarter [*ekol*] with kitchen, hearth and a circular night hut covered with animal hides from her own house herd. The positive valuation of white items is linked to nurturing bonds. The core is the baby's unmediated and intimate relationship with the breast of its birth mother. When its reliance on mothers' milk is replaced by cows' milk, child and calf are brought together in one equation formed around the auspiciousness of milk and whiteness. The white colour is thus particularly fit to serve as a sign for solidarity and support also in other sets of social relations. Whitish items (beads, clays, porridge, milk and animals with a white hue) are used in wedding ceremonies to cement the positive qualities which should prevail between in-laws, in purification rituals connected to births and the ends of liminal phases to clean away impurity, in peace making ceremonies between competing factions and in other rites of reconciliation to transform relations of enmity into relations of friendship.

White also marks the full social status of the married couple, initiated senior men, and pastoralists in general. In short, the categories of persons and acts contained within the white spectrum are vested with positive values. Responsibility and sociability should characterize such social bonds. Persons with 'white hearts' [*Akwunga lau*] are genuinely good and trustworthy people.

The red colour signifies the actively inauspicious qualities, such as disruption, dishonour and hostility. It is located on the west and left side of the cardinal axis. The core of the red is the enemy, primarily members of other tribes. The relationship with these people is based on competition for pasture, water and livestock. Such enmity is most extremely manifested in killings and bloodshed. The red expresses unsociability in other relations also known to be competitive. Red clay marks out warriors and young women not yet properly civilized through initiation and marriage rituals. Such junior categories are seen as irresponsible, unmanageable, provocative and disrespectful towards their seniors. However, active unsociability is primarily displayed through witchcraft, which can be traced in certain families. Although not widespread, exposure to the 'evil eye' leaves a trail of sickness and death among both humans and herds. The conventional association between hostility, blood and redness is apparent when the stomachs of slaughtered animals are investigated. Bubbles of red blood presage raids, sickness or death. Just as desperate ills call for desperate remedies, so can a 'reddish' goat be speared to prevent the fulfilment of bad omens. In most ritual contexts, however, animals with 'reddish' hues are strictly prohibited. As a fluid, blood appears in bright red that coagulates into a darker, brownish substance. This duality in tint and texture turns red into the colour of power with all its ambivalence, positively linked on the one hand with procreation, but negatively linked, on the other, with killing. Red also speaks to the sacred ability of diviners, who should not consume blood. Female diviners must keep their fertile, menstrual blood away from livestock. Red clay is smeared on the bodies of warriors during the preparation for raids, while menstruating woman must keep their hands off weaponry lest its power would be drained. But in ordinary relations, red colours connote hatred and envy. If somebody unintentionally takes part in a meal with a red-hearted person, their blood would 'shiver', and sickness or death would befall them. Persons with 'red hearts' [*Erenga tau*] are evil people.

However, these two stereotypes of whiteness and redness, the 'good' and 'evil', are obviously not sufficient to cover the whole range of moral qualities. For within collectives (such as families, networks, neighbourhoods and herding associations) where conventions insist that your dealings with others are based on solidarity, people may still be betrayed by those close to their hearts. Conversely, within relationships where lack of solidarity is to be assumed, changing alignments, the ups and downs of livestock breeding and the vagaries of real life may transform present enemies and 'outsiders' to future friends and 'insiders', and vice versa. Such ambiguous experiences are inserted into the colour spectrum of morality as further shadings: white is tinged with green and red with black.

Black is the colour of poverty, treason, distrust, jealousy, adultery, sorcery and cowardliness. It is located on the south, 'down' to Turkana, and left side of the cardinal axis. These are all affects and qualities of a more passive and concealed form of unsociability than the open opposition between enemies. 'Blackness' enters into a social relationship when someone abuses trust as an opportunity to advance particularistic interests. The core of the black is the structural tension built into an exogamous system, between the patrilineal [*awi*] and the matrilineal [*ekol*], between agnates and affines. Blackness is set in motion when husband and wife, co-wives, mother and daughter in-law, father and sons, and siblings are moved to conflicting courses of action. Blackness is brought inside the homestead by female strangers in the form of wives who enter the gate through marriage, and thus cause cattle to exit through the same gate as bridewealth given to her kin and clan. In her reproductive capacity, a wife strengthens the *awi* by reproducing, laying the foundation for future prosperity. Yet since the wife bears her children by establishing a separate maternal house, *ekol*, within the polygamous compound run by the husband, she also sows the seeds of dissension and the breakup of her husband's lifework and homestead when she joins her eldest son in the foundation of a new *awi*. As a countermeasure to possible subterfuge, Turkana turn wives into being the very guardians of the clan repertoires of customs and ritual observances. Under the stern stewardship of their mothers-in-law, brides are moulded to gain knowledge and thus develop vested interest in their new clan. Nevertheless, doubts may linger under the surface such that blackness shades relationships of solidarity and sincerity, which may turn out to contain the negation of such qualities. Black is the colour of avoidance, smouldering hostility and impoverishment. People with 'black hearts [*Ariono tau*] harbour suspicious and treacherous designs.

Green is the colour of fertility, alliances, sharing, mutuality and interdependency. It is located on the north, 'up' to Turkana, and right side of the cardinal axis. The essence of 'greenness' is the bond/friendship nurtured by frequent cattle exchanges, and the age-group, which is nicknamed 'the breastfed ones', expressing poignantly the extension of the white domain beyond the camp enclosure. Green items signify the importance of community commitments, expressed in food sharing and cemented by livestock circulations beyond the compound and clan. The colour green, associated with water, grass and the stomach contents of animals, plays a leading role, often in combination with white items, in ceremonies performed to promote common goods through the act of rainmaking and fertility rites. For instance, barren wives are asked to wear green beads in order to conceive, and those related to the clan of diviners will use green beads instead of the normal white to signify their married and thus fully social status. Persons with 'green hearts [*Apus tau*] cherish friendly feelings.

Green is related to yellow through a metonymic association created by the ways green grass turns yellow at the peak of dry seasons. Yellow is the colour of 'breath', 'dryness' and knowledge, capacities that develop in the person along with maturation of body and mind. By the same token, yellow is stretched beyond the sphere of the living and embeds life itself in the majestic landscape of northern Kenya. To appreciate the Turkana perspective, imagine standing at the edge of the Great Rift Valley escarpment: Deep below, the dry plains stretch towards a seemingly endless horizon, its volcanic hills are tinted in all shades of ochre – ash, amber, auburn – its parched soil scattered with streams and bushes. Here deserts, mountains and vast expanses of dry savannah stretch to the sky on all sides and, in the distance, the gleaming greenish Lake Turkana, its mirages shimmering under the vast, baking dome of the East African sky. Closer up, particularly toward the end of the dry season, the plains are often coated in dust and the mountains shrouded in a yellow haze. Lightning flares across the darkened sky, thunder roars and tall twisters throw up huge spirals of sand, soil and twigs as they travel across the dry plains. Then the weather breaks and pouring rain hammers the shrivelled earth, filling up streams and rivers; the dormant seeds sprout and a carpet of fresh grass and flowers will soon cover the ground.

These dramatic forces of nature, painted in ancestral yellow, constitute the domain of divinity, *Akuij* [Sky], the Many-One, who represents both feminine and masculine spirits in an androgynous blend. And yet maternal association is particularly strong since Sky and Earth are encompassed by *Akuij's* divine womb, and Turkana are very clear that a human wife's night-hut, *akai* [skeleton], where she gives birth, is but a miniature replica of the heavens, similarly dome-shaped and generative. Formed as a swarm of spirits, S/he is especially evoked in the turning of the seasons, shrouded in the yellow veils of dust and haze, the flaring red of lightning across the blackish sky of rainstorms. The ensuing rainbows display the whole colour spectrum – which is literally all life and living in all its diversity and contradictions – in one unifying vision that of a coloured bridge thrown across the Earth, *Akwap*. The earth after rains is greenness with the tall trees scattered through the landscape and rivers threading their way through it. The generative force that belongs to *Akuij* is not only evident in her orchestrating of the short-term weather cycles but in the whole geomorphology of the landscape and the life within it. S/he gestated this grand world with all its elements and species, and has helped to grow and transform them ever since by providing a space for pastoralism and people. Some buffaloes became cattle, a few giraffes developed into camels, hares turned into sheep, flocks of gazelles became goats, and zebras ended up as donkeys. S/he divided the entire collection of flora and fauna equally between the two generation-sets who chose the leopard and baboon respectively as totem animals. Indeed, the very first diviner S/he provided, *Apatapes*, started out in wild animal form as a white baboon leading a troop of black baboons, before it was captured, tamed and turned human by having blood from a goat dripped over its fur (Broch-Due 1990).

Turkana perceive the whole world as a series of interlinked physiologies of energy, aliveness and moral qualities that it is their task to manage and manipulate. Behind Turkana concerns with a multispecies physiology linking landscape and bodies, interior and exterior, through a myriad of flows, forces and affects, is a universal yearning for an eternity that transcends the transient lives of humans and animals on this earth. This deep desire for permanency is poetically expressed in a Turkana imagery of their cosmos, essentially *Akuij*, as the silhouette of a containing maternal body by day, dissolving its contours into a dark surface spotted with red by night, which simultaneously represents the fires of the dead and the most auspicious skin configuration of Turkana cattle.

By tying their theory of ethics and personal psychology so tightly not only to the animals they exchange, but also to the landscape itself, Turkana deeply naturalize their sociality and sensibilities. The habitus of trust becomes embedded in a cosmology wrapped in lyrical imagery all the more powerful for being a play on the world itself, collapsing the difference between primordial time and present time.

The Shaping of Human and Animal as Moral Subjects

Turkana summon up everything in their life world in their continued efforts to negotiate forms of sociality that include many species and environments. Having herds in such harsh natural surroundings brings life and death close to everyone's experience. In these conditions the visceral quality of human and livestock reproductive cycles become closely interwoven. The key to the morality which infuses the pastoral economy is the host of intimate, visceral and emotional experiences that tie humans and animals together in Turkana minds. The closely observed realities of animal procreation, the birth and death of livestock, the carefully observed pregnancies, the washes of blood and water at birth, the swollen udders, the tiny calf struggling to stand up, the decaying of bodies at death – all unavoidably connote the same essential processes in the human world. The more so in that all major social events in that human world depend completely on these events in the life of their herds.

The development cycle of herds lies at the heart of a web of events that are ecological, physiological, social and symbolic all at once: the seasons, reproduction, herd size and movements, the redistribution of animals in exchanges, marriages and inheritance, and the shared consumption of meat, blood and milk. All aspects of this web – which is the intimate web of Turkana personal universes – are part of their moral universe as well, and 'the good' only emerges from an individual's capacity to make the appropriate moves with his or her animals. In other words, 'the good' in the Turkana world is a complex quality relating to the person's ability to manage a whole range of physical and social processes. It is essentially about how successful your *path-making* is.

Recall how our healer scrutinized the goat-belly map to find the animal witch's interior path, a replica of exterior pathways. Physical paths [*erot*] are also the social pathways along which people and livestock move, creating a 'roped path' [*eropit*], between donors and recipients. The metaphor of pathways extends beyond the physical and social worlds to include individual anatomy and physiology. What one eats moves along 'food paths' [*akimuij erot*], and the image of paths and flows goes on to characterize the inner workings of the body, including the essences of human life – breath, knowledge and power. If these vital flows move freely along the interior pathways, a person is healthy, the outward signs being a willingness to move animals along the exterior paths and to participate in food sharing systems. If the person neglects the circuit of reciprocal exchanges of food and livestock, the movement of life-sustaining forces and flows is constrained, resulting in illness, misfortune and poverty. The 'blackness' of these conditions becomes a stigma from which it is difficult to escape. In contrast, vitality, well-being and wealth, conditions characterized as 'green' or 'white' are all linked to the movement of a wide range of assets along multiple pathways. On this moral high ground it is not difficult to grasp why the possession of animals is the key to the positive valuations of people, their trustworthiness, and 'good' sociality. Those who lose their animals cease to exist as worthy of sympathy and support in the Turkana moral imagination. They are pushed to the edges of the social map and risk being excluded from the pastoral economy altogether (Broch-Due 1999).

Animals are also active players in the moral game in their own right and must follow the 'good' pathways too, or risk being side-lined, rendered anonymous or killed. Viewed as subjects rather than objects or possessions, animals not only project the identity and fame of human subjects, but crucially *represent* them, positively or negatively, through their own behaviour and path-making. Like a human being, an animal being is an agent capable of trust or treason. Like a human child, a calf too must be trained in order to turn out well behaved. Indeed, the socialization of children and calves works in tandem: both are shown similar care, affection and encouragement. The birth of a new animal life is a blessing; its death bodes misfortune. Animal and human newborns are subject to the same care. Premature kids and lambs are removed from the pen and placed in wooden vessels kept in the night-hut. Here the wife, acting as surrogate mother, will feed the newborn with dam's milk through a pipe made from sheeps' leather, which imitates the umbilical cord. The foster kid is secluded for five days until it recovers, exactly the same time a human baby and its mother are sheltered after delivery.

The newborn kid is nurtured and caressed by the wife as if it were a child, and indeed the term for a newborn goat, *Ikale nice,* is also deployed as a nickname for human babies of both sexes. Toddlers will tumble around on the ground with the young animals in camp, and when they are about four years old, boys and girls will be given a young animal to look after. For the next years they are close to the young animal, spending considerable time in the corral snuggling and singing lullabies to it. Children will continue to imitate the sound and behaviour of their charges as the two mature together. Indeed the two 'children', animal and human, pass through similar stages of maturation and are referred to analogously; a bride is 'a heifer' a wife is politely addressed as 'a cow', a warrior is know by his ox name and so on.

Those milking the cattle can build extremely affectionate bonds with specific dams, who will often come to show such strong preferences for a particular pair of hands and a specific style of manipulation that they will refuse to let strangers milk them. At dawn and dusk, a wife goes to the corral and calls out the name of each dam, who then rushes eagerly towards their caretaker. During milking she sings sweet words, presses her temple against the animal's flank, and fondles the swollen udders. This caressing makes the dam release her milk readily, her teats needing only the slightest touch with the fingers. Calves and castrated oxen are similarly caressed and fondled by their caretakers. Intimate touch-talk exchanges between people and stock parallel the dialogues between parents and children. The animals are addressed and discussed as family members.

By the same token, humans go to considerable lengths to care for, supervise and train their herds. Daily care and disciplining of livestock are, to my mind, the single most important aspects of pastoralism. Social training relates to what Gudrun Dahl has coined as 'the reproduction of animal domestication' (1987: 6). Wives carefully teach their young stock in camp with quasi-Pavlovian techniques. Animal trainees are taken outside the corral and placed some distance from their trainer, who, having equipped herself with tufts of grass and a bowl of water, attracts the animals with sound signals, which are species specific. The animal is trained to respond to distinctive whistles for waiting, coming, feeding, drinking and resting. When the animal acts correctly it is rewarded; if not, it is gently hit on the nose. According to Turkana, cattle and goats are the 'clever pupils in class', responding to training much faster than 'stupid' sheep and 'naughty' camels. After proper behaviour is instilled, each animal is trained to respond to its individual name. This is a turning point in the animal's life. It is now old enough to follow the adult herd on the open range. Herders then take over training, teaching the young members to react to human voices and keep together under the leadership of particular beasts who have bells made from turtle shells tied around the neck.

A herd of well-behaved and individuated livestock not only makes grazing and watering in treacherous terrain easier, thus saving human labour, but also facilitates the crucial role beasts play in the exchange arena. The representational load of a domestic animal is heavy; by embodying its human caretaker through its tattoos, it makes sure that the donor stays active in the memory of the recipient, and by moving to new camps it helps bind several sets of caretakers together. To illustrate: An older camel belonging to our healer was used as such an *erochit* – 'to bind strongly'. It was first obtained as a share of the bridewealth of Ebei's half-sister. Ebei used it as part of the bridewealth for his own wife. The recipient donated the camel later as part of his bridewealth, and so it went on until the camel had participated in the marriages of five wives. Beyond that, the camel, which along the road had obtained the honourable title *Erereng* [the blessed one], had also managed to link together in a circular chain four Turkana clans.

However, as with human affairs, animal affairs do not always proceed along the same white and green pathways as the honourable camel mentioned above; sometimes they slide down the 'black' and 'red' pathways of divorce, death and other misfortunes. Those unfortunate events stick to the beast, and it too starts to get a bad reputation, and may even be stigmatized. This is because an animal is reared with great care to create social relationships, not to break them off. When people exchange beasts, they are thus careful to get a detailed account of the animal's personal biographies and whereabouts. As was dramatized in the opening case, it is risky to deploy an animal for marrying a wife that has previously been involved in a divorce case, which means that it has to be returned and the gift-rope thus ruptured. The bad fortune of such an animal is highly contagious and risks affecting the fertility of the new wife, and thus her capacity to create strong bonds with her own in-laws through the birth of children. One can still use a blemished animal for regular transactions not involving significant life-giving events such as birth, initiation and marriage – but what about the black cow-witch?

Social Transformation and Misgiving

The problem with the black cow, discovered by the old healer *Ebei* to be the source of misfortune, was simply its anonymity. Having been bought on the marketplace it lacked any social records, good or bad. Its origins in the distant lands of Rendille – thus having been reared among a people that sometimes turn up as enemies – did not help matters either. One simply could not know anything about the true disposition of this cow, its trustworthiness or otherwise. Without the necessary intimate details of how it had been reared and the biographical events it had been involved in among its previous caretakers, the black cow was inherently suspicious, its good intentions already in doubt. Perhaps its black colour did it no favours either in the particular situation in which it found itself: a homestead troubled by smouldering resentment between the two wives and a blameworthy husband. The black cow fell victim to a web of bad relations and meanings that were projected onto it and ultimately condemned it to death. It was decided that its mischief was of a strong kind and that it should be subjected to the most long-drawn-out method of killing available: its 'blackness' was literally to be suffocated out of it to ensure its extinction and the ensuing purification of the humans affected.

After having researched all the cases in the area involving animal witches like the one above, the link to the market became very clear to me. They all had been purchased. This does not mean that all cattle bought on the local livestock market were victims of witchcraft accusations but all those accused were indeed from the market – and their number was growing. Most significantly, it was a completely novel phenomenon to cast animals in the role of witches, at least in the real world outside the fictional realm of myth. This speaks volumes about the ambiguity and mistrust involved in the increased commodification of cattle. Commercialization severs the close connections between intimacy and wider sociality in the Turkana habitus of trust, which binds people and animals so tightly (Broch-Due 1999).

In order to appreciate why accusations in this specific area of northern Kenya were increasingly settling on cattle, rather than goats or people, a little more contextual information is necessary. Since colonial times, the processes of commodification throughout the vast pastoralist expanse of northern Kenya have been neither unilinear nor cumulative, but have given rise to boom and bust cycles occurring unevenly across the homelands of different pastoral communities. On the north-western frontier populated by Turkana segments, different spheres and goods within the local economy have, since the 1930s, been commoditized only to be 'de-commoditized' at different historical junctures. These historical shifts resulted, on the one hand, from changing colonial and postcolonial taxation and fiscal policies and, on the other, from Turkana people's own ideas about their position in Turkana society and in relation to the world at large. By the same token, in this area certain material goods – in particular, cattle – have consistently remained beyond the reach of market forces and monetized relations. This is because colonial and postcolonial policies put in place an embargo on cattle exports and sales which, as it happens, largely coincided with Turkana notions about cattle and their appropriate uses. Quite by accident, colonial and local views collaborated to ensure that Turkana cattle remained outside the realm of commodity exchange. However, since taxes had to be paid in sheep or goats, these small-stock were freely exchanged from an early date, and were rapidly drawn into the developing regional market both in the form of commodity and currency. Indeed, the huge potential for natural accumulation constituted by goats and their rapid reproduction provides any person with a highly convertible form of capital for procuring food, cash and cattle (Broch-Due 2000).

On the eastern frontier, in contrast, pastoralist groups were pacified decades earlier, brought under colonial control and the influence of money and missionaries. Here markets for both cattle and goats have been in operation ever since, and although communities like Samburu, Rendille and Borana also continue to treat cattle as 'social beasts', they have erased much of the branding and marks that used to be etched into their cattle's skins simply because a clean surface is thought to fetch a higher price. The colouration of cattle has likewise become more standardized through breeding so that the white or light colours dominate. A typical Turkana cattle herd, in contrast, is bred to display the whole diversity of coloration and patterns nature can afford in addition to be being elaborately branded and decorated.

What is highly significant for our investigation is that the community built around the Turkana healers at the heart of our case are recent immigrants into the eastern region in the vicinity of Isiolo. Here they live interspersed with long-established communities of Samburu, Borana and Turkana, many of whom have left pastoralism altogether to live in shanty towns were they scrape a living from tourism and commerce. There has always been a lot of fluidity and movement across the boundaries of clans, tribes and regions amongst all the nomads of the north. However, prolonged periods of endemic violence and recent political upheavals have increased the flow of pastoralists coming from the western heartland of Turkanaland where they did not have any previous experience of cattle marketing.

Abruptly inserted into a new environment made up of a mixture of foreigners, where cattle are treated like goats and driven through the market place, their social history erased from their flanks, the habitus of trust of these immigrant Turkana had clearly been shaken. The new 'cash cows' they were exposed to were ill-equipped to take on their role as 'social beasts' and to carry the social identities and core values of people and cosmos. The long-term cycle of cattle exchange had been disrupted. The short-term goat-cycle however, geared towards the satisfaction of more immediate needs, desires and interests of individuals, remained in operation and the guts of the goat continued to reveal vital information about the social world.

Reflections on Trusting and its Tensions

What more can be inferred from this Turkana story of intimacy, trust and the social? The *anomie* of the cattle market at the heart of our witchcraft case seems to go against Western theories after Hobbes, which saw such security in the market and put so much trust in notions of 'the contract' and market mechanisms. In the capitalistic worldview, the Market and its contracts simply create trust and faith. Game theory, where rational actors engage in calculated risk taking before entrusting their assets to others, seems equally far from Turkana. Perhaps it is too much to expect that the moral philosophy of the enlightenment brand, which concerned itself with the formation of a modern citizenship forged from a new politicized divide between the 'public' and 'private' spheres, would be able to cast much light on the life-world of the East African savannas. Whatever the case, the disagreement runs deep and seems to touch on widely divergent definitions of humanity itself.

There is a long line of thinkers, stretching from Hobbes, Kant, Herbert Spencer up to a contemporary theorist like Gareth Hardin, who share the premise that human beings are essentially egoistic and competitive, needing all sorts of enforced procedures and institutions to behave in a trustworthy fashion (Ystanes, this volume). Turkana operate from the very opposite premise: subjects are assumed to carry the social world within them at the core of their being and are thus inherently trustworthy until their actions prove otherwise. These pastoralists are thus in perfect agreement with the philosopher David Hume, who argued that 'No quality of human nature is more remarkable, both in itself and in its consequences, than that propensity we have to sympathize with others'. Turkana take this sympathizing a significant step further, incorporating animal subjects into the circle of trust and concern.

Whilst most anthropologists would agree with Turkana about the social nature of humanity, the way reciprocity is often theorized in anthropology would be significantly out of synch with local theories. The seminal model proposed by Marshall Sahlins, for example, sets up concentric circles of reciprocity with the strongest 'generalized' reciprocity placed at the family core. Then reciprocity is gradually weakened as its circles expand outward to finally become 'negative' at the farthest reaches away from the domestic core (Sahlins 1974: 199). In other words, at the intimate core, trust is a taken-for-granted value, but it gradually turns into mistrust as we reach the margins of social circles. In sharp opposition, the Turkana model of sociality, with its white/black duality, alerts us to the ambiguity, even danger, which lurks within the homestead itself. This interplay between intimacy and danger is precisely the dynamic driving the most robust African witchcraft regimes into ever new regions, as so decisively argued by Peter Geshiere (this volume). And although the egalitarian, decentralized and nomadic organization of Turkana society has historically been less prone to widespread witchcraft accusations, the seeds of witchcraft clearly lie dormant within it and can germinate at times when established notions of sharing and sociality are put under pressure and called into doubt.

Local Turkana perceptions question the above anthropological theory on other scores too. The white/green band of trust and morality extends generalized and balanced forms of reciprocity to the widest circles of friends, acquaintances and associates, even strangers. Turkana have a thoughtful and refined perspective on the complexities of human affairs. They recognize that the red/black of mistrust can colour all social relations, whether close or distant.

Whilst Turkana would most likely sympathize with Hume's position, they would be even more enthusiastically in line with the sixteenth-century French philosopher and essayist Michel de Montaigne. Like them, he was enthralled by the power of personal presence in moral life, and equally fascinated with how people act on, affect and sway one another through their sheer physicality. And, like Turkana, Montaigne included animals in this affective web. In one classic aphorism Montaigne asked cunningly: 'When I am playing with my cat, how do I know she is not playing with me?' He went on to elaborate how animals themselves form 'a certain acquaintance with one another' and greet each other 'with joy and demonstrations of goodwill'. Most significantly, he anticipated Bourdieu's contemporary theory in a commentary appended to the final edition of his *Essays*. After having extended the circles of trust from animal-to-human to human-to-human, Montaigne concluded that subjects, human and animal, could not help but express themselves and communicate their being. For it is not only words that speak; our physical movements also have the capacity to converse and discourse (Frampton 2011). Indeed, this tacit communication, extending across species, is deeply entrenched in our evolved habitus (Panksepp 1998).

According to both Turkana and Montaigne, trust thrives best with physical proximity, but it does not have to be of an intimate kind. Trust can thrive in large-scale networks as long as there is something of the absent person present to trigger the memory of a relationship and its obligations. For pastoralist Turkana, who spend much time travelling around creating partnerships across their vast grazing range, that something is the animal exchanged, which binds together people by its physical presence: a cow is a sensory reminder of the person it represents. But the point about the significance of proximity, physical or social, goes to the heart of how exactly a habitus of trust is formed and, by the same token, why it is that danger and intimacy are so closely linked.

In their everyday life, pastoral Turkana draw upon animal instincts in their training efforts but also animal genetics in their breeding strategies. Through being so deeply involved with the continual *reproduction* of animal domestication in their camps, they know from experience that animals are responsive to social gestures. It would come as no surprise to Turkana minds to learn about the 'mirror neurons' first discovered in the brains of macaque monkeys, firing not only when their fellow monkeys grasped food, but when they saw the human caretaker grasp it too. This recent breakthrough in neuroscience makes clear that mammals, including humans, have an in-built imitative and emphatic capacity, which facilitates the comprehension of intentionality in others even across species. One enthusiastic researcher labeled the cells 'the neurons that shaped civilization', precisely because human culture involves the continual transfer of complex skills and knowledge across generations (Gallese et al. 1996).

This evidence of a primary intersubjectivity and sociality, operational from the first day of life in both child and calf, resonates powerfully in the breast milk imagery Turkana employ. This is the core referent of the white spectrum of morality and is further extended into the greenness of the age-group of young men who are nicknamed 'the breast-fed ones'. Milky fluids continue to link calf and child, human and animal, physiologically, socially and symbolically. Women carry their babies for months and breastfeeding is on demand. Mother and infant form an unmediated dyad: their mutual rhythms of gazing, vocal intonations, touch and gesture are 'attuned' to each other. Turkana rearing practices are very successful in achieving strong attachment between mother and child (and caretaker and calf). There is growing evidence from infant research that attachment, and the failure of it, affect autonomic, neurochemical and hormonal functions in a growing brain. Yet the Turkana child's primary attachment is not necessarily limited to its mother and can be extended to anybody – men, women and children – who cradle infants in camp with great pleasure, passing them around from one lap to another, caressing, dancing and singing lullabies. As evocatively explained by the neuroscientist Antonio Damasio in his *Self Comes to Mind* (2010), this intersubjective music and movement of early life establishes a sort of corporeal metrics, the motor-sensory beats of self and other, that accompanies early emotional development, creating a sense of well-being, an affective precondition for trusting (see also Stern 1985; Panksepp 1998).

Toddlers spend much time in the company of older siblings and grandparents so the supportive network surrounding Turkana childcare is tightly knit. Within it, the tiny child is allowed to experience both pain and pleasure as s/he stumbles around on bare feet, tipping over and crying out in surprised hurt only to be gently encouraged to stand up again by its older supervisor who wipes away the tears. Children play happily together with the lambs, kids and calves in camp; they cavort and gambol and tumble about in an interspecies fusion of laughter, bleating and mooing. Within an atmosphere of trust, children are trained to be independent, fearless and endure discomfort with grace. When they are about five years old, they are given command of a small flock of kids and lambs, themselves trainees of the camp, as we have seen, which the children proudly take for grazing in the vicinity. Turkana strongly believe that trust and social competence is something that needs to be gradually moulded in child and calf alike through everyday practice and relationships.

This point about cumulative experience is significant and can partly explain the variation we see across different cultures in the scale and quality of social trust in communities, or the proliferation of mistrust. Moreover, Turkana teaches us that trust formation in the public sphere is not separate from trust formation in the domestic sphere: they are deeply interdependent. Even at the personal level, trust develops from primordial affect and the quality of primary attachment. The early templates of our social relations and embodied experiences with others lay down unconscious memory traces – pre-linguistic traces which form links between primary affects, emotions and memories (Schore 1994). While recent breakthroughs in neuroscience, genetics and epigenetics show that biological mechanisms are at play in perceptions, those perceptions are equally shaped by past experiences mediated in the intersubjective space of language and culture. And so, in the succinct words of Siri Hustvedt: 'illusions and delusions enter the playground. The person who was neglected as a child will read the wandering eyes of the other differently from the one who was not' (2012: 207). The pioneering work of Margaret Mead comparing infant rearing and socialization practices across cultures supports the claim that whether the dominant sentiment of communities is that of trust or mistrust to a large degree hinges on the make up of the habitus in question and its psychosocial structures.

However, we are still left with the part of the puzzle about why intimacy and danger appear so deeply linked across societies and cultures, even among the otherwise trusting and egalitarian Turkana. Let us briefly turn to psychoanalysis and the inspiration it has reaped from cultural anthropology. For it is within such theorizing that we can get closer to the edge between danger and intimacy across which trust must somehow leap.

Let us consider for a start the insights Sigmund Freud (2003 [1919]) gleaned from the double semantic capacity carried by the German term *Heimlich* [homely], to also mean its negation, the *unheimlich* [uncanny]. The shades of meanings slide from the familiar, friendly, comfortable, intimate and tamed to the concealed, secret, unfamiliar, awkward, foreign, wild and unknown. Thus the twinned terms signify the development of signification in the direction of ambivalence, from that which was familiar and homely to that which has become unfamiliar, estranging. To cut the story short, those uncanny feelings stem from lingering infantile anxieties about loss, from which humans can never completely escape, resurfacing from the unconscious as discomfort and disorientation. The taboos of incest and death arise from uncanny effects, according to Freud, but at the heart of the drama is the move from the unmediated, intimate relationship between the infant and the maternal breast, which has to be broken at some point and replaced by a mediated, social relation with the world of words and with other subjects and objects.

Matching Freud with Mary Douglas's theory of natural symbols as 'matter out of place' and the pollution of things placed 'betwixt and between', Julie Kristeva has developed the concept of 'the uncanny' as the sense of 'abjection', the horror of not knowing the boundaries distinguishing 'me' from 'not-me'. This primary uncanny is generated by the fear and dread of being overwhelmed by the maternal intimacy of shared flesh. The abject can be conveyed by bodily substances such as tears, saliva, faeces, urine, vomit and mucus emitted from the mouth, eyes, anus, nose or genitals – all bodily openings constituting the corporeal interface between inside and outside, subject and object. As part of the necessary separation from the maternal body, the nascent subject must expel this 'matter out of place', but to purify oneself completely is impossible because these transitional substances remain the preconditions of a corporeal, material existence. The duality of the abject, as being both inside and outside, speaks to the precarious grasp the subject has over its identity and bodily boundaries. The abject finds expression in rituals of purification; these rituals, argues Kristeva (1982), lay the foundations for instituting social differentiation and social order.

From the 'thick' ethnography of Turkana presented above, shot through with visceral imagery of bodies and nested physiologies extending from the individual out to the limits of the cosmos itself, one would assume that the inherent danger of intimacy would be particularly critical and thus culturally elaborated. Whilst the containing maternal body of cosmos and landscape, and its maternal equivalent here on earth in wife and cow, are celebrated in a whole corpus of stories representing the normative auspicious, there is also a subversive genre of stories nested around *Napeysekina* [the one-breasted one], whose murderous acts dramatize for the Turkana the ever-present possibility of sliding back into the engulfing corporality out of which not only infants but their entire world was formed.

Since ideas about the divine *Akuij* and the monstrous *Napeysekina* are woven from the womb, which may produce the same (femaleness) but also difference (maleness), these figures are both androgynous, alternating between feminine and masculine modes. When *Napeysekina* is mobilized as male agency and armed to the teeth s/he signifies the red qualities, as for example when s/he in one evil act uproots people and banishes them with her violence, knives and acid tongue. In this story, the beneficial force of Akuij subdues her destructive force. When mobilized in the female mode, the typical scenario is of a mother living alone with her daughter. Often, as in one story in which a daughter is visited by some girls, a chain of events is set in motion which progressively reveals *Napeysekina* as a grotesque and terrifying destroyer of motherhood, trust and proper sociality. After a series of horrible events, these subversive stories always end with her wild body being blown to pieces, each part being transformed into other things – pools, plants, gourds, trees, animals and children – apparently benign but harbouring her polluting substances, with which unsuspecting humans who come after must contend. Most significantly, the *Napeysekina* corpus clearly depicts a wild landscape formed and animated by the destructive interior energies of an originary body, which has exploded and been everted. In several stories her wicked substance enters a black cow through grazing, which in turn carries the bad qualities inside the compound, where mistrust and fear continue germinating from its dung (Broch-Due 1990, 2004).

The cosmic Turkana physiology of nested bodies of different species and their supposedly benign, nurturing relations are repeatedly questioned in these stories and myths, reminding us that stories, imaginaries and rituals are deeply embedded in everyday experience and relationships, and reflective of their ambiguities. As part of social practice, symbols produce their own effects in the world and these too are often ambivalent, as in the case with our animal witch detected in the guts of a goat. While the safe distance between image and referent remains fixed in most situations and in most people's minds, so that a compelling story remains within its fictive universe, in times of heightened uncertainty the image and referent may move so dangerously close to one another that they collapse into chaos, affect and unpredictable behaviour. The present day marginalization of many Turkana produces precisely this heightened uncertainty. Clearly, as Mary Douglas remarked in *Purity and Danger*, 'margins are dangerous … [I]f they are pulled this way or that the shape of fundamental experience is altered. Any structure of ideas is vulnerable at its margins' (Douglas 1966: 122). Marginalization is reshaping Turkana sociality in ways that foreground the danger of intimacy. For people's hearts are 'blackened', many informants complained, making them more selfish and envious. In the process, it is as if many Turkana are losing trust in the capacity of cattle to rope them together in a world turned unpredictable. The black commoditized cow-turned-witch is the perfect expression of this new uncertain reality created by the reconfiguration of intimacy, trust and the social. It also highlights a universal point about the precariousness of trusting itself; for although trust is the glue of all intimacy and sociality, it is easily lost, and when lost it can only be rebuilt with difficulty.

References

Bourdieu, P. 1977. *Outline of a Theory of Practice*. Cambridge University Press.
Broch-Due, V. 1990. *The Bodies within the Body: Journeys in Turkana Thought and Practice'*. Doctoral dissertation. Bergen: University of Bergen.
—— 1993. 'Making Meaning Out of Matter: Perceptions of Sex, Gender and Bodies among the Turkana'. In V. Broch-Due, I. Rudie and T. Bleie (eds), *Carved Flesh/Cast Selves: Gendered Symbols and Social Practices*, 53–82. Oxford: Berg Press.
—— 1999. 'Remembered Cattle, Forgotten People: The Morality of Exchange and the Exclusion of the Turkana Poor'. In D. Anderson and V. Broch-Due (eds), *The Poor are Not Us: Poverty and Pastoralism in Eastern Africa*, 50–88. Oxford: James Currey.
—— 2000a. 'The Fertility of Houses and Herds: Producing Kinship and Gender among Turkana Pastoralists'. In D. Hodgson (ed.), *Rethinking Pastoralism: Gender, History and the Myth of the Patriarchal Pastoralist*, 165–185. Oxford: James Currey.
—— 2000b. 'A Proper Cultivation of Peoples: The Colonial Reconfiguration of Pastoral tribes and Places in Kenya'. In V. Broch-Due and R. Schroeder, (eds), *Producing Nature and Poverty in Africa*, 53–93. Uppsala: The Nordic Africa Institute Press.
—— 2004 [1999]. 'Creation and the Multiple Female Body: Turkana Perspectives on Gender and Cosmos'. In H. Moore, B. Kaare and T. Sanders (eds), *Those Who Play with Fire: Gender, Fertility and Transformation in East and Southern Africa*, 153–184. London: Athlone Press.
Dahl, G. 1987. 'The Realm of Pastoral Women: An Introduction', *Ethnos* 52: 5–7.
Damasio, A. 2010. *Self Comes to Mind: Constructing the Conscious Brain*. New York: Pantheon.
Deleuze, G. and F. Guattri. 1987. *A Thousand Plateaus*. Minneapolis: University of Minnesota Press.
Douglas, M. 1966. *Purity and Danger: An Analysis of the Concepts of Pollution and Taboo*. London: Routledge and Kegan Paul.
Frampton, S. 2011. *When I Am Playing with My Cat, How Do I Know That She Is Not Playing with Me?: Montaigne and Being in Touch with Life*. London: Faber and Faber.
Freud, S. [1919] 2003. 'Das Unheimliche', *Imago* 5(5–6): 297–324.
Gallese, V., L. Fadiga, L. Fogassi, and G. Rizzolatti. 1996. 'Action Recognition in the Premotor Cortex', *Brain* 119: 593–609.
Haaland, G. 1979. 'Beer, Blood and Mother's Milk: The Symbolic Context of Economic Behavior in Fur Society'. Bergen: DERAP working paper.
Hustvedt, S. 2012. *Living, Thinking, Looking*. London: Sceptre.
Kristeva, J. 1982. *Powers of Horror: An Essay on Abjection*. New York: Colombia University Press.
Panksepp, J. 1998. *Affective Neuroscience: The Foundations of Human and Animal Emotions*. Oxford: Oxford University Press
Sahlins, M. 1974. *Stone Age Economics*. London: Tavistock.

Schore, A. 1994. *Affect Regulation and the Origins of Self: The Neurobiology of Emotional Development*. Mahwah, NJ: Lawrence Erlbaum.

Stern, D.N. 1985. *The Interpersonal World of the Infant: A View from Psychoanalysis and Developmental Psychology*. New York: Basic Books.

Vigdis Broch-Due is Professor of Social Anthropology and International Poverty Studies, University of Bergen. She is currently employed as Scientific Director at Centre for Advanced Study (CAS), Oslo. Her academic career has taken her from teaching positions in anthropology at the Universities of Oslo and Washington (Seattle), to the Directorship of a Poverty and Prosperity Research programme at the Nordic Africa Institute, Uppsala, to senior research positions at the Universities of Cambridge, SOAS and Rutgers. Her books include the co-edited volumes, *Carved Flesh/Cast Selves: Gendered Symbols and Social Practices* (Oxford: Berg, 1993); *The Poor Are Not Us: Poverty and Pastoralism in Eastern Africa* (Oxford: James Currey, 1999); *Producing Nature and Poverty in Africa* (Uppsala: the Nordic Africa Institute Press, 2000); and *Violence and Belonging: The Quest for Identity in Postcolonial Africa* (Abingdon: Routledge, 2005). She has published articles on gender and embodiment, trauma, pastoral development, cultural models of the relations between animals and people and changing property relations.

 5

'SHARING SECRETS'
Gendered Landscapes of Trust and Intimacy in Kenya's Digital Financial Marketplace

Misha Mintz-Roth and Amrik Heyer

This chapter explores gendered articulations of trust in Kenya's digital financial marketplace. As we researched the recent expansion of mobile money services among the country's urban population, we were confronted with the question of why the adoption of new products and technologies such as Safaricom's M-Pesa differed across gendered lines and whether this reflected particular household patterns of communication and intimacy expressed in gendered terms.

Safaricom is Kenya's state-sponsored telecom company, and its mobile money platform, M-Pesa ('Pesa' being Swahili for money) has expanded rapidly in recent years. Patterns of mobile money usage have become significant in Kenyans' ability to sustain livelihoods in strenuous urban environments and maintain communications with and send financial support to family and friends in rural homes. In our study of these patterns it became clear that there were substantial gender differences in the ways these technologies were being used. Women more readily professed to using their phones and mobile money applications for communication and cash transfers: men were less enthusiastic about the technology and its life possibilities. Throughout our interviews, we noticed differences in how men and women described trust in the services and brands they used and in the ways in which they discussed money transfers to family, business colleagues or friends. Women often described a more intimate attachment to their phone and the people to whom they transferred money.

Whereas much has been written about the transactional efficiencies that drive the adoption and impacts of mobile money, little attention has been paid to the role of trust in these dynamics. Our focus on the relationship between gender and trust has highlighted for us the ways in which mobile money is enabling new economic and political possibilities for particular subgroups of Kenya's urban populations.

Few scholars have accounted for the kinds of trust and social networks that build themselves from empathy or compassion, with many, instead, focusing on trust within a contractual framework of obligation (Barber 1983; Giddens 1986, 1990). By adhering to a moral order, they argue, people participate in social processes, unspoken agreements or institutions that preserve fields of justice and fairness. Ethnographers have employed this logic of trust and obligation in examining the fields of reciprocity and exchange in sub-Saharan Africa. Parker Shipton, for example, in his work with the Luo in Western Kenya, describes a system of 'entrustment' between households in the exchange of livestock, labour and land. Relationships of trust and obligation between male agnates are subject to close negotiation, alternately hidden and displayed, and emerge from repeated transactions over multiple generations. As Shipton writes, 'the entrustment and obligations surrounding farmland pertain not just to individuals but also to families and the lineages that grow out of [certain long-term arrangements]' (Shipton 1995: 173). Trust, in this circumstance, surfaces as a *product* of transactions rather than a precondition for exchange; it must be continually and perilously (re)produced, due its contestability and central role in organizing social relations.

In the context of mobile money, the rapid growth of new technologies and services is partly driven by contractual arrangements. But it is also driven by articulations of trust that diverge from what has been considered in such studies. In our discussions with urban Kenyans, perspectives on trust ranged from obligations and contracts to more feminized expressions of responsibility and care. We found the two discourses about trust at times overlapping and intersecting, but also undermining each other and repositioning authority within the household often from men towards women. Many of the early adopters of Kenya's M-Pesa were male urban labour migrants, and Safaricom advertised the product accordingly, with appeals to the masculine sentiment of obligation and duty. Men could find in M-Pesa a new way to remit money from the city to the country, where wives and children managed household assets such as land and livestock. For male migrants using the service, M-Pesa supported their investments in rural land and assets organized around patrilines under the guardianship of rural wives. However, as M-Pesa infiltrated and created new financial markets and urban networks, it gave rise to another kind of trust and commitment, articulated through women and children's networks of accumulation and assistance. Mothers, in particular, seemed to occupy a central focus in family communication and financial transfers 'back home'. The privacy which M-Pesa enabled allowed children to send money to their mothers independently of their fathers, thereby strengthening the maternal bond, motivated by an ethic of care rather than obligation. Mothers demonstrated power and authority to make claims on their children, drawing on emotional bonds and their children's economic opportunities.

While the study of these matrifocal relations remains on the margins of studies about reciprocity and exchange, it prevails in the discourse of feminist theorists and psychologists. Annette Baier offers a description of 'moral prejudices' among women that emphasizes maternal forms of care over contractual arrangements. Building on Carol Gilligan's classical study of female moral development, Baier urges scholars to consider the 'ethics of care' as a building block for trust among men and women in reference to their guardians and parents. Trust, in this regard, is cultivated and nurtured 'slowly and imperceptibly' over an extended period of time (Baier 1995: 105). It emerges from compassion and empathy rather than from a contract or material obligation. Owen Flanagan and Kathryn Jackson, in addition, argue that women develop long-term trust with each other based on previous signs of commitment and care, dependent on 'interconnections among parties involved, on their particular personalities, and on their weal and woe' (Flanagan and Jackson 1987). When we asked our urban female interviewees about their financial networks, we found that many were indeed connected to long-term intimates, including sisters, friends and mothers – those who, as one respondent said, they can 'share their secrets with'. Women alternated between the roles of giver and receiver, increasingly taking on a leadership role among family and friends, and strengthening their own economic and social relations. So while the spread of M-Pesa in Kenya may underscore the growth of remittance networks to 'send money home', as the M-Pesa slogan would suggest, it also supports the extensive lateral relations that women utilize to make opportunities for themselves, in defiance of 'traditional' patriarchal institutions.

Our study falls against the backdrop of a rapidly changing economy for financial services available through Kenyans' mobile phones. The exponential growth of Safaricom, and its mobile money platform, M-Pesa, has led a number of policy holders and private-sector stakeholders to invest in mobile money platforms and related products. (A number of Kenyan vendors, for example, now accept M-Pesa transfers as payments in commercial settings.) But it has also led Safaricom revise its assumptions about intimacy and trust as a factor in delivering its financial products. Questions have emerged regarding people's willingness to pay fees to 'abstract' corporations associated with the state and/or foreign capital. Especially in the aftermath of Safaricom's initial public offering, which coincided with the financial market crisis of 2008 and Kenya's 2007/2008 political crisis, consumers' trust in financial services has been shown to fluctuate along with their confidence in the state. Products, not to mention state guarantees, traditionally considered safe or trustworthy, have now been called into question. Against this backdrop, the easy integration of M-Pesa into people's everyday lives should not be assumed.

Methodologically, we collected data from a series of interviews and focus groups in Nairobi and Mombasa as well as from urban and rural areas in central Kenya. In some cases we interviewed and observed individuals over a period of months, accompanying them to their work, home and church. Our set of questions concerned peoples' lives and professions and their weekly usage of phones and mobile money products. We sought to know on whom they relied for money in time of need and how mobile money services impacted on their networks of financial support. Our informants revealed that their routines were quickly changing in light of digital media and the ability to stay in contact with family and friends. In addition, questions regarding why people chose to stick with, or switch from, certain brands and their products opened another outlet of debate. What follows is a discussion about the ways in which ethnographers might reconceptualize forms of trust and its uses in everyday contexts among women as well as men. In Kenya's digital media marketplace, we find there to be far more sentiment behind the building and sustaining of trust than mere contracts or abstract systems and institutions, which have long dominated the field's discourse (see Barber 1983 and Giddens 1990). We find instead a trust based on care and emotion, gendered in its expression and nurtured over time.

'N'iko na Safaricom': **Kenya's Digital Community**

Safaricom launched its M-Pesa service in 2007. It recruited three hundred of its existing airtime agents to register new customers and perform e-money cash-in and cash-out transactions and payment transfers. By offering cash deposit and withdrawal services, agents earned fees, and were, in essence, intermediaries between Kenya's cash market and Safaricom's electronic currency, a position that brought new economic status and customers for a miscellany of merchandise they might sell. Contrary to popular perception, M-Pesa agents are not Safaricom employees, and must apply for a license to enter the market. As independent business persons they re-sell pre-purchased Safaricom e-money, which Safaricom backs up by a pool of assets. They also keep an activity log on top of transaction records that Safaricom monitors. Many own shops or stores beside bus stages and markets. They cultivate relationships with customers, and keep a highly visible lime-green Safaricom sign to designate their agent status.

In looking back at Safaricom's advertisements and marketing strategies, one can discern the company's need to build trust among customers, harnessing the message of obligation and contract to cultivate a 'community' of subscribers among a group of people for whom the concept of e-money was otherwise a risky proposition. Through the use of radio, billboard and print advertisement schemes, Safaricom rallied citizens around the slogan 'send money home', a catchphrase that closely mirrored the rhetoric of Kenya's first president, Jomo Kenyatta, and made the acts of account registration such as producing national ID less suspicious and burdensome. It supplied a vision of Kenya as a nation of migrants and remitters, and simultaneously proclaimed itself as integral in this project of household- and nation-building. Once M-Pesa users 'top up' their accounts, they can send or receive money instantly and receive a text message to confirm a money transfer or receipt. To some, the e-money system will always be a point of suspicion. Power outages cause delays, long lines for M-Pesa agents are often difficult to avoid, and Safaricom's fee structures, as we were told repeatedly, are too high for many people of modest means. But Safaricom has made repeated attempts to campaign on the ground in local communities to protect its image. Projects, funded by its charity arm, the Safaricom Foundation, support company rhetoric and images of goodwill and assure Kenyans that Safaricom, a state-sponsored enterprise, exists for the benefit of citizens. Under its previous CEO Michael Joseph, the foundation administered a plethora of grants to build schools and initiate programs focusing on livestock management, water treatment, schools and so forth. It routinely sponsored charity projects with the Kenya Red Cross Society, an organization with uniquely popular appeal among Kenyans. In 2008, for example, after the country's election crisis, which left several hundreds of thousands of people displaced, the company donated KSHs 15 million towards emergency relief and utilized an M-Pesa account to collect donations (Vodafone Group 2008).

It is something of an irony that Safaricom succeeded in using the image and sentiment of nationhood to appeal to consumers in a country that is otherwise fractured by political corruption and ethnic violence. However, from our discussions and observations, it is clear that Safaricom's 'imagined community' of mobile communicators and remitters has achieved a widespread salience. During the time of our fieldwork, Safaricom released a new television commercial campaign under the banner *Niko na Safaricom* ('I'm with Safaricom'). The commercial had an all-black choir, composed of young men and women wearing tunics with the colours of the Kenyan flag, singing atop natural landmarks such as Mount Kenya and Ololokwe's summit. Filmed in seven of Kenya's eight provinces, the commercial captured Kenya's cultural and geographical diversity within a montage of close-ups and aerial shots. The lyrics, according to the commercial's composer Gabriel Omondi, were 'about Kenya and Safaricom being the same thing' (Safaricom Kenya 2010).

> Nafurahia undugu na ukoo wetu
> Nasherekea kazi na bidii yetu
> Tuvute pamoja tushirikiane
> Bega kwa bega tujikaze tusaidiane
> ...
> Niko na uwezo
> Niko na Safaricom
> [I delight in our brotherhood and bond
> I celebrate our work and effort
> Let's pull together to unite
> Shoulder to shoulder we strive to help each other
> ...
> I have the power
> I am with Safaricom]

The song's success helped to cement the notion that the advent of mobile phones has been a major positive development for Kenyans and that Safaricom has been integral in the process of developing the country's digital communications capacity. It is not uncommon to hear young children singing the song outside schools or churches. One informant in Nairobi jokingly called it Kenya's 'unofficial national anthem', while another admitted that he set the song as his ring tone because it made him feel 'patriotic'. Safaricom has thus achieved its status of being representative of the country's collective potential, while maintaining the perception that it is separate from the corruption and discontent that most Kenyans associate with the political and business class. Kenya's 'telecom revolution', according to one young man, is proof that the government cares about the 'small people'. Safaricom has successfully capitalized on (if not crafted) this sentiment on a wide scale. Today, there are over forty thousand M-Pesa agents working in Kenya (one in every thousand Kenyans) and nearly fifteen million operational M-Pesa accounts (Central Bank of Kenya & FSD Kenya, 2013).

Contracting with Safaricom

Throughout our discussions, we found that not all Kenyans concede their faith in Safaricom and its products. Safaricom is a 'necessary evil', one woman explained, as she spoke about its ability to maintain a monopoly despite the emergence of competitors including India's Airtel and France's Orange. 'It is not "the best option", she said in mocking one of its ubiquitous slogans. It is the *only* option'. Many today are quick to cite the Safaricom initial public offering (IPO) of stock in 2008 as an example of the company's profiteering at the expense of its customers. As one man told us, Safaricom is managed by 'liars', and is just another government effort to 'disempower the people'. At the time of the stock offering, many Kenyans purchased shares with exuberance only to see the stock price quickly slide. Jabir from Mombasa explained to us that his family was very soured by their decision to purchase Safaricom shares once they came to understand the stock's marginal payoffs and volatility – something evidently not explained to them at the time of the offering. 'We always hear about the company making millions, but we only get a dividend cheque for 100 shillings' (one dollar).

Even from those who appreciate Safaricom's benefit to Kenya, the company is met with a mixed reception. Few of the people we interviewed, for example, found Safaricom able to transcend Kenya's troubled political landscape. Amid the ethnic tensions that roil the country, Safaricom has fallen subject to accusations that it is owned and managed by politically powerful Kikuyu families. Jabir himself worked as an M-Pesa agent in Kenyan coastal towns and said that he was turned off by the ethnic favouritism in the company. He told us of the time he was deprived of an M-Pesa agent license in Lamu, a coastal town sixty kilometres south of the Somali border. He was denied this license, according to him, because he would outcompete other agents in Lamu who were from Kenya's politically dominant ethnic group.

> I have had a hard time getting registered, because I am not Kikuyu. They [Safaricom's employees] won't allow me. To them, they know I will be competition because I know everyone [in Lamu]. They know people trust me ... They know I would do it better.

Jabir's disenchantment with Safaricom found an echo among many young men we spoke to trying to earn wages or maximize short- and long-term economic opportunities in urban environments. Their overall feeling may be best summed up by the comment made by a young newspaper vendor, in Nairobi's Mathare slum, named Taitas who admitted that 'Safaricom is a pace setter', but also felt disempowered and distrustful of the country's corporate capitalist sectors. 'Whoever is head of Safaricom must be a very clever man. You can't blame someone for their creativity, even if they swindle you'.

Over the course of our interviews, by far the majority of complaints against Safaricom and its 'swindling', 'fleecing' and 'cheating' arose from men, and echoed their own discontent with a political economy where, to use one man's words, 'one must cheat to get ahead'. Discussions evolved into debates about company employees and profits, safety and security, and the changing nature of Kenyans' finances, marriages and families. The relations that one undergirded Kenya's patriarchal institutions, in other words, were slowly eroding. Many were ambivalent, if not scornful of M-Pesa, asserting that they used M-Pesa only when they had to. They cited certain material conveniences, especially in terms of street-vending businesses, where people could top up each other's M-Pesa accounts instead of having to carry cash around. This was a safety benefit for young men who roamed Nairobi 'hawking' second-hand clothing or selling streetside charcoal. But there were many ramifications of using M-Pesa that were detrimental to their lives and, by their estimate, to Kenya. Many expressed an outward distrust of the company and the corporate world, which was 'full of liars [and] cheaters'. Some like Matua, a shoe shiner, also from Mathare, worried about the company's integrity, given its size and profit base. 'I knew someone who sent money to the wrong number', he said, 'and never could get it back'. Safaricom employees, he said, could not be concerned with his satisfaction or cares as a customer. 'They are too distant and unfamiliar with me – why would they care?' The company, however, knew information about Matua, and this made him nervous. He reasoned that Safaricom employees were the ones sending around fraudulent SMS messages requesting that he and others transfer money to some unknown account. The system, to him, was neither fool-proof nor capable of ever being so.

Other forms of discontent emerged around changes in everyday life. Men expressed a cynicism toward mobile phones that bore similarity to a general host of urban grievances. Phone theft, to take one example, was the most common negative effect. 'Don't you know?' Taitas joked. 'The thieves really own our phones'. In contradiction to the stated benefit of not carrying cash, numerous men cited crime as a reason why they did not top up their M-Pesa accounts with more money. (This was a fear almost never mentioned by women.) While Safaricom provides many anti-theft measures to guard against strangers accessing M-Pesa, multiple men said they felt unsafe about thieves 'hacking' into their phones or 'car-jacking them and asking for your secret PIN'. Phones were not immune to fundamental urban insecurities.

But by the far the most resounding message harkened back to the dwindling dominance of men's status within households that were transforming socially and economically. Among our informants, men most often complained that they were continually the ones sending money to their friends, wives, children and relatives, never receiving money in return. As Taitas explained, 'the last time I received money it was only 50 shillings, and it was sent to me accidentally'. Via its campaign messages, and its early adopter segments, M-Pesa strengthened relationships with rural homes as sites for the investment of (urban) capital. Through its first campaign slogan, 'send money home', M-Pesa captured a ready market for the service in the form of male urban labour migrants who regularly send money to their rural wives. But the popularity of and possibilities stemming from mobile money transfers have set in place new expectations among men to travel to cities and earn money and accumulate rural assets. Among low-income households, in particular, with members lacking advanced education or job skills, mobile money provides a feeling of unmet responsibility, not just opportunity. 'All African men', said Felix, a clothes salesman from Nairobi, 'believe that wealth comes from the soil'. There is a tremendous amount of pressure for men to buy and use land to produce food for their family, he explained. 'Today, African men feel the weight of their entire family on their shoulders. It is leading to the point that men must wait until they are very old until they can find a wife. Once they are thirty-five, if they haven't made enough money and found a wife, most people will give up on them'.

As contestable as this assertion might be, they speak to the way that in which M-Pesa, by virtue of its digital technology and ability to collapse travel time and distance, has changed the nature of men's household authorities. Men no longer have to physically visit their rural homes to bring back capital. They can much more easily and cheaply send money at the touch of a button, which, in turn, cuts them off from regular visits to rural homes and undermines the marital bonds on which their strategies of accumulation and investment have rested. Migration and movement, combined with the possibility of sending money instantaneously and privately, has lessened people's dependence on land controlled within the patriline. Mothers, in particular, are now able to make claims on their children (and husbands) working afar, and women themselves are more able to depart from their husbands or fathers and demand access to financial support via products such as M-Pesa. In this respect, M-Pesa has made visible a tension in local household networks expressed through an underlying dynamic of matrifocality, or relations of solidarity that revolve around children's emotional ties with and economic support for their mothers.

'Mamas Need Some Help...': The Gender of Trust

New digital networks emerging among women, mothers and children help locate the tensions in Kenyan households and underscore the changing dynamics of patrilineal institutions and the growing significance of local networks of trust and support. We encountered numerous cases among urban women that revealed how they were integrating mobile financial service products into pre-existing spheres of relations. Networks were often formed from lateral relations with other friends and kin, sustained through contact and digital money transfers. Trust formation, we found, was based on a different sentiment from the contracts or obligations that characterized patrifocal relations. Instead, women described their mobile money activities and affinities toward each other in the language of care and responsibility. The sentiment began with the mobile device itself—with the ability to have a device that allowed them to communicate frequently with confidantes, siblings and cousins. Whereas men saw it as a symbol of alienation and insecurity, women spoke about selecting ring tones; whereas men spoke anxiously about the changing social landscape brought on by M-Pesa, women spoke about Safaricom's new products and life possibilities.

Ring tones were discussed by women as a mode of self-expression. 'Ring tones say who you are. They express you', Florence, whom we met in Nairobi's Kawangware, explained. Many women chose particular songs that revealed their favourite artist or eclectic tastes. One woman chose a popular love song called 'Mapenzi', while another explained that she preferred Bollywood music, a popular genre in Kenya thanks to the country's history of Indian immigration. Women saw their phone as an extension of their own personality, a signature touch. Linda, who hailed from the Kibera in Nairobi, chose a cock crow as her ring tone because it signified her humour and rural upbringing. Joyce, a visiting pastor from Embu, seventy-five miles north of Nairobi, liked to use the song 'Daddy Was a Preacherman' as her ring tone because it reflected her real life story. When asked why men did not identify with their phones the same way, women posited that it was because men needed to 'act professional'. As Florence joked, 'they need to appear serious in public'. If a man had a ringtone, it was an act of self-emasculation, as he would be perceived as weak. 'Men who do have ring tones are always thinking about love', Florence added.

These seemingly superficial differences between men and women mask a more profound process taking place within and across urban and rural households along gendered lines. Increasingly, the reality is that women (as wives and single mothers) have built up their own sources of survival and accumulation through which they run their households independently of men. Women's relationships to households are particularly significant where men's sources of capital are constrained. In these contexts, cross-generational transfers to rural homes via M-Pesa are geared not only to supporting fathers' control over property, but also mothers' capacities to nurture and safeguard an increasingly scarce asset base. Many women defend their roles as responsible household managers, establishing their commitment to the household and their children's needs as a gender-specific trait. Their descriptions reinforce a belief that the home orients itself around matrifocal relations. While men hold wealth in land ownership, women develop long-term bonds with children, who function as the mother's wealth, becoming, in essence, future income-generating assets. According to Michael, a young man in Kibera, 'it is wiser to send money to women [mothers], if it is to be shared appropriately within the household. Men will take a big cut for themselves or spend it'. Similarly, Fred, a security guard in Nairobi, professed that you send money to your mother because 'she is the one who knows everything'.

We found that some of the most severe comments laid against fathers and husbands were in discussions surrounding men's alleged tendency to diffuse wealth away from the household and toward other people and activities. According to Nancy, 'if you empower the mother, you empower the father. But if you send [money] to the father, then men eat and drink the money so the family can't have it'. Doris, an elderly lady whom we met in Nairobi's Kawangware, complained that her husband had previously taken money that she sent him and offered it to his nephew. Many women bitterly described men's diffusion of wealth through extra-marital relationships. And when husbands or fathers die, rather than sustaining their bereaved wives and children, their wealth is claimed by voracious in-laws. Through matrifocal households, which have long co-existed with men's lineal networks of obligation and expansion (Heyer 2004), women's wealth is contained, geared to safeguarding the assets of their children, as opposed to being mobilized through a diffuse set of polygamous and patrilineal obligations to expand an (increasingly tenuous) asset base.

In our conversations, we found that transfers to mothers were described emotively, evoking a very different dimension of trust from the 'entrustments' and 'obligations' that characterized lineal and formal contracts. In contrast to money sent to fathers, which carried a sense of 'obligation', women said they sent money to their mothers 'because it is our wish'. 'Mamas need some help', said Florence. Damares told us that she does not give or borrow from her father in the same way as she does with her mother. She does not have that rapport with him, but her mother, she trusts. 'Children send money to their mother to show how much they appreciate her', said Doris. Linda described how 'girls are close to their families', and talked about how much she 'loved' her mother. Money sent to mothers carried a sense of responsibility and recognition of the nurturing role they play, as well as a sense of deep emotion and care. The maternal trope is evoked to describe significant sources of support.

The matrifocal ties which inspire gifts and exchanges outside the patriline have diffused outward to strengthen female networks more generally. Female circumvention of male authority is also evident through the niche groups that women have created with each other. Christine, a self-employed woman from Nairobi, mentioned that she cultivated a stronger relationship with her sister in Mombasa because they can speak to each other. 'In the past I didn't have much contact with her. But now, because of M-Pesa, she is always contacting me to ask for money'. She added, 'I now have a business on the side, which I run with my neighbour. It is very easy because she and I can send each other money by M-Pesa any time of the day or night'. We encountered numerous cases among women that revealed how they were integrating mobile financial service products into their networks of business, family and friends. These networks were often formed from lateral relations with other friends and kin, and sustained through phone contact and digital money transfers.

Unlike relationships with parents and grandparents, which carry a strong history of emotional and social obligation, relationships with friends and even siblings can be either close or distant. In this looser context, entrustments and obligations rest on a history of emotional ties cultivated through time – with a childhood friend or a sister in trouble. Transfers accentuate affective bonds and create positive cycles of interdependency. And while we found these more characteristic of women's relationships, they were also very significant for younger men. 'Not many people can easily help you', a youth explained. 'If you do not have a job you cannot easily be helped' (quoted in Johnson 2014: 10) For young men in particular, negotiating uncertain futures with few assets at their disposal, cultivating 'real' friendships through exchange relations from their wide networks of connections enables them to gain leverage on the few opportunities available. Through borrowing and lending, a friend becomes a 'real' friend; a brother or sister can also transform to a 'real' sibling (Johnson 2014).

> I realized that he is a friend because if someone gives you money without repaying with interest he is good. He is a real friend ... You know in this world you cannot survive without friends and not everybody can be your friend and you can't be good to everybody and the one whom you can understand is the one who can be your friend, even if he is in Europe and he is your friend he can help you. You can have brothers but they cannot help you. (Quoted in Johnson 2014: 10–11)

Mobile money has keyed itself into and stimulated the context of changing political and economic relationships. As a new medium of exchange, it is enabling people to cultivate different kinds of relationships: ones which strengthen lateral ties (between siblings and friends), as well as relationships with their natal homes that are orchestrated through mothers as well as fathers. In the context of lateral and matrifocal relationships, M-Pesa articulates a form of trust which is based not so much on the externally sanctioned contracts and obligations that characterize formal banking or customary exchange within patrilines. Rather, these transactions are based on a discourse of emotive ties, care and responsibility.

Over the course of fieldwork, we came to know Mildred, a woman of thirty from Western Kenya, whose personal and family story seemed emblematic of the greater trends we were uncovering. Mildred was one of seven siblings living in Busia, a small town near the Ugandan border, and, having lost the right to what was once her family's plot of land, was accustomed to relying on household members to get by. No longer relying on her father, who left the family after eloping with another woman, she and her mother and sisters formed a new set of bonds that seemed to replace the solidarity that the land-owning patriarchal institution once guaranteed. They found ways to support each other when they could, and relied on the help of 'aunties' in the interim. At the time that her father left, as Mildred explained, her eldest sister had just married and 'dipped' into her in-law's incomes and wealth to provide for the rest of them.

There was not much of a possibility for Mildred to sustain a livelihood by staying in Busia. The family did not have claim to land, nor would they survive on their rural incomes alone. Her mother worked as 'a fishmonger' in a nearby market and was herself reliant on female colleagues. Mildred described her mother as a 'business lady', a legacy that Mildred says she has inherited. After working in temporary jobs in Busia, Mildred decided to move to Nairobi out of a desire for 'greener pastures' and the ability to provide for her sisters and mother. Since arriving in Nairobi, she had attended a business program and found a job at the National Bank of Kenya to sign up and manage low-income client accounts. She earned KSH 13,000 (USD 130) per month, plus commissions, a far more enviable salary than many of the women she grew up with.

Mildred stepped in as the main provider for her mother and four sisters. She was in communication with her two brothers, but explained that they too had drifted from the family. Since each family member could afford a mobile phone and airtime, Mildred spoke to her mother at least three times a week, to make sure that she had enough to eat and had paid her debts to friends and colleagues. 'I want to help her out if she is in a fix', Mildred said. When asked if she would do the same thing for her father, Mildred said that she stopped sending money to him a while ago. 'Whatever I send to him is not enough', she said. Like many other sons and daughters we spoke to, Mildred mentioned that her sentiment for her mother defied the terms of a contract: 'Mother brings us up; she mentors us'. Recalling the hardship her mother had suffered, including her HIV diagnosis, Mildred described her as wanting to help Mildred and her sisters whenever she could. 'No matter what we passed through, she was there for us'.

Mildred's responsibilities had driven her to form various lateral relations with her siblings and office colleagues. She had taken it upon herself to pay for her younger sisters' education, with one sister living with Mildred in her single room. Her sisters had become Mildred's life force. She was proud that 'at home if there is a problem I am the one they now call'. She said that she felt the need to stay and work in Nairobi even though she missed being around family. To overcome financial hardships, Mildred had integrated herself into a network of colleagues at her office who let her borrow money interest-free until her next pay cheque. She explained to them her support for her mother and sisters and found help. 'They know what I am going through', she said, feeling assured that they would keep the connection even if she left the bank.

Today, because of the digital money revolution and its conveniences, someone like Mildred is able navigate her world through a separate gendered sphere of relations. Moving from rural to city economies, connected by mobile communications and money transfers, women have located new networks of support based on care and responsibility. Mildred's economic investment in her family is not a calculation, but a moral obligation. She is responsible for supporting the network that supported her. 'If I fail', Mildred said, 'I fail them all'.

Conclusion

Discourses on trust in political philosophy and sociology focus on the question of contracts, justice and the preservation of civic society. In anthropological literature, scholars have investigated systems and institutions of reciprocity to explain the process by which trust is sustained through values and gifts. However, a literature is yet to emerge that explores the gendered dimensions of trust. We have used field data from Kenya and its market for digital financial services to make points and pose questions about gendered forms of trust and the social networks it sustains. Even as scholars question trust as factor in the spread of financial services, we contend that there are many dimensions to trust, and these must be picked out and explored.

In order to gain trust among its potential consumer base, Safaricom built brand recognition by supplying an image of male remitters and a unified nation. But as some of our findings suggest, these men are not Safaricom's most loyal clients, even if they represent (by a slight margin) the majority of its registered users. For these sentiments do not mark the day-to-day experience of M-Pesa users. A considerable number of female customers have adopted M-Pesa and used it to forge their own economic road ahead. In this sense, women's relationships of trust emerge alongside the contracts enshrined in patrilineal institutions, and even come to challenge the latter's very foundation.

Against this backdrop, it is understandable why scholars associate mobile money with the possibility of empowering women. Women's ability to communicate in secrecy and instantaneously would seem to undo masculine hierarchies, and make women capable of circumventing male structures of trust and authority. For this reason developmentalists have advocated for neoliberal interventions in the transition toward a more egalitarian future. The Consultative Group to Assist the Poor (CGAP) reported in 2009 that mobile phone technology in Kenya grants women new 'autonomy' and 'bargaining power' (Morawczynski and Pickens 2009; Jack and Suri 2014). Opportunity International found that newly introduced financial services such as M-Pesa can prove 'crucial to the success of women' (Opportunity International 2011). This may well be true. But we would posit that women's authorities do not emerge from the new technology alone, and that this discourse forgoes a more in-depth study of women's relations with each other and the possibility that these relations existed before the advent of a certain technology. Such 'novelty' narratives presuppose women's past static subordination, a postulate, we believe to be mistaken, not only in its tendency to misconstrue the nature of women's roles in the household and society, but it also for misreading the very nature of the networks undergirding women's growing economic opportunities today. Mobile phone technology has not produced a new sphere of relations from scratch. It has keyed itself into pre-existing social geographies of trust and intimacy. These relations and networks, as this study argues, fall along gendered lines, and are conceived in different language and sentiment from what was previously imagined.

References

Baier, A. 1995. *Moral Prejudices: Essays on Ethics*. Cambridge: Harvard University Press.

Barber, B. 1983. *The Logic and Limits of Trust*. New Brunswick: Rutgers University Press.

Bohannan, P. 1957. *Justice and Judgment among the Tiv*. Oxford: Oxford University Press.

Central Bank of Kenya and FSD Kenya. 2013. 'FinAccess National Survey 2013: Profiling Developments in the Financial Access and Usage Landscape in Kenya'. Kenyacic.org [online]. Available at http://www.kenyacic.org/sites/default/files/13-10-31_FinAccess_2013_Report.pdf (accessed 19 October 2015).

Flanagan, O. and K. Jackson. 1987. 'Justice, Care, and Gender: The Kohlberg–Gilligan Debate Revisited', *Ethics* 97(3): 622–637.

Giddens, A. 1986. *The Constitution of Society: Outline of the Theory of Structuration*. Berkeley: University of California Press.

—— 1990. *The Consequences of Modernity*. Stanford: Stanford University Press.

Gilligan, C. 1982. *In a Different Voice: Psychological Theory and Women's Development*. Cambridge: Harvard University Press.

Heyer, A. 2004. '"Nowadays They Can Even Kill You for That which They Feel Is Theirs": Gender and the Production of Ethnic Identity in Kikuyu-speaking Central Kenya'. In V. Broch-Due (ed.), *Violence and Belonging: The Quest for Identity in Post-Colonial Africa*, 41–59. London: Routledge,

Jack, W. and T. Suri (2014), 'Risk Sharing and Transactions Costs: Evidence from Kenya's
Mobile Money Revolution', *American Economic Review* 104(1): 183–223.

Johnson, S. 2014. 'Informal Financial Practices and Social Networks: Transaction Genealogies'. FSDKenya.org [online]. Available at http://fsdkenya.org/wp-content/uploads/2015/08/14-04-11_Informal_financial_practicessocial_networks.pdf> (accessed 19 October 2015).

Mauss, M. 1967. *The Gift: The Form and Reason for Exchange in Archaic Societies*. New York: W. W. Norton & Company.
Morawczynski, O. and M. Pickens. 2009. 'Poor People Using Mobile Financial Services: Observations on Customer Usage and Impact from M-Pesa', *CGAP.org* [online]. Available at <http://www.cgap.org/sites/default/files/CGAP-Brief-Poor-People-Using-Mobile-Financial-Services-Observations-on-Customer-Usage-and-Impact-from-M-PESA-Aug-2009.pdf> (accessed 5 November 2012).
Opportunity International. 2011. 'Banking on Women with Access to Microsavings', *Opportunity.org* [online]. Available at <http://www.opportunity.org/blog/banking-on-women-with-access-to-microsavings/#.Ukggm2CeD0A> (accessed 29 September 2013).
Shipton, P. 1995. 'Luo Entrustment: Foreign Finance and the Soil of the Spirits in Kenya', *Africa* 65(02): 165–196.
—— 2007. *The Nature of Entrustment: Intimacy, Exchange, and the Sacred in Africa*. New Haven: Yale University Press.
Safaricom Kenya. 2010. *The Making of Niko na Safaricom* [video]. Available at <http://www.youtube.com/watch?v=I-lVhWfRCiQ> (accessed 29 September 2013).
Vodafone Group. 2008. 'Safaricom Limited, with the Support of the Safaricom Foundation and the Vodafone Group Foundation, Together Donate KSHs 15,000,000 towards Humanitarian Relief', *CRS News*, 10 January. Available at <http://www.csrwire.com/press_releases/16966-Safaricom-Limited-with-the-support-of-the-Safaricom-Foundation-and-The-Vodafone-Group-Foundation-together-donate-KShs-15-000-000-towards-humanitarian-relief> (accessed 10 October 2015).

Misha Mintz-Roth is a PhD candidate in history at Johns Hopkins University, where he researches Indian Ocean migration and urban culture in Eastern Africa during the nineteenth and twentieth centuries. In 2012 he worked as a consultant for the Financial Sector Deepening (FSD) Trust of Kenya, conducting field research on mobile money and banking services in Kenya.

Amrik Heyer directs research on financial inclusion at Financial Sector Deepening (FSD), Kenya. An anthropologist by training, she is now involved in applied research to support the development of inclusive markets. Her PhD was on gender, economic development and the state in Central Kenya.

 6

EDDIES OF DISTRUST
'False' Birth Certificates and the Destabilization of Relationships
Jennifer M. Speirs

In this chapter I explore aspects of trust in the context of social relationships in the field of anonymous donor insemination (DI) primarily as it has been practised in the UK. I use the concept of trust as one way of shedding some light on difficulties that have emerged in relationships both within the family built using DI and between other stakeholders who have a personal or professional involvement. I am interested in what happens to trust over time, when it may be transformed into or suddenly replaced by distrust, as well as what may be the impact of the passage of time on relationships originally constituted in or characterized by trust. The chapter focuses particularly on the substitution of trust in people with trust in documents, in this case the birth certificates of donor-conceived people. I base my exploration on Mellahi and Wood's definition of trust as 'an expression of confidence that one will not be harmed or put at risk by the actions of another party' (Mallahi and Wood 2003: 370), using it to frame how secrecy and anonymity in DI has created tension unintentionally in relationships traditionally considered to be trustworthy.

My ethnographic data is based on discussions and unstructured interviews with medical practitioners, other health professionals and social workers, currently or formerly working in clinics providing DI services in the UK; with men who donated semen between the 1960s and early 1980s, mostly when they were medical students; and with donor-conceived people and their parents. This is anthropology at home and the field is therefore one in which I share tacit understandings of trust with my informants and have had my own experiences of trust and distrust as an enquirer into an area of controversial sociality.

Introduction

Donor insemination became subject to regulation in the UK by the Human Fertilisation and Embryology Act 1990, which provided for any child born as a result of DI to which both a woman and her husband had consented to be treated as their legitimate child, and also for the identity of gamete donors to be kept from the children and their parents. There had been profound public disagreements about whether to legislate against anonymity and these continued after the legislation came into force. They also continued after regulations were introduced in 2005 which allowed donor-conceived people to access identifying information, although not retrospectively, about their donor(s) (Department of Health 2004). The arguments focused on whether it is necessary to protect donors from potential emotional and financial claims from their donor offspring; whether donor-conceived people have the right to such information; and on perceptions about what constitutes a parent, particularly a father. The use of donated human semen in the UK had been developed by medical practitioners from the late 1930s as a means of circumventing male infertility and helping childless women to achieve a pregnancy. Prior to regulation, practitioners insisted on anonymity of the donors because of the uncertainty about the legal status of donor-conceived children and their moral concerns about the possible effects on the marital relationship of the recipients if the husband was not treated as the 'real' father. The birth certificates of these children recorded the mother's husband as the father of the child, not the donor. In effect, this entailed an illegal act by the person registering the birth.

However, since 1990 donor-conceived people in the UK and a number of other countries have become increasingly vocal and active in demanding not only that they should be informed of their conception status but also that they should have access to identifying information about their gamete donors. Their claims were made explicit in 2008 at a meeting in Toronto, Canada, where representatives from a number of organizations working to educate and support donor-conceived people, prospective parents, parents of donor-conceived people, and egg and semen donors came together to form the International Network of Donor Conception Organisations (INDCO). The organizations were based in the US, UK, New Zealand, France and Australia, and also included an international organization called The International Donor Offspring Alliance.

The INDCO issued the following list of objectives:

1. End donor anonymity.
2. Track all recipients, donors and births and safeguard all records in a central government data bank indefinitely. Information to be accessible to all involved families.
3. Mandate reporting of donor-conceived live births from each donor.
4. Limit the number of births conceived with the sperm or eggs from any given donor.
5. Require donors to regularly update their family medical history. Medical information to be included in donor data bank.
6. Mandate genetic testing for donors and include genetic information in donor bank.
7. Push our respective governments to inquire into followup health histories of egg donors.
8. Require mandatory third party counselling for all prospective donors and parents.
9. Require legal and financial protection for anonymous donors so that they may feel safe to come forward.

As these aspirations show, the organizations involved in the network support the principle of donor-conceived people having access to identifying information about their donor or donors. The information is to include direct access by donor-conceived people and their families to medical information about the donor and the donor's family of origin, without any mediation or editing by medical personnel. They themselves should be able to track down information about the donor or donors with the help of state-run registers. The International Donor Offspring Alliance (IDOA) had already decided to go further, and to push for birth certificates to indicate the fact if a person was donor-conceived. The IDOA was formed in 2007 and now has members in the UK, US, Canada, France, Japan, New Zealand, Australia, Argentina and Germany. It exists 'to act as an advocate for those conceived through the use of donor gametes' (that is, eggs or sperm). The IDOA states its beliefs as follows:

> The organisation believes that everyone has the right to know the truth of their biological parents. Where the state is involved in providing or regulating donor conception, it must not cause, promote or collude in deceiving people or depriving them of information about their own origins; nor may it discriminate against particular groups in terms of the provision of significant information about their own lives. It follows that the birth certificate of a donor conceived person must enable them to know the identity of their biological parents. (IDOA 2008)

How has this situation come about and what are the practical and theoretical implications in terms of trust? I shall focus on the UK, although there are global entanglements, because donor conceived people in the UK have discovered and are in contact with half-siblings who live overseas. Firstly I give an historical perspective as background to the continuing arguments and debates about access for donor-conceived people to identifying information about their donors, and as illustration of the moral framework about marriage and the family within which the disagreements have taken place. I then note the commitment of infertility specialists to DI services, followed by an exploration of the emergence of distrust amongst those personally and professionally involved.

Historical Perspective on DI

In the years of debate in the UK about whether or not to make anonymous donation illegal, and whether to reinstate it after it had been prohibited, the arguments from those in favour of anonymity have tended to be framed within a discourse of human rights and especially the rights of the parents and donors to privacy versus any possible right of donor-conceived people to know the identity of their genetic parents. In these arguments, privacy has been held as more important, and knowledge about genetic origins has been argued to be unnecessary. Some infertility specialists have claimed that there is nothing about genetic origins needing to be known, because the donors were so carefully selected that there is no risk of their offspring inheriting any medical problems. This trust is not well-founded given what is known about how donors were recruited, the scant history-taking by a number of clinics before the introduction of regulation, and the variable knowledge about how to elicit an accurate family medical history (Speirs 2008). Even contemporary donor-recruitment methods have been criticized in cases where anonymity has prevented the notification of donor offspring at risk of serious inherited disease (Bioedge 2013).

Concerns about a wide range of risks in DI were voiced as soon as the practice came to public attention after publication of an article in the British Medical Journal in 1945 (Barton et al. 1945). The concerns were repeated in a number of publications and reports of official enquiries over the years which consistently note the perceived problems with donor anonymity on which the INDCO and the IDOA are campaigning. A commission of enquiry was set up in response to the BMJ article by the then Archbishop of Canterbury (Church of England 1948). In their report, the commissioners condemned the practice of Artificial Insemination by Donor (A.I.D.) as an institution, and its effects on those involved. In their view: '[it involves] a breach of the marriage. It violates the exclusive union set up between husband and wife. It defrauds the child begotten, and deceives both his putative kinsmen and society at large' (ibid.: 58). The effects of A.I.D on the family are perceived to be damaging, involving an attack on the marital relationship, a cheating of the donor offspring with regard to who his genetic father is, and the deception of the wider family and beyond through the pretence that the husband of the child's mother is the genetic father. Finally the commissioners stated that there were dangers in the secrecy inherent in the practice of A.I.D.: 'For the child there must always be the risk of disclosure, deliberate or unintended, of the circumstances of his conception' (ibid.).

A UK government-appointed committee set up in 1958 noted that A.I.D had already been practised for several decades in the UK, US, Australia, South Africa, France, Germany, Scandinavia, Belgium, the Netherlands and Israel (Feversham Report 1960) and that none of these states had introduced legislation to regulate or criminalize the practice. Nevertheless the report concluded that, in the view of the committee members, artificial insemination by donor was undesirable and caused a 'grave injustice' to the child (ibid.: 79). In the UK at that time it was carried out as an open secret and was not illegal but legally ambiguous. Donor-conceived children were considered illegitimate, and the semen donor and the recipient were at risk of being accused of adultery. Donors were thought to be financially liable for the children. One way of avoiding these problems, in that pre-DNA era, was for the semen of the husband to be mixed, before insemination at the clinics, with the semen of one or more donors (creating what is now described colloquially as a sperm cocktail), so that the pretence could be upheld that it was the husband who was the biological father of the child. This practice continued in the UK until the 1970s, at which time the medical profession itself became concerned about the need for traceability in case of genetic problems being passed on from donor to offspring.

According to the Feversham report, a justification for the practice of semen-mixing was that not all of the husbands were completely infertile, and if a man's semen was used as part of the insemination material, then he and his wife could assume that there was a chance that a subsequent pregnancy might be due to the husband's sperm. This practice was termed A.I.H.D., meaning artificial insemination by husband and donor (Feversham Report 1960: ii). Douglas Cusine notes that the mixing of a husband's and a donor's semen together before insemination was sometimes called AIM – 'mixed artificial insemination' (1988: 125). Another term was CAI – 'confused artificial insemination'. Cusine reports that some doctors were against the practice because it reduced the chances of conception. Witnesses to the Feversham committee who provided an A.I.D. service advised that they kept some kind of confidential record of the link between the donor and a pregnancy, but obviously that was impossible with sperm mixing. Some records were kept in code known only to the doctor and the clinic nurse or private secretary, but many records are known to have been destroyed shortly after the births of donor-conceived babies, if all appeared to be well.

In 1971 a panel was set up by the Annual Representative Meeting of the British Medical Association in 1971, to enquire into 'the place of A.I.D. (artificial insemination by donor) in our modern society' (Panel on Human Artificial Insemination 1973: 3), following an increasing number of requests to the BMA's headquarters for information about A.I.D. The panel's report noted that since the publication of the Feversham Report, there had been no changes to the legal status of the children born as a result of A.I.D. The children remained illegitimate whether or not the mother's husband had given consent to the procedure. The content of the report focused particularly on issues of protection and negligence for medical practitioners of A.I.D. For example, practitioners should take adequate care to ensure that donors did not transmit disease in their sperm and that couples fully understood what A.I.D. involved and what emotional repercussions they might later experience. The report referred to the possibility of A.I.D. practitioners being sued, in line with what had recently occurred after pregnant women treated with the drug Thalidomide had given birth to children with physical malformations, and with an apparent increase in the practice of A.I.D. it was even more important for the medical profession to have proper standards and safeguards in place. The panel noted that A.I.D. was still considered controversial by the public and the medical profession at large.

A number of these reports noted the worry about unwitting incest because of the anonymity of A.I.D. and the related problem of how many donor offspring should be permitted for each donor. The Feversham committee had decided that the danger of genetic half-siblings unwittingly meeting and marrying each other was minimal (Feversham Report 1960: 12), and would remain a remote possibility even if the practice of A.I.D. increased substantially – and in any case would be much smaller 'than that resulting from fornication and adultery' (ibid.). Apparently most doctors limited the number of donor-assisted conceptions to ten per donor and few had even reached that number. This was partly because donors did not want to continue donating over a long period of time and partly because most pregnancies were not achieved until after several inseminations. During my fieldwork a clinical scientist told me that he recalled going to a meeting in 1981 about the ethics of sperm freezing, and learning that the number of offspring was usually limited to ten live births by UK doctors because of the potential hazard of siblings committing unwitting incest. He recalled that the Eugenics Society was concerned about this too. Indeed a round-up in *Eugenics Review* had noted its concern at the time of the Archbishop of Canterbury's commission: 'If the children are kept in ignorance of their origin, so much greater will be the chances of their marrying half-siblings or other very near relation' (Anon. 1948: 123). It also complained that 'the family and society as a whole have the right to trustworthy genealogical records' (ibid.), which secrecy would prevent.

However, medical practitioners continued to insist that DI must be kept secret, partly for their own protection against legal liability if anything went wrong, but also in order to protect the marriage of childless couples from the stigma commonly assumed to be attached to male infertility. This stigma has a taken-for-granted quality and is not unique to the UK (Lasker 1998; Thompson 2001, 2005). It was believed therefore that the implications of not keeping DI a secret would have adverse implications for the marriage and for the child, and concealing the fact that a child was donor-conceived was thought to be best for the protection of the family. It was also believed to be necessary for the protection of the semen donor from accusations of adultery and from claims for financial support of the child. Importantly for the issue of trust, couples were advised not to tell their donor-conceived children, or anyone else, about the nature of the conception. One practitioner wrote that it was for the child's sake that he believed that nobody should know about the DI except the parents: 'My last advice to the parents is that under no circumstance should they, or need they, ever tell the child the method of conception – in fact they should forget about it themselves' (Bloom 1957: 207).

Role of the Medical Profession

Given the many difficulties with anonymous donor insemination, why did the provision of the service not only continue, but increase? One typical explanation was offered by a retired clinician responsible for an infertility clinic in the 1970s and 1980s, who explained to me that it was because of the professional medical response to the needs of patients:

> Clinician: Couples are desperate. If you work in infertility you see that desperation. People are prepared to do almost anything.
> Jennifer: Why are they desperate?
> Clinician: It's a basic human need to reproduce. Also, it means that you are the same as others.
> Jennifer: Is there social pressure?
> Clinician: There's both social pressure and a biological urge. And parents put pressure on couples. The desperation is almost like an illness.

The sense of 'desperation' is summed up by an infertility specialist, a clinician who has been working in the field since 1984 and who was one of my (non-donor) research informants:

> The despair felt by some disappointed patients is unbelievable until you are touched by its potency. The hopelessness, the sense of failure, of biological rejection, often turns the infertility clinic into a minefield of emotion and distress. (Cowan 2003: 16)

The desperation has been commented upon by social anthropologists from research in the UK (Franklin 1997; Konrad 2005). In her analysis of anonymous ova donation, in a description with Biblical and therefore ancient connotations, Konrad notes 'the lamentations', the emotional phenomena in the background of commercial IVF services (2005: 239). The particular distress of male infertility is described by another specialist, a clinical scientist specializing in male infertility whom I had met before my fieldwork started: 'A diagnosis of male infertility is shocking, not only because of its social stigma but also because those who seek a second and third opinion find themselves becoming confused, isolated and frustrated' (Lee 2003: 73). He adds, in stark terms:

> In recent years I have become the harbinger of doom. They [the patients] sometimes tell me that they do not wish to hear my information, which may have the ring of a death sentence, but some do thank me for taking off their rose-tinted spectacles. (2003: 74)

The provision of DI finally received public endorsement in the report of the Warnock Committee, which led to the introduction of the regulation of infertility services by the Human Fertilisation and Embryology Act 1990. As the committee's chair, Baroness Warnock, explained, the committee decided that it would be wrong for doctors 'on compassionate grounds, not to offer assisted conception to those who sought to overcome their infertility, in other words that the medical profession had a duty ... to continue to provide assistance' (Warnock 2002: 42).

The medical profession itself appears not to have taken steps to lobby for legislation until the development in the 1970s of *in vitro* fertilization (IVF), possibly because the practice of anonymous donor insemination involves a challenging and fundamental contradiction between the perceived need for secrecy and possible long-term genetic issues for donor-conceived people. The infertility specialists were preoccupied with immediate service provision. They were concerned about the safety aspects of semen donation, and about what they thought was in the best interests of the recipients, but these were focused on the short term. Donor Insemination only became subject to regulation as a result of the introduction of legislation primarily addressed to the concerns of the public and the medical profession about the technologically more complex and risky practice of IVF. Little or no attention was paid to the possible long-term implications of encouraging patients to introduce deceit into their family life, perhaps because there were thought to be no such implications.

However one clinician told me that he believed that there was an inconsistency in the practice of anonymous semen donation: it meant that donor-conceived people would have very little access to information about their 'genetic pedigree', as he put it. He added:

> By and large, up until recently, it's been a wee sort of voice in the back of one's mind saying, heh, this isn't quite right – but the voice is sort of suppressed, you are focused so much on the couple in front of you and their needs, and welfare of the child is assumed, in the context that it is born and it is healthy, and its welfare is being attended to, really. But I think now people aren't quite so sure about that.

Donors of semen themselves are not all so sure either. My research explored what it meant to donors that they had donated when they were young, mostly as medical students. At the time that I met with them and their families, it was twenty to forty years since the time of their donating. Some of the men were curious to know how many donor offspring they had, and what they looked like, but were ambivalent or opposed to the idea of there being any contact or exchange of information with them. A few were open to the idea of contact, and even with meeting, imagining that it would be possible to pass on information about the donor's family history. One had registered with UK Donorlink[1] in case any of his donor offspring also registered in the hope of finding out about him (Speirs 2012). The donors had all been promised anonymity when they donated, and they trusted that this promise had been kept by the clinic where they had donated. For some it was like a contract – 'that was the deal' – and they presumed that there was no way that donor-conceived people would be able to trace them.

There were a variety of reasons for the donors' mixed feelings about contact, including distrust of the motives of donor-conceived people. They also worried that such contact would take away from their time and energy for their family. This is a clear example of Janet Carsten's findings from her study of adopted people, that kinship and relatedness require effort in their creation and maintenance (Carsten 2000). One donor and his wife raised both emotional and material concerns about connection. Referring to the 2004 regulations that would make people donating from 1 April 2006 identifiable to their donor offspring, the donor's wife commented that non-anonymity of donors would be worrying. She was concerned that the donor offspring 'might turn up if they were unhappy. You hear of that, in adoption'. Her husband agreed. There would be 'no control' in that situation, he said, and 'maybe they would be wacko'. I replied that several donors had mentioned that concern and then asked if he was worried about a 'knock on the door' because 'you aren't sure if donor-conceived people were brought up to be considerate? What are you saying about the parents?' The donor looked shame-faced and replied, 'I assume that they were brought up in loving families'. Later in the discussion I asked what would happen in the unlikely event that someone did 'turn up':

> Donor: Maybe I'd help financially. The person is not a complete stranger. Not an alien. If I thought they were OK, trustworthy.
> Donor's wife: Tick boxes there!

The donor's wife was observing that her husband's acceptance of the donor offspring's claim was conditional on the person being trustworthy. She also was suggesting that a donor offspring might be looking for emotional support, if life with their parents had been difficult, as she believed sometimes happens in adoption. She had heard of stories of adopted people going in search of their birth parents because of being unhappy. Whereas she suggested that donor offspring might be looking for emotional support, her husband made the assumption that donor offspring would be looking for financial support from him. I found it interesting the number of donors, all of them well-off financially, who were concerned that donor-conceived people might make contact in order to ask for financial help, or to ask for a share of the donor's inheritance. There was a lack of trust there, which appeared to be irrational, since there is no evidence that donor-conceived people want money from donors. When I was discussing this chapter with a donor-conceived person and said that I had never heard of a donor-conceived person wanting money from a donor, he commented with a chuckle, 'Well, they might not say it!' but added that indeed it was probably not a problem. Of course it could be a metaphor: the hypothetical demand may be for something other than money, which donors found difficult to put into words, or understand, such as information about the donor as a person, perhaps even a relationship. This distrust of donor offspring compares with the stereotype of the birth mother who, in searching for her adopted child, according to Jonathan Telfer, may disrupt the sense of completeness for adoptive parents (Telfer 2004: 254). Telfer notes that there is distrust of birth mothers, despite whatever positive personal qualities they may have, because of the disruption to relationships that their searching activity might cause. The mother is 'cast as the custodian of secret dangerous knowledge' (ibid.: 254), namely, information about the origins of the adoptee which may have been kept from the adoptee by the adoptive parents. The mother who relinquished her baby to adoption 'becomes an artifice of disaggregation' (ibid.).

The Emergence of Distrust

The history of the development of DI services in the UK shows that although there were expressions of concern about telling lies to children, as well as about children's right to know of their origins and their need for information so as to avoid unwitting incest with a half-sibling, it seemed best to infertility practitioners to collude with the pretence that the birth certificate was a record of genetic parentage. They did not trust society to deal kindly with childless couples, and hence strongly advocated secrecy and anonymity in order to avoid the negative perceptions about donor conception at that time, as well as to guarantee that the donor would never be able to interfere with the upbringing of his biological child. That would ensure a stable marriage, protection of the child from stigma, and a family that seemed like any other.

However it has not worked out like that. The parents of donor-conceived children began to ask infertility counsellors and social workers in the 1990s whether it was necessary to keep the status of the child a secret, because the pressure to keep the secret was causing a strain on their marital relationships. Some parents began to question whether the infertility specialists had the authority to recommend or even insist on the secrecy, and began requesting information about the donors that they thought that their children would welcome in future. The transformation of secrecy into deceit and the challenges that this posed for couples had already been noted in research in the 1970s on the experiences of parents of donor-conceived children (Snowden et al. 1983). Formal research and the stories of donor-conceived people began to reveal how often the secret of their conception was being let out, sometimes in sad or traumatic circumstances such as the divorce of their parents or the death of their father. When that happened, the donor-conceived people have spoken of their rage, bewilderment, shock and sadness (Ellis 2007) and the damage caused to their relationships with their parents has been visible. It appears that the stronger the previous trust, the stronger may be the subsequent sense of betrayal (see Rossetti 1995).

Doctors working in infertility clinics have also been at the receiving end of anger from donor-conceived people, for having carried out anonymous DI in the past, and then for having lobbied to maintain anonymity. In one situation that I witnessed, the anger was returned, with a fertility specialist mocking donor-conceived people at a conference. This led to a shouting match between the doctor and a donor in the audience who was in favour of donors not having anonymity. The same doctor at another conference described donor-conceived people as 'damaged goods' (psychologically disturbed). On neither occasion were the doctor's outbursts curtailed or commented upon by other medical colleagues, implying that they might have been in agreement. Infertility specialists in general appear to have found it difficult to engage with donor-conceived people in discussions, and distrust seems mutual. The introduction of the 2004 regulations ending donor anonymity in the UK has been resisted by a number of infertility specialists, notably clinicians. They have expressed anger against the social science researchers, members of the donor conception community, the regulatory authority and the government, who variously lobbied for, supported and introduced the change in the law. A few have treated members of the donor conception community with a contempt that has astonished and sometimes elicited anger and bitterness in return. These strong attitudes and feelings suggest that values are being challenged. An added complication is the open secret that a number of infertility specialists donated semen anonymously in their youth, making their trustworthiness as neutral commentators open to question.

Some clinicians did not believe that the regulations would be introduced and they responded to them as if their professional authority was being challenged. Furthermore, by their own admission clinicians do not like change and especially if the idea was not theirs in the first place. The need to keep donors secret, anonymous to the donor offspring and their parents, was fundamental to the delivery of DI services, and for some infertility specialists, particularly clinicians, it remains so. One explanation can be offered in terms of Goffman's theory of stigma. 'By definition, of course, we believe the person with a stigma is not quite human', he states (1963: 15), and it is this belief which cause us to discriminate against a stigmatized person in various ways. The person is inferior and a danger. Social contact between the 'normals' and people perceived to be stigmatized can be fraught with uneasiness. If a stigmatized person does not behave in a situation of contact as expected that they should, by 'cowering' (ibid.: 29), but rather by bravado or aggression, then the 'normals' may try to act as if he were a non-person. What the removal of anonymity has revealed is the problem, for infertility specialists in particular, of how to treat with members of the donor conception community, who for so long have been stigmatized for being different: the (social) parents for being infertile, the semen donor for being a *quasi* adulterer and the donor offspring for having a father who was only 'as if' he were the genetic father.

Individual INDCO and IDOA members put different emphases on the need for identifying information about donors. For some of them, access to medical history is perceived as important or even vital (Montuschi 2011). The difficulty in obtaining such access is perceived as discriminatory, and this is what motivates many donor-conceived people to continue lobbying for identifying information to be made available as a right. They point to the situation for adopted people who now have access to their original birth certificates in all four nations of the UK. Yet the activism of the IDOA and individual donor-conceived people has brought a sour note to the well-meaning actions long ago of their parents and the doctors who helped to achieve pregnancies. Some parents actively supported removing the right of gamete donors to donate anonymously, and have encouraged other parents to be honest with their children about how they were conceived (Montuschi and Merricks 2000), but have not been in agreement that donors' names should be recorded on birth certificates. Instead they place their hope on education and support for parents in talking to their children about their origins. This activism on the part of parents has been greeted mostly with silence or avoidance by infertility specialists. Perhaps some of them view the activism as a breach of trust given that parents recall that they were told at the clinics never to tell anyone about the DI, and especially not their child. For some parents, that was a condition for being accepted for treatment. Even after regulation of DI in 1990, some infertility clinics' information leaflets for patients gave the firm assurance that it was acceptable for the parents never to tell the child about his or her origins because there was no need for the child to find out. Despite this, an increasing number of parents have told their children about their conception status but it is the support group for families created following donor conception, the Donor Conception Network, which has worked to provide education and support for parents, not the infertility clinics.

As already described, the views of donor-conceived people about their perceived needs and rights have at times been pathologized and they have also been marginalized and disregarded even in research (Turkmendag et al. 2008). Baroness Deech, who was chair of the UK Human Fertilisation and Embryology Authority from 1994–2002, provided an example of donor-conceived people being told what was right for them, and of the concern about the perceived ambiguous place of a genetic father who is not the nurturing father:

> During my chairmanship the authority discussed the issue thoroughly on several occasions and remained firmly of the view that anonymity was right. This was not only in order to ensure volunteers, but out of respect for the husband of the baby's mother, who would assume the role of real father to the child in social and emotional terms. (Deech 2006)

Deech's emphasis on the social father as the 'real' father highlights a belief that kinship can be created and maintained simply through what Jeanette Edwards describes as 'intimacies of care and effort' (2000: 27). Yet tracing connections through shared substance 'be it blood, genes, flesh or bone' (ibid.) is also what her research informants did, though not exclusively. In their discussions about donor-assisted conception, these informants were able to make an interplay between the social and the biological, but this flexibility is not what everyone involved with donor-assisted conception understands or agrees with.

Part of the problem for donor-conceived people is that they are not being trusted to remain loyal to their parents. It is as if they are not capable or desirous of maintaining enduring ties of affection to their parents, particularly their fathers. They have also been accused of ingratitude towards their parents for seeking information about their donors, and even of the derogatory 'genetic essentialism' (Nelkin and Tancredi 1989), although there is no evidence that donor-conceived people give priority to genetic relationships over and above social ones. Seeking information about one's genetic parents can be seen not as a sign of a genetic determinism but rather as a belief in an enriched sociality (Speirs 2013). The search for information about and possible meetings with donors and other people conceived by the same donor are an endeavour to add to relations, to enrich networks of relatedness (Blyth 2012). Donor-conceived people are not bent on replacing the relationships with their parents by ones with the donors. Indeed, it is the fact that they are *not* prioritizing their genetic parents over their social parents that makes the actions of donor-conceived people so unsettling for those who cannot conceive of having meaningful connections with 'two fathers'. If donor conceived people were not embedded in their families already, the search for genetic relatives might prove easier. As one donor-conceived person explained:

> Despite my sense of injustice, I love and am loyal to my family. But it is still a very sensitive and prickly issue, and relationships can feel deeply strained at times. (Rose 2008)

Another who was told by his father at the age of twelve that he had been conceived using the sperm of an anonymous donor observed:

> My father and I were, I think, closer and better with each other, eventually, than we would have been had the lie been sustained – but our relationship was forever subject to a sort of conditionality, a sense of choice that does not exist between my daughters and me. (Gollancz 2007a)

Discussion

Trust in other people, especially parents, implies predictability of future behaviour. Trust in parents is not meant to involve emotional risk. In contrast to Margit Ystanes' findings (this volume), the family has been idealized in the development of DI services. The role of parents carries certain expectations and values: parents are 'supposed' to be trustworthy. As one donor-conceived person described for me: 'Trust is not just about truth and lies: children rely on their parents to be protective, not to be deceitful. They are in charge of the child's welfare'. Discovering that parents have withheld information or have given false information has caused a crisis for some donor-conceived people, to the extent of them seeking professional counselling (as have some parents). The abruptness of the revelation of the nature of their origins stands in contrast to the length of time, perhaps decades, when the donor-conceived person was living in ignorance of them. Intimate relationships imply mutual knowledge, but in this case the knowledge has never been mutually established. Yet intimate relationships change over time, for many reasons (cf. Bodenhorn 2000) and this was not taken into account in the development of DI. People find it hard to keep secrets, parents (especially wives) tell their friends about the DI, parents get divorced or the husband dies and then the mother no longer feels an obligation to hide her husband's infertile status. Whereas the passing of time should strengthen trust, with a continual reconfirmation of trustworthiness, in the case of anonymous DI in the UK there is evidence that trust in intimate relationships has been eroded and replaced by distrust and even cynicism.

A continuous thread in the history of DI in the UK has been the insistence by infertility specialists that they have a primary duty of confidentiality towards patients. This professional principle has led to guarding the stigmatizing diagnosis of male infertility and to active support for donor anonymity. The mantra 'trust me, I'm a doctor', however, is no longer seen as justified by donor-conceived people and even by an increasing number of parents, who perceive it as out-dated and no longer appropriate nor relevant. A useful analysis of contemporary tensions for professional confidentiality is made by Chris Clark and Janice McGhee who note that the concept is in a 'state of flux' as a consequence of a number of significant changes in UK society (2008: 231). Service delivery is now more complex than ever, involving many professions and increasing technology, so that confidentiality is no longer mainly about secrecy but about who needs to know what, and when. Attitudes to privacy are also changing, and it is no longer clear what personal information is shameful or disgraceful and therefore requiring to be hidden. Perhaps controversially, Clark and McGhee assert that the concept of professional confidentiality 'is rooted in a conception of privacy still very largely derived from the mores of 19th century bourgeois society' (2008: 233), and is not in tune with other significant contemporary changes, such as the Internet, with its opportunities for individuals to reveal personal information and, I would add, to search for and be contacted by lost or previously unknown genetic relatives.

Clark and McGhee therefore propose that professional confidentiality be reconceived in a 'trust-based approach' (2008: 235), in which professionals act as trustees, using their discretion for the benefit of the trustor. Privacy and confidentiality are implied in our Western inheritance of liberal individualism, but the latter at times may be in conflict with other values, such as meeting the obligations that arise from relationships. I suggest that this analysis helps us to understand the complexity of the eddies of trust and distrust amongst and between people with a personal or professional involvement in anonymous semen donation, where harm was never intended to relationships.

The process of DI started with secrets: with trust that the identity of the donors and recipients would be kept hidden from each other, and that the fact of DI likewise would be kept hidden from the donor-conceived children and their parents' social networks. It also depended on trust between doctors and patients that DI was the right course of action in the face of unwanted childlessness caused by male infertility. The secrecy became entrenched in a society that simultaneously stigmatized male infertility, semen donation and the illegitimacy of donor offspring. Yet secrecy itself depends on the ability and need of individuals to keep secrets, and some of this this has changed over time. The importance of access to medical knowledge about genetic forebears has been recognized (Turnpenny et al. 1993), and many parents of donor-conceived children have been unable or unwilling to keep their use of DI a secret. Semen donors themselves have begun to question the authenticity of the doctors who recruited them (Speirs 2012) and to offer identifying information about themselves to donor offspring through voluntary contact registers (Crawshaw et al. 2013). What remains is the distrust by donor-conceived people in parents' ability to tell their children how they were conceived, and in the willingness of the infertility treatment providers to ensure that identifying information about donors is made accessible. This distrust is what prompts the members of the IDOA and their supporters to agitate for a new kind of birth certificate, even if the practical difficulties of recording donors' names on birth registration documents are considerable (Blyth et al. 2009).

The claim that the birth certificates of donor-conceived people are false and should be redesigned to record the name of the gamete donor makes the phenomenon of DI an example of the tensions over trust which have arisen in the intimate spheres of human procreation, parent–child relations and the state's guardianship of genetic inheritance knowledge. Believing that parents cannot be trusted to tell their children about their conception status, and that infertility specialists cannot be trusted to encourage parents to do so, the IDOA are putting their trust in a new system of birth registration. It will provide documents that will record the truth and force others not to hide the truth. Unlike people, these records will be trustworthy, once and always. Paradoxically, given their criticism of the complicity of the state in the system of 'false' birth certificates, activist donor-conceived people are recommending that trust be placed in documents and systems which will have to rely on the integrity of state employees (the staff of the offices of the Registrars of Births Marriages and Deaths) and on the security and reliability of state-managed digital data transfer systems (Blyth et al. 2009: 226). There is an interesting link here to the relatives of the disappeared in Chris Kaplonski's paper (this volume), whose trust in state documents leads to a recapturing of knowledge about a long-lost relative. For donor-conceived people, the documents which they claim to trust will lead to gaining knowledge which may become part of a process of redefining the donor as a social person, transforming a biological source of genetic substance into a living person and facilitating the connection to new relatives such as donor-conceived siblings. However, in contrast to the secret police in Mongolia, the staff of the three General Registrars of Births Marriages and Deaths in the UK (for Scotland, Northern Ireland, and England and Wales) are held in some respect, anecdotally at least.

I suggested at the beginning of this chapter that it would point to a substitution of trust in people with trust in documents, in this case the birth certificates of donor-conceived people. In conclusion I do not think that this is the whole story. There may be many examples of mutual distrust between infertility specialists, parents and donor-conceived people, but they are all aiming at sympathetic policy makers in order to press variously for the reinstatement of anonymity, support for education programmes, or annotated birth certificates. The state itself is acquiring the status of a person with responsibility. In a parliamentary debate on the Human Fertilisation and Embryology Bill 2008, Robert Key MP addressed the question of what should be put on a birth certificate, and stated, 'I think that the state has a moral duty not to be party to a deliberate deception about a person's genetic history' (Key 2008), but the response in the subsequent legislation could be described as cautious. David Gollancz, a lawyer who was conceived by donor insemination in the 1950s, also asserts that the state has been involved in deception, because it has colluded with parents who have registered false information about parenthood (Gollancz 2007a, 2007b). He describes birth certificates of people like himself as a 'statutorily sanctioned fraud which ... must be abolished and replaced with a document of record which puts each person's personal history in their own hands' (Gollancz 2007a). From the perspective of the IDOA activists, the current form of the birth certificate symbolizes all that is wrong with DI: lack of respect for the need for information about one's medical heritage and deception at the heart of the family. Since parents and the medical profession cannot be trusted, perhaps the state needs to be.

Acknowledgements

The doctoral and postdoctoral research upon which this chapter is based was funded by grants from the UK's Economic and Social Research Council. I am grateful to Dr Tom Ellis and Mr David Gollancz for their time in helping me to clarify some of the theoretical insights in this chapter.

Note

1. A pilot voluntary register set up by After Adoption Yorkshire in 2004 and funded by the UK government until 2012, in order to facilitate contact between donors and their donor-conceived children conceived before 1 August 1991. The register is now run by the National Gamete Donation Trust. See http://www.hfea.gov.uk/5524.html (accessed 8 October 2015) and 'Donor Conception: Ethical Aspects of Information Sharing', p. 25, available at: http://nuffieldbioethics.org/wp-content/uploads/2014/06/Donor_concep tion_report_2013.pdf (accessed 10 October 2015).

References

Anonymous. 1948. 'Notes of the Quarter', *Eugenics Review* 40(3): 119-124.
Back, K. and R. Snowden. 1988. 'The Anonymity of the Gamete Donor', *Journal of Psychosomatic Obstetrics and Gynaecology* 9: 191–198.
Barton, M., K. Walker and B. Wiesner. 1945. 'Artificial Insemination', *British Medical Journal*, 13 January, 1: 40–43.
Bioedge. 2013. 'Danish Sperm Donor Privacy Controversy'. Available at http://www.bioedge.org/index.php/bioethics/bioethics_article/10455 (accessed 11 October 2015).
Bloom, P. 1957. 'Artificial Insemination (Donor)', *The Eugenics Review*, January, 48: 205–207.
Blyth, E. 2012. 'Genes r us? Making Sense of Genetic and Non-genetic Relationships following Anonymous Donor Insemination'. *Reproductive BioMedicine Online*, 24(7): 719–726. Available at http://eprints.hud.ac.uk/14478/ (accessed 11 October 2015).
Blyth, E., L. Frith, C. Jones and J. Speirs. 2009. 'The Role of Birth Certificates in Relation to Access to Biographical and Genetic History in Donor Conception', *International Journal of Children's Rights* 17: 207–233.
Bodenhorn, B. 2000. 'He Used to be My Relative: Exploring the Bases of Relatedness among InÄupiat of northern Alaska'. In J. Carsten (ed.), *Cultures of Relatedness*, 128–48. Cambridge: Cambridge University Press.
British Medical Association. Annual Report of the Council. Appendix V: Report of the Panel on Human Artificial Insemination. (Chairman: Sir John Peel). British
Medical Journal Supplement, 1973, 7 April, vol. 11: 3–5.
Carsten, J. 2000. 'Knowing Where You've Come From: Ruptures and Continuities of Time and Kinship in Narratives of Adoption Reunion', *Journal of the Royal Anthropological Institute* (N.S.) 6: 687–703.
Church of England. 1948. 'Artificial Human Insemination', The Report of a Commission Appointed by His Grace the Archbishop of Canterbury. London: Society for the Propagation of Christian Knowledge.
Clark, C. and M. McGhee. 2008. 'Conclusion'. In *Private and Confidential? Handling Personal Information in the Social and Health Services*. Bristol: The Policy Press.

Cowan, D. 2003. 'Assisted Reproductive Technology and the Fertility Clinic'. In J. Haynes and J. Miller (eds), *Inconceivable Conceptions: Psychological Aspects of Infertility and Reproductive Technology*, 11–16. Hove, East Sussex: Brunner-Routledge.

Crawshaw, M., C. Gunter, C. Tidy and F. Atherton. 2013. 'Working with Previously Anonymous Gamete Donors and Donor-conceived Adults: Recent Practice Experiences of Running the DNA-Based Voluntary Information Exchange and Contact Register, UK DonorLink', *Human Fertility* 16(1): 26–30.

Cusine, D. 1988. *New Reproductive Techniques: A Legal Perspective*. Aldershot: Gower Publishing Company Limited

Deech, Baroness. 2006. 'Competing Interests in Sperm Donor Secrecy', Letter to the Editor, *The Times*, 23 September.

Department of Health. 2004. 'Human Fertilisation and Embryology Authority (Disclosure of Donor Information) Regulations 2004', Statutory Instrument 2004 No.1511. London: HMSO.

Edwards, J. 2000. *Born and Bred: Idioms of Kinship and New Reproductive Technologies in England*. Oxford: Oxford University Press.

Ellis, T. 2007. "I Feel so Betrayed Because I Don't Know Who My Father Is", *Daily Mail*, 2 August, p. 50.

Eugenics Review 1948. 'Notes of the Quarter', Vol 40, No. 3, October.

Feversham Report. 1960. 'Report of the Departmental Committee on Human Artificial Insemination', Cmnd 1105. London: HMSO.

Franklin, S. 1997. *Embodied Progress: A Cultural Account of Assisted Conception*. London: Routledge.

Goffman, E. 1963. *Stigma: Notes on the Management of Spoiled Identity*. Englewood Cliffs, NJ: Prentice-Hall.

Gollancz, D. 2007a. Memorandum to the Joint Committee on the Human Tissue and Embryos (http://www.publications.parliament.uk/pa/jt200607/jtselect/jtembryos/169/169ii.pdf Draft) Bill Volume II: Evidence, Ev. 44: 366–368 (accessed 11 October 2015).

Gollancz, D. 2007b. 'Time to Stop Lying', *The Guardian*, 2 August. Available at http://www.guardian.co.uk/g2/story/0,,2139678,00.html (accessed 11 October 2015).

International Donor Offspring Alliance. 2008. 'Human Fertilisation and Embryology Bill: Birth Certificates: The Case for Reform', Briefing for Members of the House of Commons. Available at http://web.jaguarpaw.co.uk/~tom/idoa-briefing-latest.pdf (accessed 11 October 2015).

International Network of Donor Conception. http://intentblog.com/international-network-donor-conception-organizations/ (accessed 11 October 2015)

Key, R. 2008. Hansard, HC, 12 May 2008, 475(92): col. 1114. Available at <http://www.publications.parliament.uk/pa/cm200708/cmhansrd/cm080512/debtext/80512-0012.htm> (accessed 11 October 2015).

Konrad, M. 2005. *Nameless Relations: Anonymity, Melanesia and Reproductive Gift Exchange between British Ova Donors and Recipients*. Oxford: Berghahn Books.

Lasker, J. 1998. 'The Users of Donor Insemination'. In K. Daniels and E. Haimes (eds), *Donor Insemination: International Social Science Perspectives*, 7–32. Cambridge: Cambridge University Press.

Lee, S. 2003. 'Myths and Reality in Male Infertility'. In J. Haynes and J. Miller (eds), *Inconceivable Conceptions: Psychological Aspects of Infertility and Reproductive Technology*, 73–85. Hove, East Sussex: Brunner-Routledge.

Mellahi, K. and G. Wood. 2003. 'From Kinship to Trust: Changing Recruitment Practices in Unstable Political Contexts', *International Journal of Cross Cultural Management* 3: 369–381.

Montuschi, O. 2011. 'Calling All Former Donors'. Blog post, available at http://oliviasview.wordpress.com/2011/06/16/calling-all-former-donors/ (accessed 11 October 2015).

Montuschi, O. and W. Merricks. 2000. 'Why Children Need to Know'. Presentation at PROGRESS/ESHRE Conference on *Gamete Privacy: Should Egg and Sperm Donors Be Anonymous?* London, 4 December.

Nelkin, D. and L. Tancredi. 1989. *Dangerous Diagnostics: The Social Power of Biological Information*. New York: Basic Books.

Rose, J. 2008. 'I Could Have 300 Siblings', *The Guardian*, 14 November.

Rossetti, S. 1995. 'The Impact of Child Sexual Abuse on Attitudes towards God and the Catholic Church', *Child Abuse and Neglect* 19(12): 1469–1481.

Snowden, R., G. Mitchell and E. Snowden. 1983. *Artificial Reproduction: A Social Investigation*. London: Allen and Unwin.

Speirs, J.M. 2008. *Secretly Connected? Anonymous Semen Donation, Genetics and Meanings of Kinship*. PhD dissertation. Edinburgh: University of Edinburgh. Available online at https://www.era.lib.ed.ac.uk/handle/1842/2649 (accessed 10 October 2015).

—— 2012. 'Semen Donors' Curiosity about Donor Offspring and the Barriers to Their Knowing', *Human Fertility* 15(2): 89–93.

—— 2013. 'Anonymous Semen Donation: Medical Treatment or Medical Kinship?' *Cargo* (Medical Anthropology in Central East Europe) (Special Issue) 9.1-2 (2013): 73-90.

Telfer, J. 2004. 'Partial to Completeness: Gender, Peril and Agency in Australian Adoption'. In F. Bowie (ed.), *Cross-cultural Approaches to Adoption*, 242–256. London: Routledge.

Thompson, C. 2001. 'Strategic Naturalization: Kinship in an Infertility Clinic'. In S. Franklin and S. McKinnon (eds), *Relative Values: Reconfiguring Kinship Studies*, 175–202. Durham: Duke University Press.

Thompson, C. 2005. *Making Parents: The Ontological Choreography of Reproductive Technologies*, Cambridge: MIT Press.

Turkmendag, I., R. Dingwall and T. Murphy. 2008. 'The Removal of Donor Anonymity in the UK: The Silencing of Claims by Would-be Parents', *International Journal of Law, Policy and the Family* 22(3): 283–310.

Turnpenny, P.D., S.A. Simpson and A.M. McWhinnie. 1993. 'Adoption, Genetic Disease, and DNA'. *Archives of Disease in Childhood* 69(4): 411–413.

Warnock M. 2002. *Making Babies: Is there a Right to Have Children?* Oxford: Oxford University Press.

Jennifer M. Speirs obtained her PhD in 2008 from The University of Edinburgh for her thesis 'Secretly Connected? Anonymous Semen Donation, Genetics and Meanings of Kinship'. She is a research associate at the University's Centre for Research on Families and Relationships, where she recently held a postdoctoral fellowship and where she has tutored and taught in social anthropology, social work and medicine. She has been a Lay Clinic Inspector for the Human Fertilisation and Embryology Authority, and is a support and intermediary worker in the post-adoption field and in services for people affected by post-donation issues.

 7

Intimate Documents
Trust and Secret Police Files in Post-socialist Mongolia

Chris Kaplonski

Badamtsoo, a woman born in 1930, talked in 2009 with an interviewer from the *Oral History of Twentieth Century Mongolia* project about the rehabilitation of her father, who had been arrested, charged and executed as a counter-revolutionary in 1930s Mongolia.[1]

> Sainbileg [the interviewer, asking about Badamtsoo's father's education; he had graduated from a military school]: What city in Russia [did he graduate from]?
> Badamtsoo: I don't know. I just saw it on one repression document.
> Sainbileg: Ah, you only saw it on the rehabilitation material?
> Badamtsoo: Yes. The rehabilitation … when he was rehabilitated, they said he didn't commit any crime or anything. I only saw that. Apart from that, I don't know anything.
> Sainbileg: When you looked in the archives, what crime was he accused of, what did it say?[2]
> Badamtsoo: There was nothing like that.
> Badamtsoo's husband: It just said that a certain military decree was overturned. He was rehabilitated along with his younger sibling. The father, his younger brother … three or four people were arrested from the city.
> Sainbileg: Would you tell us about what you were thinking?
> Badamtsoo: What I know about when he was arrested … He put on his *deel* [the traditional Mongolian robe].
> Sainbileg: Did they arrest him at home?
> Badamtsoo: Yes. We were all there. My mother was crying endlessly, my father … my mother was crying, I just heard the crying, but I didn't know why. They said my father had been sent away. I didn't really know much.
> Sainbileg: Ah. Then, did your mother know about what was going on?
> Badamtsoo: She knew.
> Sainbileg: Did your mother tell you then about what was going on, or did you figure it out later?
> Badamtsoo: Oh, only now of course. When my father was taken like that, my mother was very scared and didn't say anything.
> Sainbileg: So, your father disappeared without a trace?
> Badamtsoo: Yes.

Sainbileg: No news came after that?
Badamtsoo: No. Nothing at all.

Badamtsoo's story is unfortunately all too common in Mongolia. In the late 1930s, in the space of about eighteen months, somewhere between 35,000 and 45,000 Mongolians were arrested and the majority executed as counter-revolutionaries or Japanese spies. Most disappeared without a trace, and the only knowledge that many people have of their relatives are not stories handed down by parents, who were often afraid to talk, but rather, scraps of information gleaned from the documents issued when a person is rehabilitated: when their case is reinvestigated, overturned, and they are declared to have been the victim of a politically motivated sentence. Through providing information about disappeared relatives and confirming their innocence, the rehabilitation process serves as a means of recovering or even discovering personal history and connecting with the past. This connection is not a simple or direct one. People learn of their relatives through documents created during the rehabilitation process. These documents, in turn, are based on older documents, contemporaneous with the repression itself.

These older documents are at the heart of a tension in the rehabilitation process I examine here through the lenses of trust and intimacy. The tension is the need to rely on documents that, at some level, are not reliable. There is a need for them to be simultaneously reliable and unreliable. I have addressed one aspect of this issue elsewhere, arguing that the effect of this tension is 'not to *represent* the truth, but *create* it' (Kaplonski 2011: 432). That article, 'Archived Relations', demonstrates the relations between various documents drawn upon and created in the rehabilitation process, a process that has previously been unexamined from such an approach. It explicates the creation of a past through the rehabilitation process. The documents the rehabilitation process created serve to overwrite the 'truth' of the original documents that the new documents were based on. Thus, the original documents apparently had to be true enough to base a decision upon, but not so true that they couldn't be replaced with a new truth. Indeed, they needed to be judged not true in some way for the entire process to work. In this chapter I move my examination of this productive tension forward by shifting focus to the relations between documents and people. Having previously looked at how documents interact with each other, I now look at how they interact with people, and what this means.

'Trust' is a useful concept here. Since writing 'Archived Relations', I have shifted from thinking about the tension on which rehabilitation rests in terms of truth to thinking about it in terms of trust. Such a shift resolves one level of the tension, the apparent fact that the documents need to be both truth and untrue. More importantly, it opens up new avenues of thinking about this tension, and reveals the myriad ways in which trust is an integral part of the rehabilitation process. There are multiple levels of trust, almost entirely unacknowledged and unexamined by the people involved, that are vital to the process. As unacknowledged and unexamined, 'trust' was not a word that was used in conversations about rehabilitation, although I do believe it is an accurate description of what is taking place and an enlightening one. In this chapter, I unpack and explore these multiple levels of trust. At the heart of this examination is the productive tension between trust and non-trust necessitated by the documents themselves, but which works to create a sense of connectedness to the past, and help recreate the repressed relative as a social person.[3] The decision to trust the documents, in short, enables the repressed person to exist as a social being.

This chapter contributes to the growing field of the anthropology of documents and archives (for a small sample see Burton 2005; Riles 2006; Stoler 2009; Kaplonski and Trundle 2011). What this chapter brings to the debate is the concept of trust. Historians, of course, have long been concerned with whether or not documents are genuine, and have long been aware that all documents come with biases, omissions and lacunae. Whether or not to trust such documents, and to what extent, is arguably an implicit part of evaluating documents. Here I want to make this explicit, and look at the ramifications of doing so.

In this chapter, I approach trust as an affect or emotional commitment, rather than a rational choice. This allows us to bring people back into the picture of the processes of rehabilitation in an explicit way. In the last part of this chapter, I link the relations between documents and people to other questions raised by the rehabilitation process. In doing so, I also hope to offer some thoughts on broader issues of materiality and intimacy.

Before turning explicitly to trust and the relations between documents and people, I first sketch out the rehabilitation process, both why it exists and how it works. This is necessary to understand more fully the tension I seek to explore here, as well as highlight some of the multiple levels of trust in the process. I then consider trust more explicitly, as well as how and why people put their trust in the rehabilitation documents, before turning to consider the relations this helps create between people and their own past.

The Road to Rehabilitation

The winter of 1989/90 saw a peaceful democratic revolution sweep Mongolia, which had been a socialist country since the early 1920s. The first public demonstrations calling for open elections and faster reform, akin to the Soviet Union's *perestroika* and *glasnost*, were held in December 1989 (see Kaplonski 2004: ch. 3). By April 1990, the Politburo had resigned, and the first democratic elections were held soon after.

As elsewhere in the (post)socialist world, the opening of Mongolian politics had been accompanied by an opening of the archives of the past, both figurative and literal. One topic that was now openly acknowledged in a new, more critical light was that of the mass repressions and killings of the 1930s, and political repression during socialism more generally.[4] The entire country had been caught up in the violence of the late 1930s. One major focus of attention had been the Buddhist establishment, which, even a decade and a half after the socialist revolution of 1921, still constituted a significant threat to the government's power. Total estimates for those killed range from 36,000 to 45,000 and of those, about 18,000 were lamas. A similar number were Buriads, a Mongolian ethnic group that was seen as particularly suspect for a number of reasons. (The two categories, of course, overlapped.)

Demands for acknowledgement of what had happened (and by some, for responsibility) and for the rehabilitation of those repressed accompanied the new openness of the late 1980s and early 1990s. People wanted acknowledgements that their uncles, fathers and grandfathers had been innocent victims.[5] In a few cases, rehabilitation had even preceded the democratic revolution. Other political figures who had been repressed in the 1960s – expelled from the Party and fired from their jobs, denounced, jailed or sent into exile – were quickly rehabilitated for their political import (Kaplonski 2004: 67). In other cases, rehabilitation documents indicate that the rehabilitation process began in the months before the first protests. Some people had been rehabilitated during the socialist period itself, but these rehabilitations were kept secret until the 1990s. Although rehabilitations took place throughout the early and mid 1990s, it was not until 1998 that a law specifically governing the rehabilitation and compensation of the politically repressed came into force after much debate (Kaplonski 1999). In practical terms, this merely ensconced in law the practices that were already in use.

The Rehabilitation Process

The rehabilitation process in Mongolia, as elsewhere, depends upon documents and the law. Not everyone who may be considered from a social perspective to have been politically repressed would be legally defined as such. Some children of people killed in the 1930s claim to be 'more' repressed than people actually convicted of political crimes in the 1950s and 1960s, as they felt they suffered more than later victims. The children did indeed suffer. Not just through loss of a parent, but often through confiscation of all the family's belongings, expulsion from school and even being entered into government registers as people to be watched. An entire, chilling register exists from the late 1930s listing children of 'counter-revolutionaries' and their educational information (State Central Historical Archives 1939). Yet legally they are not eligible for rehabilitation or compensation, as those arrested for political crimes in the 1960s are.

To be legally defined as politically repressed, one needs to have been sentenced by one of a number of Special Commissions that operated during socialism to handle cases related to state security, or convicted under specific sections of the criminal code. A person convicted of spreading counter-revolutionary propaganda, a large, catch-all crime, would qualify for possible rehabilitation. Someone convicted of violating the law separating religion and state, a relatively common charge against lamas in the 1930s, would not qualify.

If a person passes this first hurdle, there is a second, more substantive one their case faces. It must be documented. There must be extent records of the original process. If they do not exist, one may call the person in question 'repressed', but they are not legally defined as such, nor, under the law, are they (or their relatives) eligible for compensation. Estimates range from three to six thousand people for whom this is the case. In some cases, there originally was documentation that was later lost. In others, it may well never have existed, as people were sometimes hauled off the street to make up a quota of arrests.

In recognition that rehabilitation is as much a political or social issue as a legal one, the head of the rehabilitation commission told me in an interview in August 2011 that he had asked the *Ih Hural* [Parliament] to render a decision on these cases, but nothing had yet been done. As I return to below, such an appeal to the political authorities actually runs counter to the logic of rehabilitation.

The final hurdle in the rehabilitation process is the process itself. Rehabilitation is not automatic. It is essentially a reinvestigation of a case, complete with a prosecutor, judges and a legal decision at the end. Assuming the case for rehabilitation is made, the prosecutor calls for the original charges to be overturned (lit: *hüchingüi*, made powerless). This decision is then accepted by the judges, and the people involved are declared rehabilitated. Their relatives, who asked for the rehabilitation, are given a small certificate and a copy of the court document overturning the original charge, as well as a short covering letter from the secret police archives. Compensation is paid: 500,000 *tögrög* (roughly $600 at the time the law was passed) for those sentenced to prison, twice that amount for those killed. The rehabilitation process may have social and political significance, but it is at its root a legal one that relies on documents.

It is at the point of determining eligibility to be rehabilitated that the tension I want to highlight comes in. Researchers go into the archives, and re-evaluate the evidence that was used in the original case. The evidence mostly comes in the form of the secret police files. While other material may be drawn upon, it is the still-classified case files of what, in the late 1930s, was called the Ministry of Internal Affairs that provide the bulk of the material for most of the cases. This is particularly so where the person was sentenced by a Special Commission, as their case was handled outside the normal channels of the legal system.[6]

This is a point that must be kept in mind, since it is a source of the tension in the process: the rehabilitation process relies upon documents that may well have been created through the use of torture or were at least partially fabricated. The Ministry of Internal Affairs apparently did not record what methods were used in their files, but from the few published versions (e.g., Dumburai 1991) and traces in accessible archives, we can follow in heart-breaking steps the breakdown of a person's will, and embellishment of their interrogation from confused protestations – 'I don't know why you arrested me' – to full confession to a range of counter-revolutionary plots and crimes.[7]

Since the secret police documents are not accessible by the general public or even relatives (although the rules sometimes seem to be bent), a degree of trust is required. The relatives who have asked for the rehabilitation must trust that the rehabilitation committee is doing its work conscientiously: that documents that are said to either exist or not truly do, and they are genuine, not recent forgeries. While people have mentioned missing documentation to me in interviews, no one has questioned whether this is actually the case. At this level, trust seems relatively unproblematic to the people involved. This, upon reflection, may seem a bit strange. Why should people believe the secret police when they say records – damning to their institutional memory – are missing? I think at least part of the explanation for this lies in the resolution of missing documents. While missing documents prevent a legal rehabilitation, a statement can be issued instead, stating that the person can nonetheless be considered repressed. There is still an acknowledgement, if not a legal clearing of his name. This in turn enables the emotional connection with the past to be made.

It is worth pursuing this a bit further, however, to contrast it with Jennifer Spiers' work on birth certificates (this volume). As Spiers notes, in the case of donor insemination, birth certificates become a contested site of creating and challenging intimate relations and are not trusted. There are two points which I think help illuminate this difference in trusting official documents. The first is that the birth certificates themselves are about a different sort of intimate relation. The birth certificates, I would argue, are about ultimately creating or recognizing familial relations. This is not what the rehabilitation certificates do. These latter give social life to an acknowledged, or at least unproblematic relation. It is possible that through the rehabilitation documents a person may learn they had a relative they did not know about. More commonly, however, they will provide information on someone who was at least known to exist – a husband or grandfather or other relative. This, I would suggest, is substantially different from learning that a person listed as your parent on a birth certificate is not. The rehabilitation documents may re-create a repressed person as a social being, but they had already existed as a historical fact: I had a grandfather who was killed. The birth certificates, in contrast, seem to challenge the historical as well as social being of the people involved.

The second point is simply that the birth certificates challenge or break intimate relations. The Mongolian rehabilitation documents do not. They, instead, give affirmation to a relation that people want to exist. To put it bluntly, at this level, the documents are trusted because they tell people what they want to hear.

To return to the rehabilitation process: assuming that there are documents, a decision to rehabilitate or not is made based upon the existing evidence, whether from the secret police or elsewhere. At the decision level, the outcome is binary: a person is rehabilitated or not, and this is made clear in a court resolution. The actual rehabilitation documents may go into some length explaining the logic of overturning the conviction, and this can be revealing. The basic decision, of course, is that they didn't do what they were said to have done. Yet the facts may be more complex. A case may be dismissed with the simple declaration that the basic charge was wrong: 'Agvaanjam'yan didn't have connections to a foreign intelligence agency' (Supreme Court 1990a). Other times, it is a lack of evidence that enables rehabilitation: documentary proof of guilt does not exist. A person was convicted only on hearsay, and that should not have been enough. In still other cases, the resolution reached is murkier, and in terms of the tension, more interesting. Take for example, the rehabilitation decree of the Yonzon Hamba, probably the most prominent lama in Mongolia when he was executed in October 1937. It says, roughly: 'it is probable that they were carrying out these [counter-revolutionary] activities'. It goes on to say: 'But there is no clear evidence about anyone. Because there is no legal evidence, but only suspicion, the [court] decision was imposed on flimsy grounds' (Supreme Court 1990b). Everyone involved in this particular case was rehabilitated.

Taken as a whole, these rationales for overturning convictions seem striking. It appears that the documents often hinted at something real, but the evidence was also being ignored. Legally, this is clear – the conviction is nullified for lack of sufficient evidence. But epistemologically, it seems murkier. What constitutes 'legal evidence' in this case? Why is some evidence accepted (trusted), while others not? I have read the trial transcripts, the newspaper coverage of the Yonzon Hamba's trial in 1937 and even classified reports on the interrogations by the secret police. The Yonzon Hamba and others confessed, often in vivid detail. We are almost certain, of course, this was obtained through torture, and so the records are suspect to say the very least. Yet here, and elsewhere, records are clearly being relied on at the same time they are disregarded. They are used as evidence to deduce that there was counter-revolutionary activity, just not good enough evidence for a conviction. In other words, to use my initial approach: the documents need to be true enough to be judged untrue. We must trust them enough to know they can not be trusted. If they were not judged valid at some basic level, they would not suffice as evidence to overturn themselves.

Attempts to unpack this conundrum by asking people in Mongolia involved in the process to expand upon how such decisions were reached were unhelpful. 'You just know' was the essence of the replies I received. This will be a feeling familiar to anyone who has worked in archives, and while it may be at one level profoundly unenlightening, at another it highlights the issue of trust. 'You just know' suggests some things can be trusted, some can't. It is a matter of experience or intuition which is which. But let me leave the explicit consideration of trust aside for the moment, and mention a larger issue linked to the documents and their context.

The entire rehabilitation process is built upon accepting the general process of what we now call political repression as legitimate. The cases that now are called repression are the system out of control, which is an indictment of those who used the system, not the system itself. (In the parlance of contemporary politics, 'mistakes were made'.) That is, the rehabilitation of a specific individual is only possible by asserting that it was possible for people to be justly and rightly convicted under the same sets of laws and procedures. The laws in force at the time can not be seen as illegitimate; only their application in a specific situation is. The rehabilitation process *must* not call into question the laws and procedures of the specific era. It can question a specific case and argue the law was misapplied, but the laws themselves are recognised as legitimate.

This is a basic point that I think is all too seldom appreciated. The old, socialist system must first be accepted as valid for rehabilitation to work. From this perspective, the move to handle the thousands of cases for which no documents exist in a political manner would undermine the entire system. A successful appeal based on sentiment or political expediency – which is what such a move would entail – would effectively render all previous rehabilitations if not strictly null and void, pointless. If the system in place in the late 1930s (to focus on the period of the greatest violence) is simply ignored for some cases, it suggests the cases that have proceeded through the rehabilitation process have done so needlessly. A political handling of the repressions would imply that all documents are simply false or irrelevant. The rehabilitation process at some level attempts to interrogate the past. A blanket political decision would simply ignore what traces of the past remain.

Yet if an appeal to sentiment for those without documents threatens the entire edifice, affect – and in particular, trust – helps us to think about what is going on in a new way, and helps link the rehabilitation process back to the relatives of the repressed.

Trusting in Trust

It was after a conversation with my colleague Paula Haas about her work on trust among the Barga Mongols of Inner Mongolia (see her contribution to this volume) that I realized that perhaps this was a way past the tension of truth / non-truth that I was puzzling over. It seemed to offer the possibility to turn an apparent tension into something productive. The shift from talking about 'true' documents to ones that are trusted is a key movement. Pieces of the puzzle began to click into place. What is taking place in the rehabilitation process is better understood as a multi-tiered process, rather than a single-layered paradox.

There are a number of areas I now want to explore through thinking about trust. I start with a shift from thinking about the documents upon which the rehabilitation process is based as 'true' to thinking of them as objects which must be trusted. Here 'trust' implies a relationship, an attachment to the past that is embodied in the document. This does not negate the legal aspect of the rehabilitation process, but rather sets it aside for the moment. This in turn reflects how rehabilitation documents are encountered and understood by the relatives of the repressed in Mongolia.

In talking about trust, I adopt an approach similar to that argued for by people such as Lahno, who describes trust as 'an emotional attitude' (2001: 174). I find this approach useful for a number of reasons. We gain nothing in the current context from seeing trust as an assessment of risk, a calculated gamble. At one level, the outcome of misplaced trust in the original documents would be a person wrongly rehabilitated, or perhaps refused rehabilitation. But while this may deny comfort to their family if rehabilitation was denied, it is hard to see how a falsely rehabilitated person would constitute a risk in any meaningful sense. More generally, to see relying on the documents as a risk or a gamble seems merely to call more attention to the tension I am addressing, rather than resolving it. It is an intellectual distancing, not an emotional commitment. In Mongolia, I have argued, the importance of personal memory is key in understanding how the legacy of political violence has been handled in the post-socialist context (Kaplonski 2008; see below for a fuller discussion). The link to the individual past is what matters. From this perspective, the rehabilitation documents are an affirmation of what the relatives of the repressed already believed.

At a more abstract level, I find the link Lahno makes with faith, and with the affective state of feeling a 'connectedness', enlightening. This enables us to move from simply trusting the documents to building on that trust, and seeing where it leads us – the eventual reconstruction of a social person. The first part of this, the link with faith, finds echoes in Möllering's reading of Simmel on trust, and in particular his attention to what he calls 'suspension': 'the bracketing of the unknowable which represents a defining aspect of the nature of trust' (2001: 417). Indeed, I want to suggest that at the very heart of the relation between people and the documents is a Kierkegaardian leap of faith, to trust, at some level, the secret police documents, and in so doing, to enable a connection to the past and a long-lost relative. This act, however, requires implicitly bracketing off an entire range of possible interpretations and readings of the documents, all ultimately unknowable.

Finally, trust is a useful concept as it explicitly returns agency to the present. A person may or may not be trustworthy, but the decision (conscious or otherwise) to trust is ultimately ours. Neither people nor documents can force trust. As Collingwood puts it of writing history: 'the historian is his own authority and his thought autonomous, self-authorizing, possessed of a criterion to which his so-called authorities must conform' (1992 [1946]: 236). This calls to mind the comment by people involved in the rehabilitation process, of which documents to trust: 'You just know'. Ultimately, it is the actor in the present who controls the reading of the past. In our context, the documents are useful because we decide to trust them, as any historian must do. In this context, I think it is telling that I have not encountered anyone who doubted any aspect of the rehabilitations documents. I do not simply mean that people take them as evidence that their relative was innocent. Rather, no one has ever suggested that while the outcome was correct, details were wrong. Part of the explanation, of course, is that there is often no other source of information to contest what the rehabilitation documents report. But that would not preclude an emotional or gut-level refusal to accept some of the facts. In other words, once people trust the documents, they seem to do so completely.

Having said this, I do go somewhat against the grain in thinking of relations between people and the state in Mongolia, where both ethnographically and analytically, 'respect' is a much more common trope than 'trust'. The state has, in the post-socialist milieu, established ceremonies of worship or respect to the state (Dulam and Bianquis 2010). These, to some extent, recall old traditions. In my experience, however, they tend to be seen by Mongolians as political manoeuvres or symbolic gestures rather than necessarily deeply held beliefs about the state and one's relation to it. The state is not mentioned, explicitly or otherwise, in the talk of the rehabilitation process. It is an unspoken presence since it is ultimately the state, in the form of judicial authorities, that authorizes the rehabilitation. But in my experience, these elements are seen as discrete from an abstraction of the state. Just as the rehabilitation documents do not indicate respect for the state, neither are they received as embodiments or enactments of the state. Rather, it is the archives themselves that are mentioned and seen as important.

The Materiality of Trust and Knowledge

Before I take up the relations between people and documents, let me unpack further a few reasons why documents are trusted. A key element of this, I want to suggest, is the materiality of the documents themselves. They offer traces of the past where otherwise there would be none. More than simply providing evidence, these traces create a link to the past, collapsing abstract knowledge of the past into lived truth. For those who have no other remains or knowledge of their relative, the existence of the archives offers reassurance that they actually existed. The memories or stories passed down by the older generations are not phantoms.

It will be recalled that documents must exist as a physical artefact to move the rehabilitation process forward. This materiality of the document is what actually matters. Content is, momentarily at least, irrelevant. In the context of rehabilitation, the document becomes the person. Documents are the nuclei around which the past can crystallize. This, rather than the content itself, is where trust and a greater emotional attachment to the past are rendered possible.

This is not quite as odd as it may seem. It is well known that the physicality of documents – their 'thingness' – can matter as much if not more than the content. One can think of the physical American Declaration of Independence, of which the US National Archives writes: 'it has been viewed with respect by millions of people, everyone of whom has had thereby a brief moment, a private moment, to reflect on the meaning of democracy'.[8] Here it is the physical document, not the content that matters. Similarly, in the Mongolian case, it is the knowledge that a version of the past exists that matters. Being often the only version of the past that is even semi-documented, it matters all the more.

Yet this is an odd materiality, for it always remains an invisible one to the family. For the relative of the repressed, or any other outside observer (such as an anthropologist) the existence of the original documents must be taken on faith. We must trust that they exist. During, and after, the rehabilitation process, the only people to see the actual case files (if there are any) or other documentation that will be used to judge the merits of the case are the researchers reinvestigating the case. The family of the repressed do not see the documents. Nor, as far as I have been able to ascertain, are they entered as evidence or produced at the rehabilitation ruling. At this stage of the process, in other words, the trust must be a blind trust. (Certain records – such as court cases – may be held in the central historical archives, which can be accessed by the public, and would provide some information. They are, however, written in a different alphabet than is used today, and relatively few can read the old script.)

This trust is relatively unproblematic when the individual is rehabilitated. Why question a desired outcome? Yet, as noted earlier, I have not encountered – in conversations or readings – anyone who seriously questioned missing documents or suggested information was incorrect. Even the lack of materiality seems trusted. People may complain about how their relative can not be rehabilitated, but they do not seem to doubt that the records are indeed missing. Part of this can be understood, as I have noted, through the fact that the person's social standing as a repressed person is still acknowledged. Another reason is that the rehabilitation process in Mongolia is not a reckoning or coming to terms with the past such as a truth commission attempts. It is focused solely on the individual, and was intended to avoid issues of culpability or blame. While it is a public recognition of repression, it says nothing about larger social or legal processes.

There is an additional twist, or perhaps it is an irony. That is, the rehabilitation process is dependent upon the secret police and their current successors (who have been reported to drag their feet at times, slowing investigations). The standard historical accounts, at least in the West, have been that the socialist security apparatus was among the most untrustworthy of sources. Yet the rehabilitation process argues against this. Once again, the documents are trusted, but they are also trusted to be shown, in the final analysis, to be untrue.

This faith in secret police archives is not new or unique to Mongolia. As Cristina Vatulescu has noted in her work *Police Aesthetics*: 'The opening of the [secret police] archives has been dominated by an avid search for the truth about the past, which betrays an enduring belief in the authority of their holdings even on the part of the staunchest critics or victims of the secret police' (2010: 13). Ann Stoler makes a similar, if more inclusive argument about state secrets (2009: 25–28). Something invites us to trust such sources, even against what should perhaps be our rational better judgement. A secret *must* be worth knowing; truer it seems precisely because it has been kept secret. (One may also think of the long European traditions of belief in secret societies and secret knowledge underlying and controlling the everyday world.)

There is a gaping presence at the centre of the rehabilitation process. It is not a transparent process, but rather one shrouded in opacity. Yet this is all that remains for the relatives of the repressed. This, if anything, increases the need for trust as an emotional commitment, or even renders it inevitable. The past is said to exist in the form of documents, but they can not be verified or even proven to exist by the relatives. Ultimately physical existence can not be a reflection of truth. A leap of faith is required, and the lack of other information, or even closure, compels the leaper forward. Thus materiality matters greatly. It offers a tangible connection to the past, a platform from which the leap can be made.

Another possible source for trust is the archives themselves, although this, I suggest, is merely a different version of what I have been arguing concerning materiality. In reading interviews from the *Oral History of Twentieth Century Mongolia*, I was struck by how often archives are appealed to as a source of information or authority. 'It's in the archives' was brought out several times as evidence that something was true or trustworthy, even when discussing issues such as salary or awards conferred during the socialist period. Even if inaccessible, the archives represent a source or form of authority. Knowing documents exist is enough.

In talking about one of the first schools of the socialist period, one person interviewed said: 'Then on 15 September 1924, they started teaching with ten-odd children. At this place. Then in 1925, 25 children were taught. The register of those 25 children is in the state archives'.[9] The archives are appealed to as both an authority (the documents exist there, so they are trustworthy) and as a source of additional information (the names, not given, can be found there).

Rather than respect for an abstraction of the state, what is important here was that the documents were known or believed to exist. They were a tangible fragment of the past, and by existing, must themselves be trustworthy. This belief carries over even when discussing rehabilitation and the knowledge and relations the rehabilitation process enables.

Intimacy and the Personal

Let me turn now to entangled tensions of intimacy, trust and the social and shift from speaking about trust, to thinking briefly about a form of intimacy and the individual and the social. The rehabilitation documents, it seems clear, serve to create a new past for the families involved and in doing so, recreate the repressed relative as a social person. Even those who remember the person who was arrested and never returned home have only faded memories, and perhaps a photo or two if they are lucky. Most, if not all, of the family's property was usually confiscated. It was not unusual for a sentence to include the confiscation of all property, apart from the minimum that the family needed to live, and this was often interpreted quite severely. (To cite one example several people reported: even tea kettles and cups would be confiscated.)

These slight remains and memories, however, were subject to doubt. People usually told me that they first began to question the mass arrests of the 1930s when their own relative was arrested. They often had assumed other people really were spies or traitors. But when their father or uncle was arrested, whom they knew to be innocent, they began to doubt. Yet secret police reports at the time suggest at least a few people harboured, if only temporarily, suspicion even about their own husbands or fathers.[10]

In such a context, the rehabilitation documents reaffirm what people had told themselves, or perhaps had heard from relatives. Their relative really was innocent. But they can also do much more. For many people, the documents may provide new information. A covering letter is supplied with the rehabilitation papers. This may provide a bit of extra information, such as the amount of livestock the person held at the time of his arrest, if they were literate, and a few other details. In the case of a lama named Suur', whom I shall return to shortly, we learn among other things that he had ten head of livestock and a *ger* [the Mongolian traditional felt tent] to his name, and had two disciples, but had never been abroad, never been convicted of a crime and never attended school (General Intelligence Agency Special Archive 2009).

It is not enough to paint a portrait of a person never known, but it serves to humanize them, to provide proof, as it were, that they were more than just a name.

Recall Badamstoo's comments at the start of this chapter:

Sainbileg: So, your father disappeared without a trace?
Badamtsoo: Yes.
Sainbileg: No news came after that?
Badamtsoo: No. Nothing at all.[11]

It was only from the repression documents that Badamtsoo was able to recover any information about her father; not only his eventual fate, but the fact that he had studied in Russia.

The repression documents don't always offer much information, but they do offer some, and that is important. Others echoed this point, with one noting that it was only when they applied for rehabilitation that they learned that their father had been shot, thirteen days after his arrest. But for them, from when he was arrested in 1937 until receiving this information there was no information).[12]

This knowledge is important, and it – or perhaps the documents – has several functions. The most basic and important function the documents provide is simply the knowledge itself. At a very fundamental level, this knowledge works to recreate the person as a social being, to re-establish a closeness. It was from the scraps of knowledge that at least some sense of knowledge of and a link to the past could be clutched at.

The sense here is one of closure, but it is also more than that. It was a relief for many of the people I talked to over the years to know what had happened. Even if they suspected their relative had been killed, to finally know for sure was a relief, however sorrowful. One woman told me her mother had died more than fifty years after her husband had been arrested, still hoping he would return home.

The knowledge seemed to restore the person to the present. In addition to the sadness that accompanied our interviews, the main feeling when talking about rehabilitation seemed to be one of relief. It seems to me that it was as much acknowledging that the person had existed, had lived, as that he or she had been wrongfully convicted that mattered. The papers were proof and the proof was what mattered.

Manduhai Buyandelger has written of how, among the Buriads of rural northern Mongolia, ancestors killed in the 1930s, who had been denied proper burial and mourning, reappeared in the 1990s as *üheer*, malevolent spirits who haunt the living. They are lacunae in historical and personal knowledge (Buyandelger 2007). The topic of ancestor worship or propitiation has never come up among the people I have talked to, nor was it even implied. I thus do not want to stretch the *üheer* parallel too far. Yet it seems to me that linkages that the rehabilitation process creates, acknowledging the person existed, is almost the exact opposite of the lack of knowledge that creates *üheer*. Buyandelger noted that the way to 'remake üheer into proper original spirits or reincarnate in a Buddhist fashion' would be precisely to discover their history, to document their existence (personal communication). The rehabilitation papers, simply through their existence, perform a similar function. In this case, however, since the relative is known about, it is not that a relationship is created, but rather that a level of intimacy is reinforced, expanded or intensified.

The documents also work in a much more tangible, physical way, which serves to recreate the social person. As we have seen, most relatives of the repressed have few, if any, material reminders of their relative. A few will have memories of them; perhaps a few snatched from childhood. But given the time that has elapsed, most people will never have known their repressed relative. For them, the slip of paper that is the rehabilitation certificate is a very real connection to the past. Many interviews I conducted with a relative of the repressed resulted in them bringing forth the certificate, or a photocopy of it, often in tears. A few activists I knew thought this was slim comfort indeed: how could one tiny slip of paper saying, in effect, 'Sorry, we made a mistake' atone for all the loss? They had a point. Yet it was a point out-weighed by the comfort such documents did bring to most people I knew. Some, with noted relatives, or perhaps simply a story that had caught someone's eye, had a newspaper clipping or two to complement the certificate and the copy of the court resolution that they were given as a result of the official process. These were all carefully kept in a plastic folder, placed with other important papers or memorabilia. For many people, the rehabilitation document served as, in essence, a keepsake, a memento. Its very physicality served to prove that the person once existed, and by existing, mattered.

In this regard, an incident from the summer of 2011 is telling. I had met with an old lama, who was from a region I would be visiting. He, like so many of the people I have talked to over the years, had with him a folder of rehabilitation documents, in this case relating to an uncle, Suur', who had also been a lama. We chatted for some time, about his various relatives who had been repressed, and cases of other lamas. It was only, however, when I asked if it would be possible to make copies or scans of the documents he had been showing me that he finally broke down into tears. As I hastily tried to apologise for upsetting him, he reluctantly agreed, saying he wanted other people to know about his uncle. For him, the documents were clearly freighted with much more meaning than merely being a documentary record. The documents were, in some very real way, a proxy for the missing uncle. It was only asking to make copies of the documents, to somehow engage more directly with his uncle, as it where, that provoked the tears. The tears may have been an extreme reaction, but it was not atypical. The documents, when they were brought out by the lama, and other people I talked to, were treated with respect. It would be a step too far, I think, to say the documents functioned as a form of a relic of the repressed relative. At times, however, they did seem to come close to this in the way an old woman would stroke the papers as she told the story of her husband. It is clear that the documents mattered, and mattered a great deal.

Intimacy and the Social

This physical link to a past that is both remembered and created has a flip side. This is a final point I wish to briefly take up, to link it to other work I have done on rehabilitation and the memory of individuals in post-socialist Mongolia. This is the distantiation from a fuller social engagement with the issue of repression. Despite what a passing familiarity might suggest, Mongolia as a country has never deeply or systematically addressed the issue of political violence. While there is a repression commission and a research centre associated with it, they are underfunded. There is a memorial museum, but that was created largely through the individual power and persuasion of a single woman, the daughter of a Prime Minister from the 1930s who had been killed. The space devoted to the displays in the museum has shrunk since her death in 2003, and I cannot recall meeting a single visitor there in the last several years that I have visited. In this case, the public space and recognition – the museum – was largely a monument to the individual – Prime Minister Genden – and indeed the museum was located in a house where he once lived. My point is that while officially, legally, the repressions are known and commemorated in Mongolia, in actual practice, they have not played as large a part in the social sphere as say, the question of lustration did in Eastern Europe, or the Truth and Reconciliation Commission played in post-apartheid South Africa.

The rehabilitation process, through the documentation of the individual it creates, and the intimate links it makes possible with the past, also serves to reinforce what I have elsewhere called the 'singularity of memory' in Mongolia (Kaplonski 2008). By this phrase I highlight the predominance of personal memory over social or political commemoration in Mongolia. Quite understandably, very few people were interested in the larger questions that surrounded the repressions of the socialist era. Very few cared who, ultimately, was to blame or why it all happened. They wanted, even needed, acknowledgement that their relative had lived, and had been wrongfully convicted. This need to remember a relative as a specific individual, rather than as a part of a larger event, lead to an emphasis on *who* rather than larger social questions of *why* and *what* or even *how*. What matters is that their specific relative is acknowledged to have been wronged. The geopolitics of the matter, or 'coming to terms with the past', can wait.

This is not to suggest a traditional split between public and private, personal and social. The different spheres inevitably bleed into each other. The personal in this case prevents the social addressing of the issue of repression in Mongolia. There is no Mongolian Gauck Commission (the Commission established in Germany to deal with the Stasi files) because to establish one would require subsuming the personal into the social. This Mongolians are unwilling or unable to do, and I do not blame them. In terms of political repression, the documents they clutched or stroked as they told me their stories created for them an intimate link to a lost loved one, and that was more important than any broader reckoning. In this way, the repression museum, founded by the Prime Minister's daughter, was a private document writ large.

What I have shown in this chapter are the ways in which it can be fruitful to think of a particular set of documents, created by the rehabilitation process, in terms of trust and the relations they engender. The rehabilitation process, through these documents, enables the creation of a disappeared, repressed relative as a social person. Trust, usually thought of something as taking place between individuals or groups, is here applied to documents, but documents that in the end enable relations between people.

The rehabilitation process gives the relatives in the present a connection that functions on multiple levels to recover a past many of them had never known, and to create intimate links to it. It is the ironic and chilling need to trust the secret police files, which may record false confessions and torture, that makes this past possible. Trust opens a possibility to the past, and through its affective nature, renders this past all the more important and all the more real.

Acknowledgements

Many thanks are due to Paula Haas and Manduhai Buyandelger for their feedback, discussions and insights. The presenters and organizers of the workshop, 'The Entangled Tensions of Intimacy: Trust and the Social' at the University of Bergen, who kindly discussed and provided comments on my paper even when I was unable to attend, are also kindly thanked. An earlier version of this chapter was also presented as part of the panel 'Trust as Traces: Past, Present, and Emotive Relationships' at the 2011 American Anthropological Association meetings in Montreal.

Notes

1. Oral History Interview 091201A, *Oral History of Twentieth Century Mongolia*. Available at <http://amantuuh.socanth.cam.ac.uk/search/view_transcript.php?Interview=091201A&Person=990473> (accessed 11 September 2013). Mongolians traditionally only use one name.
2. This is a bad phrasing by the interviewer; the relatives do not see the archives themselves.
3. I am indebted to Manduhai Buyandelger for this phrasing.
4. In this chapter, I focus my attention largely on the 1930s, since this is a central research concern of mine.

5   I here purposefully use the masculine. Out of the thirty-six thousand or more people killed, only nineteen are known to be women.
6   I use 'secret police' and 'security services' somewhat loosely and interchangeably to refer to what has at various times been the Office of Internal Security, the Ministry of Internal Affairs, the Ministry of Public Security, and so forth: the Mongolian equivalent of the NKVD / KGB.
7   See Chapter Eight in Kaplonski 2014 for a fuller discussion of this case and the interrogation records.
8   'Declaration of Independence: A History'. Available at <http://www.archives.gov/exhibits/charters/declaration_history.html> (accessed 9 November 2011).
9   Oral History Interview 090734B, *Oral History of Twentieth Century Mongolia*. Available at <http://amantuuh.socanth.cam.ac.uk/search/view_transcript.php?Interview=090734B&Person=990286> (accessed 11 September 2013).
10 I am indeed aware of the irony of 'trusting' secret police reports in this context.
11 See note 1.
12 Oral History Interview 080807A, *Oral History of Twentieth Century Mongolia*. Available at <http://amantuuh.socanth.cam.ac.uk/search/view_transcript.php?Interview=080807A&Person=990041> (accessed 11 September 2013).

References

Burton A. (ed.). 2005. *Archive Stories: Facts, Fictions, and The Writing Of History*. Durham: Duke University Press.

Buyandelger, M. 2007. 'Dealing with Uncertainty: Shamans, Marginal Capitalism, and the Remaking of History in Postsocialist Mongolia', *American Ethnologist* 34(1): 127–147.

Collingwood, R.G. 1992 [1946]. *The Idea of History*. Oxford: Oxford University Press.

Dulam, S. and I. Bianquis. 2010. 'Major State Rituals and the Reinvention of Tradition in Contemporary Mongolia, Part 2'. In I. Charleux, B. Brown and G. Green (eds), *Representing Power in Modern Inner Asia: Conventions, Alternatives and Oppositions*. Bellingham, WA: Western Washington University.

Dumburai, A. 1991. *Dechin Gegeenii hiidiin Tiv Lam B. Agvaanjam'yan* [Tiv Lama Agvaanjam'yan, of Dechin Gegeen Monastery]. Ulaanbaatar: UABHEG-yn töv arhiv.

General Intelligence Agency Special Archive. 2009. D. Suuriin tuhai [About D. Suur']. Ulaanbaatar, Mongolia.

Kaplonski, C. 1999. 'Blame, Guilt and Avoidance: The Struggle to Control the Past in Post-socialist Mongolia', *History and Anthropology* 11(2): 94–114.

—— 2004. *Truth, History and Politics in Mongolia: The Memory of Heroes*. London: RoutledgeCurzon.

—— 2008. 'Neither Truth nor Reconciliation: Political Violence and the Singularity of Memory in Post-socialist Mongolia', *Totalitarian Movements and Political Religions* 9(2): 371–388.

―――― 2011. 'Archived Relations: Repression, Rehabilitation and the Secret Life of Documents in Mongolia.' *History and Anthropology* 22(4): 431–444.
―――― 2014. *The Question of the Lamas: Violence, Sovereignty and Exception in Early Socialist Mongolia*. Honolulu: University of Hawai'i Press.
Kaplonski, C. and C. Trundle (eds). 2011. 'The Political Life of Documents: Archives, Memory and Contested Knowledge,' *History and Anthropology* (Special Issue) 22(4).
Lahno, B. 2001. 'On the Emotional Character of Trust', *Ethical Theory and Moral Practice* 4(2): 171–189.
Möllering, G. 2001. 'The Nature of Trust: From Georg Simmel to a Theory of Expectation, Interpretation and Suspension', *Sociology* 35(2): 403–420.
Riles, A. (ed.). 2006. *Documents: Artifacts of Modern Knowledge*. Ann Arbor: University of Michigan Press.
State Central Historical Archives. 1939. Folder of documents on children of counter-revolutionaries studying in schools. 6-2-400. Ulaanbaatar, Mongolia.
Stoler, A. 2009. *Along the Archival Grain: Epistemic Anxieties and Colonial Common Sense*. Princeton: Princeton University Press.
Supreme Court of the Mongolian People's Republic. 1990a. 'Buyan-Orshih Ovogtoi Agvaanjam'yan, (Jam'yantiv) Galsanbaldan ovogtoi Gonchigdoo, Lamjav Ovogtoi Damdinjav naryn hereg talaar' [About the case of Buyan-Orshihyn Agvaanjam'yan (Jam'yantiv), Galsanbaldanyn Gonchigdoo, and Lamjavyn Damdinjav]. Supreme Court Resolution 08, 23 August 1990.
Supreme Court of the Mongolian People's Republic. 1990b. 'Yonzon Hamba Ts. Luvsanhaimchig naryn 23 hünii hergiin tuhai' [About the case of the Yonzon Hamba Ts. Luvsanhaimchig, with 23 people]. Supreme Court Resolution 07, 25 July 1990.
Vatulescu, C. 2010. *Police Aesthetics: Literature, Film, and the Secret Police in Soviet Times*. Stanford: Stanford University Press.

Chris Kaplonski is currently a Lecturer in the Division of Social Anthropology, University of Cambridge. His is a social anthropologist focusing on political and legal anthropology, and has carried out fieldwork in Mongolia since the early 1990s. His work encompasses the remaking of history after socialism; the role of narrative, bureaucracy and archives in reconstructing the past; political violence and its aftermath; show trials; and remembering political violence. His most recent project, *The Question of the Lamas: Violence, Sovereignty and Exception in Early Socialist Mongolia*, examines the use of political violence and the state of exception in contingent political systems through a study of violence by the early socialist state against the Buddhist establishment. He currently works on the intersection of consumption, sustainability and the sense of taste through a study of wine-making and consumption in Austria and the UK.

Trustworthy Bodies
Cashinahua Cumulative Persons as Intimate Others
Cecilia McCallum

Introduction

One's first impulse is to ask: how to trust a stranger? Blanche, a tragic character in Tennessee William's play 'A Streetcar Named Desire' famously said 'I have always relied on the kindness of strangers'. The poignancy of her assertion seems to lie in the sad circumstance that she could not depend upon family or friends. Yet many people would put the question the other way around: how is it possible to trust kin, to put faith in one's most intimate day-to-day companions? The ethnographic record is compelling – and a number of recent studies have once again laid this bare in the starkest terms. In Africa, fear that close family might transmute into witches is widespread and represents a creative adaptation to 'postmodern' times (Geschiere, this volume). For some Amazonians, too, sorcery is the flip side of kinship (Figueiredo 2010). In Guatemala, despite an ideology that teaches that safety resides at home, experience speaks otherwise. There, says Ystanes (this volume), trust and mistrust, intimacy and distance, succeed and replace each other, never being finally settled within persons, spaces or the social body.

Geschiere critiques the assumptions about moral communities made by development workers and others in Africa, reflecting that it will not do to imagine that they are havens of 'good sociality'. As he notes, in the mid twentieth century anthropology fuelled this tendency to make banal associations between safety, trust and intimacy. Sahlins' (1974) notion of generalized reciprocity led many to essentialize an imagined altruistic sociality in certain kinds of small-scale society characterized by intimate co-residence. But, as he argues, trust and mistrust are not conditions or ontological statuses produced by prolonged intimacy among relatives: rather, they are historical in nature, epistemological outcomes emerging from structured flows of events that range to a global scale. Like other contributions to this volume, Ystanes and Geschière highlight the temporal and spatial instability of trust and mistrust, their fugitive quality, the need to constantly reconstitute the modes of relatedness in which they emerge, and the structured quality of these modes within and across domestic, local and global spaces and temporalities. The present chapter follows along these lines, through a discussion of the imbrications of trust and mistrust, intimacy and distance, in an Amazonian context, among the Cashinahua, a people whose approach to life is shaped by the ontological approach known as 'Amerindian perspectivism'.

Amerindian thought has a strong tendency to collapse spatial and temporal distance, taking the body as the axis of this compression. The Huni Kuin [Real People], as the Cashinahua call themselves, treat trustworthiness as embodied, that is, as integrated into organs and body systems materially as thought, emotion and memory. They think of the bodies of real people as purposefully fabricated over a lifetime and also moulded by unintended experiences. Trustworthiness emerges biographically in an empirical sense. Like other Amerindian perspectivists, Huni Kuin consider the body as both material and immaterial, soul integrated into matter, and know it as a point of transience between distinct spatial and temporal planes of the cosmos. Intimacy with radically different kinds of being from these various planes is internalized in human bodies, rendering them, from the point of view of living Huni Kuin, more or less human, more or less trustworthy.

The ethnographic discussion that follows seeks to clarify how the unstable quality of trust is directly linked to this perspectivist view of the body. After describing how the Amazonianist literature has tended to treat the topic of intimacy from a sociocentric perspective, I suggest the appropriateness of taking an ethnography of the body as an analytical starting point, due to its pivotal role in the constitution of relatedness. I open the ethnographic account with a description of the historical context, characterized by deep mistrust between Huni Kuin and Nawa [non-Indians], and an episode in my relationship with a key informant, Pancho Lopes. This successful leader founded a community but was later abandoned by many followers. His life story provides a running thread to the chapter.[1] The ambiguity of trust is sketched in terms of the tense relation between alterity and sameness, to consider the part that distinction between kinds of bodies – real human, non-human, Nawa – plays in this scenario. This leads to an ethnographic discussion of the fabrication of the body. This section explores indigenous phenomenology, focusing on how 'real' – thus gendered – persons are made, that is, persons who have embodied thought, memory and emotions. Ideally, long-term fabrication creates reliable workers who willingly engage in sexual relations only with correct categories of kin.

However, each body is a unique composite. Outcomes are not guaranteed. Trustworthy bodies are those that have accumulated appropriate attitudes to past and future, a point reinforced in the following section, which returns to Pancho to trace in further detail how emotions and thoughts are materially embedded in bodies. The final section looks critically at recent debates on relatedness in Amazonia that have set out an agenda for unravelling its formal aspects through a focus on the fractal person and perspectivist ontology. It argues that closer consideration of the phenomenological processes considered in this chapter is now required. The conclusion returns to Pancho's life story to suggest that the process whereby he became a successful leader and then lost his people's trust be read from this angle.

Intimacy in the Amazonianist Literature

The question of intimacy has been central to debates on sociality and personhood in the literature on the indigenous peoples of lowland South America. The analytic starting point was sociocentric, in effect marginalizing the salience, for Amerindian regimes of trust, of the duality of intimacy accumulated in transformable bodies. Approaches differed markedly with regard to the heuristic status of intimacy, depicted either as a constitutive part of the social configuration of collective or physiological bodies, or, alternatively, as its effect. Yet they shared a common conception of intimacy as the outcome of prolonged interactions between conscious, human subjects, and associated it with mutuality, conviviality and lived sociality in communities structured by ties of kinship and affinity. For the style of analysis led by Joanna Overing, which Viveiros de Castro (1996) branded 'the moral economy of intimacy' and linked to a view of Amazonian sociality as irenic, intimacy is the pivot in the constitution of the social order. Eduardo Viveiros de Castro, known for his later unravelling of Amerindian perspectivism, is a key figure in the development of the alternative 'symbolic economy of alterity' approach. Here, intimacy is an epiphenomenon of wider structuring processes that draw their energy from sources external to those social domains where conscious human subjects interact. For him 'moral economists' place emphasis on morally achieved solidarity and privilege discussion of internal social relations within groups conceived as social monads, at the expense of wider networks of relatedness. His alternative approach, a development of Lévi-Straussian structuralism, sees sociality as determined by relations of alterity: the external encompassing the internal, distance setting the conditions of being for intimacy. In response, Overing and Passes (2000) emphasize that the notion of 'good living' is central in Amerindian sociopolitical thinking. To live well, people must trust co-residents; but sociocosmological relations with outsiders, spirits, or animals are also vital (Overing 1999; Santos Granero 2007).

In this chapter I take the posited divergences between these two approaches to sociality among Amazonians to be a matter of theoretical emphasis rather than substance (McCallum 2013). The argument developed below is that specific regimes of trust and mistrust emerge within particular modes of conceptualizing relatedness – indeed, within modes of *doing* and *undoing* relations – to which due attention must be paid. Methodologically, this entails taking the inherently unstable body that is both the seat of perspective and the social fulcrum of relatedness as an analytic starting point. I show below that for the Huni Kuin relatedness is seated in the body, materially, as a possible outcome of embodied experience. It is to this that the notion of 'cumulative body' refers. I argue that for Huni Kuin relatedness pivots on the necessary location of human perspectives in bodies whose interactions forge connections, as for other Amerindians. Trust is thus a possible but fragile outcome of an activated history of relatedness: a person, animal, plant or spirit body can only be known as trustworthy at the moment when her or his particular embodied history is put into action.

Ethnographies of perspectivism play a key part in the recent 'ontological turn' in anthropological theory (Costa and Fausto 2010). But in line with other chapters in this book, the Huni Kuin material suggests that more is at stake here than ontology, for the body within which relatedness comes to be embedded is framed in the terms of an indigenous form of phenomenology. Key aspects of relatedness, such as feelings of trust, or the knowledge that some person, entity or thing may be trusted, emerge from engagement with the phenomenal world, which is both material and immaterial. To understand the unstable imbrication of trust and intimacy it is necessary to grasp the contours of Huni Kuin phenomenology. Trust and mistrust of intimates and strangers have similar origins in affects and properties that are materially embodied in the person over time and extrapolated in intentional thought and action.

Trusting Others

Huni Kuin live most of their lives in close contact with the same persons and have developed sophisticated means for organizing relations amongst themselves: exogamous moieties, Kariera-type kin classification and a compatible alternate-generation naming system (Kensinger 1995; McCallum 2001). They favour settlement endogamy and try to persuade teenagers to marry their cross-cousins, who represent alterity yet are the most intimate of others. Here intimacy and trust are connected. To *know* to what degree a person may be trusted, whether she is in the habit of lying, stealing or aggression, one must have lived with that person or know someone who has. A person with whom one has lived closely is more likely to be trustworthy than a stranger, but this is not always the case. Equally, someone with whom one is intimate might be a source of danger.

While Nawa [foreigners, non-Indians, non-humans] are invariably untrustworthy, with few exceptions, Huni Kuin know each other as potentially and variably inconstant. After two years living with Huni Kuin, I knew myself to be a transformed, partially domesticated Nawa (McCallum 2010). When upbeat, I might claim to have embodied something of their way of being, and to be worthy of their trust (a condition I imagined, optimistically, to be reciprocal). So it was with chagrin that I experienced such inconstancy, in 1991, during a visit to Acre, the Brazilian state in Amazonia where about half the Huni Kuin population resides. Pancho Lopes, the leader of Recreio village in the Alto Purus Indigenous Area, where I had lived during the 1980s, made me a promise and then reneged on it. Thus I discovered that I could not trust someone who had been a key informant during my doctoral research, and who, some eight years previously, had included me in his circle of trust, as his *xanu* [cross-cousin] and as a co-resident of his family.

It was 1991. I had arrived in Rio Branco, the state capital, and, as required by law, checked in at the local branch of the National Indian Foundation, FUNAI.[2] I learnt that a new rule obliged visitors to Indigenous Areas to obtain prior consent from a local leader. Pancho happened to be in town and he promised to support my planned trip to Recreio. However, when I went into FUNAI to obtain final authorization for the visit, an official informed me that he had refused it and added: 'He said he will give his consent only after you obtain U$100,000 in development money for the village'. (That year, as part of Inter-American Development Bank financing of a main road linking the state to the rest of Brazil, Acre was awash with funds for projects aimed at 'protecting' indigenous peoples. Also I myself had recently failed to obtain funds for a project supporting the Alto Purus Huni Kuin.) Later, I complained to Pancho's nephew about his uncle's actions. He shrugged and replied, simply, 'My uncle is like that – one day he is good, another bad'.

In what specific Huni Kuin sense can a person be both good and bad, or fluctuate between the two? This chapter argues that Paulo's comment can be referred to a particular theory of agency, which holds that particular capacities to act permeate the body [*yuda*] in a material sense. Agency put in motion in correct action is both a condition for and a consequence of making 'real' bodies: that is, bodies able to engage in productive and reproductive action. Being properly human – or, if you like, personhood – depends upon such embodied knowledge and capacity.

Pancho let me down despite his past work in making me more of a real person, despite having spent some years transforming my original Nawa *yuda* into a more amenable entity, one conducive to Huin Kuin styles of sociality. It was work done so that I would be able to contribute positively to the ongoing constitution of social life in Recreio. During doctoral fieldwork and on later research visits, I held many discussions with him, kept his company, travelled with him, joked with him as does a man's female cross-cousin (McCallum 1997). From arrival on the banks of the Purus river I had depended on his support. After months in his house I moved into my own, some twenty metres away, but continued to eat meals with his family. In exchange, I offered what I could: apart from gifts, I worked with his family, helping prepare food and serve it, harvesting crops with his wives and daughters, as well as other tasks (McCallum 2001, 2010). He saw many advantages in my presence and often sought to exploit my perceived power as a Nawa for his and the other villagers' benefit. All this afforded me a tiny measure of shared, remembered and embodied intimacy, from both our perspectives.

From a Huni Kuin perspective, in my body, such intimacy is registered as *xinan* – a term that can be translated as 'thought', 'memory' and also 'trust' (Montag 1981: 405). With respect to our own relationship, I could not say that I had *xinan* for Pancho in the sense that I really 'trusted' him, but it would be correct to say I 'knew, recognized, remembered, thought of' him.

By Pancho's own account, his past was marked by disputes. Born in Brazil, until the late 1970s he resided in Peru. His down-river return was motivated by a dispute with an alleged poisoner. He claimed that he himself had murdered several people before his conversion to evangelical Christianity, which he took seriously. When first I lived in his house, he was fond of turning on an evangelical radio station to listen to sermons (in the early hours) and he held regular services or 'cultos', declaring himself to be a pastor of the faith. He assiduously studied a Huni Kuin translation of the New Testament. As elsewhere, these practices did not represent a 'conversion' in the sense of the radical discarding of one tradition in favour of another (Vilaça 2006, 2011). Pancho saw himself as a defender of 'real' [*kuin*] practices: styles of raising children, naming and marriage; eating and working together; curing and ritual. He and other self-declared converts expressed their new faith as a way of fostering correct living [*jive pe*] among the Huni Kuin, not as a rejection of the ways of the *xenipabu* [old ones]. There was no rupture on religious grounds with those co-resident kin who declared themselves Catholics or (in a few cases) 'pagan'.

Distinctions between Huni Kuin and Nawa were by contrast sharply etched. In the 1980s there was a general climate of ethnocentrism in Acre. However, indigenous people had some friends among the Nawa. They could count on the Catholic Josephine sisters of Manuel Urbano, who offered support and hospitality to Huni Kuin and other visitors (like myself). However, one night around 1987 Pancho and other Huni Kuin stayed in the simple wooden house the sisters usually made available to them. In the morning, the body of one of the visitors was discovered in the garden. After this, the sisters no longer wished to offer their hospitality to indigenous visitors.[3]

From a Huni Kuin perspective, Pancho's personal history left distinctive marks on his capacity for and attitudes to social action. He was a good speaker and clear thinker, able to formulate projects [*xinan*] and persuade people to follow him.[4]. He had the classic qualities of indigenous leaders in Amazonia, such as instigating collective undertakings through persuasion rather than coercion and he had brought a sizeable group of migrants with him from Peru in the late 1970s. In 1984, on a visit there, he inspired dozens more relatives to join him downriver in Recreio. As a result, the population surged briefly to several hundred (McCallum 1990). Pancho also engaged in national pro-Indian politics (once visiting Brasilia by bus) seeking legal demarcation of the Purus indigenous territory and economic aid, education and healthcare. He was skilled at organizing day-to-day life, inspiring groups of men to work or hunt together, initiating specific ritual cycles and so on. He elicited the cooperation of his father-in-law as chant-leader, and of his wife as *ainbu xanen ibu* [female leader]. She organized women in collective tasks and they acted jointly as pivots for collective meals involving up to twenty or more adults – sometimes on a daily basis (McCallum 2001). These practices establish relatedness in an embodied sense and are related to the Huni Kuin habit of speaking of kin as *nukun yuda* [our body] – a point explored in greater detail below.

Pancho's kin viewed him ambivalently. He could be overly authoritarian, sometimes incarnating the anti-social qualities of the Nawa bosses who once ruled in autocratic fashion over indebted rubber tappers. By 1990 Recreio had split up, about a decade after its foundation. By the time the researcher Lagrou last visited (1995), Pancho lived 'alone' with his wives, young unmarried children, one married daughter and his son-in-law.[5] His adult sons lived elsewhere. After years of intimacy, the conditions for renewing it had evaporated. But why had Pancho been such a successful leader? And why did his relatives eventually seem to lose faith in him? To answer these questions I return to the topic of the body and to the embodiment of thought / trust.

The Cumulative Person

Huni Kuin do not go as far as the Huaorani, who consider children as 'guests' on birth, before time and intimacy foster their transformation into kin (Rival 1998). But they do consider that humans are not born but made, slowly and cumulatively, through the progressive and deliberate moulding of the form and content of the body: the bones, teeth, flesh and skin of the child. This takes place through immersion in sensory fields of meaningful sound, sight, smell and touch. Knowledge and memory are integrated materially into the body through a series of techniques, as part of ordinary and extraordinary experience in the environing world, to form Real [*Kuin*] People [*Huni*] who are able to act upon the world and interact with others in a proper, productive (real, true) way. A real man [*huni kuin*)]and a real woman [*ainbu kuin*] have passed through experiences that allowed them to embody distinct sets of capacities and knowledge, so becoming equally human but differentially gendered. Though gender is not essence, not 'biologically determined', it does sit materially in the body as a capacity for moral and social action. Instilled in any real person, like other residues of experience it makes up part of his or her existential individuality (McCallum 1996b, 2001).

Around her twelfth birthday, Nara's mother began to complain about her unreliability. She did not think, was feckless, running wild [*unainsmapa*]. She avoided carrying crops and helping in food preparation. She did not absorb her mother's lessons in weaving design well. One day, she and a friend stole a pineapple from a neighbour's patch. In short, she could not be trusted to behave as a proper young woman and her mother was upset. She decided to intervene. So one morning she began to harangue Nara, listing the qualities required of a young woman, striking her on her arms as she did so. 'Do not be lazy, work hard', she said, as she repeatedly struck her upper and lower arms. This was not a punishment as one might first think, but rather a way of instilling knowledge and reason into the arms themselves. The mother's intent was to materially modify the quality of her daughter's body. Her words too were informed by this purpose. Nara's adult relatives later stressed the gravity of taking other people's fruit and the need to work hard to help her mother feed kin and affines. 'Do not tell lies!' they admonished. Such words are held to penetrate the ears and transform into 'ear knowledge', enabling a person to think better, remember others and behave in a trustworthy fashion. In short, sound has material effect on the body and its capacity for moral action. Thus are the bodies of kin built up gradually out of material experiences.

This is an empirical approach to personhood, then: each body is the site of accumulated past experiences. The cumulative person is rendered socially potent through a properly directed past. Each involves, ideally, a steady progress – a series of micro-additions to the originally formless base – an epistemological accumulation that unites immaterial and material. Real persons should be able to engage fully in the constitution of living sociality through engagement with like others (and distinct others) in productive and reproductive activities. The process involves a plethora of interactions over distinct temporal and spatial environments, engaging external (non-human, other body) and internal (our body), to produce embodied agency. There is no guarantee that the outcome will be the ideal cumulative person. Progress is only assured by constant attention to detail, daily repetitions of words and other acts, never-ending work. Ingestion of food, application of medicines, body painting, using clothes, hammocks and other objects, the material absorption of homiletic words, the externalization of skills in productive activities, the internalization of capacities generated in physical, sexual and reproductive interactions, all contribute to this cumulative personhood.

From the perspective of the constitution of 'real' persons, the pivotal relationships involved are those with co-residential kin. To say someone is a real man or woman is to say his or her history of becoming a person involved close exchanges with consanguineal and affinal kin who were 'real' in this sense also. Real persons are pronominal bodies: our *yuda*. The whole process is structured within the organization of relations of kinship and affinity. The eight-group alternate-generation namesake system is integrated into an exogamous moiety system. A limited stock of names are divided between Inu and Dua moieties. They are bestowed according to a principle of 'parallel transmission'. Marriage practices, fundamental to the reproduction of the system, are compatible with a Kariera-type kinship terminology. Offspring of marriages between bilateral cross-cousins inherit names in the right categories and such 'correct' marriages are encouraged (Kensinger 1984; D'Ans 1990; McCallum 2001: 21–27). As well as parents, namesake grandparents are key figures in making children grow. Thus a girl's MM (mother's mother) often looks after her on a daily basis and boys develop close ties with their MF (mother's father), namesake to their cross-cousins. Later, sexual partners, ideally bilateral cross-cousins, continue the process, 'making' their spouses' real bodies, for example, through the sharing of words, sexual substances and food.

Nara's unmarried friend Rai had a crush on the schoolteacher, her distant parallel cousin. His youthful good looks, natty dress sense (tight jeans, colourful T-shirts) and constant good humour inspired Rai to flirt openly with him, though he was married and a father. One day she asked me to accompany her to the edge of the village. 'Let's go defecate!' she said. So I went along, finding to my surprise that the schoolteacher was waiting for us in the forest. 'Here!' Rai whispered, handing me her elder sister's baby, whom she had been nursing. Then she attacked the grinning young man, pinching him hard and prodding, giggling wildly, intent on having sex with him. Luckily, the baby howled so loudly that she was forced to stop. On another occasion, her parents asked me to keep an eye on her during a fertility ritual during which men and women flirt openly, focusing on potential partners (with whom they often have sex after the singing and dancing ends). Aware of her crush on the schoolteacher, they worried about the consequences. However, a month later as I walked through the forest with her exasperated father, a respected connoisseur of plant medicines, he told me that she was pregnant. She could not marry her parallel cousin, so we were looking for abortifacients. He said that young girls are sexually voracious, so the best solution would be to find her a husband of the correct category, with whom she could 'mutually fornicate' and thus reshape her desire. Until her body had thus been altered she could not be trusted.

The process of making real bodies is not smooth. There are set-backs, disruptions, deviations, departures of a variety of sorts. Illness, death, madness, strong emotions and physical distancing from those with whom one has been intimate engender transformations of the body, its capacities and its content, as elsewhere in Amazonia (Vilaça 2005). Desire propels the body forward into actions that may not be constitutive of sociality (in the sense of living well) but emotions shaped by memory and past experiences also modify intentionality. Maira was born in the Jordão river area, but married a Purus man. Unusually, she left her close kin and settled in her husband's home. Yet she missed them deeply: 'I always miss them [*En hatu manumiski*]', she said, using *manu*, which also means 'to feel thirsty'. One night she began to dream intensely of her kin, their images [*yuxin*] appearing to her vividly. After this she began to suffer the physical symptoms of sadness: heaviness, a lack of appetite, tears welling up. Past intimacy sometimes manifests itself in this way, threatening a person's well-being. When a close person dies, people try to erase such mental images. Maira tried to get closer to her distant kin by taking *nixi pae*, a hallucinogen normally avoided by women. 'I could not visit them in person, so I wanted to see them another way', she explained. Thus, she altered her body, temporarily activating another form of perception (that of her eye [*yuxin*]) to bring back visions of her kin to her waking self.

Such voyages must be undertaken in controlled fashion, given their inherent dangers. A wrongly transformed body becomes other, no longer a true person – perhaps a Nawa, an animal, or a *yuxin* [spirit]. Excessive grief can be deadly; and knowledge of socially destructive techniques disruptive, for poisoners or sorcerers may no longer act as true kin. There is no simple path to proper, embodied personhood. But alterity is central to the process of becoming a person. Growth results from being brought into contact with that which is different, and often dangerous, through diverse relational engagements: as predator or prey, as interlocutor or spectator, friend or partner. Since these encounters affect the body materially, altering its very content beneficially (or otherwise), one may not equate cumulative personhood with a condition of finished *identity*. Each person is different: there are no self-same Huni Kuin, only composite, cumulative bodies that solidify the history of their own making, momentarily, over a life's span, before the dissolution brought about by the process of dying (McCallum 1996a, 1999).

The process of making a true person is teleological, a working towards an ideal end, but the product is not reified, since bodies – hence persons – are eminently transformable. (This point is well established in the literature, though anthropological attention to the notion of cumulative person has sometimes been taken, falsely, to indicate a preoccupation with self-identity and fixed moral order.) Thus in Huni Kuin 'reverse anthropology', a Nawa can begin to be transformed into some approximation of a real man – or woman (McCallum 2010). In indigenous Amazonian aetiologies, more generally, sickness may be understood as the transformation of people into animals or spirits (Vilaça 2011), while the Huni Kuin consider the insane to be *yuxin* [spirits], not real persons.

Trust and the Cumulative Body

When a Huni Kuin baby is born, therefore, her status at each moment of her passage through life cannot be predicted or guaranteed. In theory she might become anything or anyone. Pancho is a case in point. As a child, he suffered the corporeal transformations consequent on adoption or abduction by Nawa. He was partially brought up by a mestizo family of canoe-builders who lived several days downriver from his kin. The story of this part of his childhood is Dickensian. He recalled mistreatment, punishments, unpaid work and impoverished living conditions. By way of compensation, he learnt Spanish and obtained a general comprehension of mestizo ways that later served him in good stead. His astute insights into the local Nawa were based in part on these unpleasant childhood experiences.

From a Huni Kuin perspective, the specific make-up of Pancho's body – his accumulated person – derived in some measure from his time in this mestizo household. In that harsh setting he embodied Nawa as well as Huni Kuin agency. In later life, domineering, angry or avaricious behaviour was understood as emanating from his own, specific bodily inflection: it was his individual body that had the capacity and/or tendency to perform anti-social deeds as well as to do and instigate proper social action. It had its own 'way of being', like the Wari' 'kwere' (Vilaça 2011). When put to good use – to the benefit of real people – no matter, all to the good. But his particular past gave added instability to his body as a real person.

So in what sense was Pancho *xinanika* [trustworthy, thoughtful] to his own people? As should be clear by now, no individual body is wholly trustworthy, whatever his or her personal history. This is a consequence of the corporeal instability of thought [*xinan*]. Trust as thought has a liquid quality. In a recent synthesis on the topic, Belaunde (2005) shows that for many Amazonian peoples the circulating blood is the active vehicle of consciousness. It is how thoughts flow through the body. Although I never heard anyone say precisely this, the general logic seems to be applicable in the Huni Kuin case. If this is accepted, one could infer that thoughts [*xinan*] are carried through the body's veins and arteries in liquid form – and indeed there is some evidence for this. Thus, a healthy active body has *xinan paxa* – fresh, green thoughts – where *paxa* is a term used to describe new corn when it is still soft and sweet [*xeki paxa*]. Blood is a powerful and dangerous substance imbued with transformational capacity. Hemophagy is a disgusting thought to Huni Kuin and they cook meat well to avoid it. Blood must never be eaten in raw, liquid form, except on very restricted ritual occasions (Lagrou 2007: 352, 1998). If my inference is correct, then to eat blood would be to consume the thoughts of other bodies. It follows that the ritual eating of the blood of other bodies is to eat their thoughts. Although it is not explicitly said to be *yuxin* [spirit], blood certainly is a most powerful shamanic substance, as Lagrou insists. Thoughts irrigate the distinct organs where particular emotions, knowledge and capacities are concentrated and from whence particular thoughts take shape and flow out, such as the genitalia, the heart, the liver and the skin (Kensinger 1995; McCallum 1996b; Lagrou 1998, 2007). The liver holds thought in an especially concentrated form and it is there that emotions condense.

A person who is sweet [*bata*] thinks well, remembers others, acts generously. A good leader is a *bata ibu* – a sweet parent or owner. He and his wife, the female leader, together make the bodies of co-residents come together and share in the correct and desired human way. Their conscious thoughts, transformed from such incorporated substance, from thought (blood) to words and deeds, are necessary to the creation of trust. Memory of care, of affection, of sociability, takes the form of fluid thought. Thus embodied, thoughts are a necessary condition for making social intimacy, and the quality of the thought (sweet or bitter) produces distinct outcomes, constitutive or destructive of sociality.

Emotion-thoughts can either weigh one down or lift one up into an aerial feeling. Sadness and grief thicken the blood, so one grows dull and heavy. Happiness is felt as a lightness of being, described as *xinan chankan* [light thoughts]. Life cannot be based on mere lightness though, and a leader or parent needs some weight to the thoughts coursing through her or his veins. She needs gravitas to give purpose to action, direction to thought, or, one might say, to give it intentionality. One needs clear conscious perspective of others to motivate their actions. In this sense, to be *xinanika* [trustworthy] is to exert a centripetal force upon a field of intimacy, characterized by substantive if unstable (because liquid) memory.

Pancho was able to do this for the many years that he acted more often as a *bata ibu* than as a Nawa boss. The force he exerted, in conjunction with his wives and (eventually) son-in-law and daughters, constituted what may be described as an 'expanded person' (Cesarino 2010), a collective body (our *yuda*) wherein the flow of intentional beneficial substances takes the form of food and sexual fluids, rather than blood. The community as living *yuda* is built on the image of the blood/thought-filled body. It is a social arena where trust is desired, but not guaranteed. Formed on the basis of conjugal collaboration, the collective body derives from leaders' body-forming activities just as children derive metonymically from their parents. In this sense, the two leaders, male and female, are literally the *ibu* [parents, owners] of the village, which is captured in the expression translated as leader, *xanen ibu*. The empirical thinking that results in the notion of a cumulative body, therefore, should not be comprehended as limited to the confines of discrete biological bodies. It comprises a circle of intimacy within and between certain bodies. In so far as a body is always intentional, its thoughts directed at others, it can encompass or at least penetrate them. If these thoughts are sweet and spring from a solid fount of positive affective memory, the thinker might also be trustworthy.

Thus trustworthiness is a form of affective thought that generates particular kinds of action. It is inherently unstable, a condition that is linked to its generally liquid quality, as an agentive force that circulates in the blood, concentrates in certain organs, and gives energy and meaning to a person's actions with respect to others. And since it originates in intentional engagement with the environing universe, it is also phenomenological.

Perspectivism, Relatedness and the Body

This formulation can profitably be related to the understanding of the body set out within 'Amerindian Perspectivism' (Lima 1996; Viveiros de Castro 1998). The expression is usually understood to refer to a systematization of indigenous ontologies by these authors whose starting point was the 'symbolic economy of alterity' framework. The focus falls on relations with the outside, where many beings we perceive as animals or spirits or plants are imagined to see themselves as 'human'. Each different kind of body is at the centre of a specific way of being, or ontology. The body is the seat of the perspective, its origin, and those species that see themselves as human also understand themselves to possess human culture. Rather than a cosmos comprised of a single nature and multiple cultures, then, indigenous people think of it as comprised of a single culture and multiple natures (Viveiros de Castro 1998). In formal terms, there is only one kind of subject, whose self-perception is as human. The indigenous way of expressing this formal identity is to ascribe a 'soul' (or souls) to these self-identifying humans. This is not a body–soul distinction: souls also have bodies. The body, which is the seat of distinction, envelopes the soul as if it is a piece of clothing or a diving suit that may be removed or changed. The soul may be transferred or transformed into another body, of an animal, plant or spirit.

The Huni Kuin may be considered perspectivist (Lagrou 1998). They identify a variety of plants and animals (not all) as *huni* [persons] and direct much of their energy to maintaining clear boundaries between themselves and these others. Much of this work is focused on bodies. For Viveiros de Castro the 'diving-suit body' is the locus of 'affects' – that is, of capacities or dispositions, ways of being that constitute a kind of habitus. Each species has a distinct habitus. Thus appearance is not a measure of identity: one may only know another body as different from the way it behaves, not from the way it looks. For example, a person who eats raw meat is, perhaps, a jaguar; a child who grinds her teeth whilst sleeping is becoming peccary. These becoming-jaguar or becoming-peccary bodies shift the way of being that they 'wear', so to speak, in line with shifts of perspective. That is, their bodies' styles of behaviour alter, as they move to another perspective. Body transformation is concurrent with shift in point of view. From the stance of those watching, even though one may 'know' how to identify other bodies as apparently human, only behaviours (the effect of habitus) provides some kind of guarantee that their perspectives correspond. It would seem that when bodies imbued with consciousness (perspective) come together as pronominal collective bodies [*nukun yura*] then trust becomes possible.

For the Huni Kuin, the *yuda*, with all its affects, is thoroughly imbued with spirit (human consciousness), a point that can also be put the other way around. Whilst alive, a person's *yuxins* (spirits, including that which includes consciousness, thought, memory and trust) are thoroughly imbued in his or her body. Indeed, when 'disembued', spirits take corporeal form, as bird, animal or human. A single body is in fact multiple in this sense, a container containing other bodies, all of which may see themselves as human. But these aspects of Huni Kuin thinking about personhood should not lead one to focus on bodies as static entities. It is not as finished anchors for a human perspective that Huni Kuin see bodies, but, when at rest, as potential human action and, when in movement, its realization or negation. It is what they do or do not do that makes them more or less kin, more or less human, more or less part of the collective body.

Thinking of bodies as potential or actual (non)human action as Huni Kuin do, rather than as static entities that can be fitted into convenient classificatory slots, in Linnaean fashion, undermines a substantialist reading of this ethnography. In social anthropology substantivism treats social relations as interactions between morally and physically discrete subjects, implying that indigenous socio-logic is rooted in a bio-logic: society as the outcome of relations between individuals conceived as biologically separate autonomous entities. The notion of 'cumulative personhood' on the other hand lays stress on the active, intentional body and its spirits. It does not imply a finished totality, the end-product of a series of infinite and material additions to a unitary subject, but rather seeks to highlight the concepts and practices behind indigenous phenomenology.

Recently, Amazonian personhood has been viewed as fractal, and concepts originally developed by Strathern (1988) and Wagner (1975) in relation to Melanesian ethnography have been developed in relation to studies of the Amerindians (Viveiros de Castro 2001; Kelly Luciani 2001; Vilaça 2011). This analytical model is compatible with the notion of the cumulative person, rather than opposed to it (McCallum 2013). While the fractal model lays emphasis on the ontological aspects of personhood, formulating itself through abstraction of indigenous conceptualizations, the latter makes indigenous styles of phenomenology the analytical starting point. Application of a notion of fractal person can capture the centripetal forces at work – or rather the recursive and repetitive movement from outside to inside, the historical or biographical incorporation of potential for action. Indeed, fractality provides startling insights to the formal aspects of the history of a body's composition. What is missing from this model is the body in movement, in the expenditure of the energy and knowledge thus obtained.

Many ethnographic discussions have reaffirmed Seeger et al.'s (1987) framing of the relation between corporeality and social form and process in indigenous Amazonia. The authors noted that indigenous socio-logic is above all a physio-logic, expressing itself in corporeal idiom, upon and through bodies. These are bodies in motion, fluid and transformable, a point that has received considerable emphasis recently (Vilaça 2005, 2011). However, analysts have paid less attention to the knowledge, dispositions and capacities for action inherent in the shaped, if transformable, body, which I have referred to as 'agency'. Sahlins (2011) suggests that the term implies the imposition of a Eurocentric notion of a unique, bounded individual as the source of action, but evidently this was not my intention. In the Huni Kuin context, one may say that agency is a fractal condition, embodied relatedness, if it is anything at all. There, social thinking concerns itself with the body's actions, and capacities for action, with its ability to be involved successfully in production as well as reproduction (Belaunde 2005). Real People, having cumulative bodies, are capable of entering into appropriate, socially productive action – that is, they are understood to be imbued with a specifically human agency. Lived sociality may or may not be the outcome of the structured (structuring) conjunction of such agencies (among which, male and female agencies are the main, complementary variants). So the logic that is at once physiological and social is dependent on a particular indigenous phenomenology, which manifests itself in practices that capacitate living persons for social action in an ontogenetic sense.

One may put this differently by saying that trustworthiness originates in socially produced and corporeally sedimented ontogenesis. It should inhere as solidly as possible in a body's capacity for socially productive action. Such action requires materially incorporated power and knowledge, as well as affective memory – the remembrance of past caring – to give it coherence and direction (Gow 1989, 1991). The origins of these capacities and emotions are diverse, but can be distinguished, according to the form of their acquisition, into two kinds: those obtained while the body is in a conscious state, and those obtained in altered states of consciousness, for example, when sleeping, during extreme illness, or when taking hallucinogens (Kensinger 1995; McCallum 1996b). If the creation of living sociality depends upon human actions – and, therefore, on these specific kinds of flesh-and-bone bound agencies – then it clearly also derives from the history of their making. That is, indigenous sociology does more than generate a theory of the body as telos in an ontological sense, but encompasses a historical phenomenology of *yuda*. It is this larger frame of meaning that I mean to evoke when speaking of cumulative body.

Indigenous phenomenology encompasses bodies (of all kinds – human, animal, spirit) and 'things', as well as actions and reactions, forces and resistances. It is a phenomenology that stands conceptually not upon an immutability of matter but upon its instability: the transformability of bodies into other bodies or things, matter into those forms of non-matter that may be felt or known through the senses (wind or sounds or sights or smells). Thus it is a phenomenology that is rooted in temporal flow – past and present, told of in history, or foretold in futurology – a flow which is a necessary condition for human existence. Most of the accounts of the 'dividual' or 'partible person' place strong emphasis on form as part of the structuring of relations through processes of endlessly recursive dynamic dualism (Lévi-Strauss 1991). If exclusive analytical emphasis is placed on the formal aspects of this dualism, there is a danger that one loses sight of the weight indigenous people attribute to the cumulative person, who as we have seen is composed of memory and experience. This is expressed as the quality of the matter that makes a body – its flesh and bones, the meat itself, as a substance that can rot and transform. Knowledge and emotion accrue to the substance and infuse it, giving it real gravity, anchoring it at a specific time-space (that of conscious reality) and a specific relational field (of exchanges with other such bodies). When asleep or in an altered state of consciousness, the anchor is temporarily cut free, and the body's eye or dream *yuxin* may distance itself from the body (as it does definitely, at death). These oscillations in consciousness correspond to successive shifts in perspective – as if from that of the living to that of the dead – and constitute the temporal flow of daily time. At death however the anchor is cut definitively, and the bodies' diverse *yuxin* make a one-way trip to alterity.

Conclusion

One may not trust the dead. They are pure alterity. All that remains, once close kin have died, is to send their *yuxin* away. So trust is a possible state of relatedness only amongst the living, being confined to the space and time of living sociality. Biographical time – which needs be stopped at death – expresses the infinite potential for individuality of living bodies. As a person goes through life, her *yuda yuxin* [body soul] acquires progressively greater weight and power. Pancho was the outcome of a series of specific events, of his personal movement across space and time, which gave him unique capacities and qualities. Resulting emotion-thoughts [*xinan*] infused his body, flowing in his blood, making him an intentional subject, one who could direct his view at others, remember them, call upon them to recognize him as trustworthy [*xinanika*]. His peculiar skills enabled him to stand out as an effective political leader. The fact that many people chose to follow him speaks to the powerful capacity of intimacy lived on a daily basis to make and unmake sociality. As this chapter has striven to show, co-residence sets the conditions for the fabrication of similarity in a material embodied sense. Having lived with him, being or becoming each other's *yuda* (in the sense of kin), co-residents shared body with him (as I had, partially, after living in his house and village).

The work of co-residents – that is, persons who are or become kin and affines – is to make and protect human bodies. This chapter has shown that trustworthiness is conceived as rooted micro-historically in these unstable human entities. The process of their fabrication depends upon the controlled incorporation of alien powers and characteristics in order to foster growth, skill and (re)productive capacity and to avoid undesirable mutations. Thus the intimacy necessary so that trust may infuse relatedness is double-faced, for this unceasing desired accumulation of proper personhood centres on intimacy not just with kin but also with dangerous non-human others: the human bodies of trustworthy kin are, paradoxically, built up out of capricious others. Living Real Persons acquire their unique body [*yuxin*] from radically distinct sources: that which is alien and dangerous and that which is safe and similar. Intimacy, as I noted at the outset, cannot be conceptualized merely as the outcome of a close and prolonged interaction between conscious persons with whom one resides over a lifetime. This chapter has made clear, then, that consciousness itself (as expressed in liquid thoughts and memories flowing through the veins) derives from intimacy with that which is other. (And so one might say that, like the character Blanche, Huni Kuin too need to rely upon strangers.)

In what has been cast here as the Huni Kuin instantiation of an Amerindian perspectivist approach – that is, where bodies are always in potential transformation – trust is something that is always in brackets. The fall-back, default position is one of mistrust. To his one-time followers and co-residents, Pancho's claims to be a worthy leader motivated such a suspension of mistrust. Eventually, by moving away again, they laid stress upon his excessive alterity. What I had heard as occasional complaints that he behaved *like* a Nawa boss were in fact allegations that he had incorporated too much of the Nawa way of being: that he no longer had (or never really had) the cumulative body of a 'Real Person'. The logic of this bracketing process can be extended across species. Thus trust across species can only ever be a form of relatedness held in suspense, momentarily potentialized but ever threatening to go awry. Conversely, trust between 'real humans' is possible, but if trust is betrayed, then from the perspective of she who is betrayed, the other's humanity is put into question. Pancho's life story is exemplary of this state of eternal doubt cast upon the humanity (real humanness) of others, especially leaders like him. But it is also the form that underlies sociality amongst humans more generally. Perhaps this is merely a story about the human condition, writ in terms of my interpretation of what Huni Kuin have taught me.

Acknowledgements

Immense thanks to Margit Ystanes and Vigdis Broch-Due, and to Luisa Elvira Belaunde and Els Lagrou for invaluable comments on an earlier version. The ESRC, the Leverhulme Foundation and the Nuffield Foundation financed research with the Huni Kuin between 1983 and 1992.

Notes

1 Francisco Lopes da Silva (1938–2006).
2 Fundação Nacional do Índio.
3 I do not infer that Pancho perpetrated the murder. The events remain mysterious and the case unsolved.
4 The verb *xinan-* can be translated as 'to think' or 'to remember' and the substantive *xinan* as 'thought', 'memory' and 'trust'. In the sense of 'to think' the term can signify 'to formulate projects'.
5 Lagrou, personal communication.

References

Belaunde, L.E. 2005. *El recuerdo de Luna: género, sangre y memoria entre los pueblos amazónicos*. Lima: FEFCS.
Cesarino, P. 2010. 'Donos e Duplos: relações de conhecimento, propriedade e autoria entre os Marubo', *Revista de Antropologia* 53(1):147–197.
Costa, L. and C. Fausto. 2010. 'The Return of the Animists: Recent Studies of Amazonian Ontologies', *Religion and Society: Advances in Research* 1: 89–109.
D'Ans, A.-M. 1990. 'La Parenté et le Nom: Sémantique des Désignations Interpersonnelles Cashinahua', *L'Ethnographie* 107: 55–87.
Figueiredo, M.V. 2010. 'A flecha do ciúme: O parentesco e seu avesso segundo os Aweti do Alto Xingu'. PhD dissertation. Museu Nacional, Federal University of Rio de Janeiro: Postgraduate Program in Social Anthropology.
Gow, P. 1989. 'The Perverse Child: Desire in a Native Amazonian Subsistence Economy', *Man* 24: 299–314.
────── 1991. *Of Mixed Blood: Kinship and History in Peruvian Amazonia*. Oxford: Clarendon.
Kelly Luciani, J.A. 2001. 'Fractalidade e Troca de perspectivas', *Mana* 7(2): 95–132.
Kensinger, K. 1984. 'An Emic Model of Cashinahua Marriage'. In K. Kensinger (ed.), *Marriage Practices in Lowland South America*, 221–251. Urbana: University of Illinois Press.
────── 1995. *How Real People Ought to Live: The Cashinahua of Eastern Peru*. Prospect Heights: Waveland Press.
Lagrou, E.M. 2007. *A fluidez da forma: Arte, alteridade e ação em uma sociedade amazônica (Kaxinawá, Acre)*. Rio de Janeiro: Topbooks.
────── 1998. 'Cashinahua Cosmovision : A Perspectival Approach to Identity and Alterity'. PhD dissertation. St. Andrews: University of St. Andrews. Available at <https://research-repository.st-andrews.ac.uk/handle/10023/1676> (accessed 3 October 2015).
Lévi-Strauss, C., 1991. *Histoire de Lynx*. Paris: Pocket.
Lima, T.S. 2005. *Um peixe olhou para mim: O povo Yudjá e a perspectiva*. São Paulo: Editora UNESP/Instituto Socioambiental / NUTI.
────── 1996. 'Os Dois e Seu Múltiplo: Reflexões sobre o Perspectivismo em uma Cosmologia Tupi', *Mana* 2(2): 21–47.

McCallum, C. 1990. 'Language, Kinship and Politics in Amazonia', *Man* 25(3): 412–433.
—— 1996a. 'Morte e Pessoa Kaxinauá', *Mana* 2(2): 49–84.
—— 1996b. 'The Body that Knows: From Cashinahua Epistemology to a Medical Anthropology of Lowland South America', *Medical Anthropology Quarterly* 10: 347–372.
—— 1997. 'Comendo com Txai, comendo como Txai: A sexualização de relações étnicas na Amazônia contemporânea', *Revista de Antropologia* 40: 109–147.
—— 1999. 'Consuming Pity: The Production of Death among the Cashinahua', *Cultural Anthropology* 14(4): 443–471.
—— 2001. *Gender and Sociality in Amazonia: How Real People are Made*. Oxford: Berg.
—— 2010. 'Becoming a Real Woman: Alterity and the Embodiment of Cashinahua Gendered Identity', *Tipití* 7: 43–66.
—— 2013. 'Intimidade com estranhos: uma perspectiva Kaxinawá sobre confiança e a construção de pessoas na Amazônia', *Mana* 19(1): 123–155.
Montag, S. 1981. *Diccionario Cashinahua* (2 vols). Yarinacochá: Instituto Linguistico de Verano.
Overing Kaplan, J. 1999. 'Elogio do cotidiano: a confiança e a arte da vida social em uma comunidade amazônica', *Mana* 5(1): 81–107.
Overing, J. and A. Passes. 2000. 'Introduction'. In J. Overing, J. and A. Passes (eds), *The Anthropology of Love and Anger: The Aesthetics of Conviviality in Native Amazonia*, 1–30. London: Routledge.
Rival, L. 1998. 'Androgenous Parents and Guest Children: The Huaorani Couvade', *Journal of the Royal Anthropological Institute* (N.S.) 4(4): 619–642.
Sahlins, M. 1974 [1965]. 'On the Sociology of Primitive Exchange'. In *Stone Age Economics*. London: Tavistock.
—— 2011. 'What is Kinship? Part Two', *Journal of the Royal Anthropological Institute* (N.S.) 17: 227–242.
Santos-Granero, F. 2007. 'Of Fear and Friendship: Amazonian Sociality beyond Kinship and Affinity'. *Journal of the Royal Anthropological Institute* (N.S.) 13(1): 1–18.
Seeger, A., R. Da Matta and E. Viveiros de Castro. 1987 [1979]. 'A construção da pessoa nas sociedades indígenas brasileiras'. In J. Pacheco de Oliveira (ed.), *Sociedades Indígenas & Indigenismo no Brasil*, 11–29. UFRJ, Editora Marca Zero.
Strathern, M. 1988. *The Gender of the Gift: Problems with Women and Problems with Society in Melanesia*. Berkeley: University of California Press.
Vilaça, A. 2005. 'Chronically Unstable Bodies: Reflections on Amazonian Corporalities', *Journal of the Royal Anthropological Institute* (N.S.) 11: 445–64.
—— 2006. *Quem Somos Nós: Os War'i Encontram os Brancos*. Rio de Janeiro: Editora UFRJ.
—— 2011. 'Dividuality in Amazonia: God, the Devil, and the Constitution of Personhood in Wari' Christianity', *Journal of the Royal Anthropological Institute* (N.S.). 17(2): 243–262.

Viveiros de Castro, E.B. 1996. 'Images of Nature and Society in Amazonian Ethnology', *Annual Review of Anthropology* (N.S.) 25: 179–200.
—— 1998. 'Cosmological Deixis and Amerindian Perspectivism', *Journal of the Royal Anthropological Institute* (N.S.) 4: 469–88.
—— 2001. 'GUT feelings about Amazonia: potential affinity and the construction of sociality'. In L. Rival and N.L. Whitehead (eds), *Beyond the Visible and the Material*. Oxford: OUP.
Wagner, R. 1975. *The Invention of Culture*. Chicago: University of Chicago Press.

Cecilia McCallum is Adjunct Professor at the Department of Anthropology at the Federal University of Bahia. She holds a PhD in Social Anthropology from the London School of Economics and Political Science, University of London (1989). She has done extensive field research in Brazil, both among the Amazonian indigenous people Huni Kuin (or 'Cashinahua') and in Brazilian urban zones. Her research interests include the study of the body and health, differences of race, ethnicity, class, age and gender. She is the author of *Gender and Sociality in Amazonia: How Real People are Made* (Oxford: Berg, 2001).

9

HABITUS OF TRUST
Servitude in Colonial India
Radhika Chopra

'There is one sort of labour' wrote Adam Smith, in his eighteenth century tract *An Inquiry into the Nature and Causes of the Wealth of Nations*, 'that adds value to the subject upon which it is bestowed: there is another which has no such effect ... The labour of a menial servant adds to the value of nothing ... Like the declamation of the actor, the harangue of the orator, or the tune of the musician, the work of [the menial servant] perishes in the very instant of its production ... and seldom leaves any value or trace behind' (Smith 1904 [1776]: II.3.1).

To our twenty-first-century eyes Adam Smith's words are harsh – but compelling. How do we trust a 'menial servant' or a domestic worker if her work leaves no trace? Fortunately, the brief appearance of the actor and the musician in Adam Smith's reflections on unproductive labour opens a set of philosophic doors that invite us to imagine traces of work. With very different intentions from Smith, language philosophers like Searle point out that musicians sing but will also be heard to sing. In the context of speech, Searle argues that even if the moment in which the musician sings a song disappears, or the instance of speaking evaporates, the song and the sentence remain as a trace – for the musician and the audience of listeners make sense of the song and when the song disappears, what is sung (or 'said') remains – the said of the saying remains behind. I might extend Searle's argument to reverse Smith's statement on menial work – the moment of its performance disappears but it retains a trace, for the work has an ocular presence: clean floors, washed dishes, tidy beds. Unlike Smith's eighteenth-century musician however, the maid in the twenty-first century is a social invisible, and there must be no trace of her within the intimacies of a modern household. A menial's social invisibility as a person is her value and it is *she* who must vanish without trace. As a communicative language of presence, her invisibility is built on a social scaffold where presence is discounted, though acts of labour imprint themselves upon objects and spaces.

Invisibility is 'managed' through a series of gestures that are communicated by employers to their servants and to their children. Children 'learn' to carefully ignore servants who surround them, conveying through stillness or downcast eyes their intense awareness of the presence of the maid who dusts and sweeps all around them. Youngsters and adults together know and learn the rituals of producing invisibility as an essential principle in the institution of servitude. Leaving aside my brutalisation of Adam Smith's theory of value and productive labour for the moment, I want to ask how this impossible relationship of proximity in intimate spaces was historically managed, and how its survival shapes servitude in our contemporary world. Taking my own middle-class world in metropolitan India as a starting point, I ask how urban middle class people imagine and manage the servitude of others. What empowers us to think of the alterity of servants and what has been the history of permission upon which we draw? Historiography of modern India has located the contours of the Indian middle class in colonial history; the master–servant relationship of colonial India must therefore be a starting point to reflect upon servitude, alterity, intimacy and trust in modern middle-class life. Historians of colonial rule have also argued that the English drew on ideas forged in eighteenth-century England to craft their relations with the colonized, and their policies had as much to do with encounter (with cultures and ideas of the colonized) as they did with debates that arose in metropolitan contexts. Delving through sources of data, including architecture, paintings and lithographs, cooking books and manuals on breast feeding, it becomes apparent that colonial structures of servitude in India were 'empowered' by ideas of contract and institutions that shaped master–servant relations in the metropolitan 'West'. It is therefore imperative for me to begin with that 'other' history and politics to reflect upon the *habitus* of servitude in colonial India and of my world.

My starting point for analysing the master–servant relationship is writings on homes and households of the aristocracy and rich merchants of England, like that of the Cadbury family home in Edgbaston, a cross between the manor house and early suburbia. Young men employed as clerks, distant relatives under training for employment in the family business, and servants were all counted as serving members of the Cadbury household (Hall 1992). Boundaries of familiarity and alterity were probably quite fluid among the emerging middle class of eighteenth- and nineteenth-century England, evident in the numerous portraits painted and poems written of servants by an eccentric aristocratic family, chronicled by Merlin Waterson in *The Servants Hall:*

A Domestic History of Erddig (1980). They were clearly unorthodox, and very rare. Neither in the late eighteenth century, nor indeed later, were servants thus honoured. Increasingly amongst the most common occupations by the mid-nineteenth century (Coser 1973), domestic service as a contractual relationship had to be 'explained' with guidebooks, magistrate's handbooks and domestic manuals, for while domestic employment was based on the idea of contract, it retained aspects of primordial connection. Equated with the husband–wife or parent–child relation, the master–servant relation was, according to the eighteenth-century jurist and Tory politician, William Blackstone, 'one of the most universal relations of the ordinary affairs of life' (Steedman 2003: 321). The detailing in handbooks was the outcome, argues Carolyn Steedman, of an increasing understanding of modern property, but also the outcome of the enormous political and philosophic effort in making the 'singular human body the locus of individuality and personhood' (Steedman 2003: 323). The transfer of labour of that singular body in service to another became the prime example of the making of property. Relationships with the servant wavered between moralities of contract and familial ties, and must have generated different forms of trust: some 'so familiar ... that ... its presence [was] scarcely noticed' (Baier 1986: 233) and others needing explicit instruction in domestic manuals and magistrate's handbooks.

But what became of the labour thus transferred? What value did it have if it could vanish without a trace? In negating the work done by domestics as not work at all – work without 'productive' value and work that leaves no trace – Adam Smith seemed to negate more than just work: in the transfer he suspended identity. The first steps toward the invisibility of domestic labour were effected at the moment of that transfer. Servants became (and still continue to be) legally, metaphorically and materially shrouded. The servant, suspended from his or her identity, was then an extension of the employer's identity – part of the employer's household, a family member of sorts, certainly living within the space of the employer's home. The servant's behaviour was a reflection of the competencies of the employer rather than a trait of individual personality. For indeed the servant was thought to have none. Quoting the sermons of an eighteenth-century English cleric – 'your time and strength are no longer your own, when you are hired ... and therefore a servant is supposed to have no will of his own, where his master is concerned; but submit himself entirely to the will of his master' – Lewis Coser brings to light the moral scaffolding upon which the contract rested (Coser 1973: 32). The master's household literally and metaphorically swallowed the servant into itself, demanding time, commitment and almost total allegiance, placing the servant as a dependent upon the master, like a child upon the parent. Conceptually speaking, the servant was clearly meant to 'entrust' his or her well-being, bodily safety and personhood to the master (Baier 1986: 236). But trust also needed to flow downward: the master (and mistress) entrusted the care of things they valued to servants – the care of children, homes or food. Trust existed and was experienced in asymmetrical relations and was also nuanced across relations within the home. Despite the theory of labour value, intimacies and trust created their own hierarchies of value within the English aristocratic household. Proximates like valets or dressers, argues Edward Hall in his theoretical work on proxemic behaviour (Hall 1963) were admitted into the intimate zones of the bedroom of the master and mistress. The valet's proximate was the master, not the other servants, and though the butler and the cook were highly paid (and therefore valued), they were not intimate in quite the same way as the valet, though the former were trusted to manage servants in their charge and not poison the master's wine (Baier 1986: 232). The groom or the 'tiger' who rode behind his master's curricle was privy to more intimate knowledge than the cook who lived in the house, albeit below the stairs. Novels of aristocratic English life are replete with instances of the licence afforded to the ladies' dresser, to whom the deepest secrets of love and life were entrusted. Georgette Heyer's novels, for instance, are an outstanding example of the minutiae of intimacy and trust between master and servant in Regency England (Kloester 2010). Value and trust in the eighteenth- and nineteenth-century household was not a unified structure, for it lay in different spaces of the home, braided into different threads that made up the tapestry of trust. Value rested, indeed depended on, an unusual form of invisibility, where presence could be discounted but work imperceptibly performed.

If understanding the transfer of labour through contract was learnt through magistrates' and domestic manuals, then invisibility, the other 'condition' intrinsic to domestic labour, needed equally careful instruction. The home as a structure of symbolic and material practices was built to communicate and learn invisibility and enable intimate relations to continue uninterrupted by the presence of servants. Architectural innovations of domestic spaces, as well as arrangements of things in rooms – screens, curtained doorways, or the positioning of chairs – created a *habitus* where proximity did not automatically translate as kinship nor shared space as trust (Yastanes, this volume). Together, the spatial and social arrangements consigned the servant to a phantom existence, present without acknowledgement.

In fact architecture was the clearest, materially substantive pedagogical guide for intimacy and invisibility. Victorian house plans (Franklin 1975), turn-of-the-century urban American homes (Roper 1996), or suburban homes in early apartheid Johannesburg (Ginsburg 2000), had spaces to keep servants at physical, olfactory and visual distance (though such spaces also allowed servants to remain 'off stage', à la Goffman, and prepare for their soft-footed public appearance in the main rooms of the employers' home). The built environment conveyed the sense of a servant's place through distance and size. Other sources of understanding were advice books or published tracts on health. American etiquette books at the turn of the nineteenth century advised that the servant's room be 'simple, comfortable and pleasant' but at the same time 'plain in decor and preferably of minimum size' (Roper 1996: 22). Often the emphasis was literally and spatially on the 'minimum'. In 1892, The British Medical Journal reported that sleeping accommodation provided for domestic servants in the fashionable London neighbourhood of Marylebone were 'dark unventilated holes in the basement' (Anon. 1892: 1129) and did not conform even to the rather parsimonious understandings and minimalist rules of the Public Health (London) Act.

Over the course of time, indoor plumbing and the servants' wing became the objects of the greatest structural change in domestic architecture. The servant's wing shrank, or was removed to the peripheries of the compound, or disappeared altogether in burgeoning metropolitan spaces. This had as much to do with the vanishing of servants into the navy or the factory, as it did on urban land price. Increasingly, the single young woman replaced the 'troops' of specialist servants (Cox 2006: 15; Franklin 1975) hired to run aristocratic or affluent homes. Samuel Pepys' diary, one of the more detailed accounts of the household in London, comments that 'Jane Birch, "our little old Jane" … stayed in all for seven years in three separate periods' (Earle 1989: 221). The exit of an entire set of servitors from the home or the whittling down to a single maid-of-all-work must have reordered the household, and changed the very nature of trust and intimacy founded on learnt invisibility. Coupled with changes in the built environment, the transformation of job markets altered the logic of servitude, trust and intimacy. The meanings of intimacy, like the musician's song, were not free-floating signifiers, but sung and heard in social space and time. Though anchored in changing conditions of labour, accounts of eighteenth-century English households became templates for understanding servitude in the colonies of empire and bear testimony to the way the idea of value travelled from metropole to colony, and, while not seamlessly nomadic, nevertheless shaped historiographies of servitude in colonial India.

Colonial India

The shrinking of the servants' room in the metropolitan west that produced a particular formation of proximity was counterbalanced by an alternate architectural and social history in the colonies. The colonial 'bungalow compound complex' (King 1976) in India is an outstanding example of spaces of encounter between white officers and native servants and two forms of stratification – race and caste. The manor house of English aristocracy was an architectural template that shaped the bungalow,[1] enclosed in its vast gardens. Specific colonial architectural features like the veranda acted as a liminal space between the home within and the generalized outside, while the servant quarters, though within the compound, were placed at a great distance from the main bungalow. The bungalow's facade imposed particular forms of invisibility and presence upon servants; the back of the bungalow produced another formation, evidence of the intricate social choreography underwritten by caste and racial segregation that governed everyday life. At this point I merely want to flag the divisions of bungalow spaces, though I will return to the back of the bungalow later in the paper.

In the photograph of the formal facade of a colonial bungalow (Fig. 9.1), the servants stand stock still, echoing the immobility of the

Fig. 9.1 British Bungalow with Servants, 1870s. Calcutta Photos n.d., available at <http://calcuttaphotos1945.blogspot.com/2010/05/british-bungalow-1870.html> (accessed 23 May 2012)

Palladian pillars, acting as the perfect backdrop for the group of officers artfully posed on the lawn. The photograph suggests a deliberate muting of the servant, ignored in the background but essential as a stage prop to ceremonies of power. It's quite clear from the formality of the servants' posed bodies that they were quite accustomed to being consigned to stillness. There is another servitor who stands off-centre to the group on the lawn. The *punkha coolie,* or the fan-man, was a specialist whose duty was to keep his master's family cool through the hot season and its long summer nights. In another image of the bedroom, in a lithograph done by Captain Atkinson in 1859, the punkha coolie sits crouched outside the bedroom, fanning his sleeping master, though he himself was clearly bereft of the cooling effects of his own labour (Fig. 9.2). Apocryphal tales and ghost stories about a phantom punkha coolie pulling the fan long after he had died held modern Indian children in thrall well after the manually operated fan had disappeared. The culmination of the story in the ghostly creaking of the fan illuminated the loyalty of the punkha coolie: encased in invisibility, but dedicated to duty even in death.

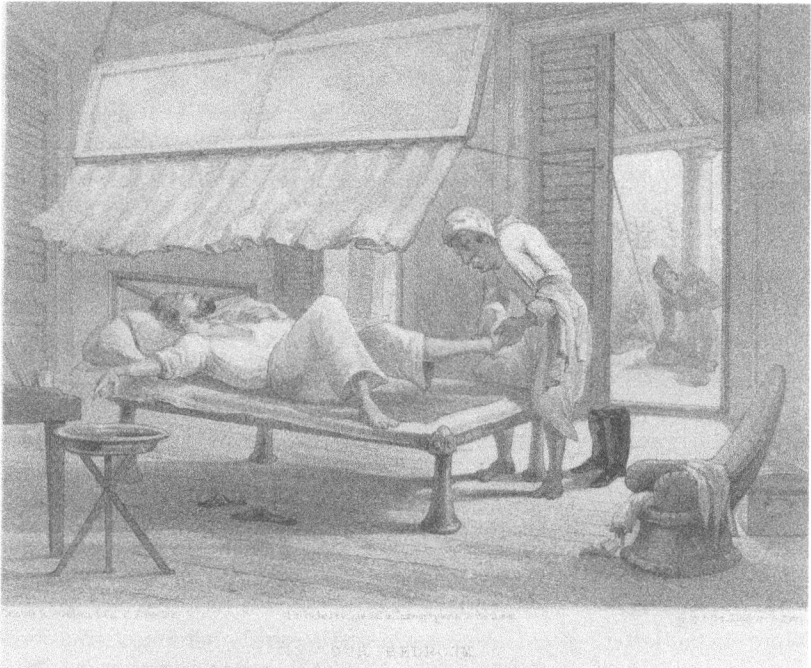

Fig 9.2 'Our Bedroom', Capt. G.F. Aitkinson. Capt. G.F. Atkinson, *Curry and Rice,* 1859 (author's own collection).

Within the interiors of the colonial bungalow, distance and invisibility were orchestrated differently. In another sketch in the series *Curry and Rice* done by Capt. G.F. Aitkinson, the white officer's body is carefully tended by a string of servants. Indian servants became adept at using what must have been unfamiliar grooming tackle, and were entrusted to produce the 'Englishness' of their *sahib* [master], wielding shaving tackle, hairbrushes and shoe polish with proficiency. There is another aspect to the care of the body that I think bears reflection. It has been established that some sartorial styles crossed cultural divides (Tarlo 1996). A few English men enthusiastically adopted entire wardrobes of the Indian elite.[2] Along with garments, it is more than likely that perfumes and cosmetics crossed the racial line, for example, the use of rose oil or 'attar of rose'. The reverse direction of clothing was equally part of structures and practices of creating familiarity within alterity. Indian princes in the late nineteenth and early twentieth century were avid consumers of English cologne and lavender water, demonstrating their bodily modernity that smelt of power. What remains unexplored is whether servants employed by colonial officers of the Raj also used the array of cosmetics from their master's dressing tables, either secretly or with his consent. Speculatively speaking, to be allowed within olfactory proximity, it might well have been the latter. The details of this form of intimate exchanges of personal things between masters and servants have unfortunately been overlooked. Though domestic accounts show that servants were paid in kind – along with money and food, *sabun tel* (literally 'soap and oil' but generically denoting body care supplies) were common forms of payment. The payment did not include the more valued English goods, and it would seem very likely that they become objects of desire and possible pilferage. I bring this up only to indicate the varied arenas of trust between master and servant that remain to be explored, without at this time, offering any evidence of such use in the colonial era.[3]

The segregated codes of two cultures, maintained quite obviously in the public domain, were reinforced within the private sphere; but some were also modified, even breached. Uniforms of servants in colonial households were a cross between overtly Indian garments and clearly English or Western styles of coats, shoes and pants, some possibly cast off and inherited from a master's wardrobe (Fig. 9.3). A servant's closeness to the master seems to have been indicated by what the servant wore in the latter's presence, a form of proxemic behaviour that created sartorial grounds for intimacy and trust. What is less clear – but no less likely – is the journey in reverse of shoe polish and nail files common to the grooming practices of English colonial elite. As much as

BOMBAY SERVANTS.

Fig 9.3 Bombay Servants. Colour Plate, 1899, author's own collection.

the difference between English master and Indian servants was clearly expressive of cultural boundaries founded on race and colonial power, it seems to me the distinction and differences among servants was equally clear. Indicators of caste and status were evident upon the bodies of servants (Fig. 9.3). The style of head gear, the wearing of loose pyjamas as opposed to an unstitched *dhoti* (a long piece of cloth wrapped around the waist and legs), shoes or bare feet – all are clear indications of region, caste and status differences among the categories of servants evident in the turn-of-the-century photograph of Indian servants in the Bombay Presidency.

Captain Thomas Williamson, describing an engraving by the artist of manners, Charles D'oyly, noted the fine divisions visually apparent in D'oyly's representations between the person who poured the water from the ewer and the one who washed the master's feet. The water bearer, Williamson observed caustically, 'will not touch a *chillumchee*, or washing vessel, under pretence of being defiled, should they come in contact with the impurities washed from the skin of a Christian' (D'oyly et al. 1813). Hierarchies of caste and precise distinctions of work meant that a single family were likely to employ at least fifteen local Indian servants ranging from the *Munshi*, or native professor of language, whose job was to translate records and documents, and the *Dufteree*, or office keeper, at the upper end of the work hierarchy, to the *massalchi*, *durzi*, *ayah* and *hookah burdar* (respectively, scullery man, tailor, nurse/maid and hookah tender). Flora Annie Steel, who lived for twenty-two years in India with her husband, chiefly in Punjab, wrote, together with Grace Gardiner, what was perhaps the definitive guide for young white women setting up household in India. They begin the chapter on the duties of servants with a 'comparative table showing the work assigned to each servant in Bengal, Bombay, and Madras' (Steel and Gardiner 2010 [1888]: 30), these being the three British presidencies at the time. The table is illuminating in the variety of tasks that were required to be done in an ordinary English household of the empire. A chapter on 'Duties of Servants' – the longest chapter in the book – is especially enlightening in listing the numbers of servants that an average colonial household would employ. So while there was an enormous cultural and racial divide within the household, it was also clear that the white members of the household were a minority within their own homes, and compelled, despite their own powerful positions, to entrust their daily lives (and those of their children) to their native servants.

Outnumbered in their own homes, the racial and class divides between white masters and 'black' servant wore very thin in daily interaction and needed constant reminder (Stoler 2001). The tensions between dominance and intimacy were perhaps even more acutely felt in plantations and forest bungalows, the provincial outposts of empire, where an assortment of servants inhabited the world of the white officer. The numbers could not be reduced, for the array of servants was expressive of the power and status of the officer. Bungalows were provisioned by the state exchequer with objects thought appropriate to the status of the officer and staff paid for by the state. The obverse was equally true. Those ranked low on the official scales of hierarchy had to make do with very few servants, or buying mismatched furniture, often at funeral auctions (Glover 2008: 169), all signs of their modest status. On the other hand, single white officers posted in plantations or forest bungalows were surrounded by servants with whom they lived and worked in close proximity. Like the valet of the English manor house in eighteenth-century London, the *khitmatgar* (loosely translatable as a gentleman's gentleman) in a plantation bungalow was the confidante of his master. Precisely because this proximity was mistrusted, single white officers and their bungalows became subjects of nervous material excess, of furniture, crockery, cutlery and even paintings that acted as aide memoires to keep racial distinction alive.[4] Food was another dimension of distinction. Native cooks were taught to caramelize custard or dress a roast duck. Flora Annie Steele and Grace Gardiner's *The Complete Indian Housekeeper and Cook: Giving the Duties of Mistress and Servants, the General Management of the House and Practical Recipes for Cooking in All its Branches*, first published in 1888, was thought to be of enormous utility, and went through ten editions. Steel's helpful guide is a rich source of recipes imparted to Indian cooks, but also, like furniture or clothing, cues of taste and distinction that needed constant reminder. The chapters of her book range from 'Hints on Breakfasts, Dinners, Luncheons, Etc.' to 'Advice to the Cook' (Steel and Gardiner 2010 [1888]). Colonial versions of curry and rice were not consumed every day but confined to Sundays or club days, when officers from contiguous districts, forest divisions or plantations met to reassure and remind each other of their whiteness, and collectively share in the transgressions of eating the food of the other without compromising the vulnerable, isolated white male self.

But servants also acted as bridges between the public 'official' status of the officer and his private life. They must have provided entertainment for bored young planters or forest officers and perhaps advised them on what to wear at a *naucht* [dance] or a *mehfil* [musical evening]. Adopting some 'native' practices was acceptable, especially if they were culled from a repertoire of local, elite life styles. For example, smoking of the *huqqa* replaced English aristocratic male rituals of after dinner pipe and port. The intimacy with local practices was tempered by signs that cocooned the colonial *huqqa* smokers into the fastness of an imagined, but materialized 'Englishness'. In D'oyly's lithograph (Fig. 9.4), the hunting print on the wall, the chair and table, and the long-tailed coat of the smoker create a sense of disengagement from localized styles of *huqqa* smoking, where smokers sat on richly woven carpets on the floor, with their *huqqas* continually replenished by expert servants. Despite the familiar sound of water bubbling through the pipes, the prints and the furniture (such as those depicted in D'oyly's lithograph) made evident to both master and servant the different cultural order to which this *huqqa* smoker belonged.

Perhaps the most critical sign of the removal of *huqqa* smoking from its Indian pedigree is the bare feet of the servant figure in D'oyly's portrait. I want to draw attention to this for two reasons. The Indian practice of removing footwear was a sign of respect, without necessarily degrading the bare-footed person: the devotee in the presence of the divine, the petitioner in the presence of the sovereign were all barefooted, but paying their respects did not demean them. In other contexts however, bare feet did indicate lower status. Lower-caste individuals, for example, could never wear footwear in the presence of upper-caste persons.

224 • *Radhika Chopra*

Fig 9.4 'A Gentleman With His Hookah-Burdar, or Pipe-Bearer'. D'oyly et al. 1813: Plate X. Available at <http://history1800s.about.com/od/thebritishempire/ig/British-India-Gallery/Englishman-and-Hookah.htm> (accessed April 2012). The illustration was originally published in a book, *The European in India accompanied with a brief History of Ancient and Modern India* by Charles D'oyly, et al., published in 1813. D'oyly captioned the print: *A Gentleman With His Hookah-Burdar, or Pipe-Bearer*.

In the context of *huqqa* smoking, bare feet was clearly not the signature of low status; quite the reverse. In the leisured but powerful spaces of a *mehfil* (intimate gathering for music, poetry and dance) of the Indian elite, or in close intimate spaces, between lovers for example, tending the *huqqa* meant that the *huqqa* attendant was an intimate within the inner circles of elite noblemen and women who smoked *huqqa* together. The *huqqa* had to be continually and expertly tended with coal embers to allow the smoke to be filtered through the heated water of the bowl at the base of the pipe. Servants moved between the *huqqa* smokers as intimates, intrinsic to the entire process of smoking, and both *huqqa* smokers and tenders remained bare footed throughout. Bare feet created symmetry in the relationship, premised on inclusion into intimate transactional spaces and initiating trust between servitor and smoker.

Other than those white officials who 'went native' (the French mercenary Claude Martine of Lucknow was an outstanding example, as were English men David Ochterlony, William Fraser, James Skinner and Thomas Metcalfe, who donned Indian clothing and routinely smoked *huqqa*), not every white officer smoked the *huqqa* in the conviviality of *mehfil* spaces. Smoking the *huqqa* in solitary splendour was a double detachment from local elite and more mundane subjects of colonial rule. The presence of the servant in such a context of isolation did not convey intimacy with the white master, but rather an erasure of presence through the renunciation of any auditory signal of presence, a self negation that lay in bare feet. The servant tending the *huqqa* in D'oyly's portrait is unlikely to have been a lower-caste person, for the valuable expertise of *huqqa* tending would have been unavailable as knowledge to lower-caste men; but caste signatures mutated into unique ignominy to reinforce colonial hierarchies of power. It seems to me that the value of tending the *huqqa* is negated by a lower 'caste' imprint that subverts the value of the work and the identity of the worker. Intimate, but excluded from his master's world, the servant standing bare-footed behind his white master's chair is placed in a position that countered the close relations of trust between local elite and their *huqqa* attendants. Colonial *huqqa* deliberately distanced itself from local practices via a stark reassignment of the meaning of bare feet and servitude.

The colonial *huqqa* smoker disappeared in the middle of the nineteenth century; the 'mutiny' of 1857 put an end to British efforts to adapt and adopt Indian cultural practices. Post- mutiny, intimacy with an Indian ethos was deeply suspect. Too much knowledge of things native was as much of a problem as too little (c.f. Colonna 1997: 70). Imperial rule sought its own inscriptions of power through difference. Apart from public and prominent sites expressive of enlightened rule and civilizing missions (the ban on *sati*5 is an example), the spaces of domesticity became critical micro-sites at which new knowledge and forms of governance materialized. The figure of the domestic servant, an embodiment of the native other in need of enlightenment, became an object of the micro-politics of imperialism. In India, as indeed in most colonies, servants were seen as dependents, rather like children, to be taught their place and kept there, no longer as proximate intimates who cared for their masters' bodies. The power of empire reached into the deepest folds of intimate family life of its subjects, remaking what family was. As dependents of colonial employers, the workers' sense of place within their own families was severely fractured. The power to exclude members of a servant's family from the employer's home, or the refusal to permit a daily commute between the homes of employment and servant's family, was a way colonial power exerted jurisdiction on intimate lives, rupturing families and creating hyphenated homes of their domestic staff. Colonial rule dispossessed people of their own families and structures of intimacy, swallowing them into the homes of their masters. New 'structures of feeling, new habits of heart and mind' (Stoler 2006: 2) produced malleable subjects and submissive servants. The imperial grip over labour power tightened, and the servant, moving into his or her white master's household, had to renounce affective ties with their own kin. The mid-eighteenth- and nineteenth-century English practices of inscribing servitude, where the servant was swallowed up into his master's home, travelled with great facility into nineteenth-century colonial bungalows in India.

Despite the absolute nature of colonial power that fixed the servant into positions of virtual enslavement, the fact that servants' work and lives were braided into everyday domestic worlds could not curb feelings of intimacy between different members of the colonial household and their servants. Sovereignty met intimacy in the kitchens and nurseries of empire, blurring the distinctions between dependence, distance and dominance. In India, *ayahs* or native nannies took care of colonial children, and *khansama* [cooks] became acquainted with the flavours of English cuisine. The persistent familiarity induced by intimacies of care translated into an imperfect balance between trust and mistrust (Baier 1986; Govier 1992). From the perspective of the state, it was not just the morally challenged alterity of the native other that was distrusted: 'vulnerable' members of the white household were also objects of doubt. White mothers, for example, were elaborately advised on moral – and thinly disguised racial – etiquette. Doctors advised strongly against the practice of the native 'wet nurse'. Steel and Gardiner's advice once again resounds with the prohibitions: 'one great point to be insisted on is, that all mothers should persevere in nursing their children ... she must not let herself be worried or imposed upon by the ayah or the monthly nurse' (Steel and Gardiner 2010 [1888]: 144). Steel warned white women to guard against 'the native's capacity for uncleanliness' (Steel and Gardiner 2010 [1888]: 88], to discipline herself and her servants in an obsessive regime of decontamination. Infants in particular were thought to be susceptible, and needed every effort to be weaned away from uncultivated spheres. Children were not permitted to sleep with their native *ayahs*, discouraged from learning their *ayah's* language, and prohibited from playing with the offspring of servants lest cultures of colour rubbed off and mutated their unformed selves. The unconditional trust of the child for their care-giving *ayah* or native nanny was a source of immense anxiety. Enforcing ruptures in this relation of care and trust became the prophylactic against the white child's submergence in the body of the native nanny. In concert, the advice and prohibitions equated children and their native care-givers as belonging to a barbaric sphere, from which the former needed to be extracted. As soon as they were able, children were sent away to English boarding schools to recover their sense of racial self, which was seen to be corrupted by close proximity to native nannies. Concern for the children's moral environment was voiced by doctors and preachers – men who envisaged the worst, and provided strident and detailed advice on how to prevent the child from being contaminated by racially inferior nannies. Their moral homilies were a way to defend society against itself by remaking the domestic, by regulating inappropriate intimacies, and by carefully monitoring the care and cultural grooming of the young (Stoler 2001: 24). The contaminated child was perhaps a reminder and an emblem of all those East Indian planters and merchants who 'went native', adopting corrupt and corrupting cultural practices and losing their manly English whiteness.

Mistrust of the self in a world populated by the contaminations of alterity was productive of a range of material cultural texts to recover the white self. Manuals produced by women for women gave helpful hints to young white *memsahibs* on a host of troublesome issues from finding a reliable *punkha coolie*, who could manually fan the heated memsahib (Steele and Gardiner 2010 [1888]), or how to deal with unfamiliar tasks: to strain milk from a herd of cows on a bungalow estate, or deal with an *ayah* for English children. *Mrs Beeton's Cookery Book and Household Guide* (Beeton 2005 [1890]) was another manual of immense importance describing in its frontispiece, '*Plans of household work. Recipes for servants ... Menus for all seasons, and for all meals*'; as was Mrs Eliot James' *Guide to Indian Household Management* (James 1879). Households of the Raj replicated their English manorial counterparts at least in terms of numbers employed, though imposing servitude without the facility or familiarity with cultural codes or a common language produced ironic twists to the Raj tale. A peculiar argot to address native servants was deployed by English women – unfamiliar to native ears, it was onomatopoeically called '*git-git*'. Between the incomprehension of custom and structures of concentrated power, the value of a servant's work vanished. 'The majority of servants' declared Steel and her co-author, with an Adam Smith-like disregard for the labour of menials, 'from Himalaya to Cape Cormorin, are absolutely ignorant of the first principles of their various duties' (Steel and Gardiner 2010 [1888]: 30).

Proximity nevertheless engendered an idiosyncratic form of trust born within suspicion. People born of mixed-race parentage were valued for their ability to translate cultural practice and local languages, and became key mediators in the public domain between white colonial authority and native subjects, but miscegenation simultaneously cast them as 'imperfect' possessors of English virtue and value. They were perhaps the epitome of Adam Smith's idea of people who added 'to the value of nothing'. As a group they could not hope to enter or transgress the segregated spaces marked as the 'English home'. Mixed race nannies for example, were no substitute for sending children away to English boarding schools and though converted Christians hired as cooks, and dressed in shirts and pants while cooking (Fig. 9.3), could be trusted to understand the intricacies of caramel custard and bread pudding, they were not included as intimate members of the white home. Mixed feeling accompanied the acknowledgement of people of mixed bloods who were partial descendants of Europeans. There was a clear sense they 'they must not be burdened with more skills than they need, but only practical know-how for the tasks to which they are geared' (Stoler 2001: 20) lest they overstep the boundaries of race and 'conceive of themselves as bosses/masters' (ibid.).

The success of the imperial project depended on successfully incorporating vast numbers of people into building railways; manning new regiments; ensuring the everyday work of administration as petty clerks or peons; and cooking breakfast. Indian labour was vital to the entire project of enlightened rule. Encounters with labour necessarily translated as encounters with caste hierarchies or gendered work. Absolute power and cultural incomprehension in concert subverted local hierarchies. Zambian nurse boys (Hansen 1989) and the army batman, who often followed his officer into retirement and into the latter's home to work as a trusted retainer under the authority of the officer's wife (Chopra 2012), are some examples of restructuring gender relations and work. But occupational categories of caste were more difficult to negotiate. Indian attitudes toward work, based on the prescriptive ideologies of impurity, made some people available for cooking, others for cleaning toilets (Frøystad 2003), while prohibiting some altogether. Domestic technologies – particularly the toilet – solidified caste within the colonial home.

At variance with the Mughal *gusalkhana* [bath house], which was a highly social room, and not at all individualized, colonial homes in the eighteenth and nineteenth centuries used their English counterparts as reference points. However, quiet unlike the outdoor privies with pit toilets of Regency England, colonial bungalows had indoor rooms and dry pattern commodes, with back entrances to enable the cleaner to enter and leave without encountering anyone. The dry pattern commode had a trap door behind it, to facilitate the removal of the full bucket and its replacement again without a sign of the worker's presence. The wall-mounted cistern that allowed fairly efficient flushing did not make an appearance in the colonial bungalow till well after its invention in the 1870s (Eveleigh 2008). Until then, portable commodes or chamber pots made a whole category of labour essential to the household. Men of the *bhangi* (loosely translated as sweeper) caste were employed only for cleaning chamber pots and commodes. Ideologies of purity and occupational segregations were critical to staffing patterns of households and were not negotiable in the way that gender became for houseboys. Indoor plumbing became more widely used in the short half century from 1875 to 1925, but this did not mean the departure of the toilet cleaner.

Accounts of the bungalow as political space (King 1984) describe an elaborate etiquette based on distinctions of authority and kinship, involving the front half of the bungalow – the veranda, the steps, the entrance and inner sanctum. The back of the bungalow was governed by an equally elaborate protocol of avoidance, not only between employer and sweeper, but between different categories of household staff among whom the toilet cleaner was a social invisible.

Conditions of servitude in England, on the other hand, were undergoing significant changes of contract and organization. Despite the fact that domestic work was deemed to add no value to objects upon which the labour was expended, literally written off as 'without a trace', workers in England were under the purview of the law of contract. However incomplete the access to law, domestic workers responded to their conditions of employment by setting up agencies and registry offices that could regulate employment. In 1897, the London and Provincial Domestic Servants Union, in a published pamphlet available for a penny, aimed to provide 'justice to both employers and employees' (London and Provincial Domestic Servants Union 1897). The Union sought to address a host of ticklish issues and to make employment more amenable for servants, and its aims included (ibid.):

1. To render it compulsory by law upon all employers to give a true and just character in writing to servants on leaving their employ.
2. To reform the system adopted by registry office keepers, so as to bring them under official supervision.
3. To prevent the cleaning of windows on the outside by women servants, and to protect the lives of servants against domestic boiler explosions.
4. To increase the rate of wages and hours for necessary out-door recreation, especially on Sundays.

In particular, the demand for a testimonial was a way of reinstating the work itself as having been performed and acknowledged, and recovering the right of property in person. In colonial India however, no such institutions existed that attempted to put forward the views of servants about their employment. Colonial constructions of Indian servants, which arose from a context of encounter between distinct races and cultural practices, tell us more about the colonizers than they do about the servants, and servants in colonial India are known primarily through the eyes of their masters. This had a great deal to do with the conditions of colonial rule that silenced a whole category of persons.

Additionally, Indian structures of *jajmani* (loosely translated as patron–client or master–servant relations) twisted into eighteenth-century ideas of value to produce newer formations of servitude. The ideas of dependence, tied work and obligation were evoked to foster relations between colonial master and his Indian servants. *Jajmani* expanded the languages of family and kinship in which the subjects of empire presented themselves as dependents of the 'parental' state (*Mai-baap sarkar* [literally, Mother-Father state], a term evoking dependence but also a sense of entrusting the parental state with the well-being of its dependent subjects). The vocabulary of dependence adopted by peasant petitioners became the template for other categories of dependents like servants, including household servants, to appeal to their employers. Kinship vocabularies did not imply the substitution or schizophrenic misrecognition of the blood family with the 'state' as family. Nevertheless, the power of colonialism to ruthlessly reorganize the family life of household servants dispossessed people from their own circles of intimacy and trust, to be replaced by a distant but powerful employer whom the servants, as dependents, were forced to trust. *Jajmani* might well have underwritten domestic codes of appeal, for the system of *jajmani* was a familiar one, and its vocabularies were deployed strategically by domestic servants in their appeals against mistreatment in similar fashion to those of their peasant brothers against excessive revenue rates. Unfortunately, within the intimacies of colonial households, this style of appeal was wholly misinterpreted and became another area in which cultural confusion produced servants not as petitioners but as complaining children in need of firm discipline.

Responses by domestic servants to the colonial Raj are hard to find, and therefore peasant petitioners become a theoretical substitute: partly because the peasantry was a source of domestic servitude, especially when colonial agrarian policies and settlements dispossessed them of rights in land use, and partly because the language of 'master–servant' or patron–client that governed caste and livelihood in agrarian society (Gould 1986) could be translated into the colonial home. The vocabulary of dependence was continuously deployed in petitions for adjustments in revenue or rent, drawing upon a system in which caste, occupational specialization and labour interlocked. It is the *jajmani* system that gives us a sense of structures of servitude in India which pre-date colonial rule, but which, as systems, did not remain unaffected by colonial policy, or indeed location. It entered the domestic as a system misheard and misunderstood, a loss that tore away the value of domestic work.

Conclusion

In what sense does the system of servitude in colonial India exist as a trace in our contemporary world? Do relations of trust look back into history, creating a *habitus* within which master–servant relations echo a past to shape the present? What place does the anti-modern institution of servitude have in globalizing India, a place of modern apartment blocks and cosmopolitan lifestyles? Many of the practices, distinctions, nuanced relations of mistrust and trust that governed the master–servant life worlds of colonial India strike notes of familiarity, like the musician's song, to my postcolonial ears. It does seem to me that for modern middle-class Indians, servants possess a peculiar value. For globalizing Indians, servants represent a form of an authentic Indian past, an 'enchanted' sign of tradition within the modern home. Like memorials, servants are part of an imagined and valued *zamana*, a time of 'core' values, of paternalism, hierarchy and bonds of trust that captures the anti-modern as a utopia brought forward into the present in the figure of the servant, to celebrate what modern Indians say they value most – deep and authentic traditions. For Indian middle-class employers, who rule the lives of those who serve them, the servant in the twenty-first century has not vanished without trace. In fact each servant serves as a sign, a reassurance – that we need never be modern.

Notes

1 The word *bangla* comes from a translation meaning 'belonging to Bengal', but it became generalized as a term for colonial homes and domestic architecture. The bungalow and its compound was a political space where power and authority were displayed for an 'audience' of the subjugated.
2 Examples could be seen among the paintings in the Asia Society exhibition, *Princes and Painters in Mughal Delhi 1707–1857*, Asia Society Museum, 725 Park Avenue, New York, February–May 2012.
3 The use of cosmetics by servants in twentieth- and twenty-first-century urban India gives an indication of this form of material culture; accusations by employers of maids using their hand creams and lipsticks are common complaints. It is possible that such usage is not merely a 'modern' Indian transaction between maid and mistress but was also a part of the covert relations between colonial master and servant.
4 Official hierarchies were reflected in the furnishings of the bungalow, a tradition that lives well beyond the colonial era. Modern civil servants of postcolonial India know to the last dish the category of crockery to which each IAS (Indian Administrative Service) officer is entitled in their official residences.
5 The term *sati* refers to the Hindu practice of the immolation of a widow upon the funeral pyre of her dead husband. Colonial debates ranged from whether it was a 'volitional' act, whether it had scriptural sanction and, most critically, how far colonial officers could prevent *sati* without arousing disaffection. The eventual abolishing of *sati* in 1829 was viewed as a 'rescue' of brown women by enlightened white men, against the barbarism of brown men.

References

Anonymous. 1892. 'Sleeping Accommodation For Servants', *British Medical Journal* 2(1664): 1129.
Atkinson, George Francklin. 1859. *Captain, Curry and Rice Or The Ingredients of Social Life at 'Our Station' in India*. London: Day and Son.
Baier, A. 1986. 'Trust and Antitrust', *Ethics* 9 (2): 231–260.
Beeton, I.M. 2005 [1890]. *Mrs Beeton's Cookery Book and Household Guide*. New York: Elibron Classic Series.
Chopra, R. 2012. 'Servitude and Sacrifice: Masculinity and Domestic Labour', *Masculinidades y Cambio Social* 1(1): 19–39.

Calcutta Photos. n.d. *From India to America, the Bungalow Re-imagined*. Available at <http://archiduct.blogspot.in/2010/05/from-india-to-america-bungalow.html>, accessed 24 August 2013

Colonna, F. 1997. 'Educating Conformity in French Colonial Algeria'. In F. Cooper and A.L. Stoler (eds), *Tensions of Empire: Colonial Cultures in a Bourgeois World*, 346–372. Berkeley: University of California Press.

Coser, L. 1973. 'Servants: The Obsolescence of an Occupational Role', *Social Forces* 52(1): 31–40.

Cox, R., 2006. *The Servant Problem: Domestic Employment in a Global Economy*. London: I.B. Tauris.

D'oyly, C., T. Williamson and F.W. Blagdon. 1813. *The European in India, Accompanied with a Brief History of Ancient and Modern India*. London: J. Dove.

Earle, P. 1989. *The Making of the English Middle Class: Business, Society and Family Life in London 1660–1730*. Berkeley: University of California Press.

Eveleigh, D.J. 2008. *Privies and Water Closets*. Oxford: Shire Publications.

Franklin, J. 1975. 'Troops of Servants: Labour and Planning in the Country House 1840–1914', *Victorian Studies* 19(2): 211–239.

Frøystad, K. 2003. 'Master–Servant Relations and the Domestic Reproduction of Caste in Northern India', *Ethnos* 68(1): 73–94.

Ginsburg, R., 2000. '"Come in the Dark": Domestic Workers and Their Rooms in Apartheid-Era Johannesburg, South Africa', *Perspectives in Vernacular Architecture* (Special Issue: People, Power, Places) 8: 83–100.

Glover, W.J. 2008. *Making Lahore Modern: Constructing and Imagining a Colonial City*. Minneapolis: University of Minnesota Press.

Govier, T. 1992. 'Trust, Distrust, and Feminist Theory', *Hypatia* 7(1): 16–33.

Gould, H.A. 1986. 'The Hindu Jajmani System: A Case of Economic Particularism', *Journal of Anthropological Research* 42(3): 269–278.

Hall, C. 1992. *White, Male and Middle Class: Explorations in Feminism and History*. Cambridge: Polity Press.

Hall, E.T. 1963. 'A System for the Notation of Proxemic Behavior', *American Anthropologist* 65(5): 1003–1026.

Hansen, K.T. 1989. *Distant Companions: Servants and Employers in Zambia, 1900–1985*. Ithaca: Cornell University Press.

James, E. 1879. *Guide to Indian Household Management*. London: Ward and Lock & Co.

King, A. 1976. *Colonial Urban Development: Culture, Social Power and Environment*. London: Routledge and Kegan Paul.

King, A. 1984. *The Bungalow: The Production of a Global Culture*. London: Routledge and Kegan Paul.

Kloester, J. 2010. *Georgette Heyer's Regency World*. Naperville, IL: Sourcebooks.

London and Provincial Domestic Servants Union. 1897. 'How Domestic Servants Can Obtain a Compulsory Character and Establish Homes and Registry Offices of Their Own'. LSE Selected Pamphlets, LSE Library Stable. Available online at <http://www.jstor.org/stable/60218261> (accessed 11 April, 2012).

Roper, S. 1996. 'Maintaining the "Cheery Fires": Servants' Space in a Turn-of-the-century Kansas House', *Material Culture* 28(3): 17–40.

Searle, J.R. 1969. *Speech Acts: An Essay in the Philosophy of Language*. Cambridge: Cambridge University Press.
Smith, A. 1904 [1776]. *An Inquiry into the Nature and Causes of the Wealth of Nations* (ed. Edwin Cannan). London: Methuen & Co. Ltd. 5th Edition, 1904 <http://www.econlib.org/library/Smith/smWN8.html> (accessed 23 April 2012).
Steedman, C. 2003. 'Servants and Their Relationship to the Unconscious', *Journal of British Studies* 42(3): 316–350.
Steel, F. A. and G. Gardiner. 1890/2010 [1888]. *The Complete Indian Housekeeper and Cook* (ed. R. Crane and A. Johnston). Oxford: Oxford University Press.
Stoler, A.L. 2001.'Tense and Tender Ties: The Politics of Comparison in North American History and (Post) Colonial Studies', *Journal of American History* 88(3): 1–41.
—— 2006. *Haunted by Empire: Geographies of Intimacy in North American History*. Durham: Duke University Press.
Tarlo, E. 1996. *Clothing Matters: Dress and Identity in India*. Chicago: University of Chicago Press.
Waterson, M. 1980. *The Servants' Hall: A Domestic History of Erddig*. London: Routledge and Kegan Paul.
Wiser, W.H. 1969. *The Hindu Jajmani System: A Socio-economic System Interrelating Members of a Hindu Village Community in Services*. Lucknow: Lucknow Publishing House.

Radhika Chopra teaches at the University of Delhi. She is the author of *Militant and Migrant: The Politics and Social History of Punjab* (London, New York, New Delhi: Routledge 2011); has edited *Reframing Masculinities: Narrating the Supportive Practices of Men* (New Delhi: Orient Longman 2006) and co-edited *South Asian Masculinities: Contexts of Change, Sites of Continuity* with Caroline and Filippo Osella (New Delhi: Kali for Women and Women Unlimited 2004). She has published widely in international journals and edited volumes; and is on the Editorial Board of *Sikh Formations: Religion, Culture, Theory* and *Culture Society and Masculinities*. She has been a Post-doctoral Fulbright Fellow affiliated to New York University; Visiting Professor at Georg August University, Göttingen; and Visiting Fellow at universities in US and the UK. She has also been co-chair of the UN Expert Group on The Role of Men and Boys in Achieving Gender Equality; curator of two film-cum-discussion series *Making Migrants: Dialogues through Film* (India International Centre, New Delhi, 15-18 January 2009) and *School in Cinema* (India International Centre, New Delhi, 2-6 August 2004); and written the text for an exhibition *Men and Masculinities* (Art Gallery, Indian International Centre, New Delhi, November 2003).

 10

'You Can Tell the Company We Done Quit'
The Destruction and Reconfiguration of Trust in the Appalachian Coalfields in the Early Twentieth Century
Gloria Goodwin Raheja

Introduction

What happens when those who control the lives of labourers attempt to discipline those workers by dissolving the bonds of sociality the workers value and the trust they may have in the judiciary and their civic institutions and their religious leaders? As industrial capitalism in the form of coal mining drew its shadow over the Appalachian Mountains in the early part of the twentieth century, such modes of disciplinary control prompted miners to form novel cross-racial bonds of trust in one another. The music the miners made registered these relationships, which drew white and African-American workers together in ways that were distinctive, musically and socially, to the coalfields in those years. In this chapter I explore this reconfiguration of the boundaries of trust and intimacy by focusing on the sonic and social landscapes of Logan County West Virginia and its environs in the early decades of the twentieth century.

Logan County lies in the Appalachian mountain landscape of southern West Virginia. Just to the east are the Allegheny Mountains with their orderly waves of ridges and valleys, but here instead are the heavily eroded remnants of the unglaciated Allegheny Plateau, its shale deeply carved by creeks and branches and rills and runnels into a jumble of unruly knobby hills, originally covered by one of the most biologically diverse temperate forests in the world, an ecosystem that evolved over the eons as the Allegheny tableland was being eroded. And beneath it all are thick seams of coal, the fossilized remains of an ancient coal swamp forest submerged and compacted by a Palaeozoic shallow inland sea and turned into coal about three hundred million years ago. (Hufford n.d.; Raitz and Ulack 1984). The hills here are generally too steep to allow much beyond a few isolated farms or home places to take root on them, so railroads, creeks, roads and coal camps are all pressed together in the narrow hollows between them. There are few long vistas if you're travelling on the roads, and depending upon how you see it or where you're looking from, you're either confined and imprisoned or held in a warm embrace by those unruly mountains.

Miners sometimes encountered 'flowers of darkness' as they called them, when the light from their headlamps fell upon fossilized ferns, spectral reminders of that long-submerged Carboniferous forest, 'caught forever in the act of dying' and imprinted on the slate that encases coal deposits (Moore 1991: 73). And they called the petrified tree trunks 'kettle bottoms', massive fossils that would crush their bodies when they dropped without warning from the roof of the 'room' where they worked at the coal face. The underground mine is a place where the life of the ancient sea that once was there inscribed itself upon the coal and shale, and where the coal itself turned against the miners and killed them. And it's a place where coal dust, 'bug dust' as the miners called it, caused them to fall ill with black lung disease, or where it spontaneously combusted in the mine and exploded, or gave them coal tattoos where it embedded itself in their skin when they'd been hurt in a mining accident. Some men thought that a coal tattoo was a sign from God and others thought that if it curved like a horseshoe it was a talisman, the only good thing about bug dust, imprinted on the surface of their bodies (Rash 2013).

Most miners knew of course that it was not the coal itself that wreaked havoc with their lives, they knew it was the coal operators and the state and county governments and religious institutions that sanctioned the predation that did the damage. And because people had different views of things, trust between husbands and wives, between fathers and sons, could also dissolve. So many different perspectives there were, on the land, on labour, on race, on place, on family ties, on religion, on civic institutions and on the unions that miners wanted to bring to the coalfields. And yet there were, among the miners and their families, struggles not only to overcome the intense hardships of life in the coal camps, but also to form new bases for trust and new forms of sociality that would contest and challenge the conditions imposed by the coal operators who had tried to decimate every form of community and every form of social capital the mining families had.

Logan County and its Environs in the Early Twentieth Century: Mining and Music

No other region of the southern Appalachians was more deeply transformed by the coming of coal mining in the early decades of the twentieth century than southern West Virginia (Eller 1982: 132). No labour struggles in the United States were more violent than those in southern West Virginia between 1912 and 1922, and nowhere was there a more compelling musical exchange between black and white rural musicians. I am interested here in drawing out the connections between popular music and the coming of industrial capitalism to rural Appalachia in the early twentieth century, and describing some of the ways the music responded to social and economic transformations of the mountain landscape.

During this critical period in Appalachian history, both black and white miners reacted to the consolidation of the coal companies' control of labour and the public sphere, to anti-union violence, to the usurpation of land rights by the coal companies, and to the hardships of life in the coalfields. This was also a critical moment in the history of American popular music. Record companies scouted for rural music, but as they did so they policed racial boundaries, insisting that black musicians strip elements regarded as 'hillbilly' influence from their music. They sequestered African-American music in 'race music' catalogues while confining white recordings, regardless of genre, to their 'hillbilly' or 'old time' series. Moreover, folk festival organizers in Appalachia in the early 1930s were engaged in promoting anti-miscegenation laws while also aiming, in their festivals, to recover an 'authentic' white rural music untouched by blues or other traditions 'tainted' by black influence (Whisnant 1983). Thus while rural whites in Appalachia were asked to embrace the capitalist order and its contradictions, they were simultaneously required to exhibit a supposedly 'traditional' white Anglo-Saxon musical heritage, as a foundation for an exclusionary nationalist American culture. Yet music that traversed those heavily patrolled boundaries was sometimes commercially recorded; these 78-rpm recordings sold well in the coalfields, and the music circulated outside of the commercial ambit as well. I would want to problematize the appropriation of black music by white coalminers, but at the same time interrogate the racial binaries in terms of which we have understood 'black music' and this appropriation, and recognize the novel and ambiguous class-based racial alliances evidenced in the coalminers' music. Coal mining transformed the sonic and social landscapes of the mountain south but the music that registered these transformations has hitherto been virtually expunged from blues historiography and it figures in only a spectral way in American memory.

White musicians who embraced the blues idiom and its aesthetics and politics in the 1920s were most numerous in the Logan County coalfields, and foremost among them was Frank Hutchison, who worked in the Logan mines for much of his life; who recorded blues and other music for Okeh Records between 1926 and 1929; who was the first white man to record a guitar blues; and who lived and worked in the shadow of Blair Mountain. The fact that blues arrived so quickly in Logan County had to do partly with the timing of the advent of the railroads and coal mines there in the early 1900s just as blues was taking shape as a musical genre further south, and with the nature of labour struggles there. Many railroad workers were African Americans from the deep South. Coal mines initially employed mainly white Appalachian workers, but labour contractors brought in black workers from the South to serve as strike breakers. This was not particularly successful, as black workers often joined whites in agitation for union representation and in defence against the violence exercised by coal operators and the county sheriffs and federal troops that defended their interests. Railroads and coal mining came into Logan County in 1904, just as the blues was developing further south. As black workers were brought there by labour contractors, they brought the blues with them. Both black and white miners embraced this idiom and they used it to question the control the coal operators tried to exert over their labour and their lives. This strategy was doubly subversive, since it challenged efforts to whiten Appalachian musical traditions and establish an exclusionary white cultural heritage as the only 'authentic' one, and it also challenged efforts to divide miners along racial lines and thus thwart unionization efforts.

This is not to say that class solidarities obliterated racism or racial identities. As Trotter has demonstrated in his research on the formation of a black working class in the southern West Virginia coalfields, the dynamics of race and class there were complex and sometimes contradictory ones (Trotter 1990). But an analysis of the music the miners made as they struggled against capitalist exploitation in the coal-mining camps provides one vantage point on the ways in which they did in fact forge alliances across the colour line, however fragile or enduring they may have been.

What Happened when the Mines Came in?

What happened when the railroads, timber industries and coal companies came to southern West Virginia? While it is problematic to assume that prior to the beginning of the twentieth century the region was characterized by social homogeneity, settlement isolation and an absence of entrepreneurial capitalism (Banks 1995; Mann 1995; McKinney 1995;

Dunaway 1995, 1996; Eller 1982: 7), it was nonetheless the case that most people lived by subsistence farming to some extent and they had a strong attachment to the land; in 1850 two-thirds of Logan County households owned their own farms and while the size and productivity of the farms varied, the gaps in wealth were not extreme (Waller 1988: 22).

Perhaps more than in other rural areas, the land itself shaped forms of sociality in the mountains. Each community occupied a distinct cove or hollow and was separated from its neighbours by a rim of hills. Land ownership usually terminated at the ridge top, reinforcing the community's identity and independence, but the hillsides were generally considered to be public land open for use by all members of the community. Many (but not all) economic and social activities were self-contained within these hollows, with individual households relying upon themselves or their neighbours for many of the necessities and pleasures of life. The land was such a dominant factor in mountain culture that neighbourhoods often drew their names from the creeks and branches that penetrated the settlement and that further divided the larger community into numerous sub-communities (Eller 1982: 7).

Aunt Jennie Wilson was born on Little Buffalo Creek in Logan County in 1900 and she learned to play clawhammer banjo when she was a very young girl. Her family managed to hold on to their land for a little while at least, before the men went into the mines. She was the daughter of a farmer in Logan County and the wife of a coal miner who died in the Logan mines in 1939. She did not record commercially in the 1920s or 1930s but she became well known in later life as a West Virginia musician, and she was interviewed on a number of occasions about her music and her life as it was, before virtually all of the farmland had been acquired by the timber and mining interests. Of her family's life as subsistence farmers she had this to say, for example.

> There was just very little that we had to buy in a store except sugar, coffee, and flour; salt, soda, and stuff like that. We had our own meat, our own milk and butter, our own eggs. Then my mother would can up lots of stuff in the fall. She'd make cans of things besides the barrels of pickles we kept. Yes, that's the way we grew up. (Spence 1976: 100)

The names of the creeks were most often the last name of the first settler there, who generally would establish a homestead at the mouth of it. As bilateral kinship groups expanded and kin moved up the creeks and runs, the communities and creeks were named for the people who settled there, and so a map of the streams and the hollows through which they flowed was almost readable as a family tree with all its forking branches. Shared access to the higher ground running up from the creeks meant that anyone in the holler could climb the mountain and search for the forest plants used as food or medicine or sold in trade: roots and leaves and nuts and fruits and fungi like ginseng, ramps, molly moochers, paw paws, black cohosh, walnuts, hickory nuts, creasy greens and yellowroot. And access to the ridgetops meant that everyone could hunt for squirrels and turkey there.

It was on those hillsides that people buried their dead, in family cemeteries up from the home place, where 'the headstones did not stand in tidy rows' on the slopes, but were 'placed companionably, as people will sit and talk – Aunt Jane beside Uncle Alec, Albion facing them beneath a spreading oak, Florrie's dead baby at his feet' (Giardina 1987: 290–291).

In countless interviews people like Aunt Jennie Wilson recalled the ways in which labour as well as land was shared, and the ways in which the line of demarcation between work and recreation was often blurred. She recalled the corn shuckings and the bean stringings to which the members of one household invited their kin and neighbours to help with the work and get it done of an evening, and the women would cook dinner for everyone and then the music and dancing would begin, because music was so often a feature of sociality and of work. Others called such events 'workings,' and they might involve planting, harvesting, or raising cabins and barns. Eller quotes, for example, from an interview with Panny Hogg Day:

> They sent out word in the neighborhood and everybody would come. They'd pitch in, and cleared up maybe two or three acres of ground for planting crops in one day. It was called 'new ground' ... and everybody pitched in and cut down the trees. They called it a 'grubbing.' It was a lot easier and nicer to work with a group and get it done than to just linger along by yourself trying to clear three or four acres of ground. (Eller 1982: 35)

Community churches and schools were generally constructed in this collective way as well (Eller 1982: 36). And religious events like 'singings', camp meetings, 'dinners on the grounds', funerals lasting several days, and revivals, all often attended by circuit-riding preachers, provided the basis for robust forms of sociality and trust (Eller 1982: 33; Waller 1988: 23).

If I seem to be romanticizing the Logan County past, before the coal mines came, it is because this is the way that people later remembered their lives and mourned the passing of their world. Their recollections may sometimes seem like sentimentalized accounts of life in the mountains and they no doubt partly are. But perhaps we can also understand these accounts as forms of social memory, forms of lament, for a world that had mostly been obliterated when the coal mines came in.

What then happened when industrial capitalism, in the form of timbering, railroads and coal mines came to West Virginia? For one thing the forests almost disappeared, and so many people lost their ability to hunt and forage for the food and medicines it had given them. And people who lived downstream from the deforestation found their water supplies contaminated and their property endangered by forest fires (Lewis 1995: 314). In 1870, two-thirds of the land in the state was covered by virgin forest – enormous stands of sycamore, sugar maple, red spruce, walnut, oak, cherry, hickory, sweet gum and poplar – but by the 1920s the mountains had been very nearly stripped bare of their timber (Lewis 1995; Eller 1982). And much of the land was rapidly being acquired by the railroad, timber and mining companies. In the late nineteenth century, typical farms in southern West Virginia were about 187 acres; by the end of the 1920s, they were mostly between 47 and 76 acres (Corbin 1981: 7), primarily due to the predatory land acquisition tactics of these industries and the northern capitalists who financed them (Lewis 1995: 312). This was especially true of the mining interests.

An attitude of no respect for the property rights of others allowed the capitalists to take what they wanted. Following the Revolutionary War, the state of Virginia had compensated its soldiers with the 'wastelands' of its western counties and sold the rest in bulk to early land speculators. By the 1880s, the deeds to both groups of land had been forfeited to the state because of the failure of the original titleholders to pay taxes on the land and to register their ownership. Virginia, and later West Virginia, reclaimed the land and sold it to the people who had settled there. The late-nineteenth-century speculators and capitalists now purchased the original deeds and sought help from the courts, claiming that they were the rightful owners.

At least twice the US Supreme Court ruled that the original deeds were invalid and that the local inhabitants were entitled to the land. The northern capitalists then found local federal judges who were noted for their 'tender concern for the rights of nonresident landowners', a concern possibly stimulated by bribery, and these judges declared that the original deeds were valid. Facing huge legal fees and years of litigation, neither of which they could afford if they appealed, the natives finally sold their claims, left, or were thrown off the land (Corbin 1981: 3).

This kind of judicially sanctioned land seizure was but one of several tactics used by coal companies to strip people of their rights to the land. Many buyers who ventured into the mountains offered to purchase only the rights to the minerals, and leave the owner rights to work the surface. Landowners initially trusted these agents but saw the consequences all too soon. First, as the value of the coal beneath the ground was realized, taxes soared and the farmers, not the coal companies, were responsible for all of them: many had to abandon their farms because they couldn't pay. And second, hidden away in the complex agreements that few could read were provisions granting the coal companies rights to use the surface in any way deemed necessary to the extraction of coal (Eller 1982: 54–57). People found no protection against these deceitful practices in the courts. In the early years of the twentieth century an enormous body of West Virginia case law evolved to protect the interests of the industrialists at the expense of farmers (Lewis 1995: 304–308) and by 1900 ninety per cent of the land in Logan County was controlled by absentee landowners. It is no wonder that so many people lost faith in the judicial system and held the judges in contempt (Corbin 1981: 3–4). The county courthouse had long been a place where people gathered together on court days to socialize, where music was played on the steps, where information was exchanged, and where jurors found it possible to reconcile their cultural values with the law in the courtroom and thus had trust in the workings of the judicial system (Waller 1988). But as courts turned against the farmers, trust in the law evaporated.

There were discursive struggles too, in which Appalachian newspapers and local and national coal and railroad interests characterized striking miners and anyone who opposed their seizures of land as 'white savages' when they stood in the way of 'progress', that is, the expansion of the new labour disciplines of industrial capitalism and the control of land and labour and the public sphere by outside capital. These characterizations were used to justify the seizure of land and the often-violent suppression of strikes and union organizing. Like many other newspapers in Appalachia at the time, the *Logan Banner* (the chief newspaper in Logan County) was relentless in its mission of portraying mountain people as backward, irrational, moonshine-drinking savages, whose lives would be reformed and their culture refined by labour in the mines (Shapiro 1978; Waller 1988). Moonshine was a particular target. Many farmers and miners who moved between work in the mines and working a bit of land made moonshine as a way of providing for their own recreation and sociality, of course, but also as a way of earning a bit of cash to supplement their subsistence farming and their mine wages (Thompson 2011). The coal operators, the newspapers, and West Virginia governors and legislators often blamed moonshine whenever miners went on strike or otherwise exhibited resistance to the disciplines and violence of the coal camps. This discursive strategy directed attention away from violations of miners' rights and directed it instead to miners' supposedly flawed 'culture' (Corbin 1981: 212; Waller 1988: 204).

Tens of thousands of West Virginia farmers became miners after losing their land. And what did they find in the coal camps to which they moved? They found that more often than not they were required to sign 'yellow dog' contracts that prohibited them from joining a union, and that the West Virginia courts and the US Supreme Court upheld the legality of these contracts (Lunt 1992). They found that the coal companies hired armed Baldwin-Felts detective agents as mine guards (the miners called them 'gun thugs') to terrorize the coal camps or, in Logan County, they found that the coal companies paid the county sheriff to hire and arm deputies to do their bidding. They found that when they went on strike labour recruiters brought in African Americans from the southern states, or Italian or Hungarian immigrants, and settled them in separate hollers in the camp, as 'scabs' to break the strike and keep the mines open. They found that although it was illegal in West Virginia, they would be paid in scrip instead of US currency, scrip that could only be used in coal company-owned stores where prices were high. They found that they would risk being fired if their wives earned a bit of cash by cooking for visiting mine officials and then went downtown to Logan to buy a hat rather than to purchase one at the company store (interview with Billie Gee Gunther, September 2006). They found that they would be paid by the ton for the coal they dug, but that they were routinely cheated when coal companies under-weighed the coal as it came out of the mine, and that the coal companies refused to allow an impartial checkweighman to verify the weights. They found that if they complained about the weights, they'd be assigned an especially bad 'place' or 'room' to work in underground, where the roof might only be three feet high and they'd have to lie on their backs to work the coal, or where they'd stand in water all day up to their knees, as punishment and warning to others. They found that during times of union organizing they were not permitted to gather together in groups of more than two or three miners and this was enforced by the gun thugs, and so forms of sociality were limited at those times. They found that if they went on strike they would be evicted from their homes and forced to live in tent colonies where they might be fired upon by the gun thugs.

The miners found that teachers in the company schools told their children that their families were backward and uncivilized if they complained about conditions in the mines. They found that the preachers hired to preach in the company churches would tell them that the unions were 'ungodly and wicked', that the coal operators were favoured by God, and that they should be content with the wages that were offered. And they found that those ministers might serve as mine guards during the week, when they weren't preaching the gospel of the coal companies (Corbin 1981: 146–155).

And the wives missed the home places they had to move away from, and they missed the sociable gatherings of women who helped one another out. Census records show that related families sometimes settled together in the coal camps to mitigate the isolating effects of the mining life, but such kinship solidarities were shattered when work was scarce and men had to find jobs in whatever mine would take them on. Miners' wives feared that their children would starve when the mines had a lay-off, they feared that their sons might have to go into the mines at the age of eight, they feared that their men would die in an explosion or roof fall or be shot at by the gun thugs or sheriff's deputies.

Miners knew that the county authorities and the judges in the state would not protect their interests when there was an accident in the mines, because there were seldom any prosecutions for mine safety violations against the operators. In West Virginia in 1910 for example there were 163 prosecutions, but 159 of these were against the miners, because coal companies argued that accidents were always the miners' fault and they disavowed all responsibility for ensuring the safety of the mines (Corbin 1981: 17).

So many of the things the miners and their wives discovered in the camps caused them to lose their trust: in the coal companies of course, but also in local and state government, in their county and state courts, in the local police, in the preachers who protected the interests of the coal operators, and in the teachers who taught their children in the company stores. And as this trust was eroded, they frequently found it difficult to rely on other people in the community (some of whom could be spying for the company), difficult to gather together to work and play music and socialize together because the coal operators said they couldn't. Kin and neighbours might lose the ability to rely on one another and place their trust in one another, as some managed to profit a bit from the sale of land while others suffered the consequences, or some wanted to bring in the union and others feared what might happen if they did. Husbands and wives sometimes lost trust in one another, because the hardships of life in the coal camps and new ideas about work and masculinity might drive them apart and cause them to see things differently. Sometimes it was because the men thought that the only chance they had to provide for their families lay in mining and women couldn't bear the thought of leaving their old homes and settling down in the coal camps. And sometimes it was because men abandoned their wives when things got too hard to bear. In 1922 a journalist named Freda Kirchwey visited Logan and Mingo counties and talked with wives of striking miners. She wrote that women had many different views on things. 'Some were on strike with their husbands; some were on strike against their husbands. Some were good-natured and easy-going even with hunger and death nearby. Some were bitter; some just tired' (Kirchwey 1922: 84). Mrs Sweet told Kirchwey about her life in a tent colony to which the miners and their families had retreated during a strike.

> 'It was hard when the baby come,' she said 'because there wasn't no work, an' then, soon as they got workin', seems like, the strike come along. Tom [her husband] went out [on strike] like the rest. The baby come four weeks ago. I had a real hard time – seems like I ought not to, don't it, with the second? – and when the baby was twelve days old, Tom went off. I can't make it out. I think an' I think about it. He seemed to care about me; he was real decent to me most times. Sometimes I think maybe he just couldn't stand to watch us get hungry an' not know how to help it nor do nothin' different. But sometimes I think he was pretty mean, seems like, to go off just when he did ... This week the union sent me two dollars, an' last week a dollar fifty; that's the first money come into the house since the baby came a month ago. They say they'll send it right along now even if Tom has lit out. I guess we can get along somehow. Maybe Tom'll stay away an' maybe he'll come back. I reckon he thinks he'll come back some time when things ain't so hard around here.' (Kirchwey 1922: 87)

And out of loneliness married women sometimes sought consolation from other men, when their own husbands were in the mines from pre-dawn hours until after dark, and were so tired when they got home that it was all they could to wash off the coal dust and eat a hasty meal before they fell asleep (Billie Gee Gunther interview, September 2006).

Logan County People Respond to the Coming of the Mines

We have few records of the voices of Logan County people who lived in these times and suffered through them. The words of Mrs. Sweet and several other women survive in scattered journalistic accounts, there are some oral history records from Logan and surrounding counties, there is an autobiography of one of the leaders of the march on Blair Mountain, and there are poems and letters miners sent to the

United Mine Workers Journal during the early decades of the twentieth century. There is a great deal of music though, recorded by musicians from Logan County and adjoining coalfield counties for Okeh Records and Brunswick records during the heyday of the 'hillbilly' commercial recordings. And there are field recordings made by folklorists in the 1930s, of songs that men sang in the mines in the 1920s and early 1930s.

We know that miners responded to the terrible burdens they bore after the coming of industrial capitalism to the mountains by moving from mine to mine in search of better working conditions, by moving back and forth from mine to farm if they could manage it and if they had access to any land at all, by struggling fiercely for the right to unionize (which was not achieved until the passing of the National Labor Relations Act in 1935), by abandoning their families when the burdens became unbearable as Tom Sweet seems to have done, or by going into the mines day after day because that was the only way they had to put food on the table. But miners and their wives also responded in music, in words that registered the conditions under which they lived and what they thought of them. In *Logan County Blues: Frank Hutchison in the Sonic Landscape of the Appalachian Coalfields*, the book I am writing, I analyse many aspects of this unique soundscape, but in this chapter I look simply at the ways in which cross-racial labour alliances were complemented and sometimes forged by cross-racial musical performances. I look at the ways in which both white and African-American miners in Logan County drew upon a blues idiom, the ways in which whites learned music from black miners and railroad workers to articulate a common critical perspective and to forge bonds of trust across those racial lines. I look at the ways in which union songs (some of which are blues and some of which are not) were expressions of the miners' perspectives on class and the experience of coal mining. I look also at the ways in which African-American religious songs were adapted as union songs by both white and African-American miners, in ways that explicitly reject the religious perspectives of the company preachers and express the miner's trust in their own miner-preachers and their own newly forged religious convictions and ideologies of class. And finally I look at music written and sung by women in the coalfields that also crosses racial boundaries, as it gave voice to their perspectives on the work their men did in the mines and the dissolution of community and trust that the mine owners tried to bring about.

In 1926 Frank Hutchison became the first white guitar player and singer to record blues music. He lived for almost all his life in Logan County, working as a coal miner in the Fort Branch, Ethel, and Daisy mining camps. He was born in 1897 and died in 1945, without ever being interviewed about his life and music, but Sherman Lawson, a friend who had performed and recorded with him on the fiddle, talked with Mike Seeger about him, and there is also an interview with Aunt Jennie Wilson, who was once engaged to Hutchison. They and the relatives of Hutchison I interviewed all vividly remembered the names of the African-American workers who showed Frank how to play the blues and they remembered the stories he told them about it. They remembered that he talked about first hearing blues music when he was six years old in 1903, from Henry Vaughn, who worked for the Chesapeake and Ohio Railroad when the trains first came to Logan. They remembered that he talked about Bill Hunt, a crippled man and probably a former coal miner who played blues music at the company store on payday when the miners could afford to give him some coins. Frank would walk up the mountains above the coal camp where he lived, in the late 1910s and early 1920s, and learn blues songs from him. In most of the other areas of the south, white musicians who knew some blues could say only that they learned a song 'from a darky on Decatur Street' or from a 'nigger singing in a field' but Frank, like other coalfield musicians, could tell the stories of the individual men from whom they learned to play; the narratives of encounter with black musicians were different and far more intimate there in the coalfields. And although white and black miners were almost always segregated in different hollers in a coal camp by coal company policy, they worked together underground, they struggled together for union recognition, and they all frequented the company store and bought blues records there (Garland 1969: 90).

And in the 1920s, while very few white musicians in the south outside the coalfields would play with black musicians, Hutchison and other coal miners did. He played, for example, with Howard Armstrong, when he and the other members of the string band called the Tennessee Chocolate Drops travelled through the coal camps, and Armstrong told an interviewer how Frank did not insert those markers of whiteness like yodelling in his music because he did in fact play 'solid blues' (Moore and Lornell 1976). In other parts of the South, when white musicians recorded blues, the lyrics were often sung in a mocking or jesting tone, or they included yodelling, as if the singers were reminding listeners of their whiteness, as if to announce that they were not taking the blues aesthetic seriously. And just as the blues sung by African Americans were often critical of labour conditions in the cotton fields and prison farms further south (Barlow 1989), or critical of southern racial violence (Gussow 2002), so did the coalfield blues sung by both white and black musicians in Appalachia often articulate a critical commentary on mining, violence and class relations there. Despite efforts by the coal companies to divide miners along racial lines, the music made by the miners can thus be read as a sign of the forging of new forms of cross-racial class solidarity and trust in the mines.

In addition to borrowing the blues form and the blues aesthetic to critique working conditions in the mines, Hutchison also borrowed from African-American song traditions about the sinking of the Titanic, in which black bluesmen sang about a trickster hero who outwitted the white passengers on board the ship and ended up 'shooting craps in Liverpool' as the ship went down, even as he ridiculed white pretensions and racial hierarchies. But instead of critiquing racial hierarchies, Hutchison uses the Titanic song genre to comment critically on class relations in Logan County. Although some other Titanic songs have references to the different accommodations of the rich and the poor, Frank Hutchison's 'Last Scene of the Titanic' is unique in being squarely though obliquely about class relations aboard the ship. And, through shifts in perspective from the upper deck to the lower deck, the square dance calls (which Frank often performed at dances in Logan County) and changes in the music, as well as some of the language, it evokes the coal-camp landscape in which Hutchison lived and mined coal and played music for his neighbours in oppressive conditions. It's actually a three-minute drama about the events that transpired before the iceberg was sighted, as an image of class relations in Logan County coal-mining communities and the ways in which the poor, 'on the lower decks', suffer from the arrogance and inattention of the rich. He has in effect transported Logan County to the decks of the Titanic, using the metaphor of shipboard hierarchies to comment on class hierarchies in the communities in which he lived.

When miners found the class relations oppressive, they turned to one another and to the unions, and once again the boundaries of community and trust crossed racial lines. Nimrod Workman (1895–1994) lived the first years of his life on his father's farm in Martin County Kentucky, but like so many other Appalachian men he had to leave that way of life and go to work as a miner when he was fourteen years old. He worked in the Chattaroy West Virginia mines for almost forty-two years; he was a union organizer who said he witnessed the Battle of Blair Mountain in 1921; and in later years he spoke out in Washington for the rights of miners suffering from black lung disease, with which he too was afflicted. He knew Frank Hutchison and other Logan County musicians, and he was himself a storyteller and a singer of unaccompanied ballads from the Scotch-Irish tradition, of Baptist hymns, of old Appalachian songs, and of songs he wrote himself about unions and coal mining, some of which he sang in the mines for his fellow miners as they sat on the underground tracks and ate their lunches (Wilson 2011). Much of his music survives because he was interviewed and recorded extensively by Alan Lomax, Mike Seeger and Mark Wilson; the recordings are housed in the American Folklife Collection at the Library of Congress and elsewhere, and some of Workman's songs have been released on LPs and CDs.

Many of Nimrod's songs were of his own making, and they drew upon long traditions of Appalachian music and on African-American field hollers and blues that he learned from black agricultural workers and miners. For some of the coal-mining songs he wrote like 'Coal Black Mining Blues' and 'Chattaroy Holler' he seemed to have had an endless number of variations and an endless number of laments and verses that he inserted into the songs as he saw fit in any given performance. When musician coal miners like Frank Hutchison recorded blues and 'hillbilly music' for the commercial record companies in the 1920s, very little of the inventiveness and specificity that Nimrod displays in his descriptions of life in the mines would have been tolerated by the record producers; they wanted music that would sell well in the commercial market, and songs with too much specificity about that life of labour would have limited their profitability. When Nimrod was recorded by field researchers he was under no such constraints, so in many of those songs we can hear what miners sang about their own lives, while they worked or ate their lunch or drank moonshine with their friends (Wilson 2011).

'Coal Black Mining Blues' is one of the songs that Nimrod sang most frequently and he wrote it when he was working for the Buffalo Coal Company in Chattaroy in the early decades of the twentieth century; he composed it based on the blues forms he heard African-American miners sing.

> Got the blues, got the blues, lord, lord
> Coal black miner's blues.
>
> Went to my place and I peeped in
> Slate and the water up to my chin
> Got the blues, got the blues, got the blues, lord, lord
> Coal black mining blues.
>
> Looked at old Jim and Jim looked sad
> The worse darn place that I ever had
> Got the blues, got the blues, got the blues, lord, lord
> Coal black mining blues.
>
> Sent me to the office to look at the roll.
> Chilton counted up my dollars in the hole.

Got the blues, got the blues, got the blues, lord, lord
Coal black mining blues.

Bascom at the bottom, heaping up sand
Shorty comes along says he's got another man
Got the blues, got the blues, got the blues, lord, lord
Coal black mining blues.

In these verses, Nimrod speaks first about his 'place', the small underground chamber supported by pillars of coal left there to hold up the 'roof', where one or two miners laboured at the face of the coal. He sang this verse often, a recollection of the times he'd have to stand in pools of water and slate to get at the coal with his pick. Such an image would resonate with every miner who heard it in the 1920s and every miner who heard it would imagine that assignment to such a terrible 'place' might have been in retaliation for the singer's outspokenness about conditions in the mines. In the third verse, he tells of the experiences of countless miners who went to the office to draw their pay, only to find that the deductions for rent, for mining equipment (for miners had to pay for their own dynamite and tools), and for food at the company store meant that he drew no pay at all that week, and the company just counted out how many dollars 'in the hole' [in debt] they were. And finally, in the last verse, for which Nimrod had many variations, he speaks of the experiences of fellow miners who found their 'places' taken from them, as scabs[1] were hired to replace them. In one rendition of this verse, in one of Mike Seeger's recordings, Nimrod comments in a speaking voice aside that 'he's taking his place you know, scabbie'.

Wesley J. Turner, a white miner in eastern Kentucky, also used the blues form to comment on the 'place' he and other miners were assigned to work in, on the repercussions if a man spoke out about his working conditions, and about the anti-union tactics employed by the coal operators. A typed copy of the lyrics, sent to George Korson[2] by Turner in 1935, is in the Korson papers in the Library of Congress. A few years later, in 1940, Korson tracked Turner down and recorded him singing this blues. 'Hignite' is the name of the coal company in whose mines Turner laboured.

'Hignite Blues' (partial transcription)

A mile and a half back in the mines,
Slate a-fallin' all along the main line,
   Ha, ha, got the Hignite blues.

Two men put in every place,
The way they're cramped it is a disgrace,
   Ha, ha, got the Hignite blues.

> I talked to the foreman to see about,
> He said 'Take your tools and get out,'
>   Ha, ha, got the Hignite blues.
>
> They are all afraid to quit—
> Afraid they will lose their tit.
>   Ha, ha, got the Hignite blues.
>
> I took my case up in the hall,
> The committee accepts but that was all,
>   This is the union blues.
>
> They took Walter Griffin off of the track,
> They docked him on dirt so he couldn't come back,
>   Such union blues!

'Hignite Blues', like so many other miners' blues, is illustrative of some of the most basic aesthetic and political characteristics of African American blues music:

> The popularity of blues performers and blues recordings in rural black communities throughout the South stemmed from the genre's ability to explore the shared concerns of African Americans through the details of personal experience, often presented in striking poetic images. Unlike European-derived ballads, in which a story is usually presented in narrative fashion—that is, in a linear sequence recounting the actual order of events—blues songs are more frequently like a series of evocative snapshots assembled around a theme or set of themes: lost love, sexual desire, work, violence, loneliness. (Starr and Waterman 2007: 101)

In these coal-mining blues, these same aesthetic effects are borrowed from the music of African Americans who worked in the mines and from records the miners heard in the 1920s, but the images concern a life of hardship in the mines rather than a life of racial oppression. And those aesthetic and political effects were understood and deployed by white and black miners alike.

The coal miners were in a bind, many had nowhere else to go and many of them spent all those years in the mines, as if it were a prison sentence, 'some pullin' lifetime, some pullin' ninety-nine'.[3] They could have no trust in the coal companies, no trust in the county, state, or federal governments, and so they placed their trust in the possibility that a union might bring them a better life. They had also abandoned the religion of the coal camp churches, in which preachers hired by the coal companies told them that the unions were the work of the devil and the coal operators were on a mission from God to 'civilize' them. Miners for the most part had always rejected that message, and so marriage records and oral histories tell us that miners often asked untrained and un-ordained miner-preachers to officiate at their weddings and to pray with them, on Sundays and as they worked in the mines.

'Native white' and African-American miners and their wives also appropriated spirituals and hymns and rewrote them as songs about coal mining and unionization, thus inscribing their own visions of Christianity in their music, writing over the appropriation of religion by the coal operators and the preachers they hired, and positing new forms of trust and solidarity. In 1940 George Korson recorded Sam Johnson, an African-American miner, singing his own composition 'We Done Quit' at Pursglove, Scott's Run, West Virginia. Korson wrote that 'This ballad was sung by the Scott's Run miners [both white and black] during the 1930 strike. They sang it to the tune of "I can tell the world," a Negro spiritual' (Korson 1943: 436).

> You can tell the coal operator 'bout'n this
> You can tell the company we done quit
> Tell them what the non-union have done
> Tell them that the panics have come
> An' it brought sorrow, I declare, unto my home
>
> Went up to the top house the other day
> Yes I did
> Went up to the top house to see 'bout my weight
> Yes I did, yes I did
> The checking weighman said that they dock me for slate
> Yes he did, my Lordy, yes he did
>
> Bittner told the operator the other day
> Yes he did, yes he did
> They will sign the contract or leave this place
> Yes he did, my Lordy yes he did
>
> Sam told Bittner the other day
> Yes he did, yes he did
> Befo' he sign the contract they'd all be dead
> Yes he did, yes he did

In this song and in so many others, Sam Johnson and his fellow miners used the idiom of African-American spirituals (which had often been a vehicle for critiques of slavery) to draw attention to the opposition of coal companies to the unions, to critique the unfair practices of the coal companies as they reduce a miner's pay by 'docking him for slate', that is, by falsely weighing the coal he dug and saying that his load of coal had too much slate in it and not enough coal and therefore his pay would be docked, which was one of the chief complaints miners had about the dishonesty of coal-mine operators. And, as if to remind themselves that sometimes miners could only trust one another, the song also alludes to Van Bittner, a union official who betrayed the miners by urging them to sign an unfair contract. The singer confronts him directly in the song, referring to himself in the third person, as in so many African-American blues songs.

I'll conclude with a blues song written by Aunt Molly Jackson during a 1930 coal strike, her 'Hungry Ragged Blues' that she sang when Theodore Dreiser's National Committee for the Defense of American Political Prisoners went to eastern Kentucky, near the West Virginia border, to look into the question of the relationship between miners and the mining companies and the conditions under which the miners and their families lived (Romalis 1999: 87). The committee asked many miners and members of their families to testify about their lives and Aunt Molly responded by speaking about her husband's membership in the National Miners Union and then she sang her song (Romalis 1999: 40, 87). Her songs and those of her sister Sarah Ogan Gunning are among the few surviving songs sung by women in the coalfields but they provide us with some indication of how women as well as men crossed aesthetic and social boundaries to form new bonds of trust and new modes of critique. This is how she later described its composition.

> On the seventh day of May, 19 and 30, during the strike, the miners built a soup kitchen out of slabs over in the meadow. When it was finished, I told all the wives to bring everything we had from our mining shacks and put it all together and collect vegetables from the farmers to make soup as long as the farmers had anything to give. By the middle of October we were desperate; we did not see how we were going to live. For two or three days we did not have anything to make soup out. On the 17th morning in October my sister's little girl waked me up early. She had 15 little ragged children and she was taking them around to the soup kitchen to try and get them a bowl of soup. She told me some of them children had not eat anything in two days. It was a cold rainy morning; the little children was all bare-footed, and the blood was running out of the tops of their little feet and dripping down between their little toes and running onto the ground. You could track them to the soup kitchen by the blood. After they had passed by I just set down to the table and began to wonder what to try to do next. Then I began to sing out my blues to express my feeling. This song comes from the heart and not just from the point of a pen. (Greenway 1953: 266–267)

'Hungry Ragged Blues', Aunt Molly Jackson [lyrics as transcribed in Romalis 1999: 40–41]

I'm sad and weary, I've got the hungry, ragged blues;
I'm sad and weary, I've got the hungry, ragged blues;
Not one penny in the pocket to buy one thing I need to use.

I woke up this morning, with the worst blues I ever had in my life;
I woke up this morning, with the worst blues I ever had in my life;
Not a bite to eat for breakfast, a poor coal miner's wife.

When my husband works in the coalmines, he loads a carload every trip;
When my husband works in the coalmines, he loads a carload every trip;
Then he goes to the office at the evening to get denied of scrip.

Just because it took all he made that day to pay his mine expense;
Just because it took all he made that day to pay his mine expense;
A man that will work for just coal oil and carbide, he ain't got a stack of sense.

All the women in the coal camps are sitting with bowed down heads;
All the women in the coal camps are sitting with bowed down heads;
Ragged and bare-footed, and the children cryin' for bread.

No food, no clothes for our children, I'm sure this head don't lie;
No food, no clothes for our children, I'm sure this head don't lie;
If we can't get more for our labor we'll starve to death and die.

Listen, friends and comrades, please take a friend's advice;
Listen, friends and comrades, please take a friend's advice;
Don't load no more of that dirty coal till you git a living price.

Don't go under the mountain, with the slate hangin' o'er your head;
Don't go under the mountain, with the slate hangin' o'er your head;
And work for just coal oil and carbide, and your children cryin' for bread.

This mining town I live in is a sad and lonely place;
This mining town I live in is a sad and lonely place;
Where pity and starvation is pictured on every face.

Ragged and hungry, no slippers on our feet;
Ragged and hungry, no slippers on our feet;
We're bumming around from place to place to get a little bite to eat.

All a-going round from place to place bumming for a little food to eat;
Listen my friends and comrades, please take a friend's advice,
Don't put no more of your labor, till you get a living price.

Some coal operators might tell you the hungry blues are not bad;
Some coal operators might tell you the hungry blues are not bad;
They're the worst kind of blues this poor woman ever had.

Although the members of the Dreiser committee regarded Molly Jackson's song as exemplifying the views of her Kentucky community (Romalis 1999: 42), clearly she is speaking here from a particular position as a miner's wife, and a miner's wife with a particular set of views, but all the same drawing on a long history of African-American musical traditions to do so. She is repeatedly asking the men to go on strike and not go into the mines to work for 'just coal and carbide' (the expenses for mining equipment deducted from their pay); she is expressing a point of view that was not shared by all the men, nor all the women. But, like so many other singers whose words I have tried to understand here, she deploys an African-American musical idiom to challenge the destruction of community and trust, the wages that left her children hungry and cold, and the harsh working conditions the men experienced in the mines, and to gesture towards new forms of trust and solidarity.

Notes

1 Nimrod and other miners used the word 'scab' not only with reference to men brought in to work in the mines as strike-breakers, but apparently also with reference to men who were willing to take the jobs of miners fired for insubordination. Miners could feel no solidarity with scabs of either sort.
2 George Korson was a journalist/folklorist who collected and studied coal-mining songs in Pennsylvania, West Virginia, and Kentucky in 1939 and 1940.
3 This is a line from a song called 'Coal Diggin' Blues' played and sung by the coal miner Jerrell. Stanley at Braeholm, West Virginia, and recorded there in 1940 by George Korson. (Korson 1943:234-235)

References

Banks, A. 1995. 'Class Formation in the Southeastern Kentucky Coalfields, 1890–1920'. In M.B. Pudup, D.B. Billings and A.L. Waller (eds), *Appalachia in the Making: The Mountain South in the Nineteenth Century*, 321–346. Chapel Hill: University of North Carolina Press.

Barlow, W. 1989. *Looking Up At Down: The Emergence of Blues Culture*. Philadelphia: Temple University Press.

Corbin, D.A. 1981. *Life, Work, and Rebellion in the Coal Fields: The Southern West Virginia Miners, 1880–1922*. Urbana: University of Illinois Press.

Dunaway, W.A. 1995. 'Speculators and Settler Capitalists: Unthinking the Mythology about Appalachian Landholding, 1790–1860'. In M.B. Pudup,

D.B. Billings and A.L. Waller (eds), *Appalachia in the Making: The Mountain South in the Nineteenth Century*, 50-75. Chapel Hill: University of North Carolina Press.

—— 1996. *The First American Frontier: Transition to Capitalism in Southern Appalachia, 1700–1860*. Chapel Hill: University of North Carolina Press.

Eller, R. 1982. *Miners, Millhands and Mountaineers: Industrialization of the Appalachian South, 1880–1930*. Knoxville: University of Tennessee Press.

Garland, P. 1969. *The Sound of Soul*. Chicago: NTC/Contemporary Publishing.

Giardina, D. 1987. *Storming Heaven*. New York: Ivy Books.

Greenway, J. 1953. *American Folksongs of Protest*. Philadelphia: University of Pennsylvania Press.

Gussow, A. 2002. *Seems Like Murder Here: Southern Violence and the Blues Tradition*. Chicago: University of Chicago Press.

Hufford, M. nd. 'Landscape and History at the Headwaters of the Big Coal River Valley'. In *Tending the Commons: Folklife and Landscape in Southern West Virginia*. Online collection of the Library of Congress, available at <http://www.loc.gov/collection/folklife-and-landscape-in-southern-west-virginia/about-this-collection/#overview> (accessed 4 November 2013).

Kirchwey, F. 1922. 'Miners' Wives in the coal strike', *The Century Magazine* 105(1): 83–90.

Korson, G. 1943. *Coal Dust on the Fiddle: Songs and Stories of the Bituminous Industry*. Philadelphia: University of Pennsylvania Press.

Lewis, R. 1995. 'Railroads, Deforestation, and the Transformation of Agriculture in the West Virginia Back Counties'. In M.B. Pudup, D.B. Billings and A.L. Waller (eds), *Appalachia in the Making: The Mountain South in the Nineteenth Century*, 297-320. Chapel Hill: University of North Carolina Press.

Lunt, R.D. 1992. *Law and Order Vs. the Miners: West Virginia, 1906–1933*. Charleston: Appalachian Editions.

Mann, R. 1995. 'Diversity in the Antebellum South: Four Farm Communities in Tazewell County, Virginia'. In M.B. Pudup, D.B. Billings and A.L. Waller (eds), *Appalachia in the Making: The Mountain South in the Nineteenth Century*, 132-162. Chapel Hill: University of North Carolina Press.

McKinney, G.B. 1995. 'Economy and Community in Western North Carolina, 1860–1865'. In M.B. Pudup, D.B. Billings and A.L. Waller (eds), *Appalachia in the Making: The Mountain South in the Nineteenth Century*, 163–184. Chapel Hill: University of North Carolina Press.

Moore, Mt. 1991. 'Because the Earth is Dark and Deep', *The American Voice* 22 (Spring): 73-88.

Moore, R.J. and K. Lornell. 1976. 'On Tour with a Black String Band: Howard Armstrong and Carl Martin Reminisce', *Goldenseal* 2(4): 9–12, 46–52.

Raitz, K. and R. Ulack. 1984. *Appalachia: A Regional Geography*. Boulder, CO: Westview Press.

Rash, Ron. 2005. 'The Marked,' a poem included in Silas House, *The Coal Tattoo*, p. 149. New York: Ballantine Books.

Romalis, S. 1999. *Pistol Packin' Mama: Aunt Molly Jackson and the Politics of Folksong*. Urbana: University of Illinois Press.

Shapiro, H.D. 1978. *Appalachia On Our Mind: The Southern Mountains and Mountaineers in the American Consciousness, 1870–1920*. Chapel Hill: University of North Carolina Press.
Spence, R.Y. 1976. *The Land of the Guyandot: A History of Logan County*. Detroit: Harlo Press.
——1999. 'Aunt Jennie Wilson: "I grew up with music"'. In J. Lilly (ed.), *Mountains of Music: West Virginia Traditional Music from Goldenseal*, 103-109. Urbana: University of Illinois Press.
Starr, L. and C. Waterman. 2007. *American Popular Music: From Minstrelsy to MP3*. New York: Oxford University Press.
Thompson, C.D. 2011. *Spirits of Just Men: Mountaineers, Liquor Bosses, and Lawmen in the Moonshine Capital of the World*. Urbana: University of Illinois Press.
Trotter, J.W. 1990. *Coal, Class, and Color. Blacks in Southern West Virginia, 1915–32*. Urbana: University of Illinois Press.
Waller, A. 1988. *Feud: Hatfields, McCoys, and Social Change in Appalachia, 1860–1900*. Chapel Hill: University of North Carolina Press.
Whisnant, D. 1983. *All That is Native and Fine: The Politics of Culture in an American Region*. Chapel Hill: University of North Carolina Press.
Wilson, M. 2011. Program notes for compact disk, *Mother Jones' Will* (MTCD512). Stroud, UK: Musical Traditions Records.

Gloria Goodwin Raheja received her Ph.D. in anthropology from the University of Chicago in 1985 and she is Professor of Anthropology at the University of Minnesota. She is the author of *The Poison in the Gift: Ritual, Prestation, and the Dominant Caste in a North Indian Village* (Chicago: University of Chicago Press, 1988), co-author (with Ann Grodzins Gold) of *Listen to the Heron's Words: Reimagining Gender and Kinship in North India* (Berkeley: University of California Press, 1994) and editor of *Songs, Stories, Lives: Gendered Dialogues and Cultural Critique* (New Delhi: Kali for Women, 2003). She has also written extensively on colonial ethnography in nineteenth-century India. She is currently working on two book manuscripts: *Logan County Blues: Frank Hutchison in the Sonic Landscape of the Appalachian Coalfields* and *Scandalous Traductions: Landscape, History, Memory*.

Index

abjection, Kristeva on 127
adopted people, Carsten's study of 157
adultery 113, 152, 153–4
affection, Hyden's notion of economy of 69
affective assemblages 107
affective bonds, accentuation of 142–3
African-American musical in Appalachian coalfields 247–55
Airtel (India) 137
Aitkinson, Capt. G.F. 220
alimentary process 108, 110–11
alterity
  boundaries of 214–15, 220, 226–7
  symbolic economy of 193
Alto Purus Indigenous Area in Amazonia 195–6
ambiguities
  societal trust in Guatemala 38–9, 43, 46, 47, 49–50, 54, 55
  trust in Cashinahua society, ambiguity of 192–3
  witchcraft, intimacy and trust in Cameroon, ambiguities of 71–4
American Declaration of Independence 181
American Folklife Collection (Library of Congress) 249
Amerindians
  perspectivism of 192, 193, 209
  sociopolitical thinking of 194
  thought processes of 192
anonymous ova donation, Konrad's analysis of 155

Artificial Insemination by Donor (A.I.D.) 152–4
  practice of 152–3
  sperm cocktails, creation of 152–3
artificial insemination by husband and donor (A.I.H.D.) 152–3

Baier, Annette 10, 13, 15
  trust, perspective on 91, 92, 96–7
Barad, Karen 33
Barga Mongol concept of trust 8–10, 21–2, 84–102
  anthropology and literature on trust 89–90
  behavioural choice, trust and 90
  bribery, land system and 86–7
  cadastral register 86
  categorization of forms of trust 92–3
  cognitive and performative trust, distinction between 97–8
  cognitive dissonance, concept of 88
  control
    notion of relinquishment of 91
    trust and lack of 91, 95–6
  cooperative relationships, trust and 91
  corruption
    land allocation and 86
    lying and cheating, trust and 98
  cultural differences, trust and 89
  dishonesty, concerns about rise of 85
  economic reforms of Deng Xiaoping, effects of 84–5
  Enlightenment, notion of trust and 88–9

Barga Mongol concept of trust (*cont.*)
  'entrusting,' trustworthiness and 96
  expectation, trust and 97
  functionality of trust 91–2
  good intentions/thoughts *(sain sanaatai/sain sanah)*, trust and 93–4, 100–101
  herding family, trust in untrustworthy government by 86–7, 99–100
  hierarchical relationships 96, 98
  immoral behaviour, misfortune through 97
  Inner Mongolia Television (NMTV) 86, 88
  land rental system 86
  linguistic anthropology 85
  linguistic distinctions between forms of trust 93, 94
  migration, population increase and 85–6
  modern life, omnipresence of trust in 89
  Mongolian concepts of trust 93–100
    notions related to trust 94
  moral decay, narratives of 84
  morality, notions of 90
  New Barga Right Banner 84, 85, 86, 93, 96, 97, 98, 100
  non-verbal clues, trust and 96–7
  objectivity and trust 90
  organizational harmony, trust and 89
  Oyun (Barga Mongolian philosopher) 95–6
  pastureland
    division into parcels *(nutag)* 84–5
    trust and division of 85–8
  political philosophy, trust and 88
  renting land, advantages and disadvantages of 86
  respect
    expression of 99
    threefold nature of 98–9
  risk, trust and 88–9, 90
  role-segmentation 89
  self-descriptive assertions about trust 84
  social control, trust and 91–2
  social obligation, power of 96
  social relations, risk in 89
  social trust 90
  solidarity, trust and 89
  subordination, upward requests and 96
  theoretical literature, trust in 88–93
  trust
    as action, Barga Mongol concept of 98
    Baier's perspective on 91, 92, 96–7
    control and, Mongol perspective on 95–6
    differences in conceptualizations of 85, 89–91, 94–5, 96–7, 98–9, 100–102
    future contingency and 91
    multiple associations and assumptions attached to 93
    and related concepts, definition of 93
    and trustworthiness, lack of conceptual distinction between 95
  trust relations, variables within 92
  trusting
    assessment of acts of 97–8
    untrustworthiness and 85, 86–7
  trusting the untrustworthy
    goodness in 97, 98, 100–101
    herding family as example of 86–7, 99–100
  trustworthiness
    assessments of 97–8
    Barga Mongol conceptualizations of 97–8
    disjunctions between actual behaviour and assessments of 87–8
    expectations of 86–7
    expression of 99

itgeltei and *naidvartai* in sense of 94–5, 96, 99
  social trust and 90
  Western and Mongolian concepts of, differences in 94–100, 100–101
  Western notions of trust 88–9
    Mongolian concepts and, discrepancies between 94–100, 100–101
bath houses in colonial India 229
Mrs Beeton's Cookery Book and Household Guide 227
Bioedge 151
birth certificates 148, 149, 150, 160, 164, 165
  Spiers' work on 176
Bittner, Van 253
Blackstone, William 215
Bloch, Maurice 5–6
blood
  intermixing of 52–3
  power and 113
  purity of *(pureza de sangre)*, notion of 50–52
  symbolism of 38–9, 43, 50–54
  transformational capacity of 202–3
blues idiom, white musicians and 237–8
bodily transformations in Cashinahua society 200–201, 202, 205, 207–8
Bombay Presidency, Indian servants in 221
boundaries
  of alterity 214–15, 220, 226–7
  fluidity of movement across 122
  maintenance of 44
Bourdieu, Pierre 26, 43, 106, 124
British Medical Journal 151, 217
Brunswick Records 246

Cadbury family household in Edgbaston 214–15
cannibalistic banquets in Cameroon 62
Capital (Marx, K.) 4

casino capitalism 67, 68
caste
  hierarchies of 221–2
  occupational categories of 228–9
Chesapeake & Ohio Railroad 247
Church of England 151, 154
cognitive dissonance, concept of 88
cognitivism, trust and 42–3
colonial India 218–31
  architecture of 218–19, 220, 222–3
  history of rule in 214
  traces of system of servitude in 231–2
colonialism, witchcraft and 65
colour
  ceremonial significance of green 114
  coloured bridge across Earth *(Akwap)* 115
  enmity, red colour and 112
  fertility, green colour and 114
  junior categories, red colour and 112–13
  loops in alimentary process 111
  marriage, white colour and 112
  morality, white colour and 113, 116, 123, 125
  mutuality, green colour and 114
  red colour, divination and 113
  significations among pastoral Turkana of 112–16
  social status, white colour and 112
  solidarity in social relations, colour white and 112
  white, significance of 112, 113
  yellow colour, significance of 114–15
Cooperation without Trust? (Cook, K.S., Hardin, R. and Levi, M.) 10–11
corporeality and trust in Cashinahua society 18–19, 191–210
  agency in motion, bodies and 195
  alterity, symbolic economy of 193
  Alto Purus Indigenous Area 195–6
  Amazonian personhood, fractal nature of 206

corporeality and trust in Cashinahua society (*cont.*)
  Amazonianist literature, intimacy in 192, 193–4
  Amerindian perspectivism 192, 193, 209
  Amerindian sociopolitical thinking 194
  Amerindian thought 192
  biographical time, trust and 208
  blood, transformational capacity of 202–3
  bodily transformations 200–201, 202, 205, 207–8
  Catholic Josephine sisters of Manuel Urbano 197
  co-residents, human bodies and work of 208–9
  community as living *yuda* (collective body) 203–4, 205
  conjugal collaboration 203–4
  consciousness
    circulating blood as vehicle of 202, 205
    oscillations of 207–8
  cumulative personhood 198–201, 206, 207
  dead, mistrust of 208
  emotion-thoughts, effects of 203, 208
  epiphenomenon of intimacy 193
  ethnographic discussion 192–3
  fertility ritual 200
  generalized reciprocity, Sahlins' notion of 191
  generosity, sweetness and 203
  grief, dangers of excess of 201
  habitus, bodily transformations and 205
  hemophagy 202–3
  identity, cumulative personhood and 201
  indigenous Amazonian aetiologies 201
  indigenous leadership in Amazonia 197
  indigenous phenomenology 192–3, 194, 207–8
  Inter-American Development Bank 195
  intimacy, moral economy of 193
  kinship, trust and 191
  Lopes, Pancho 192–3, 195, 196–8, 202, 203, 208, 209, 210n3
  marriage practices 199–200
  moiety system (exogamous) 199
  moral communities, Geschiere's critique of assumptions of 191
  names, inheritance of 200
  National Indian Foundation (FUNAI) 195
  Nawa (non-Indians) 192, 196–8, 201, 202, 203, 209
    distinctions between Huni Kuin and 197
    untrustworthiness of 195
  parallel transmission, principle of 199
  personhood 195
    empirical approach to 199
    ontological aspects of 206
  perspectivism
    ethnologies of 194
    relatedness and the body 204–8
  pivotal relationships 199–200
  real bodies, process of making 200–201
  Real People (Huni Kuin) 192, 201, 202, 206, 209
    distinctions between Nawa and 197
    existential individuality for 198
    fostering correct living (*jive pe*) among 197
    goodness and badness in individuals for 196
    intimacy as *xinan* for 196
    kinship relations, organization of 194–5
    perspectivism of 205
    social thinking of 206–7
    sociality, styles of 196
  recursive dynamic dualism 207–8
  relatedness, Amerindian modes of 194

self-identification, souls and 204
social form, relationship between corporeality and 206
sociocosmological relations 194
sorcery, witchcraft and kinship, links between 191
spirits *(yuxin)* 201, 203, 205, 208, 209
strangers, trust in 191
structuralism, relations of alterity and 193–4
substantivism 205–6
teleological process of making true person 201
temporal flow of daily time 208
trust
  ambiguity of 192–3
  cumulative body and 202–4
  liquid quality within 202
  temporal and spatial instability of 191–2
trusting others 191, 194–8
trustworthiness *(xinanika)* 202, 203, 208
  actions generated by 204
  embodiment of 192
  social production of 207
Viveiros de Castro, Eduardo 193, 204–5, 206
women, qualities required of 198–9
cumulative personhood in Cashinahua society 198–201, 206, 207

Damasio, Antonio 125
Darwin, Charles (and Darwinianism) 3, 17, 18
Dawkins, Richard 19
Day, Panny Hogg 240
de Waal, Frans 17–18
The Decent of Man (Darwin, C.) 17
Deng Xiaoping 84–5
Dickens, Charles 6
digital community in Kenya ('*N'iko na Safaricom*') 134–6

distrust, sperm donation and relationship destabilisation 30–32, 148–66
access to medical histories, problems of 160
adopted people, Carsten's study of 157
adultery, potential for accusation of 152, 154
After Adoption Yorkshire 166n1
anonymity of donors, debates about 149
anonymous donation, calls for removal of right to 160
anonymous ova donation, Konrad's analysis of 155
anonymous semen donation, inconsistency in practice of 156
Artificial Insemination by Donor (A.I.D.) 152–4
  practice of 152–3
  sperm cocktails, creation of 152–3
artificial insemination by husband and donor (A.I.H.D.) 152–3
Bioedge 151
birth certificates 148, 149, 150, 160, 164, 165
birth mothers, donor distrust of 158
British Medical Association 153
British Medical Journal 151
Church of England 151, 154
confused artificial insemination (CAI) 153
'desperation' in patients, sense of 155
discussion 162–5
donor-assisted conceptions, limits on numbers of 153–4
donor-conceived people
  access to identifying information for 149
  genetic relatives, search for 162, 164–5
  knowledge for, documentation and 164–5

distrust, sperm donation and relationship destabilisation (*cont.*)
  marginalization of views of 161
  shock at betrayal of secrecy 159
  trust in, problem of 161–2, 162–3
donor conception community
  medical practitioners' contempt for 159
  treating with, problem of 160
Donor Conception Network 161
donor insemination (DI) 148, 149
  distrust in process of, emergence of 158–62
  historical perspective 151–4
  infertility specialists' duty of confidentiality and 163
  public endorsement for 155
  regulation of (and aftermath of) 156, 160–61
  risks in, concerns about 151–2
  secrecy of, medical insistence on 154, 159–60, 163–4
  trust in intimate relationships, erosion of 163
donor offspring, donor distrust of 157–8
donor-recruitment, criticisms of 151
donors of semen, concerns of 156–8, 164
emergence of distrust in DI process 158–62
ethnographic data, basis for 148
Eugenics Review 154
Feversham Report (1960) 152–3
  semen-mixing, justification for 152–3
genetic determinism 161
Human Fertilisation and Embryology Act (1990) 31, 149, 155, 165
Human Fertilisation and Embryology Authority (UK) 161
International Donor Offspring Alliance (IDOA) 149, 150, 151, 164, 165
  activism of 160
  beliefs, statement of 150
  membership of 150
International Network of Donor Conception Organisations (INDCO) 149–50, 151, 160
  objectives of 150
intimate relationships, change over time in 162
legal status of donor-conceived children, uncertainty about 149
marital relationship of recipients, moral concerns about effects on 149
medical problems, possibility of inheritance of 151
medical profession, role of 154–8
mixed artificial insemination (AIM) 153
needs of patients, medical responses to 154–5
Panel on Human Artificial Insemination (BMA, 1973) 153
parents of donor-conceived children, questions from 158–9
professional confidentiality, bourgeois privacy and 163
professional medical authority, regulation seen as challenge to 159–60
Registrars of Births Marriages and Deaths 164–5
secrecy, concerns about 158–9
service delivery, complex nature of 163
sociality, enrichment of 161
stigma, Goffman's theory of 159–60
stigma of childless couples 154
transformation of secrecy into deceit, challenges of 158–9
trust-based approach to confidentiality, call for 163
trust in documents, substitution of trust in people for 148, 165

trust in parents, implications of 162
UK Donorlink 156
unwitting incest, worries about 153–4, 158
in vitro fertilization (IVF), development of 156
Warnock Committee 155
donor-conceived people
  access to identifying information for 149
  genetic relatives, search for 162, 164–5
  knowledge for, documentation and 164–5
  marginalization of views of 161
  shock at betrayal of secrecy 159
  trust in, problem of 161–2, 162–3
donor conception community
  medical practitioners' contempt for 159
  treating with, problem of 160
Donor Conception Network 161
donor insemination (DI) 148, 149
  distrust in process of, emergence of 158–62
  donor-recruitment, criticisms of 151
  historical perspective 151–4
  infertility specialists' duty of confidentiality and 163
  public endorsement for 155
  regulation of (and aftermath of) 156, 160–61
  risks in, concerns about 151–2
  secrecy of, medical insistence on 154, 159–60, 163–4
  semen donors, concerns of 156–8, 164
  trust in intimate relationships, erosion of 163
Douglas, Mary 127, 128
Dreiser, Theodore 253, 255

The Economy of Obligation: The Culture of Credit and Social Relations in Early Modern England (Muldrew, C.) 6–7

Enlightenment, notion of trust and 88–9
Eugenics Review 154

Facing Mount Kenya (Kenyatta, J.) 27
female networks
  care and responsibility, example of network based on 143–5
  strengthening of 142
Feversham Report (1960) 152–3
  semen-mixing, justification for 152–3
financial services, rapid change in economy of 133–4
flows and processes, universal physiology of 107–8, 117
Frankel, Herbert 67
Fraser, William 225
free will, servitude and 215–16
Freud, Sigmund 126–7
Friedman, Milton 5

game theory 10, 42, 122
Gardiner, Grace 222, 223, 226–7, 228
gender, trust and intimacy, e-finance in Kenya and 27–9, 131–46
  affective bonds, accentuation of 142–3
  Airtel (India) 137
  borrowing, lending and friendship 143
  cross-generational transfers 141
  cultivation of trust over time 133
  digital community in Kenya ('N'iko na Safaricom') 134–6
  e-money, risks in concept of 135
  entrustments, obligations and 132, 142–3
  female circumvention of male authority 142
  female networks
    care and responsibility, example of network based on 143–5
    strengthening of 142
  financial services, rapid change in economy of 133–4

gender, trust and intimacy, e-finance in Kenya (*cont.*)
  friendship, borrowing, lending and 143
  gender of trust 140–45
  household authority, change in nature of 139–40, 141
  households, women's relationships to 141
  interconnections between parties, trust and 133
  interdependency, creation of positive cycles of 142–3
  Joseph, Michael 135
  Kawangware in Niarobi 140–41
  Kenya Red Cross Society 135
  Kenyatta, Jomo 135
  leadership roles of women 133
  matrifocal relations 132–3, 141
  matrifocal ties 142
  men's status within households 139
  methodology, data collection and 134
  mobile money
    new technologies and 132–3
    patterns of usage 131
    political and economic relationships and 143
    women's empowerment and 145–6
  mobile phones, positivity in development of 136
  moral order
    social processes and 132
    trust and 132
  M-Pesa 27, 28–9, 131–2, 133–4, 136, 137–8, 139–40, 142, 145
    launch of service 134–5
    social landscape transformed by 140–41
    trust, articulation of emotive trust through 143
  nation-building project 135
  Omondi, Gabriel 136
  Orange (France) 137
  patriarchal (or patrilineal) institutions 133, 138, 140
  political economy of Kenya, discontent with 138
  power outages, problem of 135
  ring-tones as self-expression for women 140–41
  Safaricom 27–8, 131, 132–3, 134–6, 145
    advertising and marketing strategies 135
    contracting with 137–40
    disenchantment with 137–9
    'imagined community' of mobile communicators 135–6
    initial public offering (IPO) 137
    integrity of, worries about 138
    intimacy and trust, revision of assumptions about 133–4
    television commercial campaign, lyrics of song for 136
  Safaricom Foundation 135
  street-vending 138
  study methodology 134
  transactional efficiencies 131
  transactions, trust as product of 132
  transfers to mothers, descriptions of 142
  trust
    cultivation and nurture of 133
    gender of 140–45
    social networks and 132
    urban insecurities 138–9
  Vodafone Group 135
generative force (*Akuij*) among pastoral Turkana 115, 116, 127
Giddings, Anthony 67
The Gift (Mauss, M.) 29
goat-belly diagnostic map of Turkana natural and social worlds 105, 106, 109, 110, 117
  diagnosis of domestic trouble on basis of 105–6
  events and transformations, visual signs in 109
  goat in Turkana world, importance of 108–9
  literal comprehension of 109

good intentions/thoughts *(sain sanaatai/sain sanah)*, trust and 93–4, 100–101
Govier, Trudy 8, 10, 13, 15
Guide to Indian Household Management (James, Mrs. E.) 227–8
Gunning, Sarah Ogan 253
Gunter, Billie Gee 243, 245

habitus
 bodily transformations and 205
 Bourdieu's concept of 11, 17, 21, 26
 of servitude in colonial India 214
 of trust among pastoral Turkana
  commercialization and, problem of 120–21
  lyrical imagery of 116
  negation of, cultural universe and 111
  transformatory possibilities in working towards 109–11
 Turkana *habitus*, moulding of 106
Hardin, Russell 10–11
healers *(nganga)* in Cameroon 61, 62, 64, 75, 76
 ambiguities of 71–4
 competition within profession, development of 77–8
 drastic change, subjects of 76, 77–8
 everyday life with 77
 living with witchcraft and approach of 76
 mercantilization of 77
 recourse to 70–71
hemophagy 202–3
Heyer, Georgette 216
hierarchical relationships
 Barga Mongol concept of trust 96, 98
 trust in Guatemala and 41–2
'Hignite Blues' 250–51
Hobbes, Thomas 8
homely *(Heimlich)*, Freud's insights from 126
Hrdy, Sarah Blaffer 20–21
Human Fertilisation and Embryology Act (1990) 31, 149, 155, 165

Human Fertilisation and Embryology Authority (UK) 161
Hume, David 17, 123
'Hungry Ragged Blues' 253–4
Hunt, Bill 247
huqqa smoking 223–5
Hutchison, Frank 237–8, 246–8, 249

The Complete Indian Housekeeper and Cook (Steel, F.A. and Gardiner, G.) 223
indigenous phenomenology 192–3, 194, 207–8
industrial development, effects of 238–45
Inner Mongolia Television (NMTV) 86, 88
Inter-American Development Bank 195
International Donor Offspring Alliance (IDOA) 149, 150, 151, 164, 165
 activism of 160
 beliefs, statement of 150
 membership of 150
International Network of Donor Conception Organisations (INDCO) 149–50, 151, 160
 objectives of 150
The Interpersonal World of the Infant (Stern, D.) 16
intersubjectivity 1, 4, 16–17, 19, 24
 intersubjective space between persons 33
 language and culture, intersubjective space of 126
 sociality and 124–5
intimacy
 changing perceptions of 78–9
 epiphenomenon of 193
 inherent danger of 127
 intimate exchanges of personal things 220
 intimate relationships, change over time in 162
 moral economy of 193
 personal aspects of 183–6

intimacy (cont.)
  recent reflections on notion of 66–7
  social aspects of 186–8
  witchcraft and 64, 65–6, 66–7
intimacy, trust and sociality among pastoral Turkana 18, 25–6, 29–30, 105–28
  abjection, Kristeva's concept of the uncanny as sense of 127
  affective assemblages 107
  alimentary process 108, 110–11
  animal affairs, unfortunate events in 119–20
  animal birth, blessing of 118
  animal body marking 109
  animal domestication, reproduction of 118–19, 124
  animal physiology, pigmentations in 111
  animal sustenance 108
  animal witches 120
  animals, active players in moral game 117–18
  bewitchment 105–6
  black colour, significance of 113–14
  blood, power and 113
  bodies and livestock, images of 107–8
  body decoration 109
  bonds with animals 118
  boundaries, fluidity of movement across 122
  cattle exchanges 114
  cattle exports, problem of embargo on 121
  cattle market, *anomie* of 122
  ceremonial cure 106
  ceremonial significance of green colour 114
  co-wives, strife between 105–6
  colour, significations of 112–16
  colour loops in alimentary process 111
  colour white, significance of 112, 113
  coloured bridge across Earth (*Akwap*) 115
  commercialization, effects of 120–21
  commodification, process of 121
  common goods and personal goods, tension between 111
  community built around the Turkana healers 121–2
  conception, idiom of 108
  corporeal relationships, inventory of 107
  cosmic Turkana physiology 128
  cow (cause of domestic trouble), sacrifice of 106
  cross-species relationship, incarnation of 106
  cumulative experience, significance of 125–6
  Damasio, Antonio 125
  digestive process, management of 110
  divination 105, 106, 108
    Apatapes 115–16
    red colour and 113
  divinity, domain of 115
  donors and recipients, relationship between 110
  Douglas, Mary 127, 128
  energy, interlinked physiologies of 116
  enmity, red colour and 112
  ethics and personal psychology, Turkana theory of 116
  exchange of animals
    cycles of 122
    social relationships and 119–20
  exchanges 110
  fertility, green colour and 114
  flows and processes, universal physiology of 107–8, 117
  food pathways 108
  food sharing 110, 117
  Freud, Sigmund 126–7
  game theory 122
  generative force (*Akuij*) 115, 116, 127
  gift and goat (*akine*) in Turkana terminology 109

goat-belly diagnostic map of Turkana natural and social worlds 105, 106, 109, 110, 117
  diagnosis of domestic trouble on basis of 105–6
  events and transformations, visual signs in 109
  literal comprehension of 109
goat in Turkana world, importance of 108–9
Great Rift Valley escarpment 115
green colour, significance of 114
habitus of trust
  commercialization and, problem of 120–21
  lyrical imagery of 116
  negation of, cultural universe and 111
  transformatory possibilities in working towards 109–11
herding skills 118–19
herds, development cycle of 116–17
homely *(Heimlich)*, Freud's insights from 126
houselines, foundation of 112
human sustenance 108
Hume, David 123
immigration, effects on Turkana pastoralism 121–22
incest and death, taboos of 126
internal processes, passion for exterior projection of 109–10
intersubjectivity, sociality and 124–5
intimacy, inherent danger of 127
junior categories, red colour and 112–13
Kristeva, Julia 127
livestock
  giving and circulation of 110
  importance to Turkana lives 106
macro- and microcosmic bodies 108–9
marginalization 128
marriage
  bridewealth and 114
  white colour and 112

maternal association 115
matrifiliation, principle of 112
Mead, pioneering work of Margaret 126
memorialization 110
Montaigne, Michel de 123–4
moral subjects, shaping of humans and animals as 116–20
morality
  colour spectrum of 113
  trust and emotions, notions of 110–11
  white colour and 113, 116, 123, 125
mother-child bond 112
mutuality, green colour and 114
natural symbols, Douglas' theory of 127
nature, dramatic forces of 115
neuroscience, 'mirror neurons' in 124
pastoralism and people, space for 115
physiologies entangled 107–9
precariousness and coherence in social life, tension between 111
psychoanalysis 125–6
purification
  chyme and 111
  rituals of 127
Purity and Danger (Douglas, M.) 128
rearing practices 125
reciprocity
  anthropological theories of 123
  Turkana perceptions of 123–4
red colour, significance of 112–13
rumination, chyme and 110–11
Self Comes to Mind (Damasio, A.) 125
shared meals 110
'social beasts,' treatment of cattle as 121
social relationships, 'blackness' in 113–14, 117
social status, white colour and 112

intimacy, trust and sociality among pastoral Turkana (*cont.*)
  social transformation, misgiving and 120–22
  solidarity in social relations, colour white and 112
  subversiveness of *Napeysekina*, mobilization of 127–8
  sympathization with others, Hume's perspective on 123
  tensions of trusting, reflections on 122–8
  tortoise shell treatment 106
  trust, development of 125–6
  trusting, reflections on 122–8
  trustworthiness of humans, thinkers on 122
  Turkana *habitus*, moulding of 106
  Turkana livestock ledger 110
  Turkana society, organization of 123
  Turkana trustworthiness 122–3, 123–4
  veins and life essences 108
  warrior body painting 113
  weather cycles 115
  witchcraft
    accusations of, rise in 106–7
    unsociability and 113
  yellow colour, significance of 114–15

Jackson, Aunt Molly 253–5
Johnson, Sam 252
Joseph, Michael 135

Kawangware in Niarobi 140–41
Kenya Red Cross Society 135
Kenyatta, Jomo 135
Keynes, John Maynard 5
kinship
  assumption of synonymy with trust 68–9
  betrayal of kin to outsiders 63
  bilateral kinship groups 239–40
  claims of, elasticity of 65

family coherence and transcontinental migration 78–9
kinship relations, poly-interpretability of 61
kinship solidarity in Appalachian coalfields 244
kinship vocabularies in colonial India 230–31
locality, witchcraft references and 65–6, 79n3
Maka notions of witchcraft and 61–2, 63–5
societal trust in Guatemala 38–9, 50, 52–3, 54
trust in Cashinahua society and 191
Kirchwey, Freda 245
Korson, George 250, 252, 255n2
Kristeva, Julia 26, 127

labor relations and trust in Appalachian coalfields 26–7, 235–55
  African-American musical influences 247–55
  American Folklife Collection (Library of Congress) 249
  bilateral kinship groups 239–40
  Bittner, Van 253
  black lung disease 236
  blues idiom, white musicians and 237–8
  Brunswick Records 246
  burials 240
  carboniferous forest, remains of 236
  Chesapeake & Ohio Railroad 247
  class solidarities 238
  'Coal Black Mining Blues' 249–50
  coal camps, life in 244–5
  coal mining, realities of 236
  coal weight checking 243
  coalfield blues, importance for workers morale 247–55
  cross-racial bonds of trust, formation of 235, 236–7

Day, Panny Hogg 240
deceitful court practices 241–2
deforestation 241
discursive struggles 242–3
Dreiser, Theodore 253, 255
eviction of strikers 243
farmers becoming miners on losing land 243
forest plants, uses of 240
fossils 236
Gunning, Sarah Ogan 253
Gunter, Billie Gee 243, 245
'Hignite Blues' 250–51
'Hungry Ragged Blues' 253–4
Hunt, Bill 247
Hutchison, Frank 237–8, 246–8, 249
industrial development, effects of 238–45
Jackson, Aunt Molly 253–5
Johnson, Sam 252
kinship solidarity 244
Kirchwey, Freda 245
Korson, George 250, 252, 255n2
labour contractors 238
labour disciplines 242–3
labour sharing 240
labour unions, 'yellow dog' contracts denying membership of 243
land ownership 239
land seizure, judicial sanctioning of 241–2
Lawson, Sherman 247
Logan County, West Virginia 26, 235–6, 236–8, 239, 240–41, 242, 243, 245–55
  geography of 235–6
Logan County Blues: Frank Hutchison in the Sonic Landscape of the Appalachian Coalfields (Raheja, G.G.) 246
Lomax, Alan 249
mine guards, detective agents as 243
mine safety violations 244
mine-to-mine movement of workers 246

mining and music in southern Appalachians 236–8
mining development, Logan County people's responses to 245–55
moonshine, blame on 242–3
mountain people, press portrayals of 242–3
music of the Applachian coalfields 245–7
National Committee for the Defense of American Political Prisoners 253, 255
National Labor Relations Act (1935) 246
National Miners Union 253
Okeh Records 238, 246
propaganda attacks on mining families 243–4
property rights, capitalism and 241
racial class solidarity, music and 247–8
railroad workers 238
rural music, record companies and 237–8
scrip payments 243
Seeger, Mike 247, 249, 250
social memories 240–41
sociality, dissolution of bonds of 235
sociality, forms of 239–40
spirituals, miners' use of idioms of 252–3
strike breaking labour recruiters 243
striking miners song 'We Done Quit' (1930) 252
subsistence farming 239
taxation, effects of industrialisation and 242
Tennessee Chocolate Drops 247
Titanic song genre 248
trust, loss of 244–5, 251–2
Turner, Wesley J. 250–51
United Mine Workers Journal 246
Vaughn, Henry 247

labor relations and trust in Appalachian coalfields (cont.)
  Wilson, Aunt Jennie 239–40, 247
  Wilson, Mark 249
  women, life in coal camps for 244–5
  Workman, Nimrod 248–50
The Labyrinth of Solitude (Paz, O.) 46–7
ladino life-worlds *see* societal trust in Guatemala
Lawson, Sherman 247
Leviathan (Hobbes, T.) 8
Logan County, West Virginia 26, 236–8, 239, 240–41, 242, 243, 245–55
  geography of 235–6
Logan County Blues: Frank Hutchison in the Sonic Landscape of the Appalachian Coalfields (Raheja, G.G.) 246
Lomax, Alan 249
London and Provincial Domestic Servants Union (1897), aims of 229–30
Lopes, Pancho 192–3, 195, 196–8, 202, 203, 208, 209, 210n3
Luhmann, Niklas 67

macro- and microcosmic bodies 108–9
magical money *(mokoagne moni)* 64–5
Maka of Southeast Cameroon 60, 61–2, 63, 64, 71, 72, 76, 79n2
Mark, Karl 4–5
marriage 42, 51, 54, 138, 251–2
  bridewealth and 114
  distrust, sperm donation and relationship destabilisation 151, 152, 154, 158
  iintermarriage 50–51
  intimacy, trust and sociality among pastoral Turkana 112, 117, 119–20
  practices in Cashinahua society 199–200
  problems for *ladinos* in 53

Martine, Claude 225
master-servant relations *(jajmani)* 214–15, 230–31, 231–2
matrifiliation, principle of 112
matrifocal relations 132–3, 141, 142
Mauriac, François 69
Mauss, Marcel (and Maussian thought) 12, 29
  gift-giving, 'primitive exchange' and 68, 80n7
Mead, pioneering work of Margaret 126
memories 19, 107, 119, 124, 185–6, 192, 196, 198
  affective memory 204, 207
  of care and sociability 203
  faded memories 183
  institutional memory 175–6
  intentionality, modification through 200–201
  memorialization 110
  past down through generations 181
  personal memory of political violence 179
  singularity of 187
  of slave trade 63
  social memory 26, 30, 241
  unconscious memory traces 126
Merriam-Webster web dictionary 24
Metcalfe, Thomas 225
miscegenation 228
  anti-miscegenation laws 237
mixed artificial insemination (AIM) 153
mobile money
  new technologies and 132–3
  patterns of usage 131
  political and economic relationships and 143
  women's empowerment and 145–6
mobile phones, positivity in development of 136
moiety system (exogamous) 199
Möllering, Guido 67–8

Money and the Morality of Exchange (Parry, J. and Bloch, M.) 5–6
Mongolian concepts of trust *see* Barga Mongol concept of trust
Montaigne, Michel de 123–4
'The Moral Economy of the English Crowd' (Thompson, E.P.) 7
moral scaffolding 215–16
morality
  Barga Mongol notions of 90
  immoral behaviour, misfortune through 97
  intimacy, moral economy of 193
  moral communities, Geschiere's critique of assumptions of 191
  moral decay, narratives of 84
  moral reasoning, personhood, sociality and 25–32
  moral risks of life outside family 37
  moral subjects, shaping of humans and animals as 116–20
  social processes and moral order 132
  spatio-moral domains, unfixed trust and 54–6
  trust and emotions, notions of 110–11
  white colour and 113, 116, 123, 125
Mother Nature: A History of Mothers, Infants, and Natural Selection (Hrdy, S.B.) 20–21
M-Pesa 27, 28–9, 131–2, 133–4, 136, 137–8, 139–40, 142, 145
  launch of service 134–5
  social landscape transformed by 140–41
  trust, articulation of emotive trust through 143
Mughal *gusalkhana* (bath house) 229
Muldrew, Craig 6–7
music of Applachian coalfields 245–7

National Committee for the Defense of American Political Prisoners 253, 255
National Indian Foundation (FUNAI) 195
National Labor Relations Act (1935) 246
National Miners Union (US) 253
natural symbols, Douglas' theory of 127
The Nature of Entrustment: Intimacy, Exchange and the Sacred in Africa (Shipton, P.) 23
Nawa (non-Indians) 192, 196–8, 201, 202, 203, 209
  distinctions between Huni Kuin and 197
  untrustworthiness of 195
New Barga Right Banner 84, 85, 86, 93, 96, 97, 98, 100
Le noeud des vipères (Mauriac, F.) 69

occult
  compartmentalisation of sphere of 72–3
  global occult powers 64–5
  maintenance of compartmentalisation 73–4
Ochterlony, David 225
Okeh Records 238, 246
Omondi, Gabriel 136
Oral History of Twentieth Century Mongolia project 170–71, 183, 188n1
Orange (France) 137
On the Origins of the Species (Darwin, C.) 17
Oyun (Barga Mongolian philosopher) 95–6

Panel on Human Artificial Insemination (BMA, 1973) 153
parallel transmission, principle of 199
Parry, Jonathan 5–6
patriarchal (or patrilineal) institutions 133, 138, 140
Paz, Octavio 46–7

Pentecostalism in Africa 74–5, 76, 79
  kinship, liberation from witch-
    infested intimacy and 75
  scrutiny of preachers 75
  trust, potential for victory over
    witchcraft and 75, 76
  witchcraft, everyday life and
    strengthening effect of 75
Pepys, Samuel 217
personhood 195
  empirical approach to 199
  individuality and 215
  ontological aspects of 206
perspectivism
  of Amerindians 192, 193, 209
  ethnologies of 194
  of Real People (Huni Kuin) 205
  relatedness and the body 204–8
Police Aesthetics (Vatulescu, C) 182
Prisoner's Dilemma 42
proxemic behaviour 216, 220–21
psychoanalysis 2, 16, 26, 32, 125–6
Public Health (London) Act (1892) 217
Purity and Danger (Douglas, M.) 128

Ralushai Commission (1996) 73
Ramaredi Shaba in Sekhukuneland 73
rational choice, trust and 67
Real People (Huni Kuin) 192, 201, 202, 206, 209
  distinctions between Nawa and 197
  existential individuality for 198
  fostering correct living *(jive pe)* among 197
  goodness and badness in individuals for 196
  intimacy as *xinan* for 196
  kinship relations, organization of 194–5
  perspectivism of 205
  social thinking of 206–7
  sociality, styles of 196
reciprocity 3, 22, 29, 79, 80n5, 132–3
  anthropological theories of 123

anthropological use of term 69, 80n7
  generalized reciprocity, Sahlins' notion of 191
  negative reciprocity 68
  Turkana perceptions of 123–4
recursive dynamic dualism 207–8
Registrars of Births Marriages and Deaths 164–5
rehabilitation process in Mongolia, trust and 174–8, 178–9, 180, 181–3, 185, 187, 188
  compensation, payment of 175
  creation of past in 171
  decision-making in 176–7
  dependence on secret police and successors 182
  development of 173
  documentation of cases, requirement for 174
  eligibility for rehabilitation, determination of 175
  intimate relations, birth certificates and 176
  missing documents, problem of 175–6, 181–2
  opacity of 182–3
  original charges, overturning of 175–7
  political repression, acceptance of legitimacy of 177–8
  reinvestigatory element of 174–5
  secret police files, evidence from 175
  social and political significance 174, 175
  tension in 171–2
  trust, requirement for 175–6, 180
  truth and trust in 172
  Yonzon Hamba, rehabilitation decree of 177
relatedness, Amerindian modes of 194
relations of trust in colonial India 11–13, 213–32
  Aitkinson, Capt. G.F. 220

alterity, boundaries of 214–15, 220, 226–7
American etiquette books 217
architecture 214, 217, 232n1
bath houses 229
Mrs Beeton's Cookery Book and Household Guide 227
Blackstone, William 215
bodily care, fashions of 220
Bombay Presidency, Indian servants in 221
British Medical Journal 217
Cadbury family household in Edgbaston 214–15
caste, hierarchies of 221–2
caste, occupational categories of 228–9
children, native *ayahs* and 227
class divides 222–3
colonial architectural features 218–19, 220, 222–3
colonial India 218–31
 traces of system of servitude in 231–2
colonial rule, history of 214
cosmetics, use of 220, 232n3
dispossession 226
distinction, dimensions of 222–3
domestic architecture, structural change in 217–18
domestic labour
 changing conditions of 217–18
 steps towards invisibility of 215–16
domestic servants
 accommodation for 217
 micro-politics of imperialism and 225–6
footwear, removal as sign of respect 223–4
Fraser, William 225
free will, servitude and 215–16
Gardiner, Grace 222, 223, 226–7, 228
Guide to Indian Household Management (James, Mrs. E.) 227–8

habitus of servitude in colonial India 214
Heyer, Georgette 216
huqqa smoking 223–5
imperial power
 family life and 226
 intimacy within households and 226–7
imperial project, development of 228–9
Indian ethos, post-mutiny intimacy with 225–6
The Complete Indian Housekeeper and Cook (Steel, F.A. and Gardiner, G.) 223
Indian structures of *jajmani* (master-servant relations) 230
intimate exchanges of personal things 220
invisibility, management of 214
kinship vocabularies 230–31
labour, transfer of 215–16
licence in historical novels 216
London and Provincial Domestic Servants Union (1897), aims of 229–30
Martine, Claude 225
master-servant relationship
 analysis of 214–15, 231–2
 Indian structures of 230–31
menial labour 213
Metcalfe, Thomas 225
miscegenation 228
 anti-miscegenation laws 237
mixed blood, acknowledgement of people of 228
moral scaffolding 215–16
Mughal *gusalkhana* (bath house) 229
Ochterlony, David 225
officialdom and privacy, servants as bridges between 223
peasant petitions 231
Pepys, Samuel 217
performative traces 213
personhood, individuality and 215
property, making of 215

rehabilitation process in Mongolia, trust and (*cont.*)
  proxemic behaviour 216, 220–21
  proximity, trust and 228
  Public Health (London) Act (1892) 217
  punkha coolie, invisibility of 219
  racial divides 222–3
  sartorial styles 220, 225
  sati (Hindi practice of) 225, 232n5
  segregated codes of two cultures 220–21
  self, mistrust of 227–8
  servants, muting of 219
  The Servants Hall: A Domestic History of Erddig (Waterson, M.) 214–15
  servitude, changes in conditions in England for 229–30
  Skinner, James 225
  Smith, Adam 213, 214, 215
  social invisibility 213
  spatial and social arrangements 216
  Steel, Flora Annie 222, 223, 226–7, 228
  testimonials 230
  toilet arrangements 229
  transfer of labour through contract 216
  trust, flows of 216
  trust in asymmetrical relationships 216
  unproductive labour, Smith's reflections on 213
  value and trust in 18th and 19th century households 216
  Victorian house plans 217
  Waterson, Merlin 214–15
  Wealth of Nations (Smith, A.) 213
  Williamson, Capt. Thomas 221
  women, manuals for 227–8
  work of servants, value of 227–8
respect
  expression of 99
  importance of showing 41
  threeforld nature of 98–9
  trust and 180

Safaricom 27–8, 131, 132–3, 134–6, 145
  advertising and marketing strategies 135
  contracting with 137–40
  disenchantment with 137–9
  'imagined community' of mobile communicators 135–6
  initial public offering (IPO) 137
  integrity of, worries about 138
  intimacy and trust, revision of assumptions about 133–4
  television commercial campaign, lyrics of song for 136
Safaricom Foundation 135
Sahlins, Marshall 22–3, 123
secret police files in post-socialist Mongolia, trust and 30, 170–89
  acknowledgement and rehabilitation, demands for 173
  American Declaration of Independence 181
  'Archived Relations' 171–2
  arrests and executions of counter-revolutionaries 170–71
  birth certificates, Spiers' work on 176
  Buddhist establishment, repression of 173
  Buriads of rural north 173, 185
  counter-revolution in 1930s Mongolia 170–71
  democratic elections 173
  disappeared relatives 171
  documents
    archives and, anthropology of 172
    blind trust in, need for 181
    entangled tensions of intimacy and the personal 183–6
    intimate links within 187–8
    materiality of 181, 182–3
    past and 181
    people and, relations between 171, 181–3

proxys for missing people within 186
reaffirmation within 184–5
repression documents 184–5
social reconstruction from 185–6
faith, trust and link with 179
General Intelligence Agency Special Archive 184
intimacy
  personal aspects of 183–6
  social aspects of 186–8
memory, singularity of 187
Oral History of Twentieth Century Mongolia project 170–71, 183, 188n1
personal memory, importance of 179
Police Aesthetics (Vatulescu, C) 182
political repression and violence during socialism 173
political violence, issue of 187
politically motivated sentencing 171
politically repressed, legal definition as 174
politics and archives, opening up of 173
rehabilitation process 174–8, 178–9, 180, 181–3, 185, 187, 188
  compensation, payment of 175
  creation of past in 171
  decision-making in 176–7
  dependence on secret police and successors 182
  development of 173
  documentation of cases, requirement for 174
  eligibility for rehabilitation, determination of 175
  intimate relations, birth certificates and 176
  missing documents, problem of 175–6, 181–2
  opacity of 182–3
  original charges, overturning of 175–7

political repression, acceptance of legitimacy of 177–8
reinvestigatory element of 174–5
secret police files, evidence from 175
social and political significance 174, 175
tension in 171–2
trust, requirement for 175–6, 180
truth and trust in 172
Yonzon Hamba, rehabilitation decree of 177
repressions, place in social sphere 187
respect, trust and 180
state secrets 182
trust
  as affect of emotional commitment 172, 179
  knowledge and, materiality of 180–83
  Lahno's perspective on 179
  non-trust and, productive tension between 172
  usefulness of concept of 171–2, 180
trusting in trust 178–80
US National Archives 181
Vatulescu, Cristina 182
Seeger, Mike 247, 249, 250
Self Comes to Mind (Damasio, A.) 125
Shipton, Parker 23
Simmel, Georg 67–8, 69
Skinner, James 225
Smith, Adam 4, 5, 7
  relations of trust in colonial India 213, 214, 215
sociality 41, 42, 55, 56, 148, 236
  Amazonian sociality 193–4, 196, 199, 200–201, 203, 206–7, 208, 209
  dissolution of bonds of 235
  enrichment of 161
  forms of 239–40
  'good' sociality 191
  intersubjectivity and 124–5
  ladino notion of 43–50

Smith, Adam (*cont.*)
  moral reasoning, personhood and 25–32
  trusting and, ethnographies of 3, 4, 5, 11, 16, 17–18, 19, 21–3, 25, 26, 30, 31–2
  see also intimacy, trust and sociality among pastoral Turkana
societal trust in Guatemala 13–14, 22, 37–56
  ambiguities 38–9, 43, 46, 47, 49–50, 54, 55
  blood intermixing 52–3
  blood purity *(pureza de sangre)*, notion of 50–52
  blood symbolism 38–9, 43, 50–54
  boundaries, maintenance of 44
  catcalling 48
  civil war, effects of 39, 44–5
  closure, appraisal of 46–7
  cognitivism, trust and 42–3
  comparison in trust research 41
  competence as social actors, importance for *ladinos* of 44
  concealment and closing oneself off, management of situations by 45–6
  confianza, connotations of 25, 40–41, 43
  domestic intimacy and trust relations, complexities of 38
  domestic relationships, hierarchies in 42
  domestic violence 49
  emotion, exaggeration of displays of 46
  family and kin, trust and intimacy within *la casa* 37–8, 46, 48, 49, 54–5, 56
  gender relations, male pursuit of dominance in 48
  gendered aspects of openness and closure 46–8
  heterosexual relationships 47–8
  hierarchical relationships, trust in 41–2
  inward looking tendencies 44–5
  kinship 38–9, 50, 52–3, 54
  knowing, introspective mode of 40–41
  The Labyrinth of Solitude (Paz, O.) 46–7
  ladino conceptualizations of trust and mistrust 38–9
  ladino identities 52–3, 54
  ladino life-worlds 43–50, 54, 55–6
  language differences 40
  male sexual freedom 48
  marriage, problems for *ladinos* in 53
  moral risks of life outside family 37
  openness, depreciation of 46–7
  Paz, Octavio 46–7
  Prisoner's Dilemma 42
  public trust, low level of 37–8, 50
  respect, importance of showing 41
  ritualized politeness 41
  sexual abuse 49
  sexual purity, notion of 51
  social mobility 53–4
  social status, blood symbolism and 54
  spatial freedom 48
  spatio-moral domains, unfixed trust and 54–6
  streets *(la calle)* outside homes, dangers of 37, 46, 48, 54–5
  symbolic closure, life-world of *ladinos* and 49–50
  symbolism of openness and closure 46–7, 48–9
  trust, ethnographic approach to 39–43
  trust, experience of 43
  trust, theoretical perceptions of 39–43
  trust and mistrust, formation of 39
  Trust (Hardin, R.) 55
  trust research 40–43, 55–6
  white lies *(mentiras blancas)*, management by 45
  whitening *(blanqueamiento)*, practice of 51

women, symbolic association of openness with 47–8
South Africa, distinction between 'witch' and *sangoma* in 73
spirits *(yuxin)* in Cashinahua society 201, 203, 205, 208, 209
Steel, Flora Annie 222, 223, 226–7, 228
Stern, Daniel 16
stigma, Goffman's theory of 159–60
streets *(la calle)* outside homes, dangers of 37, 46, 48, 54–5
substantivism 205–6
subversiveness of *Napeysekina*, mobilization of 127–8
sympathization with others, Hume's perspective on 123

Tennessee Chocolate Drops 247
The Servants Hall: A Domestic History of Erddig (Waterson, M.) 214–15
Thompson, E.P. 7
Tilly, Charles 68
Titanic song genre 248
Tönnies, Ferdinand 5
A Treatise of Human Nature (Hume, D.) 17
Trevarthen, Colwyn 16
trust
  as action, Barga Mongol concept of 98
  as affect of emotional commitment 172, 179
  ambiguities of 192–3
  anthropology and 21–3
  in asymmetrical relationships 216
  Baier's perspective on 91, 92, 96–7
  capitalization on 4–7
  categorization of forms of 92–3
  cognitive and performative trust, distinction between 97–8
  cognitivism and 42–3
  control and, Mongol perspective on 95–6
  cultivation and nurture of 133
  cumulative body and 202–4
  development among pastoral Turkana of 125–6
  differences in conceptualizations of 85, 89–91, 94–5, 96–7, 98–9, 100–102
  in documents, substitution of trust in people for 148, 165
  doubt and 70–71
  entrustment and 96, 132, 142–3
  ethnographic approach to 39–43
  experience in Guatemala of 43
  faith and 67–8, 179
  flows of 216
  functionality of 91–2
  future contingency and 91
  gender of 140–45
  good intentions/thoughts *(sain sanaatai/sain sanah)* and 93–4, 100–101
  hierarchy, intimacy and 10–15
  intimacy and, recent reflections on notion of 66–7
  knowledge and, materiality of 180–83
  Lahno's perspective on 179
  liquid quality within 202
  loss of 244–5, 251–2
  mistrust and, formation of 39
  modern life, omnipresence of trust in 89
  multiple associations and assumptions attached to 93
  nebulous quality of trusting and 32
  non-trust and, productive tension between 172
  non-verbal clues, trust and 96–7
  objectivity and trust 90
  organizational harmony, trust and 89
  in parents, implications of 162
  proximity, trust and 228
  public trust, level of 37–8, 50
  rational choice, trust and 67
  and related concepts, definition of 93

trust (cont.)
  research on
    emerging field of 2–4, 32
    enquiring 'I' and 7–10
    societal trust in Guatemala
      40–43, 55–6
  risk, trust and 88–9, 90
  social networks and 132
  solidarity, trust and 69, 89
  strangers, trust in 191
  struggle on issue of 66–9
  temporal and spatial instability of
      191–2
  theoretical perceptions of 39–43
  trust-based approach to
      confidentiality, call for 163
  trust relations
    in Cameroon 67
    variables within 92
  and trustworthiness, lack of
      conceptual distinction
      between 95
  ultimate trust, God's work as basis
      for 74–5
  usefulness of concept of 171–2, 180
  Western notions of 88–9
    Mongolian concepts and,
      discrepancies between 94–100,
      100–101
    see also Barga Mongol concept
      of trust; corporeality and
      trust in Cashinahua society;
      distrust, sperm donation and
      relationship destabilisation;
      gender, trust and intimacy,
      e-finance in Kenya and;
      intimacy, trust and sociality
      among pastoral Turkana;
      labor relations and trust
      in Appalachian coalfields;
      relations of trust in colonial
      India; secret police files in
      post-socialist Mongolia,
      trust and; societal trust
      in Guatemala; witchcraft,
      intimacy and trust in
      Cameroon

Trust and Rule (Tilly, C.) 68
Trust (Hardin, R.) 55
trusting
  anthropology of, working towards
      an 24–5, 32–3
  assessment of acts of 97–8
  biological trusting 15–21
  consciousness and 2
  democracy and 1
  disposition to 1
  ethnography of 1–2, 32–3
  intersubjective worlds of 1, 33
  nebulous quality of trust and 32
  performativity of 33
  social networks and 1
  social phenomenon of 1–2, 25–32,
      32–3
  taken for granted nature of 1–2
  tensions of, reflections on
      122–8
  in trust 178–80
  trusting others 191, 194–8
  untrustworthiness and 85, 86–7
  the untrustworthy
    goodness in 97, 98, 100–101
    herding family as example of
      86–7, 99–100
trustworthiness 202, 203, 208
  actions generated by 204
  assessments of 97–8
  Barga Mongol conceptualizations
      of 97–8
  disjunctions between actual
      behaviour and assessments
      of 87–8
  embodiment of 192
  expectations of 86–7
  expression of 99
  of humans, thinkers on 122
  itgeltei and *naidvartai* in sense of
      94–5, 96, 99
  social production of 207
  social trust and 90
  Western and Mongolian concepts
      of, differences in 94–100,
      100–101
Turner, Wesley J. 250–51

Index • 281

United Mine Workers Journal 246
unproductive labour, Smith's
  reflections on 213
US National Archives 181

Vatulescu, Cristina 182
Vaughn, Henry 247
virtual reality 65, 76
Viveiros de Castro, Eduardo 193,
  204–5, 206
Vodafone Group 135

Warnock Committee 155
warrior body painting 113
Waterson, Merlin 214–15
Wealth of Nations (Smith, A.) 4, 5, 213
Weber, Max 5, 7
What Kinship Is and Is Not (Sahlins,
  M.) 80n7
white lies *(mentiras blancas)*,
  management by 45
whitening *(blanqueamiento)*, practice
  of 51
Williamson, Capt. Thomas 221
Wilson, Aunt Jennie 239–40, 247
Wilson, Mark 249
witchcraft, intimacy and trust in
      Cameroon 14–15, 60–81
  affection, Hyden's notion of
      economy of 69
  betrayal of kin to outsiders 63
  cannibalistic banquets 62
  casino capitalism 67, 68
  colonialism, witchcraft and 65
  complacency in face of dangers
      76–7
  conceptual distinctions, erosion of
      72–3
  confrontations within families 77
  courage, witches and 63
  death, witchcraft and suddenness
      of 62–3
  doubt, trust and 70–71
  enrichment, opportunities for 76
  faith, trust as leap of 67–8
  family, sociability and trust 66
  Frankel, Herbert 67

Giddings, Anthony 67
global occult powers 64–5
healers *(nganga)* 61, 62, 64, 75, 76
  ambiguities of 71–4
  competition within profession,
      development of 77–8
  drastic change, subjects of 76,
      77–8
  everyday life with 77
  living with witchcraft and
      approach of 76
  mercantilization of 77
  recourse to 70–71
intimacy
  changing perceptions of 78–9
  recent reflections on notion of
      66–7
  witchcraft and 64, 65–6, 66–7
kin, locality and witchcraft
      references 65–6, 79n3
kinship
  assumption of synonymy with
      trust 68–9
  claims of, elasticity of 65
  family coherence and
      transcontinental migration
      78–9
  Maka notions of witchcraft and
      61–2, 63–5
kinship relations, poly-
      interpretability of 61
knowledge, uncertainty and trust
      67–8
Luhmann, Niklas 67
magical money *(mokoagne moni)*
      64–5
Maka of Southeast Cameroon 60,
      61–2, 63, 64, 71, 72, 76, 79n2
management studies, trust and
      67
Mauriac, François 69
Mauss' gift-giving, 'primitive
      exchange' and 68, 80n7
Möllering, Guido 67–8
negative reciprocity 68
Le noeud des vipères (Mauriac, F.)
      69

witchcraft, intimacy and trust in Cameroon (*cont.*)
  occult
    compartmentalisation of sphere of 72–3
    maintenance of compartmentalisation 73–4
  Pentecostalism in Africa 74–5, 76, 79
    kinship, liberation from witch-infested intimacy and 75
    scrutiny of preachers 75
    trust, potential for victory over witchcraft and 75, 76
    witchcraft, everyday life and strengthening effect of 75
  'prosperity gospel' in Africa 74
  radical approach, everyday life and 76–9
  Ralushai Commission (1996) 73
  Ramaredi Shaba in Sekhukuneland 73
  rational choice, trust and 67
  reciprocity, anthropological use of term 69, 80n7
  same-sex intercourse 79n2
  Satan, struggle with witchcraft as 74–5
  Simmel, Georg 67–8, 69
  social relations, balance in 77
  solidarity and trust, family as safe haven of 69
  South Africa, distinction between 'witch' and *sangoma* in 73
  Tilly, Charles 68
  transcontinental migration, effects of 78–9
  trust, struggle on issue of 66–9
  trust and intimacy, recent reflections on notion of 66–7
  Trust and Rule (Tilly, C.) 68
  trust relations 67
  ultimate trust, God's work as basis for 74–5
  village and city, protectiveness of distance between 78
  village tribunals 77
  virtual reality 65, 76
  western highlands of Cameroon 72–3
  What Kinship Is and Is Not (Sahlins, M.) 80n7
  witchcraft
    within family 68–9
    intimacy and 60–66
    new and innovative forms of 64–5
    urban forms of 78
  witchcraft attacks, rumours of 61
  witchcraft discourse
    flexibility of 78
    subversive character of 72–3
  witchcraft of the house (*djambe le ndjaw*) 61–2, 64
  witchcraft stories, kinship in 62
  zombie spirits 63–4
women
  life in coal camps for 244–5
  manuals in colonial India for 227–8
  qualities required in Cashinahua society of 198–9
  ring-tones as self-expression for 140–41
  symbolic association of openness with 47–8
  see also female networks
Workman, Nimrod 248–50

zombie spirits 63–4

www.ingramcontent.com/pod-product-compliance
Lightning Source LLC
Chambersburg PA
CBHW070912030426
42336CB00014BA/2389